Paper Prototyping

The Fast and Easy Way to Design and Refine User Interfaces

The Morgan Kaufmann Series in Interactive Technologies

Series Editors:

Stuart Card, PARC ◇ Jonathan Grudin, Microsoft
Jakob Nielsen, Nielsen Norman Group

Paper Prototyping: The Fast and Easy Way to Design and Refine User Interfaces
Carolyn Snyder

Getting the Work Right: Interaction Design for Complex Problem Solving
Barbara Mirel

The Craft of Information Visualization: Readings and Reflections
Edited by Ben Bederson and Ben Shneiderman

HCI Models, Theories, and Frameworks: Towards a Multidisciplinary Science
Edited by John M. Carroll

Observing the User Experience: A Practitioner's Guide to User Research
Mike Kuniavsky

Web Bloopers: 60 Common Web Design Mistakes, and How to Avoid Them
Jeff Johnson

Persuasive Technology: Using Computers to Change What We Think and Do
B.J. Fogg

Coordinating User Interfaces for Consistency
Edited by Jakob Nielsen

Usability for the Web: Designing Web Sites that Work
Tom Brinck, Darren Gergle, and Scott D.Wood

Usability Engineering: Scenario-Based Development of Human-Computer Interaction
Mary Beth Rosson and John M. Carroll

Your Wish is My Command: Programming by Example
Edited by Henry Lieberman

GUI Bloopers: Don'ts and Dos for Software Developers and Web Designers
Jeff Johnson

Information Visualization: Perception for Design
Colin Ware

Robots for Kids: Exploring New Technologies for Learning
Edited by Allison Druin and James Hendler

Information Appliances and Beyond: Interaction Design for Consumer Products
Edited by Eric Bergman

Readings in Information Visualization: Using Vision to Think
Written and edited by Stuart K. Card, Jock D. Mackinlay, and Ben Shneiderman

The Design of Children's Technology
Edited by Allison Druin

Web Site Usability: A Designer's Guide
Jared M. Spool, Tara Scanlon, Will Schroeder, Carolyn Snyder, and Terri DeAngelo

The Usability Engineering Lifecycle: A Practitioner's Handbook for User Interface Design
Deborah J. Mayhew

Contextual Design: Defining Customer-Centered Systems
Hugh Beyer and Karen Holtzblatt

Human-Computer Interface Design: Success Stories, Emerging Methods, and Real World Context
Edited by Marianne Rudisill, Clayton Lewis, Peter P. Polson, and Timothy D. McKay

Paper Prototyping

The Fast and Easy Way to Design and Refine User Interfaces

Carolyn Snyder
Snyder Consulting
www.snyderconsulting.net

MORGAN KAUFMANN PUBLISHERS
An Imprint of Elsevier
AMSTERDAM BOSTON LONDON NEW YORK
OXFORD PARIS SAN DIEGO SAN FRANCISCO
SINGAPORE SYDNEY TOKYO

Publishing Director	Diane Cerra
Publishing Services Manager	Simon Crump
Editorial Coordinator	Mona Buehler
Project Management	Graphic World Publishing Services
Cover Design	Yvo Reizebos
Cover Image	Getty Images/Digital Vision
Text Design	Rebecca Evans & Associates
Composition	Rebecca Evans & Associates
Technical Illustration	Graphic World Illustration Studio
Copyeditor	Graphic World Publishing Services
Proofreader	Graphic World Publishing Services
Indexer	Steve Rath
Interior Printer	The Maple-Vail Book Manufacturing Group
Cover Printer	Phoenix Color Corp.

Morgan Kaufmann Publishers
An Imprint of Elsevier
340 Pine Street, Sixth Floor,
San Francisco, CA 94104–3205
www.mkp.com

Printed in the United States of America

07 06 5 4

Library of Congress Control Number: 2002115472

ISBN–13: 978–1–55860–870–2
ISBN–10:1–55860–870–2

This book is printed on acid-free paper.

To my parents
Clif and Lillian Snyder,
who raised me with unconditional love,
awesome siblings Nancy and Gordon,
and self-affirming wisdom like
"You never know until you try,"
"Use your own good judgment,"
"Why don't you look it up?" and
"Were you born on the side of the hill
where the doors fell shut?"
(Well, maybe not that last bit.)

Contents

Foreword

Jakob Nielsen
Principal, Nielsen Norman Group

Carolyn Snyder has written a wonderful book with all the practical information you need to make paper prototypes and get cost-effective usability data about your user interface designs. Any mid-sized design project will probably get an ROI of several thousand percent from following the advice in this book.

Yet, even though the book is great and the advice valuable and correct, there is a significant risk that you will put it all away and make this volume live out the rest of its life safely ensconced on a shelf. In my experience, paper prototyping almost never gets done in real design projects, despite its immense potential contribution to the quality of the ultimate user experience delivered by the project team.

Why don't design teams use paper prototyping? It is because it is so expensive and time consuming that the project manager regrettably made the decision to allocate the resources elsewhere and ship on time? No, paper prototyping is one of the fastest and cheapest techniques you can employ in a design process.

Paper prototyping isn't used because people don't think they will get enough information from something that simple and that cheap. It feels like you are cheating if you attempt make progress in your project without investing more of the sweat of your brows. "It's too easy; it can't work" goes the reasoning. Better to wait until we have a more perfect user interface before we show it to customers. Wrong. If you wait, it will be too late to translate the usability findings into the necessary change in direction for your design.

I am here to tell you that it does work. There are many different grades of paper prototypes, and they all give you immense value relative to the time they take to create and test. I have run studies where we had nothing but three different mockups of the homepage for a Web site and still learned a lot about how people would use the service and how the concepts communicated.

Twenty years of experience with usability engineering uniformly indicates that the biggest improvements in user experience comes from getting usability data as early as possible in a design project. Measured usability can increase by an order of magnitude when it is possible to change the project's basic approach to the problem, change the feature set, and change the user interface architecture. Usability insights also help later in the project, and there is value in fine-tuning details in the user interface, but the impact on the final user experience is not as great as the impact from fundamental changes made early in the design. It's a rough estimate, but I would say that the benefits from early usability data are at least ten times bigger than the benefits from late usability data. Late usability studies often add about 100% to the desired metrics for the final design, but early usability can add 1000% or more.

Forty years of experience with software engineering uniformly indicates that it is much cheaper to make changes to a product early in the development process. The most common estimate is that it is a hundred times cheaper to make a change before any code has been written than if the same change has to be made after the code has been completed.

Ten times bigger impact if the need for a design change is discovered early in the project. A hundred times cheaper to make the change. The experience from both fields is clear: Early is much better than late.

The benefits from early usability studies are so vastly superior that there is no doubt that you should use paper prototyping, even if you don't think the prototype is going to be as good as testing a fully developed design. If you try, you will be surprised at the amount of insights that can be derived from a "primitive" prototype, but even if you don't believe me, believe the collective experience of usability engineers and software engineers: Early beats late by so much that it outweighs the differences in quality of the prototypes.

Paper prototyping has a second benefit besides its impact on the quality of your current design project. It will also benefit your career. Consider all the other books you read about computers, Web design, and similar topics. How much of what you have learned from these books will still be useful in 10 years? In 20 years? In the immortal words of my former boss, Scott McNealy, "Technology has the shelf life of a banana."

In contrast, the paper prototyping technique has the shelf life closer to that of, say, paper. Once you have learned paper prototyping, you can employ the technique in all the projects you do for the rest of your career. I have no idea what user interface technologies will be popular in 20 years, but I do know that it will be necessary to subject these designs to usability evaluation and that paper prototyping will be a valuable technique for running early studies.

—*Jakob Nielsen*
Fremont, California
February 2003

Acknowledgments

It takes an entire village to raise an idiot. Oops, tangled metaphors, sorry. . . . I'll start over.

It takes a whole professional community to support an author. Writing down everything you know about a subject is only the first step. Writing a good book means calling upon a whole raft of people to fill in all the holes in your knowledge and experience. Fortunately, the usability community consists of some of the nicest, smartest, and most helpful people I know.

First and foremost, Jared Spool, founder of User Interface Engineering, my mentor and friend. Jared introduced me to usability and taught me most of what I know about paper prototyping—without him, I wouldn't be a usability consultant and this book wouldn't exist.

It was Mary Beth Rettger's enthusiasm that first convinced me to write this book. She has been a staunch supporter of this project from the outset, contributing many examples and much wisdom. She has been my sounding board, reality check, and cheerleader throughout.

Chauncey Wilson's encyclopedic knowledge of HCI literature is matched only by his willingness to share it, and I thank him for his help with References section. And our spirited debates on topics like in-room observers have enriched my insights as well as our friendship.

Diane Cerra is the kind of publisher every author should have—encouraging and patient. I think I could almost write another book just for the pleasure of having lunches with Diane.

I was thrilled when Rene Rittiner agreed to do the illustrations. I worked with Rene long ago when we were both software engineers, and his cartoon drawings always made me laugh.

Several people helped make the load lighter: Amy Maurer prepared many of the hand-drawn examples. Hal Shubin contributed two case studies, researching all my picky questions with seemingly unlimited patience. Jakob Nielsen encouraged me from the moment he first heard that I planned to write this book. Ann Marie McKinnon provided valuable guidance in organizing the material. Simo Säde was kind enough to mail me a book from overseas even though we were strangers.

I want to thank the following people who contributed to this book: Michael Albers, Betsy Comstock, Donna Cooper, Diana Demarco, Joe Dumas, Mitchell Gass, Andrew Gigliotti, Stacey Gilligan, Joe Grant, Kristin Grasso, Bob Hanson, Jennifer Harlow, Phillip Hash, Adam Henry, Gareth Hinds, Laura Holly, Ruth Huard, Timo Jokela, Sanna Kaartinen, Robin Kinkead, Jurek Kirakowski, Jussi Koivumaa, Lori Landesman, Samantha Lizak, Cay Lodine, Jennifer Lymneos, Michael Muller, Brent Mundy, M. David Orr, David Pearah, Mary Ann Perry, Rhon Porter, Greg Ralph, Thyra Rauch, Mary Beth Rettger, Susie Robson, Simo Säde, Rich Schaaf, Tony Schaller, Will Schroeder, Hal Shubin, Jason Silver, Rachel Smith, Jared Spool, Joel Spolsky, Ronnie Thomson, Helena Tokkonen, Tom Tullis, Bob Virzi, Neil Wehrle, Scott Weiss, Chauncey Wilson, Drew Wolff, Rosalee Wolfe, Jack Zaientz, Shawn Zhang.

One of my unanticipated frustrations in writing this book was that I ended up with more material than I could possibly use. I recognize the value of many examples and anecdotes that I couldn't fit in, and I thank the contributors for their generosity. For every person whose name appears herein, there are a dozen others who could have—many researchers and practitioners have used and written about methods similar to mine. Thanks to all my colleagues who have taught me about usability and prototyping over the years—this is your book too.

True to the spirit of paper prototyping, the first manuscript of this book was full of half-baked ideas. The reviewers—Brent Emerson, Ellen Isaacs, Mary Beth Rettger, Terry Roberts, and Chauncey Wilson—provided a wealth of thought-provoking, detailed, and constructive comments. I learned a great deal from them, and I am grateful (and humbled) to realize how much better the book became as a result of their feedback. I also appreciate the sharp eyes and editorial know-how of Suzanne Kastner during copyediting and production. Naturally, the responsibility for any remaining errors, omissions, and obfuscations rests with me.

Last but not least, thanks to Craig Duncan for his unflagging encouragement and understanding during the many evenings and weekends when this project seemingly became my life. Sweetheart, I look forward to resuming my life with you.

Introduction to Paper Prototyping

These first four chapters provide an introduction to the what, why, and how of paper prototyping—what it is, what it does for companies, why it's useful, and how to prototype various interface widgets.

Chapter 1

Introduction

Paper prototyping is a widely used method for designing, testing, and refining user interfaces. In the early 1990s it was a fringe technique, used by a few pockets of usability pioneers but unknown to the vast majority of product development teams (and often considered pretty darn weird by the rest). But by the mid-1990s, paper prototyping was catching on. People at well-known companies (IBM, Digital, Honeywell, and Microsoft, just to name a few) experimented with the technique, found it useful, and started using it as an integral part of their product development process. As of 2002 paper prototyping is not considered nearly so weird, and the technique is mainstream practice at many companies, both large and small. There are, however, still many people who've only heard enough about paper prototyping to be intrigued—this book is for you.

For much of its history, paper prototyping has been a tool clenched firmly in the hand of the academic researcher or usability specialist. Like any useful tool, though, its greatest potential can be realized by placing it in the hands of nonspecialists along with instructions for its proper use. I believe that anyone who is involved in the design, implementation, or support of user interfaces can benefit from paper prototyping because it fosters development of products that are more useful, intuitive, efficient, and pleasing. Although you can't learn everything about a topic from one book, this one gives you enough knowledge about paper prototyping to start using it.

What Is Paper Prototyping Anyway?

In its broadest sense, paper prototyping can be considered a method of brainstorming, designing, creating, testing, and communicating user interfaces. This book emphasizes the creating and testing aspects of paper prototyping, although I touch on the others as well. The technique is platform independent and can be used for Web sites, Web applications, software, handheld devices, and even hardware—anything that has a human-computer interface is a potential candidate for paper prototyping.

I'm not aware of any official definition of paper prototyping, and I've heard people use the term in reference to several different methods. Here's the definition of paper prototyping I use in this book:

> *Paper prototyping is a variation of usability testing where representative users perform realistic tasks by interacting with a paper version of the interface that is manipulated by a person "playing computer," who doesn't explain how the interface is intended to work.*

Here's how it works: You meet with other members of your product team to choose the type of user who represents the most important audience for the interface. You determine some typical tasks that you expect this user to do. Next, you make screen shots and/or hand-sketched versions of all the windows, menus, dialog boxes, pages, data, pop-up messages, and so on that are needed to perform those tasks. It is not necessary to have a working version of the interface. If you can sketch it on a whiteboard, you can make a paper prototype of it. Figure 1.1 shows an example of a hand-drawn paper prototype screen.

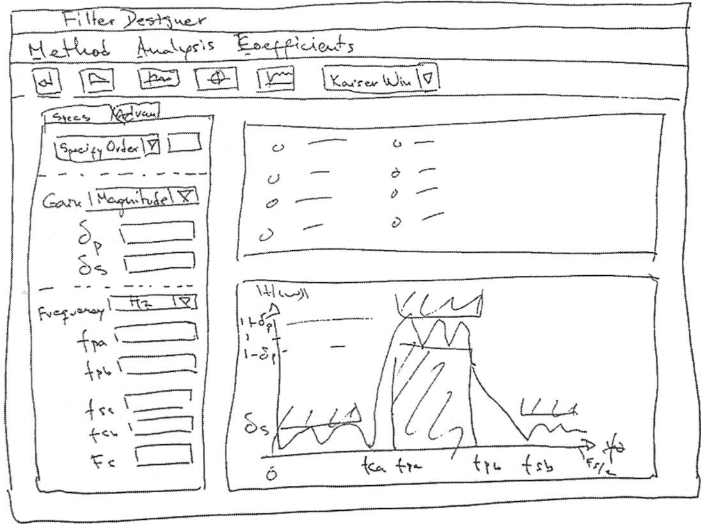

Figure 1.1 A hand-drawn paper prototype of a screen from an application used to design filters for scientific data.

After you create the prototype, you then conduct a usability test. You bring in a person who is representative of the audience you and your team members agreed on. You ask this **user** to attempt the tasks by interacting directly with the prototype—"click" by touching the prototype buttons or links and "type" by writing data right on the prototype. One or two of you play the role of **"Computer,"** manipulating the pieces of paper to simulate how the interface behaves but without explaining how it is supposed to work. A **facilitator** (usually someone trained in usability) conducts the session while other members of the product team act as note-taking **observers.**

You will quickly discover which parts of the interface work well and which are the trouble spots. Because the prototype is all on paper, you can easily modify it right after—or sometimes even during—each usability test. You can conduct several usability tests in just a day or two, and it doesn't take long to see the patterns in the feedback you're getting. Thus, paper prototypes allow you to iterate and improve a design quite rapidly based on input from real users, and this can all happen before the first line of interface code is written.

The previous discussion makes reference to four roles: user, facilitator, Computer, and observer. Figures 1.2 to 1.8 show these four people in action. (With the exception of the facilitator, there can be multiple people in each role, especially observers. So this is a minimalist example, but still a realistic one.)

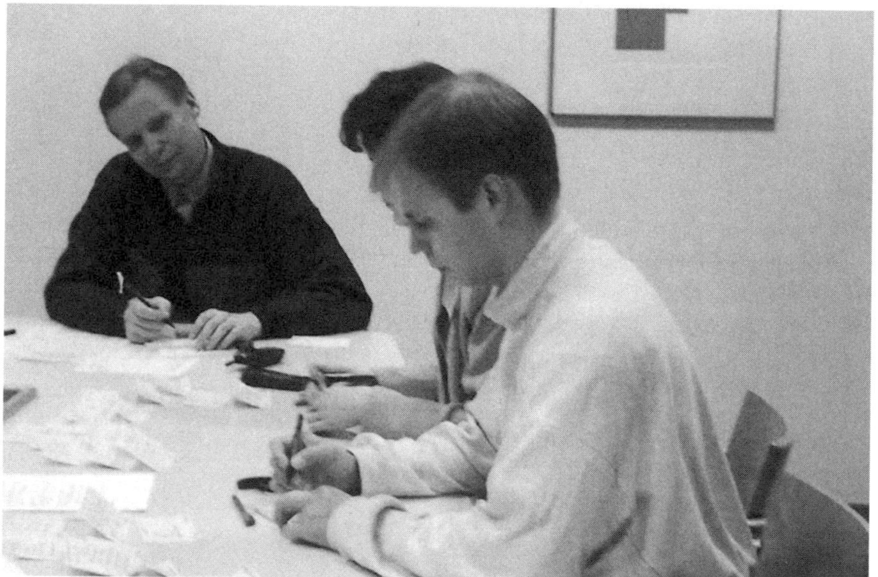

Figure 1.2 Paper prototyping is a team effort. After creating the usability tasks, the product team works together to generate a mock-up of the interface.

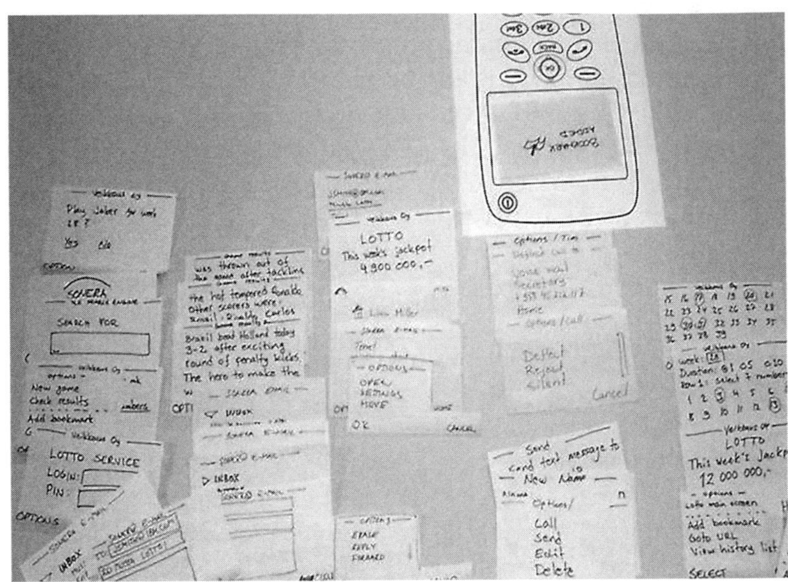

Figure 1.3 Individual pieces contain content that is relevant to the usability tasks—in this case, using a wireless phone to check lottery results and sports scores.

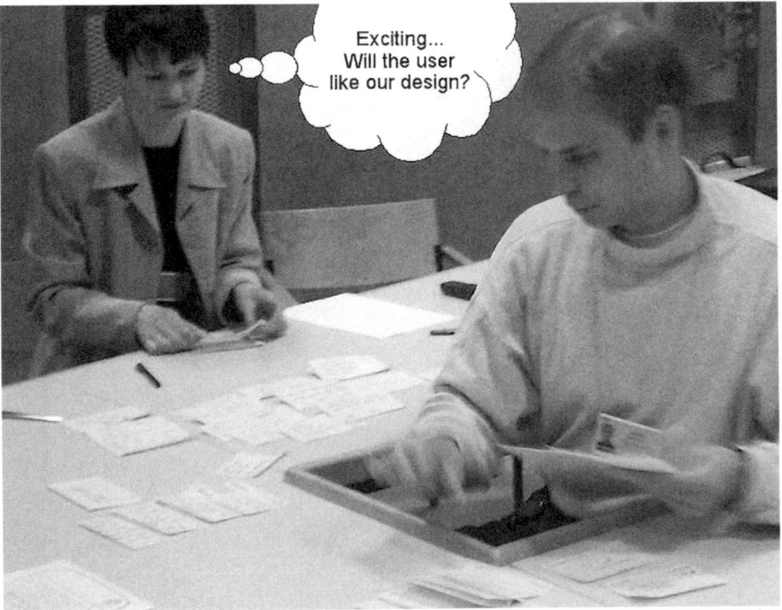

Figure 1.4 The Computer practices the tasks before the first user arrives. Another team member reviews her list of issues that she hopes the usability tests will cover.

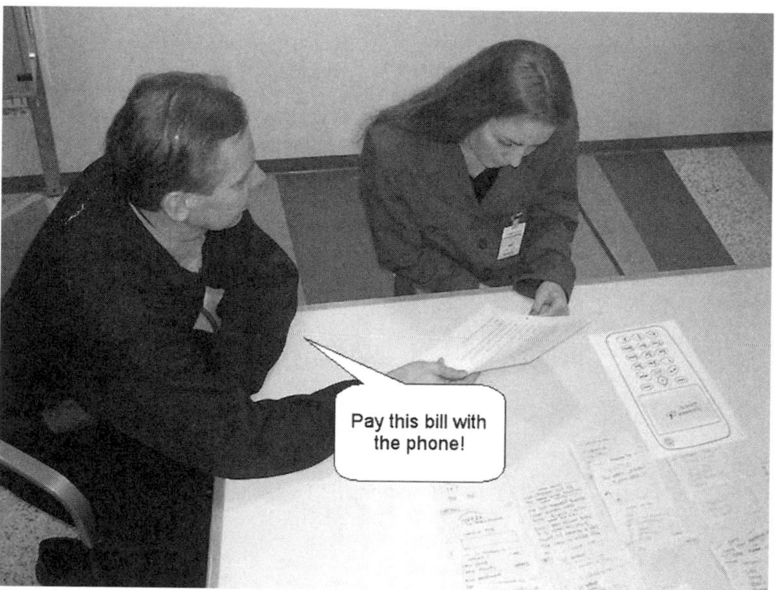

Figure 1.5 The facilitator explains the purpose of the session and how to interact with the prototype. The facilitator sits next to the user, giving each task and interacting with her as needed.

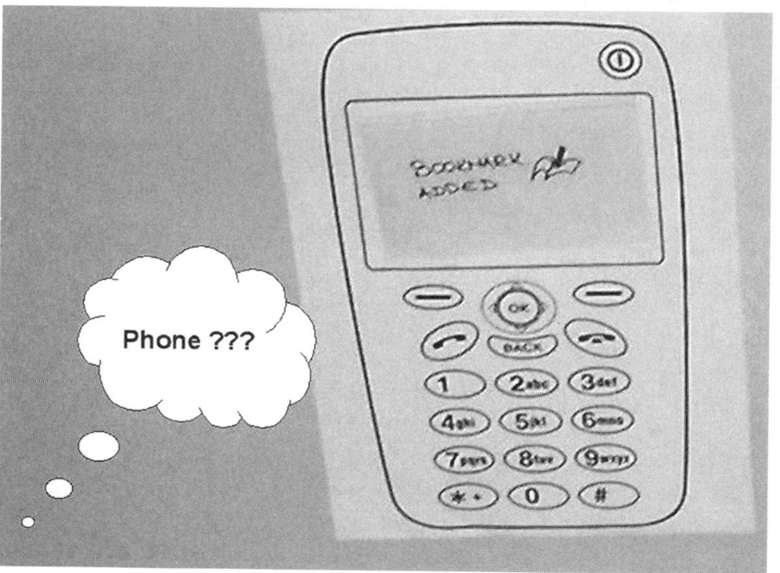

Figure 1.6 The user might find paper prototyping odd at first but quickly gets into the spirit.

Figure 1.7 The Computer highlights the item the user has just "clicked" on. Other team members observe quietly and take notes. The facilitator (not visible) is still sitting next to the user.

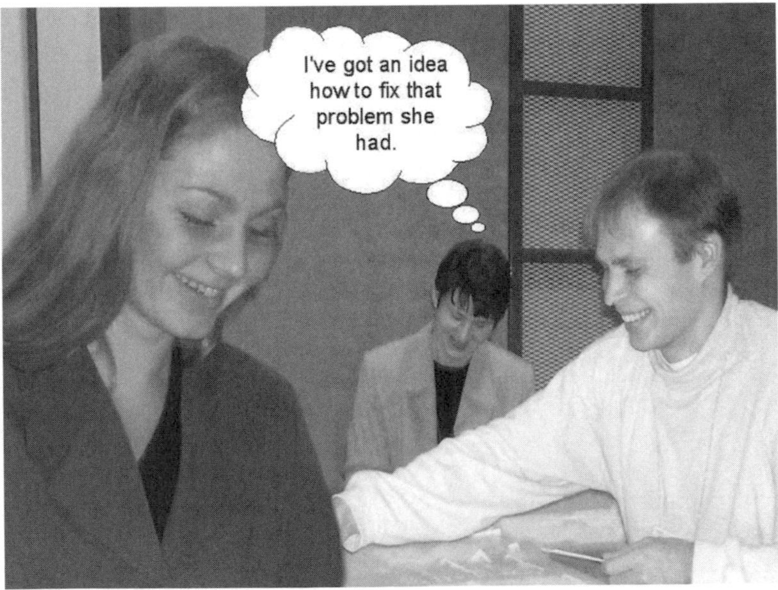

Figure 1.8 Paper prototyping is a creative activity and is often quite fun.

What Paper Prototyping Isn't

There are three techniques—comps, wireframes, and storyboards—that people commonly confuse with paper prototypes. These techniques are useful, but they usually don't fit my definition of a paper prototype, although all of them can be turned *into* paper prototypes. Here's a bit more explanation.

Comps

Comps (which is short for *compositions*) are visual representations—usually of a Web site—that show the look of the interface, including colors, fonts, layout, logos, artwork, and so on. (Figure 1.9 shows a sample of some comps.) The graphic designer or agency responsible for the visual aspects of the design might make several variations of the interface, allowing the decision makers to pick the one that best supports the current business initiatives, conveys the brand, and so forth. Some comps use nonsense words to represent the text and links. Comps are primarily used in internal discussions of a site's visual design; they usually are not intended (or suitable) for usability testing because users can't interact with them. However, if comps contained realistic content and were printed out, they might then fit my definition of a paper prototype.

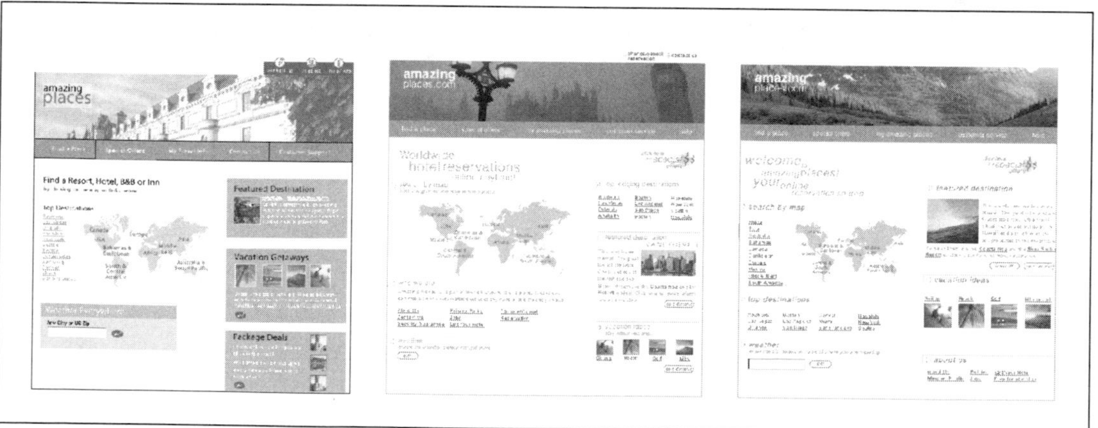

Figure 1.9 A set of comps for the home page of PlacesToStay.com. Comps are used to explore different layouts, graphics, and visual emphasis. Unlike this example, some comps use nonsense words for text and links.

Wireframes

Like paper prototype, *wireframe* can be a confusing term because people use it to mean different things. A wireframe defines the page layout for a Web site, showing what content goes where. (Figure 1.10 shows an example of a wireframe.) In the early stages of designing a Web site, wireframes are used in determining the page layout and navigation. But is a wireframe a paper prototype? It depends. Some wireframes designate the major areas on the page with labels (for example, "product information") but don't contain any content. This type of wireframe is sometimes used to get feedback from users, but this approach is of limited benefit because it's hard to tell whether the user's understanding of "product information" is the same as the designer's. Thus, a wireframe without content doesn't quite fit my definition of a paper prototype. On the other hand, with the addition of realistic content a wireframe could be printed out and tested as a paper prototype. In that case I would classify the wireframe as a paper prototype.

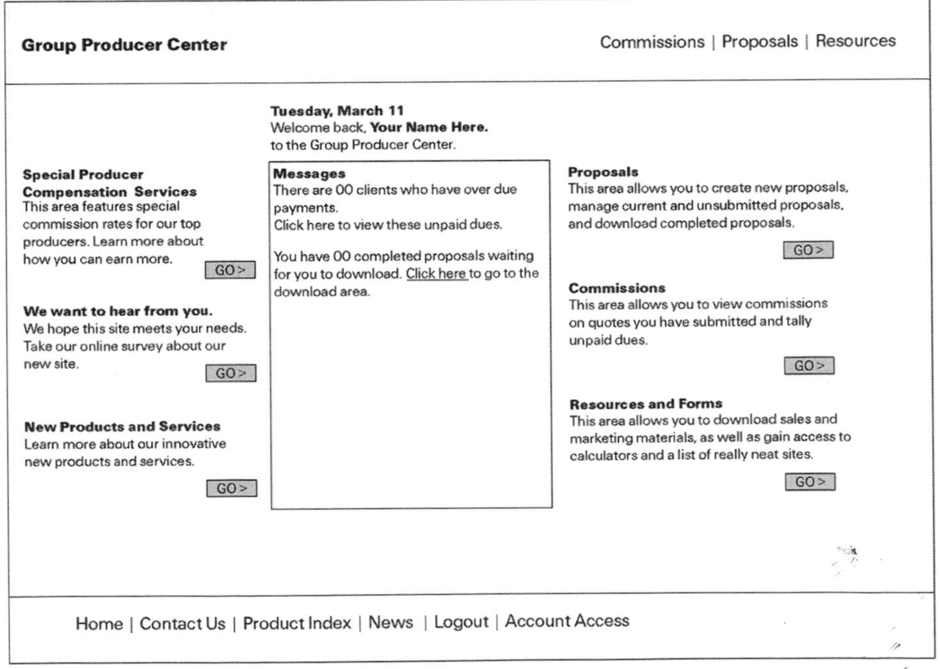

Figure 1.10 A wireframe shows the layout of a Web page, but often the content is represented by nonsense words.

Storyboards

A storyboard is a series of drawings or images that represents how an interface would be used to accomplish a particular task. It's basically a flowchart. Some storyboards, like the one in Figure 1.11, include representations of the user interface, but other storyboards are more conceptual and high-level. As the name implies, storyboards are often spread across a wall. They are typically used to understand the flow of the user's work and how the interface will support each step. Storyboards are most often used within the development organization, although sometimes users review them. Because users can't interact with storyboards (they can only look at them), I wouldn't classify them as paper prototypes. However, you could readily turn a storyboard into a paper prototype by taking it down from the wall and adding whatever data is needed to support a task scenario.

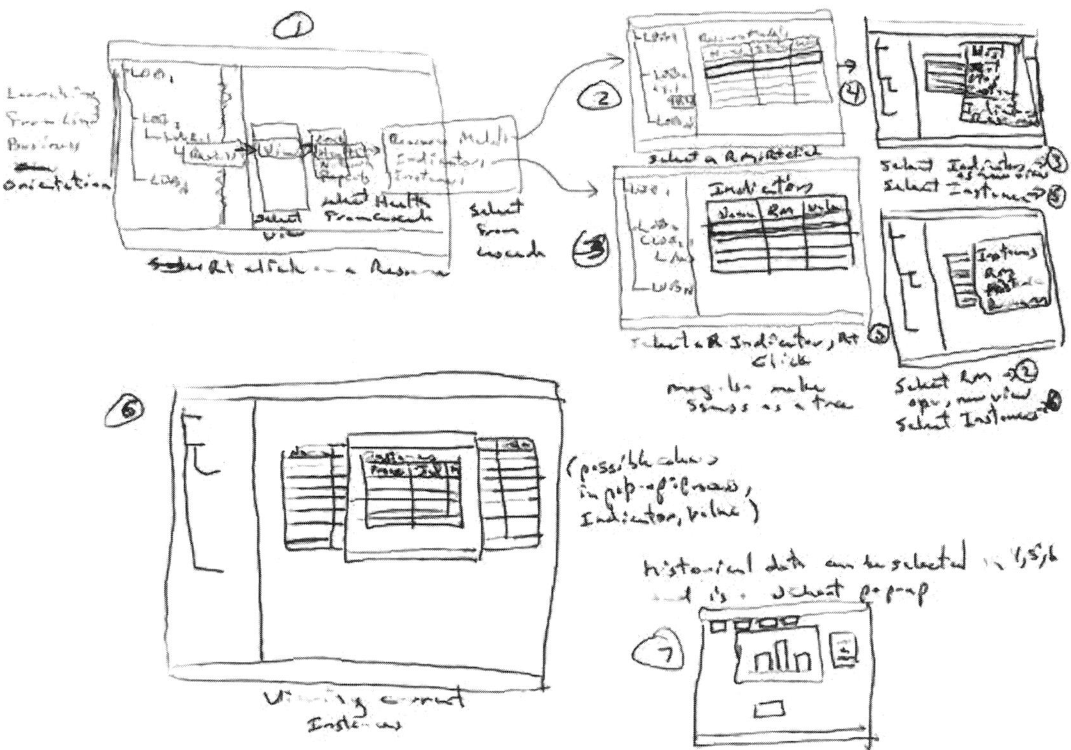

Figure 1.11 A hand-sketched storyboard used by developers to work out a sequence of screens. The annotations explain choices the user makes or processing done by the system.

Benefits of Paper Prototyping

Here's a preview of paper prototyping's advantages:

- Provides substantive user feedback early in the development process—before you've invested effort in implementation.
- Promotes rapid iterative development. You can experiment with many ideas rather than betting the farm on just one.
- Facilitates communication within the development team and between the development team and customers.
- Does not require any technical skills, so a multidisciplinary team can work together.
- Encourages creativity in the product development process.

Someone once asked me what the paper prototyping "bumper sticker" would say, and my answer was, "Maximum Feedback for Minimum Effort." That's really what it boils down to—an efficient means of getting make-it-or-break-it information about your interface. Using only a few office supplies and a dash of ingenuity, you can get all sorts of useful feedback in time to do something about it before the next release.

Of course, no technique is perfect, and this includes paper prototyping. One important drawback is paper prototyping's difficulty in detecting some classes of problems. In addition, depending on the circumstances of the project, there are cases in which the benefits of paper simply aren't very compelling.

Paper Prototyping and Usability

Entire books are devoted to usability (a.k.a. user-centered design). Although I can't summarize the entire discipline in a few paragraphs, I've found it helpful to think about usability in the following ways:

- The goal of any user-centered activity is to make the interface better for its intended audience and purpose, in a way that is consistent with the business goals of the organization producing that interface.

- Usability is like love: The more you give away, the more you have. You can help spread the love by passing along the concepts in this book to others. It'll come back to you in the form of more successful products.
- Usability is also similar to pornography in its ability to elude precise definition. To paraphrase the famous line by U.S. Supreme Court Justice Potter Stewart, "I know usability when I see it." If you do much reading about usability, you'll come across many definitions of it (some more usable than others). Don't get bogged down in the semantics; you'll be able to recognize good usability before you can define it.
- Like Don Norman says, a usable interface becomes invisible; sometimes you know you've gotten it right when your customers/users *don't* talk about how usable the product is . . . they're too busy raving about how you've made their life better.

Don Norman is a pillar of the usability profession. His first book, ***The Design of Everyday Things,*** *is 15 years old but still a classic. It's a deceptively entertaining read that will have a profound effect on how you look at objects and interfaces of every kind. Don first described the concept of an invisible computer in DOET (as it's affectionately abbreviated) and later went on to write a whole book called* ***The Invisible Computer.***

Readers familiar with usability may notice that I tend to view paper prototyping and usability testing as overlapping and often synonymous concepts. But that's a generalization, and like any generalization it isn't entirely accurate. Many companies create prototypes in software and conduct usability tests with them. Paper prototypes also have uses beyond usability testing, such as internal reviews. But most of the time when I use the term *paper prototyping,* I assume that the prototype is being created with the intent of usability testing it.

The History of Paper Prototyping

I've been using paper prototypes since 1993, but I didn't invent the technique. Neither did Jared Spool, whom I learned it from during my consulting days at User Interface Engineering. But determining where paper prototyping originated is like trying to track a river upstream to a single source. The best I can do is point out some of the tributaries.

If you peruse the References section or do an online search, you'll find the concept of "low-fidelity" prototyping popping up circa 1990 from authors like Jakob Nielsen, Bob Virzi, and Tom Tullis, to name just a few. A few people in high-tech companies were using the technique during the 1980s and earlier (Chapter 2 has some interesting examples courtesy of Robin Kinkead). As far as I can tell, the method was around for a decade or two before it showed up on the radar screen of the average person (such as yours truly) involved in product development.

Paper prototyping has an estranged cousin: participatory design. I say estranged because many authors discuss one or the other without mentioning (or perhaps even realizing) how related they are. It's probably most accurate to describe paper prototyping as a subset of participatory design. There is a whole body of literature pertaining to participatory design, which has been around for decades; this is where the river starts branching off into more sources than I can do justice to.*

And of course, prototyping in its general sense has been around for a long time in engineering disciplines and life in general. Before chiseling the first wagon wheel out of stone, I'm willing to bet that primitive humans prototyped and tested the concept using some other medium. So any work pertaining to prototyping could be considered a precursor to this book.

Usefulness of Paper Prototyping

In July 2002 I conducted an online survey of some usability professionals about their use of paper prototyping and their attitudes toward it. Figure 1.12 shows that of the 172 people (most of them usability specialists) who responded to the question, "What is the importance of paper prototyping to your work?" 86% answered either "Essential" or "Useful." ("Useless" was one of the options, but no one chose it.) Although this survey isn't very scientific (it's a biased sample because I issued the invitation on usability-related discussion lists), it's still a pretty good indication that paper prototyping is no longer a fringe technique.

But this book is not about the history of paper prototyping, or even the present. It's about the future. Specifically, *your* future in using it to develop better products.

---

* If you're interested, anything by Michael Muller is a good place to start. He's done considerable work in participatory design. Think of him as your guide to that branch of the river.

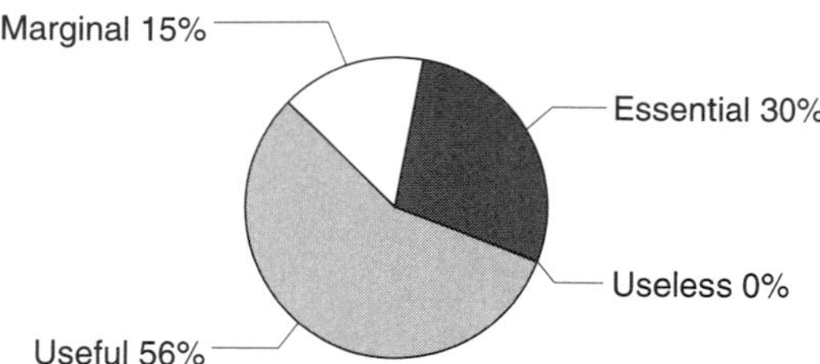

Figure 1.12 Answers to the question, "What is the importance of paper prototyping to your work?" from a July 2002 survey of usability professionals.

Audience for This Book

So let's talk about you. You're probably involved in the design, implementation, or support of user interfaces in some way. In other words, you might be any of the following:

- Software or Web site developer
- Project manager
- Interface/interaction designer
- Usability specialist
- Technical writer
- Graphic designer
- Information architect
- Marketing professional
- Quality assurance/test engineer
- Training specialist
- Technical/customer support representative
- Manager of any of these

Following are some assumptions I've made about your background.

Programming

You don't need to have technical skills to create and test a paper prototype, although presumably (if there's any intention of implementing what you're prototyping) you'll be working with someone who does. Unlike software-based prototyping tools, for paper prototyping you need only those cutting, pasting, and drawing talents you perfected as a child. So although many of you might be programmers, I don't assume any technical knowledge about software development.

Interface Design

Strictly speaking, you don't need to be an interface designer to create a paper prototype any more than you need to be an artist to glop paint on a canvas. Of course, to be a *good* artist you need some combination of talent, training, and practice. The same is true of interface design. Strictly speaking, this book won't teach you to be a good designer, but if you have the enthusiasm to learn, paper prototyping will give you a means to practice and thus refine whatever talent you may have.

Usability Testing

It was hard to decide how much material to include about usability testing. Usability specialists who read this book certainly don't need me to tell them how to conduct tests. But for every usability specialist, there are probably 100 designers, developers, and writers who wouldn't mind knowing a little more about usability. There are already some good books about usability testing, and I don't want to reinvent the wheel. However, discussing paper prototyping without talking about usability testing is like trying to gossip without using pronouns.*

My compromise is to give you a sense of how usability testing works, including some of the concepts and tips I found most helpful when I first started, but I leave most of the details to other books. I've concentrated most of the general usability

---

* The next time you throw a party, ask your guests to sing "Let Me Call You Sweetheart" sans pronouns before you'll give them back their car keys—not because it's an effective sobriety test, but because it's funny.

testing information into a couple of chapters so that it's easy to skip for those who already know it.

Usability for Everyone

For products to truly become usable, the development team can't rely on a handful of usability specialists to gather and interpret data from users; this creates a bottleneck that either slows the development process or forces usability activities to be skipped entirely (guess which). Thus, it's good for product teams to have a way to collect at least some of this usability information for themselves.

You wouldn't discourage a friend from taking singing lessons simply because he isn't an operatic tenor like Pavarotti. Similarly, I don't think it's necessary to be an HCI (human-computer interaction) guru to get started with paper prototyping. Paper prototyping and usability testing are common-sense techniques, and people in a variety of disciplines can benefit from using them. Yes, some will be better at it than others, but like my parents always told me, "You never know until you try."

On the other hand, usability specialists can spend decades developing their knowledge and skills. There is a great deal to know about the fields that comprise HCI, including cognitive psychology, social psychology, statistics, experimental design, data analysis, interface design principles, and probably others. I don't mean to summarily dismiss all that collective wisdom by implying that any idiot can conduct a good usability study. My philosophy is simply that anyone who cares about making better interfaces can benefit from learning the basics of paper prototyping and usability testing. But there is always more to learn.

Author Background

It's probably already clear that I am a practitioner, not an academic. I gained much of my experience in hard-to-use interfaces because I spent the first decade of my career *creating* them, first as a software engineer and then as a project manager. (The building controls company where I worked was full of well-meaning people, but this was back in the 1980s, when most people, including me, knew nothing about usability.) Although my software skills have fallen by the wayside, I still have some clear memories of the pressures and challenges involved in product development. I remain sympathetic toward development teams, especially knowing that technology certainly hasn't gotten any simpler.

In addition to my computer science background, I also (for reasons still not entirely clear to me) picked up an MBA along the way, which gave me a tentative grasp of business concepts.* Working at a small consulting firm (User Interface Engineering) for 6 years gave me a very practical, whack-upside-the-head grounding in sales, marketing, and finance. Like the difference between profit and cash flow—profit looks nice on paper, but cash flow is where your paycheck comes from. So I approach usability from a business perspective, trying first to understand the importance of the product to the company and to its users, then looking for ways to identify and manage the risks. After all, if an otherwise good company makes too many mistakes and goes out of business, everyone loses. Paper prototyping fits perfectly into that mind-set because it lets you make (and fix) most of your mistakes before the product goes out the door.

I am not a researcher or scientist, and I don't even consider myself an expert in HCI; it's a big field, and I'm sitting in a small corner of it. There are many good papers and articles about paper prototyping, but for the most part I've confined the references to their own section at the end of the book. I mention some of the especially interesting ones along the way, however. Although this book discusses many topics for which there is HCI research, this book isn't about the research—it's about what real product teams do. Scientific studies are a fine thing; the experience of practitioners is equally important but less often published. So I've made an effort to include many real-life examples, anecdotes, quotes, and case studies from my clients and peers—material you won't find anywhere else, because although many of these people know enough about paper prototyping to write their own books, they don't have the time.

Terminology Used in This Book

Terminology is a perennial challenge in any high-tech field; technology evolves faster than the language used to describe it. Beneath the surface of seemingly

* And also confused me because I no longer was sure which Dilbert character to identify with; sometimes I feel sympathy for the pointy-haired boss.

innocuous words such as *designer* lurks a myriad of meanings waiting to confuse or even alienate people who've latched onto conflicting ones. I certainly don't want to redefine the English language, but I should explain the conventions I've adopted in this book. In most cases I'm using a definition that may be broader than what you're used to, so keep that in mind if you take exception to how I've used a particular word. I defined earlier what I mean by paper prototyping, so here are the rest:

Computer, computer. In paper prototyping, a human being simulates the behavior of a computer. To differentiate the silicon-based entities from the carbon-based ones, I'll use *computer* when I'm talking about a machine and *Computer* to refer to a person who's simulating a computer.

Product, interface. I use the terms *product* and *interface* somewhat interchangeably—you might be developing shrink-wrapped software, an intranet site, or a handheld device. Although *product* implies something that is sold, maybe your interface isn't. I use both these terms in an inclusive sense that encompasses not just the screens but also help, manuals, training, hardware, packaging, and even tech support. If the user sees it or interacts with it, I count it as part of the interface.

Product team, development team. Using similar reasoning, *product team* means anyone who works on any of the aforementioned, including tech writers, marketing, training, and customer support. In other words, anyone who has a direct or indirect effect on the end user's experience of the product is part of the product team. Sometimes I use the term *development team,* but I'm not referring only to those who, as a programmer friend of mine puts it, "rearrange 1s and 0s all day." If you're making/testing/supporting something that users will eventually come into contact with, you're part of the development team.

Release. *Release* refers to that moment when real users obtain the official version of the interface and start using it. Release is commonly used for software, but there are synonymous terms for other types of interfaces—*launch* for a Web site, *deployment* or *rollout* for an interface with internal users.

Screen. Although the literal definition of *screen* refers to a computer monitor, I use it in a generic sense to mean any piece of the user interface, be it a Web page, LCD display, form, dialog box, and so on. When I talk about "the screens," I'm referring to whatever it is that you're prototyping.

Test versus Study. Usability *test* refers to one session with a user. A usability *study* is a series of usability tests conducted over one to several days.

Of Interest . . . Comparing Apples to Apples

In any discussion of *paper prototyping* or *low-fidelity prototyping,* it's important to agree on what is meant by those terms. People use these terms to mean different things. If someone is using a different definition than yours, you may completely misinterpret each other's conclusions about the technique. It's a good idea to keep this in mind as you do further reading on the topic of paper prototyping.

As an example, consider the article "Low vs. High-Fidelity Prototyping Debate" by Rudd, Stern, and Isensee (1996). This article thoughtfully outlines the pros and cons of high- and low-fidelity prototyping. However, the authors' definition of low-fidelity prototyping is different than the one used in this book. They assume that the paper screens will be *shown* to users rather than having users *interact* with them in the context of completing tasks. This is a very important difference, so it's no wonder that some of their conclusions about paper prototyping appear to contradict mine. If you read the article carefully, though, you'll realize that the different definitions are at the heart of the apparent discrepancies. Once you account for the terminology differences, most points of disagreement vanish.

Whenever I hear someone start talking about paper prototyping, I've learned to ask, "Please tell me what you mean by *paper prototyping.*" This often prevents me from misinterpreting what they're talking about.

Chapter Overview

In several years of teaching paper prototyping, I've found that the most natural learning sequence doesn't necessarily follow the way you'd do the activities in real life. For instance, it's easier to understand some of the strengths and weaknesses of paper after you've made and mock-tested a prototype, or lacking that experience, at least seeing plenty of examples.

This book is organized into four parts. Depending on your background and interests, it may make sense for you to read the chapters in a different order than how they appear in the book.

Part I—Introduction

The next three chapters provide an introduction to the what, why, and how of paper prototyping: what paper prototyping is, why it's useful, and how to prototype various interface widgets.

Chapter 2, Case Studies: Several detailed examples of usability studies conducted with paper prototypes are included so that you can see the sorts of things that companies learn from them.

Chapter 3, Thinking about Prototyping: A lot of reasons, both practical and psychological, are provided to help explain why paper prototyping is a useful technique. In addition, some of its drawbacks are discussed, although the details are reserved for Chapters 12 and 13.

Chapter 4, Creating a Paper Prototype: The widget-level view of paper prototypes and how to include interaction, help/documentation, and hardware are discussed. This chapter is presented out of its proper order (logically, it's part of Chapter 7) because some people find it useful to see many examples when first learning about paper prototyping.

Part II—Process: Conducting a Usability Study with a Paper Prototype

This is the practical, how-to part of the book. It assumes you've decided to try paper prototyping, so it describes how to go about it. (Those who are still undecided might want to read Part III first and then come back to this section.)

Chapter 5, Planning a Usability Study with a Paper Prototype: This chapter includes an action plan of the activities, people, and schedule you'll need when you're ready to try paper prototyping. (If you're already familiar with how to conduct a usability study, you may want to skim this chapter.)

Chapter 6, Task Design: Good usability tasks are vital in paper prototype testing. This chapter explains why and how to create good tasks.

Chapter 7, Building the Prototype: The process of creating a paper prototype around a set of usability tasks and holding internal walkthroughs to prepare for usability testing is described in this chapter. (Refer to Chapter 4 for details about how to prototype specific interface widgets.)

Chapter 8, Introduction to Usability Test Facilitation: For those who haven't previously conducted usability tests, this chapter provides enough guidance to get started. Testing with two users at a time (a.k.a. co-discovery) is also discussed. Experienced facilitators can probably skip this chapter.

Chapter 9, Usability Testing with a Paper Prototype: Everything from how you explain paper prototyping to what you do when a user tries to do something you haven't prototyped is covered.

Chapter 10, Observers: Observers are an integral part of usability testing. This chapter explores the benefits and risks of having observers in the test room and how to ensure that they will behave appropriately.

Chapter 11, Data: Capturing, Prioritizing, and Communicating: This chapter describes how to take good notes and prioritize the data you've collected and also discusses ideas for capturing and communicating what you've learned from your prototypes.

Part III—Deciding to Use Paper

The following three chapters delve into the nitty-gritty of what paper prototyping is and isn't good for, whether it might make sense to use for your project, and the sorts of objections you might face from your co-workers when you pitch the idea to them.

Chapter 12, What Paper Is Good For: Paper prototyping is a useful technique, but it is not perfect. This chapter outlines the kinds of usability problems that paper will (and won't) typically find.

Chapter 13, The Politics of Paper: It's one thing to convince yourself that paper is worth trying, but it's quite another to convince your co-workers. Common concerns about paper prototyping (validity, bias, professionalism, and resources) are discussed.

Chapter 14, When to Use Paper: Various circumstances of your project, staff, and development environment can affect your decision of whether to test with a paper prototype. (Strictly speaking, this chapter should precede Chapter 5, which also pertains to planning. I've placed it here because it may contain more detail than some people need.)

Part IV—Broadening the Focus

This section encourages you to think about how paper prototyping relates to the overall process of product development.

Chapter 15, Examples of User-Centered Design: Descriptions are provided of some real companies that use paper prototyping as one of several techniques in their user-centered design process.

Chapter 16, Final Thoughts: This is a short but thought-provoking list of my own unanswered questions about paper prototyping.

And last of all, there's a References section with all the books and papers referenced throughout the book, plus plenty of suggestions for further reading.

No Bad Examples!

There are many examples of interfaces in this book, but there are no bad examples! That's because all the examples I use are intended to illustrate techniques, not designs. In other words, I'm not critiquing anything. The point of the examples isn't to illustrate "good" or "bad" design but rather to give you ideas and insights about the *process* of improving your own design.

Companion Web Site: www.paperprototyping.com

There's a companion Web site for this book at *www.paperprototyping.com*. There you'll find downloadable versions of materials shown in this book, including worksheets, handouts, and forms. The site also contains links to places where you can purchase the supplies used in paper prototyping and links to papers and articles available online. The symbol in the margin is used throughout this book to indicate the presence of corresponding materials on the Web site.

Chapter 2

Case Studies

So what is paper prototyping good for? In a nutshell, it lets you create and refine an interface based on user feedback *before* implementing it. This chapter contains several real-world examples where paper prototypes provided that important—and often surprising—feedback.

To illustrate that paper prototyping works for a variety of interfaces, I've chosen a software application, a Web site, a Web application, a telephone display, and a small touch screen. In each example, the product team created a paper prototype of the interface before a working version was available and tested it with about a half dozen users.

You'll notice several types of findings from these case studies:

1. **Usability issues.** This broad category contains all the sorts of things you'd probably expect to find from usability testing—confusing concepts, poor terminology, lack of feedback, layout problems, improperly used widgets, or any other situation in which the users can't get the interface to work the way they need it to. But usability issues are just the beginning.
2. **Missing (or misspecified) functional requirements.** It's common for users to have some needs that the product team isn't aware of at the start of the project, or the team may have a mistaken assumption about what functionality will satisfy a user requirement.
3. **Preference for one design alternative.** Sometimes there are different ways to provide a function and it's a coin toss to developers which one is easier to implement (but instead of tossing that coin, they debate it ad nauseam in meetings). Users, however, may have a firm preference for one or the other, which will show up pretty readily in usability testing.

4. **Priorities.** No company has unlimited resources, so it's important to separate the gotta-haves from the nice-to-haves. Occasionally a paper prototype will reveal functionality that isn't as important as the team had thought—a feature that draws a ho-hum response from users can be moved lower on the priority list or even dropped, thus saving work.
5. **Issues outside the user interface.** Interestingly, paper prototypes can reveal some issues that one might think of as being outside the scope of the user interface, for example, the credibility of the company or the implications of using the interface in a social setting. When the interface and tasks are realistic enough, test participants start extrapolating to their own environment and thus they can anticipate problems. (Caveat: Not all the problems—some problems can be found only in real-life use and won't show up in a usability lab, even if you test the released product.) These issues can result in changes being made in the interface or elsewhere, such as marketing or training materials.

You'll also see that there's quite a variety in the scope of issues revealed by these case studies—everything from high-level strategic issues ("Are we building the right thing? Will the market accept this product?") to low-level and specific ("Does this control offer the right degree of magnification?"). In my experience, it's common for paper prototype tests to turn up both high-level and low-level issues, so these examples are pretty typical.

DILBERT © UFS. Reprinted by permission.

Software: The MathWorks

Contributions by Jennifer Lymneos, Mary Beth Rettger

This paper prototype from The MathWorks is of the Control Point Selection Tool (cpselect), which is part of the Image Processing Toolbox 3.0 (Figure 2.1). This application is used by scientists to align images (for example, from geographic surveys) to detect differences between them. The user works with an overview and detail view of each image, choosing comparison points at the same location on each image.

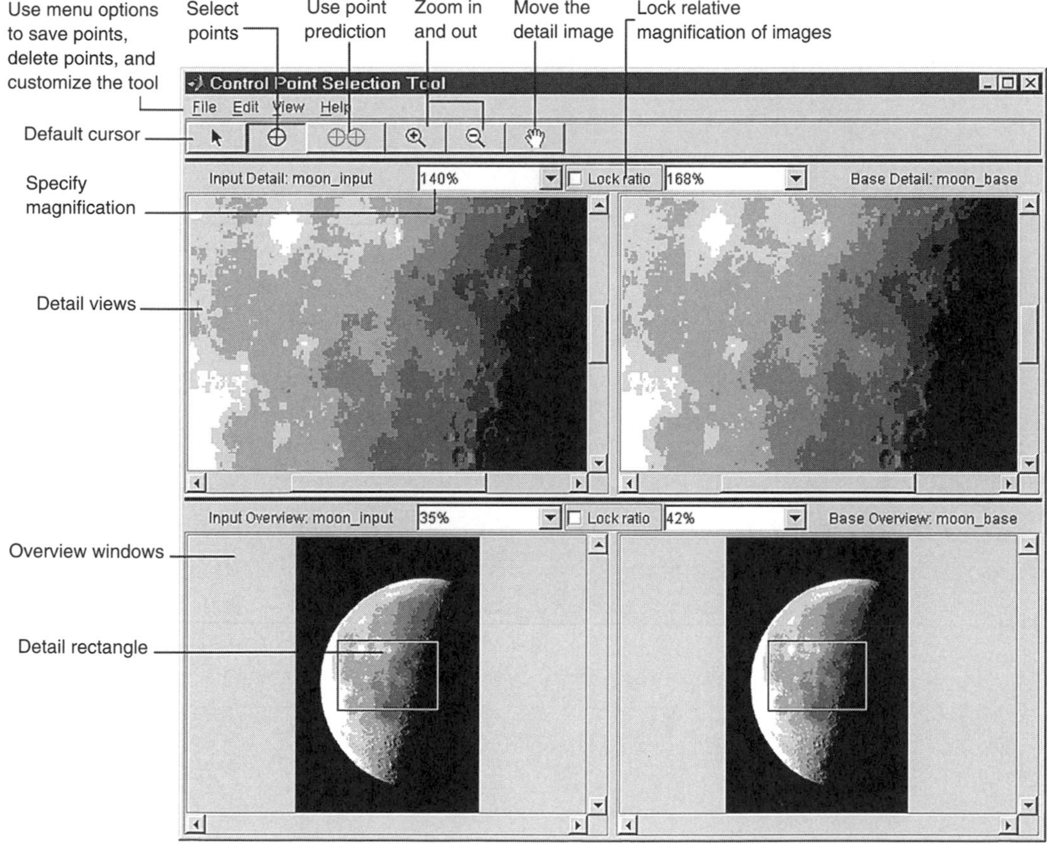

Figure 2.1 As shown by this screen from its documentation, the Control Point Selection Tool lets the user examine two images, including an overview and detail area for each. Clicking on any image adds a control point to the appropriate location in the other images.

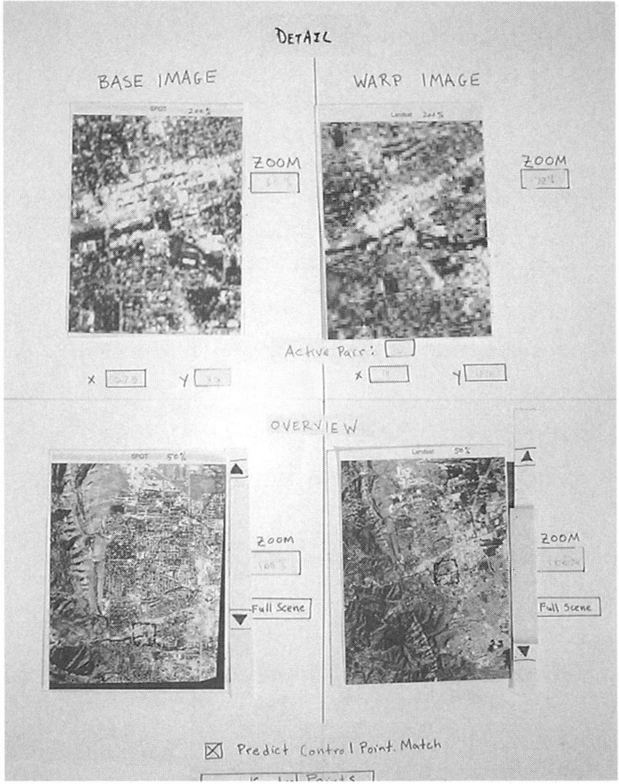

Figure 2.2 One of the paper prototypes used in testing. Not shown here are the colored dots on pieces of transparency that were placed on top of the images to indicate the control points.

In 2000 The MathWorks was working on the first release of cpselect. They had done their homework and knew a fair amount about their user population and requirements, but the developers were having a tough time getting started. In a scientific application such as this there are many technical details, and the team was getting caught up in them before they even had consensus on the high-level approach to the interface. So they created a paper prototype (Figure 2.2) and conducted several rounds of usability testing, refining the prototype as they went.

The Team Had Questions . . .

In the early prototypes, the team had a number of fundamental questions about what users needed and which design variations would work for them:

- Did the overall information display work? Did the users really need to see both a detail and an overview for each of the two images, or would just an overview do the job?
- When users dug down into the details of an image, what were they looking for? How did they want the control points to work? Initially, the team thought of control points as having two states: manually selected and predicted (that is, placed as a result of an algorithm using data from previous manual point selections).
- Did users want to specify the degree of magnification, or would a simple "zoom by a factor of 2" control suffice?
- How important was it to make the interface consistent with similar tools that their users had worked with?

. . . And Paper Prototyping Answered Them

The team learned that the four views were in fact needed and that users wanted a high degree of control over the magnification—zooming by a factor of 2 each time is conceptually simple, but it doesn't cut it when you're looking at large land masses. The team also learned that their "Fit to Window" control, which some had argued was too vague, didn't trouble users, because when they needed to manipulate the magnification they'd use the more precise tools.

Some interesting subtleties emerged in regard to the control points. The team realized that there were really several states—and combinations of states—that the points could have. For example, a point had different meanings depending on whether it had a corresponding match in the other image or was awaiting a match and whether the match was predicted or manually selected. Although users liked having the predicted points, they needed to distinguish them from manually selected points because they often had to tweak the position of the predicted point manually. Once the team understood the set of point states that users needed to see, they created a symbol for each one and a legend to help the users learn what the symbols meant.

One happy finding was that it was okay for cpselect to differ from other tools that users had worked with. The product team had worried about this because the market for technical computer software is highly sophisticated and some of The MathWorks' customers had written their own software applications to help with image processing. If customers were accustomed to a different way of doing things, they might not like cpselect. Fortunately, because cpselect incorporated the features users needed but with a simpler interface compared with the homegrown tools, its differences proved to be benefits rather than drawbacks.

Customers Are Happy

All in all, the team conducted five rounds of paper prototyping, refining the interface after each. (Although the "five rounds" may sound arduous, each round included only two or three users, and the team went from a blank slate to a ready-to-implement design in about 3 months, while working on other projects at the same time.) The resulting interface was much different than what they'd started with, and the product team believed it was also much better. Although the paper prototype didn't answer every question they had about the interface, there was a much smaller (and highly focused) set of issues to be solved later in the development process when a working version was available.

The Control Point Selection Tool shipped in April 2001, and customer feedback indicates that the tool is easy to learn and helps them do their image registration work. Their biggest request is not for bug fixes but for new tools to automate even more of the process. Jennifer Lymneos, a Usability Specialist who worked on cpselect, adds, "By the end of paper prototype testing, months before the tool was released, we were confident that the design was a good one. None of the feedback from users has contradicted what we learned from the paper prototypes, nor has it been related to fundamental aspects of the tool. In fact, many of the enhancement requests are small things like where the legend should go and what its title should be. For the first release of a brand-new tool, I think that's a pretty good indicator that we got the basics down right."

Web Application: Centra Symposium

Contributions by Ronnie Thomson, Drew Wolff

In the summer of 1996, developers at a start-up company called Centra were working on the first release of their flagship product Symposium, an Internet-based training environment. Symposium is a Web application that offers a live, "virtual classroom" environment where students with microphone-equipped PCs can hear and talk to the instructor and other students while viewing class materials on their computer screens. Distance learning was a new concept at the time,

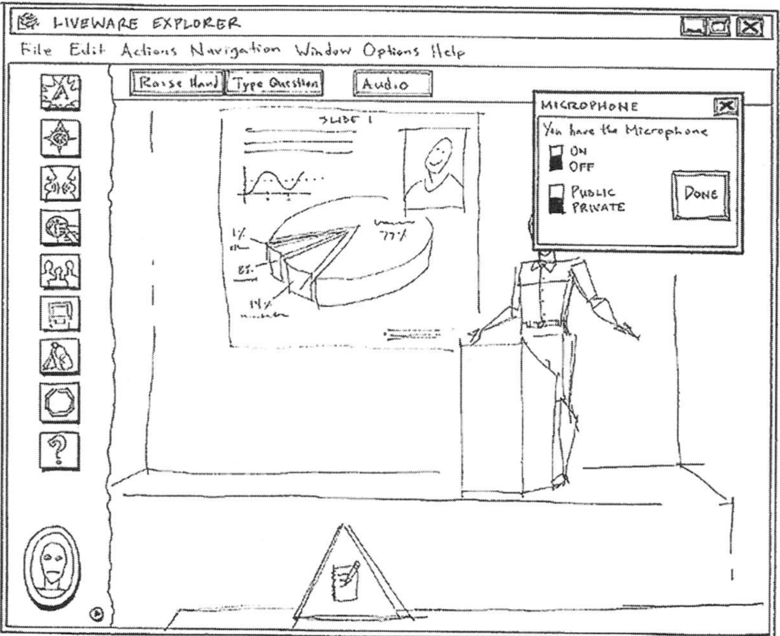

Figure 2.3 The initial paper prototypes of Symposium (called Liveware at the time) featured avatars for the instructor and students. In this example, the instructor is giving a PowerPoint presentation to the class.

and Centra hoped their product would appeal to large corporations with geographically dispersed employees, who would use Symposium from their office or home to receive training without having to travel.

The initial design was ambitious (Figure 2.3). The designers wanted to create a virtual classroom in 3D. Using avatars, students would navigate various rooms (such as a library or classroom) and talk with the instructor and each other via an audio channel. The avatars offered the potential for richer communication through facial expressions and gestures, such as hand-raising to ask a question or head-scratching to indicate confusion.

The product team had questions about whether the navigation worked, whether students could access the online course material, and how well they could participate in the classroom activities. Usability tests provided answers to these questions, and we also found a couple of surprises:

- Rather than enhancing the students' learning experience, the 3D virtual reality interfered with it.

- The product had some important social issues: Users wanted to know who could see and hear them, and they raised concerns about using the interface in a professional work setting.

A Return to Flatland

The paper prototype had stick-figure drawings of the avatars and sketches of the classroom environment. A total of eight users (two at a time) participated in co-discovery usability tests in which they were asked to register for and then take an "online" class. Although it lacked a 3D appearance, the paper prototype sufficed to show us that a 3D environment would interfere with the students' learning experience.

We discovered all manner of confusion related to the avatar, starting with the fact that some people had never heard the term before. Questions arose about the appearance of one's avatar, and users spent time fiddling with the customization controls. The 3D navigation proved cumbersome, with users voicing objections such as, "Why do I have to walk my guy into the classroom? Why can't I just take the class?" It also wasn't clear what viewpoint the avatar should show. Should the interface appear as though the user was looking through the avatar's eyes, or should the user have an outside perspective where they could see their own avatar along with everyone else's? How would the classroom "seating" be handled? (With a spatial layout, students in the back of the classroom wouldn't be visible to those in front, and students in the front might block others' view.) None of these questions had easy answers, and they all distracted users from the learning experience.

The bottom line was that the cutting-edge 3D functionality got in the way of the real purpose of the application—enabling large companies to provide training to geographically dispersed employees. The designers realized that they were jeopardizing their entire business model with an interface that felt too much like a video game.

Based on the feedback, Centra dropped the 3D functionality, which shortened their development schedule. Ronnie Thomson, Director of Engineering, explains, "Time to market was our major concern, and the 3D functionality was our biggest challenge from a technical perspective. Our original plan was to implement it in C++. When we dropped the 3D, we were able to use Java instead, which was a simpler development environment. The end result was that we released rev 1.0 sooner than if we'd stayed with the 3D and C++."

Social Considerations

The paper prototype tests were conducted with everyone—users, facilitator, Computer, and observers—sitting in the same room, so obviously the users realized that people in the test setting could hear them. But the users were able to extrapolate the test setting to real life and identify some of the social concerns that they would have if they were to use this interface alone at their desks.

Because of bandwidth constraints, it wasn't possible to support a full-audio environment. The instructor had a microphone and could "pass" a second microphone to one student at a time. In testing the prototype, we found that the test participants wanted a clear indication of when their microphone was on. (In a similar paper prototype test of a video-conferencing system, one of my colleagues found a situation in which a test participant mistakenly believed that the person on the other end of the pretend system couldn't hear him. He made a joking remark that would have been embarrassing had it happened in real life.) In both of these cases, the designers modified the interface to make the microphone indication more salient.

I learned the live microphone lesson the hard way. During a break from teaching a large class, I went to the ladies' room without turning off my cordless mic! I really wish someone would have found this problem with a paper prototype and implemented a warning buzzer that goes off once the mic moves more than a certain distance from its receiver.

When the 3D functionality was removed, the designers realized they still had to give students a way to see who else was in the class. They added what they called the "people panel"—a listing of the class by name, including visual indication of which person has the microphone (Figure 2.4).

Users also raised some interesting concerns about using the interface in a work setting. With the 3D version, people worried that their co-workers might think they were playing a video game instead of working. They also anticipated the possibility of interruptions; for example, a person looking at a computer screen and wearing headphones might appear to co-workers to be listening to music rather than taking a class. Centra eventually offered kits for students, including a "do not disturb" sign, so that co-workers would know that the person was engaged in training and thus not interruptible.

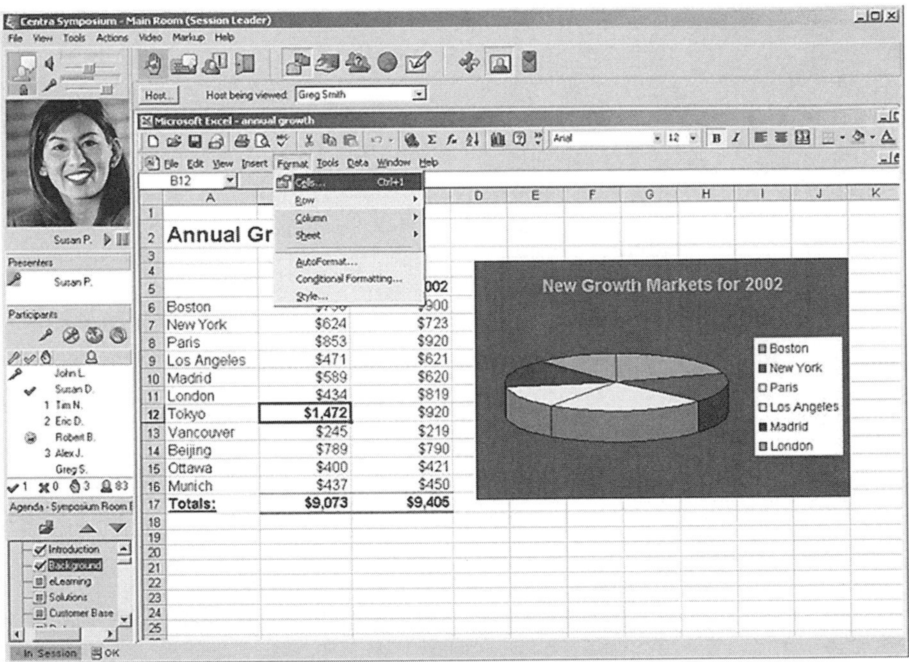

Figure 2.4 This screen shot from Symposium 5.3 shows how the instructor avatar was replaced by a live video feed and student avatars by the Participants panel. Note the microphone symbol to show which class member is speaking.

Six Years Later . . .

As of 2002 Symposium is still alive and well in only two dimensions. Ronnie Thomson, Director of Engineering, reports, "Interface changes in subsequent releases have been relatively minor—most of our focus has been on providing enhancements to the functionality such as the ability to share applications. We tried making radical interface changes in rev 5 (without paper prototyping them first), but customers hated it so we went back to what we had. We've also used the same basic UI model for other products." Drew Wolff, former Director of Product Marketing, concurs: "The target market includes a lot of people who are learning about computers and applications specific to their company. Having to learn how to use Symposium would defeat its purpose. Fortunately, the interface is elegant and intuitive—no need for a book that explains how to use it—so people can concentrate on the class material."

E-commerce Web Site: Priceline.com

In the mid 1990s Walker Digital, a small Connecticut think tank, was preparing to launch a new online service. Their name isn't exactly a household word, but the Web site they launched became one: Priceline.com. Back then, the site was several months away from its initial launch, and they were still trying to figure out exactly how this unique* method of selling airline tickets would work. There were some pretty significant risks, both with the technology and with people's willingness to do business in this new manner. The product team wanted to mitigate the risks by finding out whether average people understood this service and were willing to use it to purchase airline tickets.

For those who aren't familiar with how Priceline works, you tell them when and where you want to fly (U.S.-originating flights only) and how much you're willing to bid for an airline ticket between those cities on those dates. You also give them your credit card number. Priceline checks with several major airlines and lets you know if any of them is willing to sell you the ticket you want for the price you named. If so, bang—you've bought a ticket (usually a nonrefundable one), which is charged to your credit card. The site targets travelers who have flexibility in their plans; the customer can't select the airline or flight time but may be able to get a price that's lower than advertised fares.

Initially, the product team had been focusing on the technical challenges (which were considerable) and also on selling the concept to the major airlines. But they recognized that without consumer acceptance, their clever new business model for selling airline tickets wouldn't get off the ground, so they decided to conduct some usability tests. I worked with several members of the product team to create a paper prototype of the site. All of the pages were drawn by hand because the site was still its conceptual stages. People had some ideas about how the interface might work, but just about everything was still open for debate.

Two members of the product team participated in 2 days of test sessions by "playing computer." We recruited seven people who fit the profile of Priceline's target market and asked them to work with the paper prototype to perform various ticket-purchasing scenarios. We found several important issues, including three showstoppers:

---

* So unique, in fact, that it's patented. (Patent Number 5897620: Method and apparatus for the sale of airline-specified flight tickets. Issued April 29, 1999.)

- Asking for an email address to enter the site met with complete resistance.
- The site (including the company behind it) had to establish its credibility before people were willing to transact.
- Three days was too long to wait for an answer.

After the first two usability tests (four users total), we'd already observed so many serious issues that three of us spent a few hours that evening completely revising the prototype. The next day's tests confirmed that most of our changes were improvements. Equally important, we found some things that the team *didn't* need to worry about:

- People didn't need to see probabilities of getting a ticket; they were going to do their own homework on pricing.
- People understood the concept of submitting a binding offer. They had some questions about it, but overall they understood what the site was offering and how it might benefit them.

Following are the details of what we learned from the paper prototype tests.

Email Address

Some of the developers had already predicted that users wouldn't be willing to provide personal information up front, but the team was still arguing about it. Some of the Marketing folks insisted on asking people for their name and email address before letting them into the site. (Don't laugh. Remember, this was 1997, when the word *e-commerce* wasn't even in the dictionary* and before it was commonly understood that people would rather have a root canal than give out their email address for marketing purposes.) The feedback was unanimous. All seven users said they would either leave the site or enter bogus information. This evidence was enough to convince the proponents of aggressive data collection that it was a Bad Idea, and it was dropped.

Binding Offer, Trust, and Credibility

One of the big questions for Priceline was whether people would understand the concept of the binding offer—that by submitting a credit card they were commit-

* *E-commerce* didn't appear in the Oxford English Dictionary until September 2001.

ting to purchasing a ticket if Priceline found a suitable one that an airline was willing to sell.

The results were interesting. There were indeed problems, but not in the way we expected. On the plus side, the test participants did understand the nature of the binding offer and indicated that they'd be willing to make purchases this way if the deal was attractive enough. However, giving their credit card to an unknown Web site was quite another matter. As one user said, "Anyone can put up a Web site. How do I know these guys are legitimate?"

So we had to think of ways in which an unknown Web site (and company) could convey its credibility. In the testing, the users told us that seeing real flight information would help convince them that this site had a legitimate relationship with the airlines. Unfortunately, users sometimes want things they can't have. Priceline wasn't able to show a list of flights, but they realized they needed to do *something.* For example, even the relatively simple idea of including some company information, such as their office address, the names of company officers, and a toll-free number, helped reassure users that this was a real company (that they could then research further using conventional methods such as calling the Better Business Bureau, which a couple of users said they'd do). And in their help topics, Priceline explicitly says that they don't show flights, which may not be ideal to users but at least prevents them from looking for information that doesn't exist.

Ultimately, Priceline also launched an extensive advertising campaign featuring actor William Shatner that helped establish their brand in the minds of American consumers. I'd be very surprised if they still had the "Are these guys legitimate?" problem today (although they might face it all over again if they expanded internationally).

3-Day Response—Not!

There were significant technical challenges in matching the user's offer against the airlines' databases to see which ones would accept. The developers weren't sure how long it would take to query all the databases and respond to the user. In the paper prototype, we told users that they'd have an answer within 3 days. We quickly learned that this was unacceptable. If people couldn't know right away, they wouldn't use Priceline.

This wasn't good news to the product team because this requirement was much stricter than they'd hoped, and now they had a harder problem to solve. Fortunately, they were able to beef up their technology and the site now promises an answer within 15 minutes. However, in the absence of data about what was acceptable to people, the site might have launched with the 3-day reply and failed miserably.

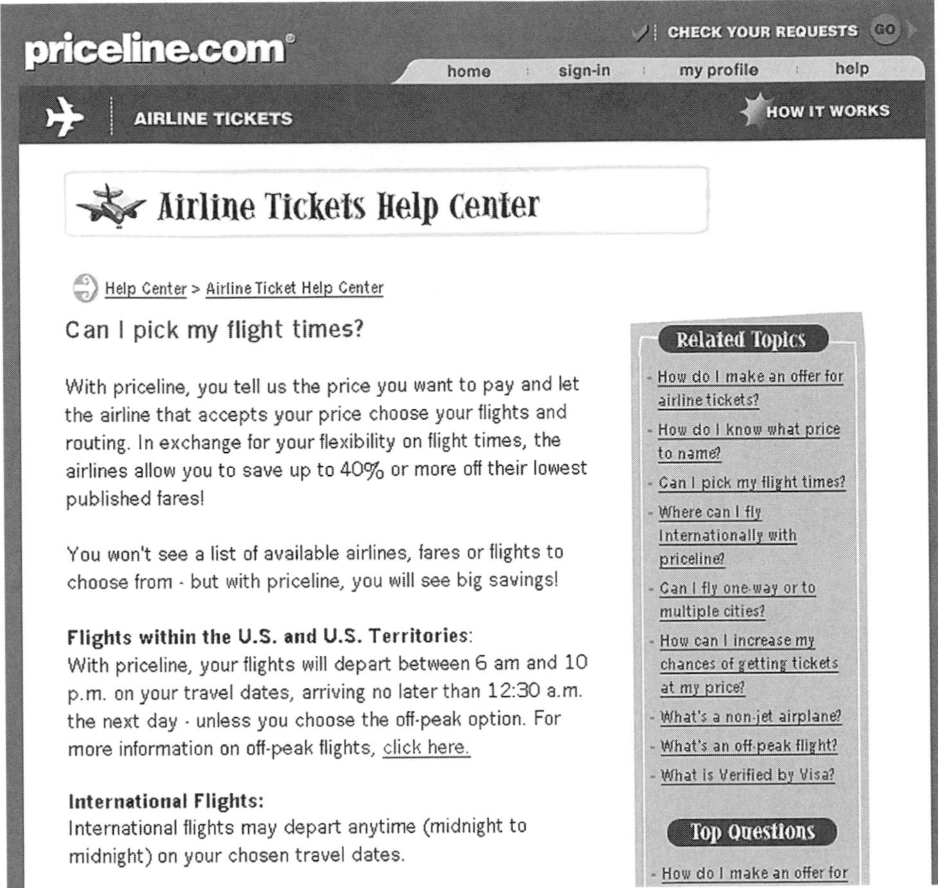

Figure 2.5 This page from Priceline.com, April 2002, explains the trade-off between flexibility and ticket cost—a question that came up in paper prototype testing 5 years earlier, before the site had even launched. Also note the explicit mention that Priceline doesn't show flights, which at least prevents users from continuing to search for this information.

Probability and Pricing

Initially, the designers wanted to estimate the probability of getting a ticket based on the user's bid. For example, for a $300 bid, there's a 50% chance an airline will accept. A nice idea, but pretty darn difficult to do with any degree of accuracy. Fortunately, after hearing all the users describe the ways in which they currently searched for the best travel deals, it was clear that most people would do their own research on lowest available fares and base their offer on that. End of problem. The developers could safely ignore this challenge instead of solving it. (Last I checked, the site simply says, "Visit other travel websites to research the fares and itineraries available on your travel dates.")

Frequently Asked Questions

One of the Catch-22s of new Web sites is figuring out what the "frequently asked" questions are going to be for a site that hasn't launched yet. But this is exactly what we were able to do. A useful output of the paper prototype tests was the set of questions that people had about how Priceline worked. For example, "Is there a fee for this service?" (The answer was no, but the site didn't say so.) Whenever a user had a question, we'd give them an answer orally, then jot down both the question and the answer for future reference. At present, the site has a help section that addresses a number of questions (Figure 2.5), including some that arose during the paper prototype tests. Naturally, the content of the help section has evolved over the years along with the site and the Web-using population.

We conducted these usability tests of Priceline in early 1997, well in advance of their initial launch. Six years later, the site is still in business. Although I can't claim that those early paper prototype tests were solely responsible for the viability of the site, I'd like to think that they helped at least as much as William Shatner's singing in their TV commercials!

Small-Screen Display: Pingtel xpressa Phone Interface

Contributions by Hal Shubin, Rich Schaaf

Pingtel is the creator of xpressa, a high-tech telephone. The xpressa phone has a user interface—a small grayscale LCD display. In addition to the usual set of telephone buttons, the xpressa phone has 11 buttons around the display whose functions change depending on the context (Figure 2.6).

Pingtel was developing this phone and its user interface in 1999. The team had written specifications to document the flow of the screens but hadn't nailed down the interface yet. The designers wanted to make the phone interface intuitive, but in some cases they had what seemed to be equally viable ideas about how to implement functionality. During the design phase a number of questions arose, for example:

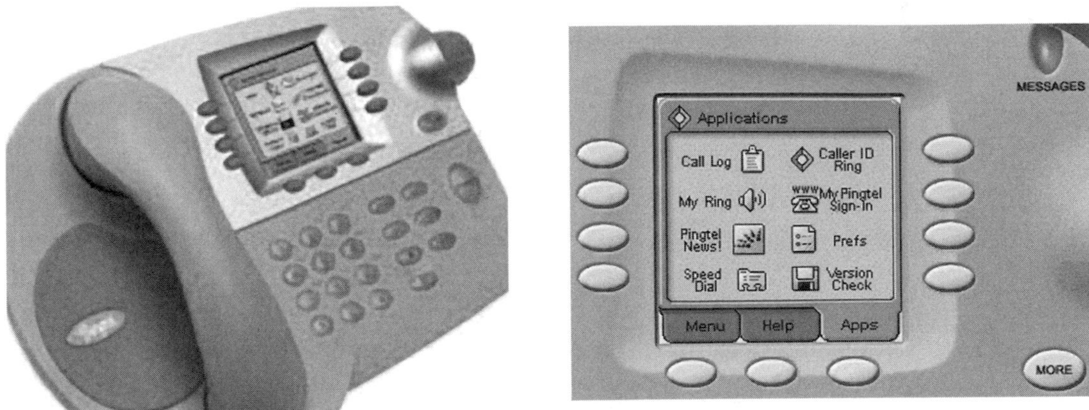

Figure 2.6 The production version of the xpressa phone and a close-up of its LCD display.

- Would users adopt an object-verb approach (for example, looking up a number first and then dialing it) or verb-object approach?
- Which was the easier method of searching for stored phone numbers—scrolling through the entire list or a divide-and-conquer method using the left-hand buttons to divide the list into successively smaller chunks? (See Figure 2.7.)
- Should they create novice and advanced modes, where only a subset of functionality would be available by default and the user would need to explicitly access the more advanced functions? Or would this just be confusing?

The right answers weren't obvious, and the product team didn't want to waste time implementing the wrong approach. They could have mocked up a version of the interface in software, but this would have taken some time. Besides, they believed it was important to see how users interacted with the physical buttons. So they opted to create and usability test a paper prototype of the xpressa interface. Because of the small display and the need to get the spacing right, they created the screens in PhotoShop using a format created by a graphic designer and used overlays for each individual screen.

The team conducted four tests of their paper prototype. Users were asked to complete various tasks (such as calling a previously stored number or transferring a call) by touching the paper prototype buttons and to explain their actions aloud as they went. One of the team members played Computer, swapping screens in

Figure 2.7 One of the paper prototype screens used in testing the search functionality, where users were asked to look up Mary Connolly's home number. The function of the 11 physical buttons around the display depends on context; in this example the four right-hand buttons are not used.

response to the users' actions. There was also a physical model of the phone sitting on the desk so that users could see what the real phone might look like, but they interacted only with the paper prototype.

Findings

The team got answers to their original questions and more. Users naturally used the object-verb method, so there was no need to support the verb-object approach. The divide-and-conquer method for searching was better than scrolling, although eventually the team came up with a type-in search method that was superior to both. The novice mode didn't work. Although hiding advanced options seemed like a good thing, it was too hard for users to find them when they were needed—they had no idea where to look.

The team also found out some things that they hadn't expected. In looking up names in the phone book, none of the users thought to use cell-phone style text entry, where you have to press the "2" key three times to get the letter C, etc. Users naturally pressed one key for each letter; for example, to enter *Smith,* they typed 76484 instead of 77776444844. This is the approach used by audio phone directories, and people tried this approach without being told that it would work this way. (The team had known about both models beforehand; what was surprising was how clear the preference was for the second approach.)

Hal Shubin, the usability consultant who worked on the design and testing of the xpressa interface for Pingtel, summed it up: "Paper prototyping removed a lot of the extraneous baggage; things the developers tended to focus on (shapes, colors, etc.) that weren't relevant to testing the interaction model. The paper prototype helped us learn a lot quickly, without writing any software." For more information on how the xpressa phone interface was prototyped and tested, see the Interaction Design Web site at *www.user.com.*

Touch Screen Interface: Jukebox Car Radio

Contributions by Samantha Lizak, Kristin Grasso

This example is a little different because it comes from a university course rather than from industry, and thus wasn't ever implemented. But this paper prototype is interesting because it simulated a touch screen that incorporated texture. Carnegie Mellon University students Samantha (Sam) Lizak and Kristin Grasso prototyped a jukebox-style music system for a car as part of a class project for a Human Factors class taught by Professor Sara Kiesler. The project's corporate sponsor had provided functional specifications (such as support for up to 1000 music albums), and the class worked in small teams to design and test a prototype interface.

The Modal Touch Screen

Because space is at a premium on an automobile dashboard, Sam and Kristin used a modal design. Depending on which of three physical buttons was pressed, the 5- × 6-inch touch screen console was used for the music system, climate controls, or other functions. For example, when in music mode, the left- and right-pointing arrows skipped over songs, and the up and down arrows controlled volume. In temperature mode, the arrows controlled hot/cold and fan speed, and the six rectangles on the bottom matched the standard airflow choices (feet, feet and face, defrost, and so forth). (See Figure 2.8.)

Before making the paper prototype, Sam and Kristin reviewed touch screen layout guidelines to ensure that their design followed the recommendations for

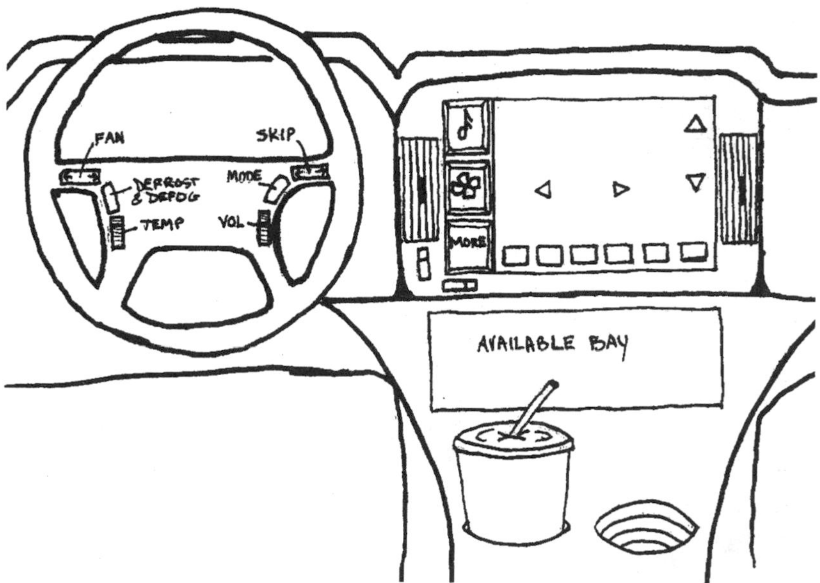

Figure 2.8 The conceptual sketch for the car music system interface. The music note, propeller blade, and "more" buttons are physical buttons that control the major mode of the display. The touch screen console is the mostly empty area above "available bay," and the triangles and rectangles represent textured buttons. (The console isn't normally blank. It displays the appropriate screen depending on the mode.)

button size and separation. (Kristin notes, "You discover how small 5 × 6 inches really is when you're trying to cram a lot of information onto the screen!") To get the spacing right, they made a template of the screen layout, copied it, and then drew each individual screen by hand.

Adding Texture

One drawback of a touch screen is that the user must look at it because the buttons are graphical rather than physical. Sam and Kristin first got the idea of incorporating texture into their interface after doing some contextual inquiry sessions (they rode around with people in their cars, taking notes about how they operated their car stereos). They observed that most people reached blindly for the radio controls and used touch to guide them to the correct one. The students believed that judicious use of textured buttons would help users operate the controls while keeping their eyes on the road.

Figure 2.9 These two prototype screens illustrate different uses of the display area and textured buttons. The left image shows the radio display, where the six buttons were used in a conventional manner for preset stations. The right image shows the jukebox, where the three bottom virtual buttons each include two textured buttons.

The textured control buttons consisted of six rectangles along the bottom edge, left- and right-pointing triangles near the center about an inch apart, and up- and down-pointing triangles along the right edge. To add texture, the students used a clear plastic overlay and damaged the plastic over the buttons by poking it with a pen. In some modes, there were two textured rectangles per touch screen button. For example, on the screen shown in Figure 2.9, the user would feel two textured buttons for the "By Band" control, but both would do the same thing. This flexible mapping of physical to virtual buttons allowed the virtual buttons to be larger on screens where fewer buttons were needed.

Successful Interface, Successful Learning Experience

The students conducted five usability tests of their prototype. They placed each screen inside a clear plastic sleeve like those used for overhead transparencies. They put all the screens into a three-ring binder so that whichever of them was playing Computer could flip to the next screen based on user actions. The user sat at a PC-based driving simulator, and one student held the prototype off to the side, about where it would be in a car.

The students actually did their first usability test in a car driven slowly around a parking lot. Professor Kiesler decided that was a little too realistic and stipulated that for safety reasons, prototypes were to be tested without driving.

Sam and Kristin observed that people did use the textured buttons as they had hoped. The users were able to keep their attention primarily on driving and still operate the controls correctly. Even with only five users, there was a consensus that users wanted some additional functionality, such as a "profile" feature to store preferences for sound levels, temperature, and radio presets. The students also learned that some features they had considered (such as playlists) were either not important to users or were not practical without a keypad, which would be inappropriate to use while driving. The feedback from their paper prototype quickly revealed which of their ideas were workable and which were not.

Because this paper prototype was created in academia rather than in industry, its success is measured not only by how well the interface worked but also by how much the students learned from it. In addition to the basics of touch screen design, Sam and Kristin gained experience in balancing design constraints. The small display size forced them to keep simplifying the functionality and interface, and the paper prototype let them experiment with ways to make the most common functions the easiest to use.

Historical Examples of Paper Prototyping

Contributions by Robin Kinkead

The idea of testing interface mock-ups has been around for decades. Long before the graphical user interface (GUI) was born, engineers and industrial designers were testing prototypes of airplane cockpits, medical equipment, cash registers, and so on. Robin Kinkead, who has worked in the human factors field since 1965, was involved in a number of pre-GUI prototyping projects. Following are two of them from the early 1970s.

1971, NCR: Postal Mail Sorting Machine

In the early 1970s, much of postal mail sorting was still done by hand, and NCR was developing a machine to partially automate the process. In machine-assisted mail sorting, a postal worker would read the zip code from each envelope and key it in so that the machine could route it appropriately. One important design question was whether envelopes should be presented in a vertical or horizontal sequence. To work as quickly as possible, operators would look at the next envelope as they typed the zip code from the current one. Robin needed data on whether it was faster to move one's eyes left to the next envelope or up to it. He and his colleagues hypothesized that the horizontal sequence might be faster because the side-to-side eye movements required were similar to reading.

To find out, Robin built a paper prototype using foam board and stiff paper. He shifted envelopes manually while the user pressed buttons to indicate which way arrows went on the simulated addresses. The answer? Contrary to what they expected, vertical was faster. It was a shorter distance, and addresses are more compressed vertically.

1974, Xerox: Stenographic Translator

The Xerox Stenographic Translator was a color-screen editing station for computer-translated stenographic (court reporter) notes. The development team at Xerox knew that the user interface was going to be complex, that users had to navigate among several screens, and that representations of particular screens would change as well while the user edited text. Back then, they had no way at all of making a software prototype of the concepts (this was pre-GUI), so paper drawings of screen states were the logical choice.

The prototype consisted of 250 pages of screen drawings (naturally, similar screens were created with the aid of a Xerox copier). Stenographers were instructed on how the device was going to work and then were asked to perform several tasks, including bringing up notes, editing them, adjusting the steno's "profile," and finally printing. Depending on the user's choice, the experimenter flipped to the correct response page.

This technique proved extremely successful. A complete, complex user interface in an almost unknown medium was designed, tested with eight people, and refined in just 4 weeks. Stenographers using the 12 beta test machines were able to quickly learn and use them for creating written transcriptions of courtroom proceedings.* Unfortunately, Xerox never took the device beyond the beta phase, although Robin did receive a patent for the user interface.

Summary

One of the fascinating things about usability tests, whether or not they use paper prototypes, is how often product teams are surprised by what they learn. The team usually has many questions going into the usability study—and maybe even some accurate predictions about where the problems will lie—but the real value in usability testing lies in its ability to surprise the product team with answers to questions they never would have thought to ask.

As the saying goes, it's not the rattlesnake you see that will bite you. It's inherently difficult to know where your own blind spots are—usability testing helps you find them. Many of the problems described in these case studies would have had a detrimental effect on the success of the product, and in some cases the entire company, had they not been found before release.

As powerful as usability testing is, a paper prototype leverages that power one step further by letting you gain all that knowledge even earlier in the project, before implementation. Although all the problems described in this chapter could have been found by testing a working version of the interface, the product teams were glad they didn't have to wait until then.

---

* Robin told me: "The beta test units worked so well that Larry Tesler, then at Xerox PARC, said after he tried it: 'That interface was *really* friendly!'" Robin believes this may have been the first time anyone ever described a UI as "friendly," soon to become the much overused "user-friendly."

Chapter 3

Thinking about Prototyping

This chapter explores two main topics—how a prototyping method supports (or interferes with) the process of creating an interface and the effects of paper prototyping on the people involved in producing, testing, and refining a design. You'll see the pros and cons of paper prototyping and learn how to compare it to whatever other method of prototyping you may be considering for your product. Other than paper, I don't cover specific prototyping methods here (in Chapter 12 I mention a few) because I think it's important to first think in terms of the concepts and benefits pertaining to prototyping. If a new prototyping tool comes along 2 years after this book, you should still be able to use the material in this chapter to evaluate it.

Creating an Interface—Look and Feel

Broadly speaking, you can think of an interface in terms of look and feel. The look comprises the screen layout, graphics, wording, and so on, and the feel is the behavior and processing. Look is pixels; feel is code. Both look and feel require work to produce, and the amount of effort varies depending on the method of prototyping. Let's examine look and feel in the context of designing a screen; for the sake of simplicity I'll choose an online order form.

The effort needed to create the form's look can be further divided into design time and rendering time. First you have to understand the purpose of the form, determine what fields it must contain, think about what order they should appear in, decide how they should be labeled, and so on. That's design time, and it's a process that happens inside your head, often with the aid of specs or other input. An order form is a relatively simple example; other screens are much more difficult to design. To get the order form out of your head and into a place where others can see it, you have to render it, either by hand or on a computer. In reality, design and rendering aren't discrete steps as I've described them here—they happen repeatedly and often simultaneously. But thinking of them separately will help clarify how a prototyping method supports the work.

The feel of an interface is, in essence, its programming—all the code that must be written to display the form, accept the user's inputs, process them, and produce some type of output. (Once you start thinking about how that output will appear to the user, then you're back to the look.) Depending on the development environment, some things are more arduous to code than others. Strictly speaking, programming also has design time and rendering time, although that distinction isn't as helpful for feel as it is for look, so I'm going to ignore it.

So we have three main activities to consider in prototyping—the time you spend

1. Designing—in other words thinking about what the user will experience
2. Rendering what the user will see
3. Coding the behavior

Now let's examine how paper and computer-based prototyping tools support each of these activities. You'll notice that each section has some questions to ask yourself while considering which prototyping method is best for you.

Designing

Design is probably the hardest activity of the three, and correspondingly it's hard for a prototyping method—any prototyping method—to support it very well. As sophisticated as computers are, they're a poor replacement for our creative problem-solving abilities, which is why interfaces are still designed and developed by humans. Prototyping methods focus mainly on the rendering and coding aspects of the process; they don't necessarily help us become better designers.

On the other hand, it's possible for a prototyping method to *constrain* the design process, as Alan Cooper eloquently explains (see Of Interest box that follows). One benefit of paper prototyping is that it imposes relatively few constraints on a design. The next chapter provides many examples of how to construct various interface widgets. For now, proceed under the premise that paper prototyping will let you make most anything you can envision.

Of Interest . . . Excerpt from "The Perils of Prototyping"

By Alan Cooper, Chairman & Founder
August/September 1994
Originally Published in Visual Basic Programmer's Journal;
available at ***www.cooper.com/articles/art_perils_of_prototyping.htm***

Software has a life of its own. It is full of little quirks and idiosyncrasies that influence how it is built. This is true whether the tools are high-level (VB or HyperCard) or low-level (asm, C). Some things are easy to build, and other things are hard to build. That this strongly influences the design is almost universally unrecognized. If you take the great risk of building something divergent from the tool's strength, you will quickly find yourself in a minefield of tactical choices: "Hmmm, let's see, if I code it this way the user presentation is better but then I have to build my own [giant-piece-of-reinvented-wheel], or I could code it the other way and have this operational conflict with this store-bought gizmo that I need to make this other part of the program easy to do, or I could roll my own and then it would be correct but I won't be able to test it for 6 months, or I could . . ." None of this has anything to do with software design!

Of course, any design process has constraints. Some things are hard to implement, and others are impractical or even impossible. A good designer doesn't ignore constraints, but on the other hand you don't want to choose a tool that introduces additional and unnecessary ones, especially early in the process when you're trying to be creative. When considering a prototyping method, ask yourself: *"What does this tool make easy (or hard) to prototype? Will this tool affect my creativity? How much will it distract me from thinking about the design?"*

Rendering

There are many ways to render an interface. You can draw it by hand or do it on a computer using Dreamweaver, Visual Basic, or any one of a myriad of tools. There are even tools like DENIM that let you *sketch* an interface on a computer by means of a drawing tablet, which may initially seem odd but as discussed in Chapter 12, it does have some benefits. There are plenty of choices here. In thinking about rendering, consider how much effort is needed with a particular method and how good the prototype needs to look. The following sections address these issues in more detail.

Effort to Render

The effort needed to render a prototype varies not only with the method but also with the skills of the individuals involved—drawing comes naturally to some people, whereas others may be proficient at creating interfaces with software. There are three factors to consider regarding the effort required to create a prototype and test it with users: creation, duplication, and modification.

Creation

How quickly can a screen be made the first time, starting from a blank slate? Some prototyping tools give you a leg up because they provide a library of widgets, or maybe you've even developed your own. Although it's possible for some people to mock up screens quite quickly using software, it's often possible to draw that same screen by hand in even less time. From what I've seen, I believe that drawing by hand is probably faster for many people, most of the time, but naturally there are exceptions.

Duplication

Does your interface have many similar screens (for example, several online product pages that all have the same layout)? How easy is it to make the variations? In software, this is pretty straightforward—you load a template, put in the unique parts, and do a Save As. With a hand-drawn paper prototype you can do the analogous process using a copy machine, so there may not be a significant difference here.

Modification

When you discover a reason to change a screen, how quickly can you tweak it? If this happens in a usability test, can you do it while the user is still present and thus get immediate feedback? An interface doesn't just get designed, it gets redesigned as well, often many times before it's done. With a paper prototype, you can make changes very quickly, even during a usability test. If a term is confusing, you can cross it out and try a different one. You can write an example next to a confusing edit field. You can write a sentence of explanation about the next step in a process. Simple changes like these can solve many usability problems.

I once saw a developer (let's call him Ed) make changes on the fly to a working Web application. During the usability tests, Ed sat in the room along with the other observers. I thought he was just using his laptop to take notes—little did I know that he had a connection to the development server. Along came a task where the users became confused and clicked the wrong link. During the post-task discussion, Ed asked the users to click Back and then Refresh. Voila! Up came a new version of the page that solved the problem. Although Ed's real-time interface changes were entertaining as well as successful, it's rare that this is feasible for developers to do with a software prototype.

With some software prototyping tools it may also be possible to make quick changes, but think carefully about the logistics of how this would work in a usability test. When the user finds a problem and you want to make a change, you might have to grab the keyboard and mouse from the user, get out of the running prototype and into the prototyping tool, make the change, and then get back into the same spot in the interface (which may have been reached after a sequence of actions) to see whether your fix works. One advantage of a paper prototype is that you can make the change without losing the user's context.

How Good Should It Look?

This is a complex question, so I'm providing only a partial answer here and will tackle other parts of the answer elsewhere in this book. The short answer is that a prototype has to look (and act) realistic enough to elicit feedback for the issues you're most worried about, but it doesn't need to be any better than that. Chapter 12 goes into detail about the kinds of problems that paper prototypes are good and not so good at finding. Chapter 13 presents evidence that paper prototypes seem to reveal about as many (and as severe) problems as you'd get by testing the real thing; as you saw in the previous chapter, there are plenty of real-life examples to back this up.

One drawback of a prototyping tool that gives you several options for specifying the appearance (fonts, colors, shading, and so on) is that it's easy to get caught up in tweaking the design to make it look nice. If you end up changing it later (and has there ever been a design that didn't get changed?) then your tweaking time will have been wasted. A sketched prototype helps you avoid the temptation to perfect the appearance because it isn't *supposed* to look finished. Time is money, so you want to weigh whatever effort you're putting into a prototype against the benefit you'll get out of it.

Coding

I once saw a demo of a tool that was touted as a fast and easy way to create interfaces. The guy conducting the demo first put several controls on the screen in just a minute or two. Then he made an offhand comment about "linking in some prewritten code" and jumped to a completed version of the interface. Being a software engineer at the time, I immediately thought, "But wait—he's just skipped over the hard part!"

Coding the behavior of an interface (and the underlying databases and processing required to produce its outputs) is where the bulk of the work lies—90%, according to Joel Spolsky, a programmer who writes a column on software development at *www.joelonsoftware.com*. I don't want to get hung up on the exact percentage because it varies depending on the type of interface and also on the tool—a software application may have very complex underlying code, whereas many Web pages have little or none. But it's a reasonable generalization that most interfaces have substantial code beneath them.

In a paper prototype, the coding effort is always zero.

Joel explained to me why creating a working software prototype can actually take longer than making the real thing. The problem is that you have to either reconstruct code or leave it out. If you leave it out, you're very restricted in the kinds of tasks you can ask users to do, and thus you may not get good feedback about the new functionality. If you reconstruct it, however, your software prototype can take longer than if you'd just coded it into the real product. Joel offers this example:

> Several years ago at Microsoft, the developers wanted to explore the usefulness and feasibility of using drag & drop to move cells in Excel. They had a couple of interns work all summer to make a prototype of Excel to support this functionality. Trouble was, to actually test it they needed to implement a healthy chunk of the spreadsheet functionality so people could perform realistic tasks—if they'd just done the drag & drop part, they wouldn't have gotten to see which

> method people naturally chose in different situations. So they ended up re-creating a good chunk of Excel in order to make their prototype functional. When they usability tested it, they found that drag & drop was indeed a useful thing for users, so they put it in the product. It took the staff programmer about 1 week to implement in the product, as compared to the interns who worked all summer on their prototype. The irony of this is that the whole purpose of a prototype is to save time.

Joel also notes that you could always put new functionality into your code and take it out later if it isn't what users need. But ripping out code can introduce bugs, not to mention that destroying one's own work is a pretty unsatisfying thing to do.

As prototyping tools become more sophisticated, they'll grow in their ability to automate the behavior of certain interface widgets—put a Submit button on a form, and it'll automatically do the right thing. But a prototyping tool that could automate everything would in essence replace programmers, and I don't think that will ever happen. In a paper prototype, a human simulates what the code would do. Thus, *the coding effort is always zero.* No matter how sophisticated the prototyping tool or how proficient one is with it, you can't get any faster than that. This is an important benefit of a paper prototype, particularly for complex software—no code to write or (sometimes even more important) rewrite until the design has stabilized. The flip side of that coin is that at some point you do have to start writing code, and paper prototypes don't help with that.

To assess the importance of the coding factor for your product, ask yourself: *"How much code is required to support everything the user sees? How much of this work does the tool do for me? How much of a pain will it be to change that code while the design is still changing? Do we plan to evolve our prototype into the finished product, or is it okay to throw the prototype away when the real coding begins?"*

Don't forget the data. As Chapter 7 explains, if you plan to conduct usability tests of your design, users will need to see realistic data to perform meaningful tasks. For example, if you want users to look up a stock quote using your mobile phone interface, you'll need some way to make that stock quote appear on the display so that users will know when they've found the answer. Depending on where the interface's data comes from, this may be easy or hard. Sometimes in an electronic prototype it's necessary to hard-code the data or create a test database; it may be easier to use a paper prototype instead because you can simply write in whatever data you need. So consider the following: *"Where does the data come from? How easy will it be to have the prototype display the realistic data needed for usability testing?"*

Finding Technical Issues

Obviously, paper prototypes don't show you whether a design can be built (of course, other prototyping methods may not either, unless they use the same development environment in which you're planning to implement). Paper prototypes aren't constrained by existing architecture, databases, bandwidth, legal considerations, business policies, the operating system, accessibility concerns, and so on. In real life, developers must consider all these constraints and more. You don't want to create a prototype that's impossible to implement.

Interestingly, even though there is no code involved in a paper prototype, it can sometimes help the development team anticipate technical problems. Although software engineers naturally tend to think in terms of database schema, software architecture, communication protocols, and the like, sometimes they get technological tunnel vision and may overlook the implications that a particular user requirement has for the design.

Here's an example from my own experience:

> In the mid-1980s I was a project manager for the development of some internal tools for my company's field technicians. We had spent several weeks hashing out database schema, processing, and all sorts of technical innards. There were also to be some reports available to the user, but we'd left them until last under the assumption that they'd be easy—reports simply take information from database records and format it nicely, so what could go wrong with that?
>
> But then the engineer assigned to program the report modules walked into my office scratching his head. He couldn't figure out where Report X was supposed to get its data. We quickly realized that, in fact, Report X was impossible to produce with the databases we'd designed. D'oh! It took our five-person team about 2 weeks to revise the databases (and the code that had already been built on them, as well as the specs) to recover from this snafu.

Would paper prototyping have found this problem? Although I can't rewrite history, I believe the answer is yes. In paper prototyping, you first create a realistic set of tasks and then build the prototype to support them, which forces you to visualize the entire process of what users will be doing. If we had done usability testing on this project, we would have included the reports because users needed them to see the results of their work. The problem with Report X was blindingly obvious the first time someone looked at it—mocking up Report X would have put it on our radar screen before we'd spent all that time developing a database schema that was incompatible with it.

Strictly speaking, paper prototyping doesn't deserve all the credit for unearthing this type of problem—it's really walking through the tasks that allows us to see an interface from a user's perspective. The paper prototype simply makes it possible for this to happen earlier in the development process, when it's less painful to make changes. In working with many product teams over the years, I've seen that it's common for technical questions about what can and cannot be coded to arise from the process of constructing a paper prototype and using it to walk through tasks.

Now let's switch our focus from prototyping tools and interface development and start talking about the people—first the users, then the product team.

Psychological Benefits for Users

Suppose you had a software prototyping tool that could read your mind—you simply plunk down all the interface elements and everything would auto-magically behave the way you wanted, without any coding, so you could test it on a computer. Even if you could do this, you still wouldn't have the advantages of paper prototyping described in this section. It turns out that there are some interesting psychological effects in terms of the way users respond to an unfinished design that's shown to them on paper.

Less Intimidating Than a Computer

Many people, especially younger ones, take computers for granted—my niece was proficient with a mouse at age 3. But there is still—and will continue to be for decades—a substantial percentage of adults who are not yet comfortable with computers. When faced with technology they find intimidating, there's an increased risk that users will feel foolish when they can't figure something out during a usability test. In contrast, with a paper prototype there is no computer to contend with, just human beings. This can help some technophobes relax, so keep this in mind if your target audience includes people who lack confidence in working with computers. (One could make the opposite argument that some people may be more comfortable interfacing with computers than with humans, so again it depends on who your audience is.)

One might wonder about the opposite situation—if your users are technically savvy, does paper prototyping seem silly to them? I've tested several paper prototypes of sophisticated scientific and engineering applications, and in my experience the answer is no. Techie types such as network administrators and software developers readily understand that the paper prototypes are being used to get their feedback before the design is cast in concrete. I've yet to see one scoff at a paper prototype.

More Creative Feedback

An unfinished design seems to encourage a more creative response from reviewers. In a paper by Schumann, Strothotte, Laser, and Raab (1996), the researchers compared the methods used by architects to present building concepts to their clients. The researchers found that many architects preferred to show their clients sketches during the early stages of design, believing that this encouraged more discussion about the building and its intended use. Most architects reserved more accurate representations such as CAD drawings for the later stages of design. (Strangely enough, the researchers were working on a tool that would take a CAD drawing and produce from it something that *looked* like a sketch—a seeming step backward that was done deliberately for the purpose of encouraging creative discussion.)

Unfinished designs can have a dramatic effect on how stakeholders become involved with the project, as illustrated by the story in the From the Field box on p. 59. Instead of being a passive viewer, a person presented with an unfinished design becomes more creatively engaged in thinking about the concepts and functionality. I've seen this happen many times. If you show users a slick-looking interface and ask for feedback, they may subconsciously think, "These guys have obviously put a lot of thought into this, so I'll keep my hare-brained suggestion to myself." But with a paper prototype, it's obvious that the design is literally still "on the drawing board" and that changes can be made very easily, sometimes even by users themselves.

No Nitpicky Feedback

A polished-looking prototype can encourage low-level feedback about the visual aspects of the design. When something appears to be finished, minor flaws stand out and will catch the user's attention. To put it another way, people nitpick. Unless you're in the later stages of development or are specifically asking for feedback on the visual design, it isn't especially useful to hear comments such as "Those fields don't line up" or "I don't like that shade of green." I've known many

From the Field: Rough Prototypes Encourage Feedback

"My company researches and develops intelligent autonomous agents and agent-based applications, generally for the United States government. I was about to present a set of preliminary designs to a government research technical review committee. Previous review meetings of this nature had left the committee with a negative view of our progress and our willingness to involve their ideas.

"The project leader and I had initially discussed taking my paper prototype drawings and either redrafting them or implementing mock-ups (in VB or Director) of them. Our goals were to (1) reinforce that these designs were preliminary, (2) encourage a dialogue with the committee about the direction of the project, and (3) get the reviewers excited about being part of the design process and to invest some of their considerable energy and expertise into the project. After thinking about what we hoped to get out of the review presentation, we decided to stick with the rough drawings instead of something more polished.

"This approach was a huge success. The reviewers got very excited during the presentation and constantly interrupted me with suggestions and meaningful critiques. Afterward we got additional positive comments and ideas—something that had rarely happened with past projects. Committee members specifically mentioned that the sketchy nature of drawings made them feel included in the process.

"Three months later we presented an implemented demonstration of the application that included a number of changes suggested by the review committee and a presentation that showed the now-familiar design sketches next to the implemented screens. The demonstration was even a larger success than the prior meeting. The committee members felt like part of the team and were excited by seeing their ideas come to life. In addition, seeing the rough design sketches presented next to the polished screen shots left them impressed by the large degree of progress made. They left excited about the future of the project. Again, this high level of collaboration between the research team and the review committee had been rare in the past and bodes very well for both the quality of the final deliverable and for future funding for the research project."

Jack Zaientz, Soar Technology

developers who ran afoul of this problem when using software prototypes in an effort to get feedback about functionality—the Of Interest box on p. 61 is a great example. Hand-drawn paper prototypes avoid the nitpicky feedback because it's obvious that you haven't specified the look yet. This encourages users to focus on the concepts and functionality instead.

My colleague Ann Marie McKinnon, a graphic designer, has experienced something similar to Joel's Corollary Two—if it looks too pretty, people can become too attached to it. After she showed a nicely designed set of screens to some key stakeholders, Ann Marie reported that they "fell in love" with that particular version of the interface because it looked so nice. They subsequently resisted making any changes to the functionality, even when the rest of the team found a clear need to do so.

Effects on the Product Team

Perhaps even more significant than the users' reactions are the effects that paper prototyping has on the product team's mindset and the ways in which they work together.

Minimizes the Invested Effort

The more effort you've put into creating something, the harder it is to accept that it needs to be changed. Say that you're a developer who has spent 2 weeks creating a prototype based on the requirements spec you got from Marketing. Upon seeing it in action, Marketing decides they want something different. What's your reaction?

a. Oh my yes, your way is obviously better. No problem, I'll change it.

b. But I did it this way because . . .

c. Sure, I'd be happy to waste another 2 weeks of my life coding something else you don't want.

d. You want changes? Step outside and I'll make some to your face.

Unless you're a saint or a psychopath, you probably answered b, maybe c on a really bad day. It's a natural reaction to defend one's hard work to avoid the need to redo it. I've also heard, and I'll confess to having done this myself, that a developer

Of Interest . . . Excerpt from "The Iceberg Secret"

by Joel Spolsky
February 13, 2002
Available at ***www.joelonsoftware.com.***

You know how an iceberg is 90% underwater? Well, most software is like that too—there's a pretty user interface that takes about 10% of the work, and then 90% of the programming work is under the covers. And if you take into account the fact that about half of your time is spent fixing bugs, the UI only takes 5% of the work. And if you limit yourself to the *visual* part of the UI, the pixels, what you would see in PowerPoint, now we're talking less than 1%.

That's not the secret. The secret is that *People Who Aren't Programmers Do Not Understand This.* There are some very, very important corollaries to the Iceberg Secret.

Important Corollary One

If you show a nonprogrammer a screen which has a user interface that is 90% worse, they will think that the program is 90% worse.

I learned this lesson as a consultant, when I did a demo of a major web-based project for a client's executive team. The project was almost 100% code complete. We were still waiting for the graphic designer to choose fonts and colors and draw the cool 3-D tabs. In the meantime, we just used plain fonts and black and white, there was a bunch of ugly wasted space on the screen, basically it didn't look very good at all. But 100% of the functionality was there and was doing some pretty amazing stuff.

What happened during the demo? The clients spent the *entire meeting* griping about the graphical appearance of the screen. They weren't even talking about the UI. Just the graphical appearance. *"It just doesn't look slick,"* complained their project manager. That's all they could think about. We couldn't get them to think about the actual functionality. Obviously fixing the graphic design took about one day. It was almost as if they thought they had hired *painters*.

Important Corollary Two

If you show a nonprogrammer a screen which has a user interface which is 100% beautiful, they will think the program is almost done.

People who aren't programmers are just looking at the screen and seeing some pixels. And if the pixels look like they make up a program which does something, they think "oh, gosh, how much harder could it be to make it *actually work?*"

The big risk here is that if you mock up the UI first, presumably so you can get some conversations going with the customer, then everybody's going to think you're almost done. And then when you spend the next year working "under the covers," so to speak, nobody will really see what you're doing and they'll think it's nothing.

It's hard to change something if you've invested a lot of effort in it. (Illustration by Rene Rittiner.)

who agrees to revise the interface may quietly postpone this effort under the (sometimes correct) assumption that in a couple of weeks Marketing will again ask for something completely different.

But with a paper prototype, the effort that went into its creation is measured in minutes or hours, rather than days or weeks. The feeling of ownership is proportionally less, as is the knee-jerk reaction to defend the design and resist changing it. If you've spent 15 minutes drafting a screen and the first user finds a huge problem with it, it's relatively easy to throw it away and try something different.

More Creativity

Veteran usability specialist Mary Beth Rettger describes an interesting phenomenon regarding how paper prototypes can result in design revolution, not just evolution. The MathWorks makes extensive use of paper prototypes during development. Mary Beth has noticed that sometimes a developer will test a paper prototype and find some minor problems—nothing too serious. They'll start to tweak the interface, then scrap it in favor of an approach that's very different and much better. It's hard to articulate, but amazing to watch. She says, "It's as if they turn the design inside out and upside down. Or keep one piece and change everything around it. It's almost organic in nature." Because paper prototypes are a flexible medium that let you see the strengths and weaknesses of a design early on,

Mary Beth conjectures that they facilitate the kind of quantum design leaps that lead to greatly improved usability.

Multidisciplinary Teams Can Participate

Interfaces aren't created by interface designers or programmers alone; there's a whole cast of characters whose insights need to be funneled into the design. Customer support reps often have a good grasp of what customers find confusing, and so do trainers. Technical writers can provide a "distant early warning" about usability problems when they run into something that's hard to document. (When I was a software project manager, I learned that when the tech writer wandered into my office with a puzzled look asking, "Can you explain to me again how this six-level alarm prioritization thing works?" it was usually a clue that we'd over-designed something.) And if the people in Sales and Marketing have done their homework, they'll have a lot of data about what the target market wants, and why.

Expertise in interface design or software development is not necessary to participate in the creation of a paper prototype. Thus, it's a technique where members from different disciplines can collaborate, including writers, marketers, trainers, customer service reps, and so on. Anyone who has knowledge of the subject area or the users can contribute directly to the design. In particular, technical writers are often valuable contributors to a paper prototype—they can get right in there and wordsmith the *interface,* rather than having to explain it in the manual or help.

I'm not implying that good design can be done by nondesigners or that the designers responsible for an interface should abdicate this responsibility in favor of design by committee. (Chapter 7 talks more about the dynamics of paper prototype creation.) All I'm saying is that paper prototyping facilitates the process of incorporating many people's ideas into a design, and usually that's a good thing.

Earlier Communication across Disciplines

Software engineers write code. Interface designers create screens. Technical writers draft help and manuals. Marketers research market segments, find opportunities, and create brands. Graphic designers create effective layouts and visuals that support the brand. Last but not least, the users themselves are going about their daily lives, unaware that you're working on something they're going to love (or hate). The trouble is, in the early stages of product development these activities are very separate. There's little means of communicating in a useful and collaborative way about the product. Paper prototyping alleviates the problem because all the stakeholders can see the same thing at the same time.

Paper prototyping is also a great way for new team members to get up to speed on the product and how it works. For example, instead of the technical writer going to the designer for an explanation of the interface, the writer can participate in the creation and testing of the prototype. The same end result—but less pain and suffering to get there.

From the Field: Fostering a Common Vision

"Our development team at RioPort is divided between California and Colorado. Typically when teams are remote they tend to see things differently—sometimes there's a communication breakdown when one person can't grasp what someone else is verbalizing. There are general issues everyone can see, but it's easy to get a myopic view when you don't have everyone in the same room, looking at the same white board.

"In the summer of 2001, the Colorado developers went to the west coast and both groups worked on the paper prototype for what eventually became our PulseOne Media Service. Walking through the flow of screens as a team before bringing in users was helpful in giving us a common understanding of the interface. When we did usability tests, it was valuable having customers echo the same issues that some of us had been concerned about, and to see their discovery and exploration process. Actually observing participants is a much richer form of communication compared to reading a report, plus we were able to ask them questions directly. This was important because our interface supported a model of online music distribution that was new to people, and we wanted to hear their impressions of it.

"As a result of the usability tests, we gained a common understanding of problems and areas that needed additional attention. The paper prototyping exercise allowed us to do this earlier in the project cycle; this accelerated communication and eliminated misunderstandings and rework that otherwise would have occurred later."

Tony Schaller, Sr. Vice President
Technology and CTO at RioPort, Inc.

Avoiding Miscommunication (The "Amelia Bedelia" Problem)

Miscommunication between any two people is inevitable at some point in their relationship. For people who come from different professions with different jargon, it can be difficult to establish a common vision of the product and how it serves its target user population.

For a developer, it's frustrating to implement something that wasn't quite what Marketing had in mind. I call this the "Amelia Bedelia" problem after a funny series of children's books about a well-meaning maid who follows her employers' instructions literally, with predictably disastrous results. It's not so funny when you've spent days or months developing the wrong thing. Interface specs—even with screen shots—don't solve the Amelia Bedelia problem because they don't

"My dress!" exclaimed Mrs. Rogers.

"It's full of holes."

"Yes, ma'am, I removed

every single spot,"

said Amelia Bedelia.

Like the children's book character Amelia Bedelia, we sometimes misinterpret what our customers are asking for. (From *Thank You, Amelia Bedelia* by Peggy Parish. New York: HarperTrophy, 1995. Reprinted by permission.)

show the behavior of the system and they also don't show you what people expect the interface to do (especially nontechnical people because they have a harder time inferring functionality). But when you put a paper prototype in front of someone and watch them use it, you'll quickly discover whether it meets their expectations. It's a good idea to get Marketing (or whoever collected the requirements and wrote the early project documents) involved in prototyping sessions and make sure they attend the usability tests.

Opinion Wars

Every development team has its opinion wars—those endless meetings where arguments go round and round about the best way for users to do something. Many opinions are based on assumptions, and particularly nasty disagreements are often based on *unspoken* assumptions. Or sometimes there's simply a lack of data—in the words of philosopher Bertrand Russell, "The most savage controversies are those about matters as to which there is no good evidence either way."

I once stopped two developers who were on the verge of a fistfight over whether there should be an Update button on a form. The interface in question was a client-server software application used by customer service reps (CSRs) while on the phone with customers. This particular form showed the customer record, including data such as address and telephone number.

	Developer A: "There must be an Update button!"	*Developer B: "No Update button, you idiot!"*
Unspoken assumption	Data integrity is paramount. If the CSR accidentally types into a field, customer data could be overwritten and lost.	Speed of customer service is paramount. If the CSR has to click an Update button and the system is slow to respond, the customer will get impatient.
Conclusion	Make CSRs click an Update button first if they need to make changes.	Let CSRs make changes directly to the customer record.

The fascinating thing about this disagreement was that neither developer was saying a word about their unspoken assumptions, they were simply battering each other with their conclusions. Once I started asking them *why* they held their position, then the assumptions came out. Now we had some tangible questions to research: How often did records get overwritten in the current system? How likely were delays in bringing up the form for editing? Did the slowness of the system cause trouble for the CSRs? (Unfortunately, none of these questions got answered because the company was bought and the entire development team was laid off 2 days later.)

Strictly speaking, any kind of usability testing gives you a way to discover whether your assumptions about the design are true or false. Paper prototypes let you get this information early, before you've invested effort in coding. When a question arises, the team can say, "We're testing the prototype next week, so we can ask some users." Then it magically becomes an issue for research, not argument.

Summary

Although paper prototyping isn't a perfect technique, it's useful in a wide variety of situations. Its main benefits are that it:

- Is fast and inexpensive
- Identifies problems before they're coded
- Elicits more and better (i.e., less nitpicky) feedback from users
- Helps developers think creatively
- Gets users and other stakeholders involved early in the process
- Fosters teamwork and communication
- Avoids opinion wars

Chapters 12 and 13 go into more detail about the kinds of things that paper prototyping is and isn't good for, as well as how people react to it.

Chapter 4

Making a Paper Prototype

I'm going to plunge into the topic of creating paper prototype widgets because most people like to see lots of examples while they're learning about paper prototyping. But in real life, before creating the paper prototype you should first define the users and tasks and then build your prototype around them. The next chapter returns to the beginning of the process and discusses all the steps in their proper order. This chapter is meant to familiarize you with how many common interface widgets (and their behaviors) can be prototyped in paper.

Paper Prototyping Materials

Although it's possible to create a paper prototype with nothing but a pen and paper, several other materials come in handy. Most of the supplies used in paper prototyping (Figure 4.1) are available from your favorite office supply store. A few items (such as the removable tape) may not be stocked in stores and are easiest to find online. See *www.paperprototyping.com* for links to the supplies mentioned in Table 4.1.

For lugging these supplies to meetings, old conference bags are ideal unless you're already using them for your groceries. You can also buy a plastic toolbox—one of my colleagues uses bright-colored ones and she notes that they attract a lot of positive attention at her company.

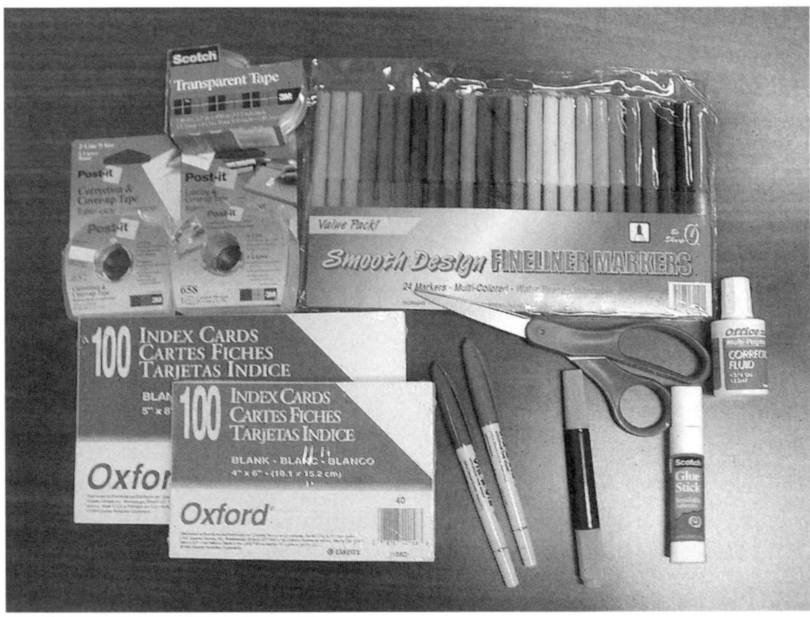

Figure 4.1 Paper prototyping makes use of common office supplies—those that are harder to find in stores are readily available online.

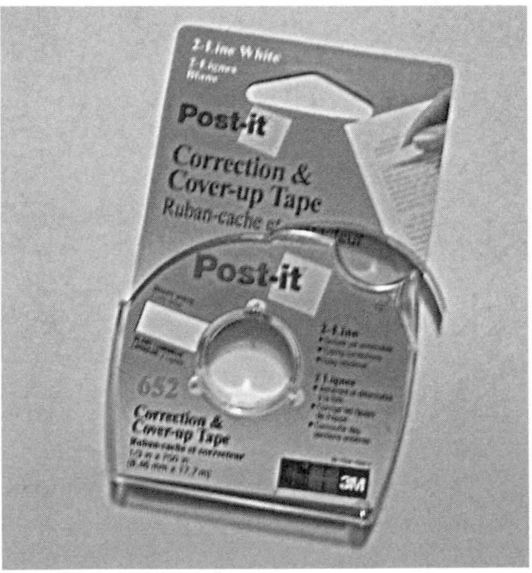

Figure 4.2 Removable tape, such as the Post-It brand shown here, is useful in paper prototyping. It comes in several widths.

Table 4.1 Office Supplies Used in Paper Prototyping

What	*Used for*	*Notes*
White poster board, about 11 × 14 inches	A fixed background upon which other paper prototype elements are placed.	Paper prototypes are usually somewhat larger than life size. I buy 11 × 14 when I can find it or cut a 14 × 22 piece in half.
Blank paper	For drawing larger prototype pieces, jotting down notes, etc.	It's okay to use a lot of paper while creating a prototype, and keeping a stack of paper on hand reminds people of that. (Bring a recycle bin too.)
Unlined index cards, 5 × 8 and 4 × 6	Useful for smaller prototype pieces: dialog boxes, pop-up messages, drop-down menus, etc.	Card stock is sturdier than regular paper and holds up better under repeated use.
Markers, pens (black and/or colored)	Hand-drawing the prototype. Choose a thick enough point so that you'll draw a bit larger than life size—regular pens may be too fine, flip chart markers are too thick, Sharpie pens are about right.	My local discount store sells sets of art markers for much less than I've found online.
Highlighter	Used with transparency and removable tape to make a highlight element.	Light-colored translucent plastic would also work.
Scissors	Used to cut screen shots into pieces, as explained in the text.	Don't run with them!
Transparent tape (Scotch tape, invisible* tape)	For attaching prototype pieces permanently, such as creating a dialog box out of two index cards. For a less permanent attachment, use removable glue.	A matte finish reduces glare, although this usually isn't a problem unless you're videotaping.

Continued

Table 4.1 Office Supplies Used in Paper Prototyping—cont'd

What	*Used For*	*Notes*
Restickable glue	Like the glue on sticky notes, it keeps elements of the prototype in place until you're ready to move them. Useful in experimenting with different layouts or if your prototype has elements that change individually, such as a Web site that uses frames.	Don't confuse it with glue marked "washable," which is not restickable. Difficult to find in stores.
Removable tape (Post-it is available in 2-line and 6-line widths)	It's opaque so you can write on it. See Figure 4.2 for an example. Use the 2-line width for edit fields (especially if the data appears elsewhere in the interface), small amounts of text that change, status line messages, list elements. The 6-line size is good for disabled buttons and quick fixes to the prototype.	A paper prototyping essential—I use enough of this stuff that I'm tempted to buy stock in 3M. Turning a corner under makes it easier to lift the tape off the paper when you want to move it elsewhere.
Transparency (overheads, acetate)	Placed over the prototype, it allows the user to "type" (hand write) data without altering the prototype. Figure 4.3 shows an example of removable tape. I use transparency when there are more than a half dozen fields to complete, otherwise I use removable tape.	Get write-on transparency rather than the stuff intended for laser printers, which is much more expensive. If you're testing in a lab with an overhead camera, transparency can cause glare—use copies of the paper forms instead.
Transparency pens, wet erase	For writing "typed" input on a piece of transparency laid on top of the prototype. Use damp paper towel or cotton swabs as an "eraser."	Permanent transparency pens work too, but since you can't erase them you'll use more sheets of transparency.

Table 4.1 Office Supplies Used in Paper Prototyping—cont'd

What	*Used For*	*Notes*
Correction fluid (Wite-Out)	For small changes to the prototype, such as a field label.	You have to let correction fluid dry before writing on it. In a usability test, I prefer to use removable tape to make quick fixes.
Fome-Cor board	For making 3D prototypes. It's polystyrene form sandwiched between two sheets of thick paper.	You'll sometimes see it spelled "foam core," although Fome-Cor is actually a brand name. Other companies make similar products.

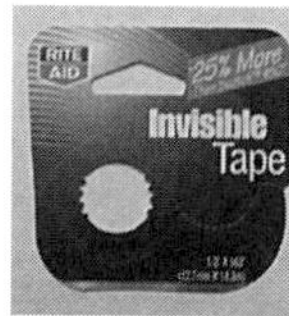

* For those who enjoy visual humor, buy a roll of "invisible" tape, remove the tape, and hang the backing card on your bulletin board.

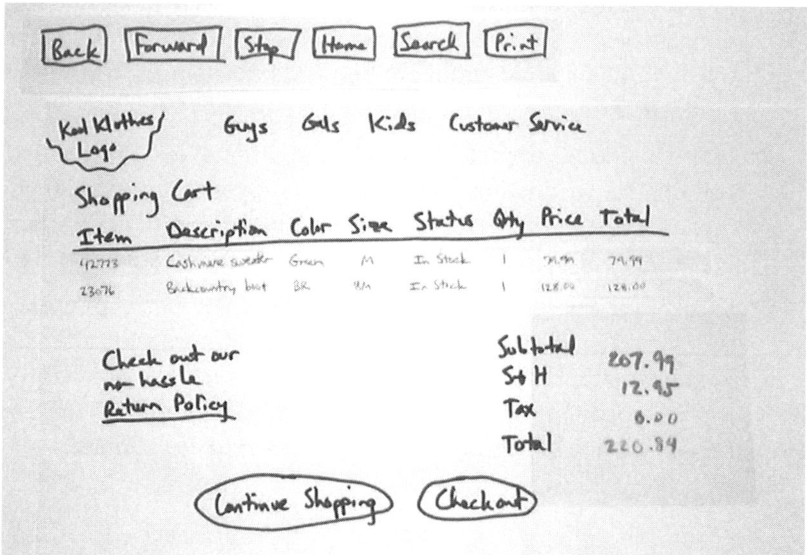

Figure 4.3 This prototype shows the use of both removable tape (line items) and transparency (the total). In this example the Computer wrote these elements on the fly to show the results of the user's actions; on screens with data entry fields the users would write on the tape or transparency themselves.

Supplies I Don't Use

There are a few items I generally don't use in the paper prototype itself, although I sometimes use them in related activities with the product team.

- **Sticky (e.g., Post-It) notes.** They don't lie flat after they've been moved a few times, so I avoid using them in prototypes. I prefer card stock and restickable glue, which essentially lets you turn anything into a sticky note. Sticky notes are often useful in group exercises (such as prioritizing the results from usability testing), however, and if they help you be creative, by all means use them.
- **Flip chart paper.** Although I suggest making paper prototypes larger than life, flip chart paper is probably too big. A colleague of mine tried it and reported that users couldn't see the whole interface without moving their heads, which introduced artificial confusion. On the other hand, flip chart paper is great for scribbling design ideas, making to-do lists for the team, and so on.
- **A ruler.** Straight lines usually aren't important for a hand-drawn paper prototype. When I was at User Interface Engineering, we used to include rulers in our paper prototyping supply kits, but we found that they encouraged people to waste time by making their prototypes overly neat. I advise using a ruler only if exact alignment is important, and if alignment is truly that important, the interface should probably be rendered using software instead of being hand-drawn.
- **Fine-tip pencils or pens.** Fine lines are difficult for observers to read, so don't use fine-tip writing instruments to create your prototype. If you feel uncomfortable working in pen because it can't be erased, pencil is okay for your earliest drafts, but then draw them in marker before testing them with users.
- **Laminator.** I've heard of people who laminated their prototype pieces to make them sturdier and/or so users could write on them with a wet-erase pen. A fine idea if you happen to have a laminator handy, but I wouldn't buy one just for this purpose. One drawback is that you can't alter a laminated piece as easily as paper—removable tape works, but correction fluid doesn't.

Creating a Background

It can be helpful to create a background to go underneath your prototype pieces. I usually use a piece of 11- × 14-inch poster board for the background because it's both sturdier and larger than a piece of regular paper. The background stays on the table, and you put the other pieces of the prototype on top of it. Why might you use a background?

- It helps orient the users that they're looking at a representation of a computer screen or other electronic display. This isn't always necessary, but it may be helpful with less tech-savvy users.
- If controls appear on every screen, you can draw them on the background and omit them from the individual screens. (And if you change those controls, you only have to change them in one place.)
- When you're usability testing, you'll have prototype parts spread out all over the table—the background helps you keep track of what is currently visible to the user versus what you've set aside.
- It provides a reality check for screen real estate. In paper prototypes of software or Web sites I normally don't worry about exact proportions. But if an interface is composed of multiple windows and the prototype pieces spill way over the boundaries or users repeatedly move pieces on top to see the ones beneath, it's time to start worrying about screen real estate.
- If you're videotaping, you can tape the background to the table so that the prototype will stay in the camera's view.

A background is not always necessary. If you're testing a Web site and you've made screen shots that include the browser buttons, you don't need a separate background. On the other hand, if you're prototyping the display for a small-screen device, you'll probably want a background or blinder (as described later in this chapter).

Software Application Backgrounds

First, decide whether the background should represent the underlying operating system or just your application. If your application is the only thing you'll be testing, you can use its main window as your background. You might want to start from the operating system if you're testing multiple applications at once and/or want to verify that the user can launch the application. In this case, draw enough of the familiar operating system elements to orient users. For example, for a Windows desktop, I'll draw the Start button and clock at the bottom and a few common desktop icons like My Computer. Figure 4.4 shows an example of a Windows application background where the desktop elements were not deemed necessary.

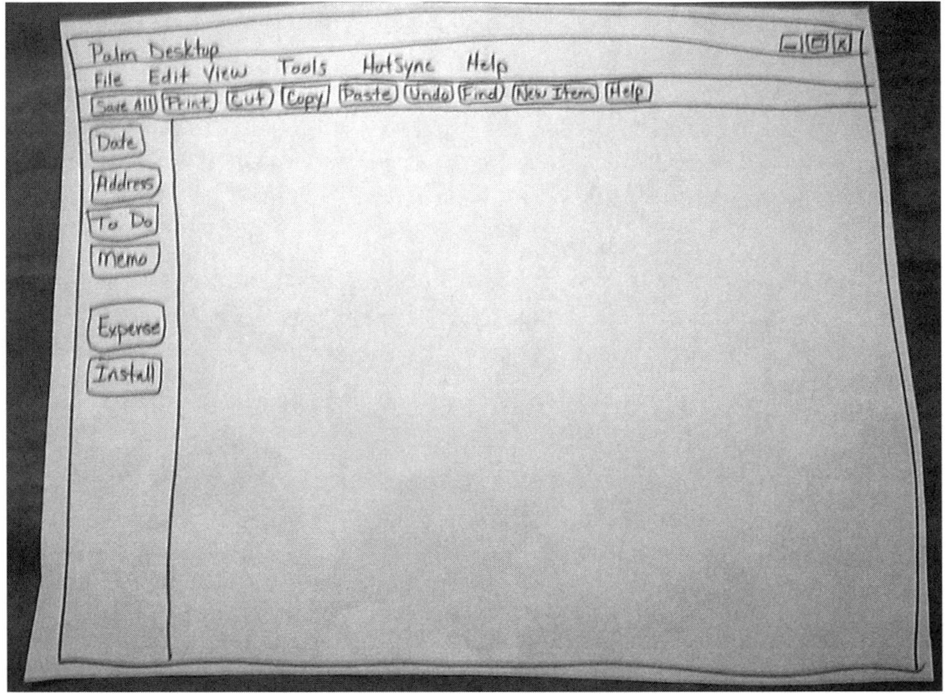

Figure 4.4 A background for a Windows application (the Palm Desktop) drawn on a large piece of paper. The menu bar, toolbar, and left-hand buttons appear on every screen. All other prototype pieces are placed on top of this background. Note that the toolbar icons have been replaced by their corresponding words.

Browser Backgrounds

For a Web browser, the version or brand isn't relevant in paper prototype testing. As a rule, you need only the most common browser buttons: Back, Forward, Home, and maybe Print or Search. In my experience, users understand these buttons just fine when they're drawn by hand; a screen shot of real browser buttons is often harder to read. Figure 4.5 shows an example of a browser background.

I usually omit the buttons for Stop and Reload—these browser controls aren't needed for paper prototype usability tests because there is nothing to "download." Similar logic applies for omitting bookmarks and the URL field—if you're testing a specific Web site you've probably made the assumption that the user got there by some means that's outside of what you're trying to test. I typically start the usability test by telling users, "You've opened your favorite Web browser and typed in *www.whatever.com.*" In my experience most users don't navigate within a

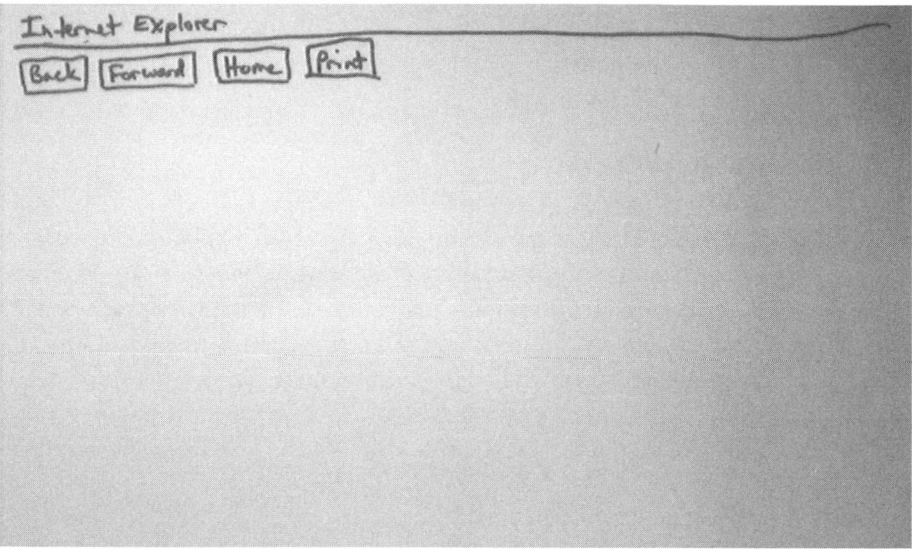

Figure 4.5 A background for testing a Web site can consist of just the most common browser buttons. The browser brand or version isn't important—this background says "Internet Explorer" simply to inform users they're looking at a Web browser.

Web site by hacking the URL field (and if we're trying to test the site's navigation, we don't want them to), so I feel pretty safe leaving it out.

Beware of making assumptions about how users will access your site because your assumptions may be wrong. It can be an eye-opener to start a usability test by showing users the ad or direct mail piece used to promote the site and asking them, "How would you investigate this?" One of my former clients was a start-up company that had just mailed 100,000 brochures for the purpose of driving traffic to their site and then brought me in to do some usability testing. Unfortunately, the URL was so hard to pick out of the brochure that most users (who were quite interested in the concept of the site) couldn't tell me what they'd type in to get there. Start-up companies can't afford many errors like this one; last time I visited the site, the fine print explained that the original company "ran through millions of dollars and went out of business."

A note for both software applications and Web sites: If you're placing several prototype pieces on a background, users sometimes get confused as to whether they're looking at several different windows or one window that happens to be made up of several pieces of paper. When I see this happen, I simply tell users, "This is all one screen," which usually alleviates the confusion.

Small-Screen Interfaces

In prototyping a small-screen device such as a personal digital assistant (PDA) or wireless phone, sometimes pixels count. When screen real estate is scarce, you may want to incorporate display constraints even for your initial prototyping efforts. It depends on what you're trying to learn from usability tests; in the early stages when you're still trying to understand users' needs or nail down the functionality, size may not be as critical as it is in the later stages of the project. Following are examples of two people who chose to do things differently, and why:

From the Field: The Importance of Screen Real Estate

"My company develops applications for PDAs such as Pocket PC and RIM, and also for wireless usage. I've found that sometimes it's important to have the look and feel of a specific environment—in our case the developers have experience with other platforms but they're not always familiar with how various widgets appear on the Palm vs. Pocket PC, etc. By creating platform-specific widgets in a graphics application, it helped them understand exactly what they needed to implement."

Phillip Hash, HiddenMind

"We used a paper-only interface back when we were still in the early stages of designing a browser/phone combination. We wanted to understand what tasks worked well in this type of interface, and to determine the appropriate set of buttons that would work for both navigation and phone functions. It would have been premature to worry about screen size too much while we were still in the exploratory phase."

Timo Jokela, formerly of Nokia

If you decide you need to worry about size constraints, one way to do it is in a graphics program: Start with a photo or screen shot of the device, create a file for each individual screen, and then print them out for testing. For example, here's how Phillip Hash created the prototype just described: "My approach for handheld devices is to first grab screen shots of applications running on those devices, such as my Pocket PC. Then I'll open those images in Fireworks and overlay widgets on top of them." The paper prototype of the xpressa interface shown in Chapter 2 was created in a similar way. Hal Shubin started by downloading a Palm Operating System Emulator (even though he wasn't prototyping a Palm interface, it gave him something of about the right dimensions to work with). A graphic designer created a mock-up of the entire telephone and gave him back a set of GIF files. Hal used PhotoShop to create the paper prototype—the phone image was the background and he created overlays for each different screen.

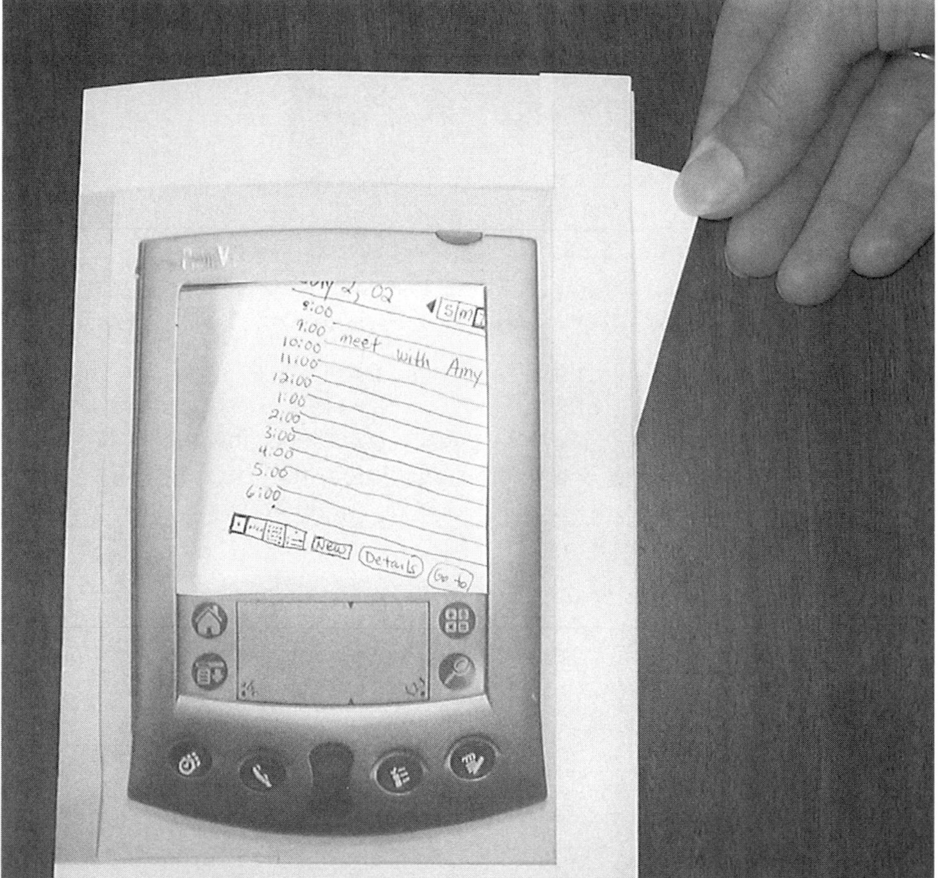

Figure 4.6 For a small-screen device where size constraints are important, you can make a blinder using a photograph of the device, somewhat larger than life. Use hand-drawn content on an appropriately sized grid for the display.

It's possible to avoid using a graphics package altogether but still keep screen constraints in mind. In his book *Handheld Usability,* Scott Weiss describes how to make a "blinder" for a small-screen device: "The key component of a prototype of a handheld device is the *blinder,* which is a sheet of card with a drawing of the hardware device with a cutout where the display would be. The size of the cutout is important because it models the amount of data that can be displayed without requiring scrolling. In order to support scrolling, the card must be larger than the drawing of the hardware device" (Weiss, 2002, p. 139) (see Figure 4.6). By using a grid (such as graph paper) for the display area, it's possible to accurately represent the number of characters that are visible but still draw them by hand. (Or, if it's faster, figure out an appropriate size font and type the data instead.)

How to Prototype Interface Widgets

Once you've created a background, the next step is to create each screen that will be placed on top of it. Figures 4.7 through 4.15 demonstrate how you can prototype the most common interface widgets.

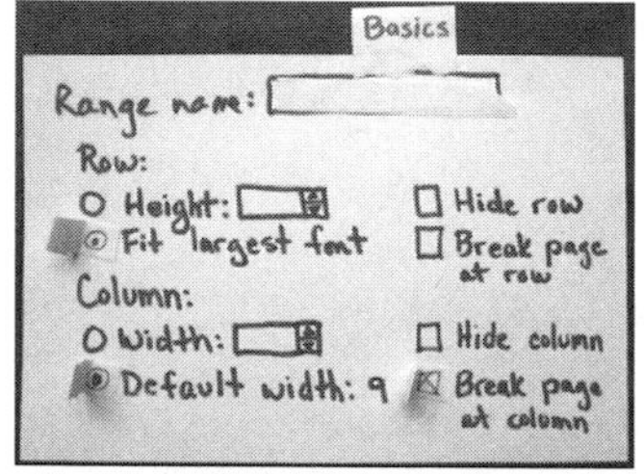

Figure 4.7 Radio buttons/checkboxes.

Buttons and checkboxes

Removable tape works well for radio buttons and checkboxes—the user touches the desired option, and the Computer moves or adds the piece of tape. Sometimes users will catch on and simply move the radio buttons themselves.

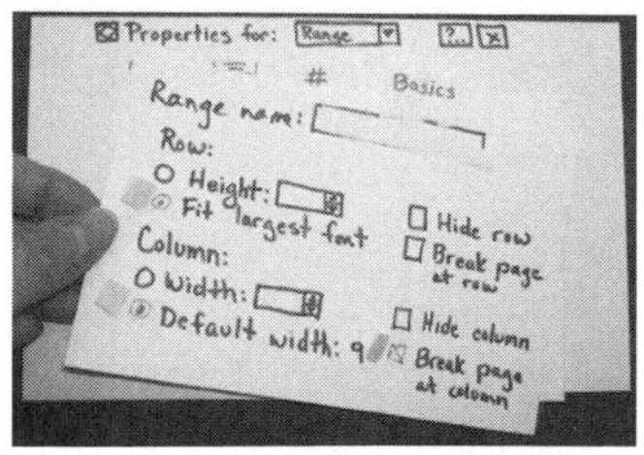

Figure 4.8 Tabbed dialog boxes.

Tabbed dialog boxes

Because a tabbed dialog box is a metaphor for a stack of index cards, prototyping them with a stack of index cards works quite well. Draw each dialog box on a separate index card, then stack them on top of each other, using removable tape to make the tabs. When the user clicks one of the tabs, simply move that card to the top of the stack. Multiple rows of tabs can get a bit cumbersome—you can still use this approach, but you'll spend more time aligning your stack of cards.

Figure 4.9 Text fields.

Text fields

Removable tape works well for text fields. The user writes on the tape, which the Computer can reuse elsewhere in the interface. In this example, the user is naming a table, so this name might appear in the list of defined tables. *Note:* For forms, it may be easier to place a piece of transparency over the entire form and have users write on that or to let them write directly on a paper copy of the form.

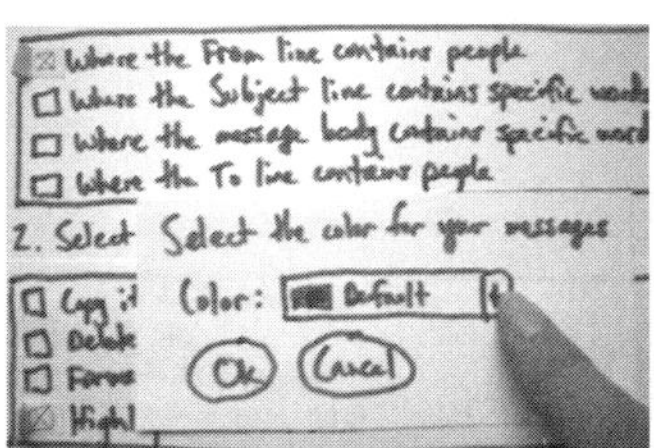

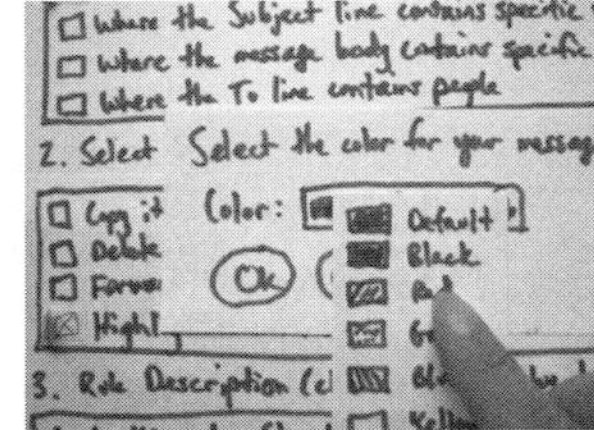

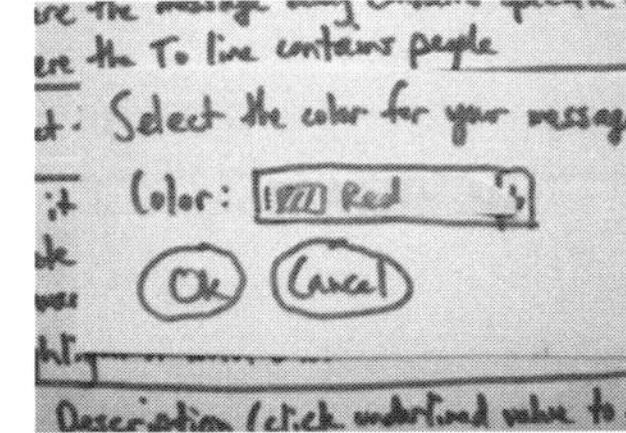

Figure 4.10 Drop-down lists.

Drop-down lists

Write the default selection on the paper prototype (for example, "choose one") and put the list on a separate piece of paper. When the user clicks the down arrow, the Computer shows the list. Once the user makes a selection, the Computer writes it on a piece of removable tape and sticks it on top of the default. (The Computer may want to prepare the options that the user is likely to select ahead of time, or the Computer can create them on the fly.)

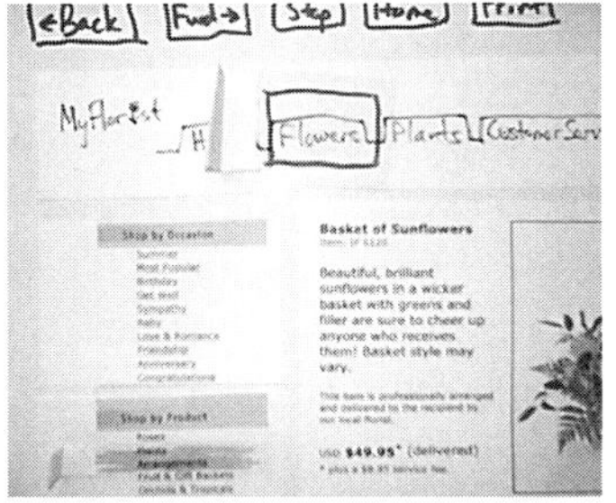

Figure 4.11 Selection bar/highlight.

Selection bar/highlight

To show which element in a list is highlighted, make a highlight from a piece of transparency that you've colored with a light-color marker. (Some markers don't work well on transparency—the ink will puddle—but all you need is a hint of color.) In addition to the highlight at the lower left to indicate the Arrangements section, this image also shows a dark color rectangle that is used to highlight the Flowers tab.

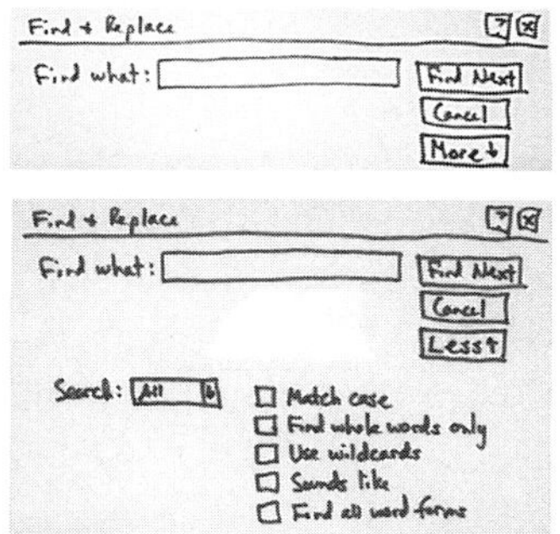

Figure 4.12 Expandable dialog boxes.

Expandable dialog boxes

For a dialog box that has a More button or is otherwise expandable, you can cover the expanded part with blank piece of paper containing the button that causes it to expand. (Or you can fold the screen so that the additional options are not initially visible—a dab of restickable glue helps it lie flat.) When the user clicks the button, remove the blank paper or unfold the screen to reveal the expanded part, and change the button, in this case to Less.

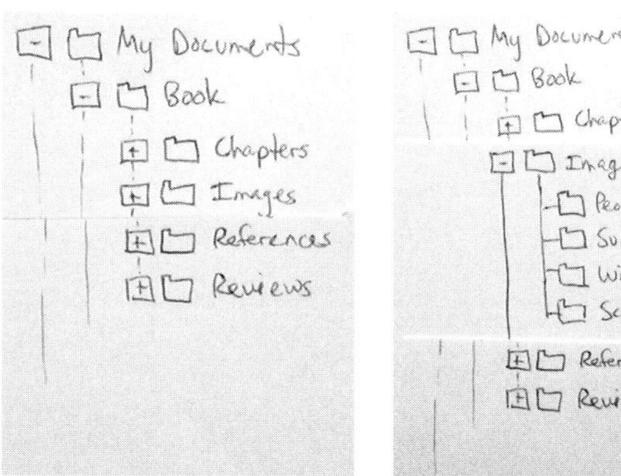

Figure 4.13 Expandable lists.

Expandable lists

Cut the list into pieces and use removable tape (or glue) so that you can separate parts of the list and add the expanded portion. You don't necessarily have to support the expansion of the entire list; after you've created the tasks and walked through them a couple times, you should have some idea of which items the user may wish to expand.

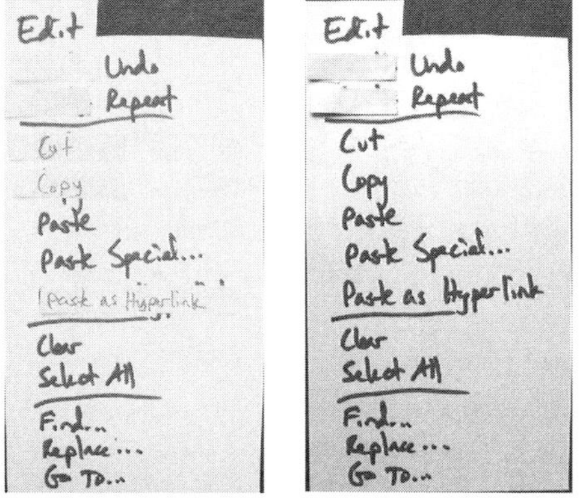

Figure 4.14 Disabled ("grayed-out") controls.

Disabled controls

If a menu option, button, or other control is initially disabled until the user does something, make a version on removable tape with a gray marker and place it over the same element in black. Once the user has done what's necessary to make the functionality available, remove the grayed version to reveal the enabled version underneath. (In the example shown, there is still tape covering the word "Can't" before Undo and Repeat.)

Figure 4.15 Cursors.

Cursors

I don't bother to prototype the standard arrow or I-beam cursors—this level of detail isn't needed for most paper prototype tests because the user's finger (or pen) shows where they're clicking or typing. If your application uses cursors to convey information (for example, an image editing application that displays a different cursor depending on the mode), draw them on small pieces of paper or transparency and place the current one somewhere on the interface as a visual cue for the user.

You'll probably want to have an hourglass cursor for those times when the user is waiting for the Computer. If you draw the hourglass larger than life on an index card, users will laugh and say, "Hey, just like my real computer!"

Representing the Users' Choices

You might be wondering how important it is to accurately represent the state of each radio button, list, selection, and so on. Usually it's pretty important because otherwise you're asking the users (not to mention the Computer and the observers) to remember all their choices. This cognitive effort makes the task harder and can result in artificial confusion. Sometimes it's also possible to miss subtle problems unless you have responded to all the user's actions in the exact order they happened.

Figure 4.16 shows a prototype of a screen used to create a rule for filtering email. As the user selects each Condition and Action, the Computer writes it on removable tape and places it at the bottom. Note that the removable tape initially says, "where the from line contains people." After the user clicks on the link and selects a name from the address book, the Computer places another piece of tape on top of the word people to show the selected name. In this manner the user sees the rule being built one component at a time, much as it would appear on a computer. Because many actions are possible on this screen and they can be done in any order, the pieces of removable tape at the bottom help everyone keep track of exactly what the user has done.

You might also be wondering how hard it is for the Computer to remember each correct response. The good news is that I believe it's probably easier to make and use a paper prototype than to read about how to do it. The Computer is usually someone directly involved in the design and thus knows a lot about it. As

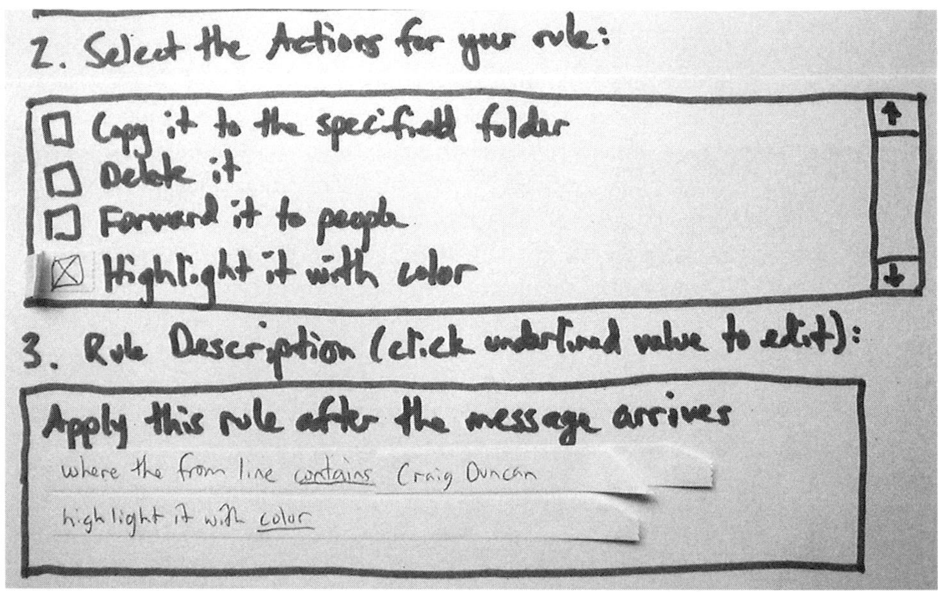

Figure 4.16 As the user specifies each component of the mail filtering rule, the Computer writes it on pieces of removable tape so that all the user's actions, in the sequence they happened, are shown in the interface.

explained in Chapter 7, the Computer practices the tasks before the first usability test, and this also helps. (As a consultant, I have helped product teams make paper prototypes of many interfaces that I initially knew nothing about. After watching a few run-throughs, I usually learn enough about how the interface works that I could be Computer if necessary.)

Hand-Drawing versus Screen Shots

Of all the examples of paper prototypes in this book so far, you may have noticed that most of them are hand-drawn and rather messy. That's deliberate; I wanted to emphasize that you don't need much artistic ability to create a paper prototype. Paper prototypes are very good at unearthing problems with concepts, terminology, workflow, content, and so forth. These types of problems are often readily apparent even without an exact visual representation of the interface. Although you may ultimately need artistic ability to create a good interface, you don't necessarily need it to create a paper prototype.

Similarly, it's usually appropriate to draw in monochrome and to fake most of the images and art—instead of the company logo, draw a box with the word "logo" in it, use a word instead of an icon, and so on. The only time I recommend against faking graphical content is when it conveys information needed for the tasks. For example, on a clothing Web site I'd use pictures of the products (perhaps cut out of a catalog) because it's important to users to see pictures of the merchandise.

If you're wondering whether it's okay to use screen shots in a paper prototype, the answer is yes. Chapter 7 provides more information about whether to use screen shots or hand-drawn paper prototypes.

Note: When I say that paper prototypes can be hand-drawn, messy, and monochrome, some people get the mistaken idea that I don't believe in the value of professional graphic design. Nothing could be further from the truth. Graphic design is both a skill and an art, and I have a great deal of respect for people who do it well. I've found that good graphic designers often embrace paper prototyping because it gives them valuable input for creating the layout and look of the interface. Usability testing will show them which design elements need to be emphasized or downplayed through the use of color, font size, white space, images, and so on. So I'm not anti-designer—in fact, people who see graphic designers as the ones who make an interface pretty are the ones who trivialize the skill.

Simulating Interaction

The paper prototyping motto is: "With a little imagination, you can simulate almost anything." There are many aspects of human-computer interaction that a human being can simulate well enough that usability testing provides useful feedback. But complex or subtle interaction usually can't be simulated perfectly; as Chapter 12 discusses in detail, this is a drawback of paper prototyping.

- **Tooltips/mouseovers.** Tell users at the start of the test that the real interface will have tooltips (a.k.a. "those little yellow boxes that pop up") to explain the icons. Tell them that if they want to see the tooltip for an icon, they can point to it and ask, "What is this?" and you'll tell them what the tooltip would say.
- **Rollover/pop-up menus.** These are conceptually similar to tooltips but are harder to simulate orally because a whole menu pops up instead of just a word or three. On a computer, I've found that what most users do is click to make the menu drop down, and then click again to make the selection. This works well

enough to show you what option the user would select, but it will also mask some of the subtle problems that can occur with rollover menus.

- **Beeps.** Simply say "beep" whenever the computer would, for example, when the user clicks outside a modal dialog box.
- **Drag & drop.** This interaction is a bit difficult to simulate perfectly. Keep in mind that many users never even try to use drag & drop in an unfamiliar interface—they use the menus instead—so it may not be something you need to worry about. But if drag & drop interaction is an integral part of your interface, ask users to specify what they're dragging and where they're dropping it. The Computer then talks through the visual changes that occur during this process. ("As soon as you move into this area, the cursor changes to this, and when you release the mouse you see . . .")
- **Right mouse menus.** Tell users at the start of the test that right mouse menus exist, and if they want to see one they should tell you that they're clicking the right mouse button, and then you'll display the menu. As with drag & drop, don't be surprised if no one tries to use right mouse menus in an unfamiliar interface.
- **Sliders, progress indicators.** I don't usually bother to make widgets for progress indicators because they can be simulated verbally, for example, by telling the user, "A progress indicator comes up. It says 20% . . . 60% . . . done." (Or "1% . . . 2% . . .") If you need a slider for some other purpose (such as a user input device), cut two slits in a piece of paper and use a strip of paper for the slider.
- **Animation and video.** Rapidly changing images can be hard to simulate. Sometimes it's easiest to describe to the users what they'd see on the screen; other times a still picture (or a series of them) will suffice. For short video clips, consider using a video player to show the video, as one product team did when they were testing their multimedia Web site.
- **Web site links.** When I first started paper prototyping Web sites, I'd take a highlighter and highlight everything that was clickable—text links, buttons, image maps, and so on. As you might imagine, the pages looked pretty garish and all that highlighting proved to be more distracting than useful. It was also extra work, so I dropped that idea. Now I tell users at the start of the test that they if they're not sure whether something is a link or just a picture, they can point to it and ask, "Is this a link?" and we'll tell them yes or no. (Or, "It wasn't originally, but apparently it should be.")

◇ **Scrolling.** On some Web pages, there is important information "below the fold" and you're interested in knowing whether users can find it. Although scrolling is a bit cumbersome to simulate with a paper prototype, there are a couple of ways to do it. The first is to fold the paper so the user initially sees only part of the page, and unfold it if they tell you they'd scroll down. This method is good enough for gathering gross data about whether users scroll on a particular page or not. If you need to do something fancier, make a cutout in a large piece of cardboard that's the size of the monitor display. Put the page underneath and slide it up or down as the user "scrolls." (Figure 4.17 shows an example.) But many development teams make a deliberate decision not to include scrolling in their tests, leaving this question to later tests with the actual design.

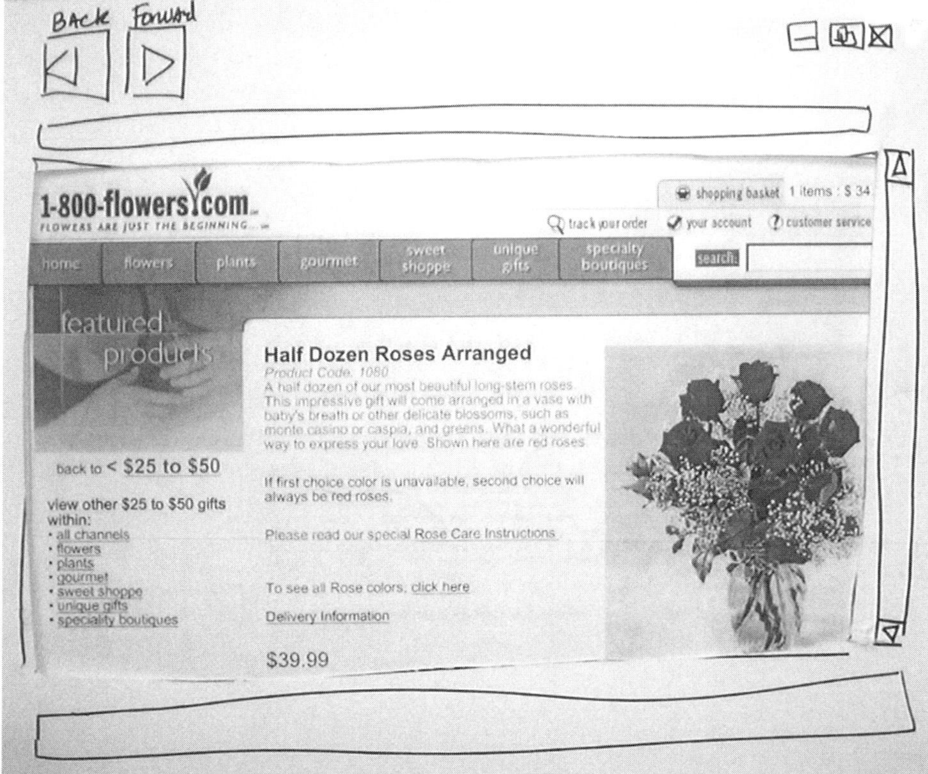

Figure 4.17 It's usually not necessary to get fancy about simulating scrolling, but if you need to do it you can use a cutout and move the scrolled piece beneath it.

Beyond the Computer Screen—Incorporating Other Elements

A user interface isn't just what appears on the computer screen—in the broad sense it includes everything that users interact with during the process of accomplishing their goals. That could include printed manuals, online help, other reference materials, hardware devices, and even human beings. And some interfaces have buttons and knobs instead of graphic user interface widgets. So let's look at how you incorporate these elements into paper prototypes.

Hardware Props

Sometimes the interface includes hardware devices in conjunction with software or a Web application. For example, portable gadgets (such as PDAs, digital cameras, and audio players) have a cable connecting them to the computer, and these devices have interfaces of their own. If a hardware device is an integral part of a product, you may want to include it in your paper prototype tests (see Figure 4.18). Obviously, users will be able to see that the device isn't connected to anything, but you can still learn a lot about how they'll interact with it. Here are some examples:

- **Tape backup system.** The development team wanted to know the point at which the user inserted or removed a tape, and when and how they labeled it. So we put a tape drive on the table next to the prototype, along with some blank tapes and a pen, and asked users to use these items as needed. One of the developers wrote "Whirrrr!" on a card to represent when the drive was making noise—funny, but also useful feedback for the users during testing.
- **Portable MP3 player.** We wanted to know when users would connect the physical device during the process of downloading music and whether they'd use it or the Web application to perform functions such as deleting individual songs.
- **Touch screen control panel.** This example is ironic because we used a computer as a *prop* for a paper prototype test. To correctly install a touch screen, the users (computer technicians) had to plug it into the same port they had chosen in the installation software we were prototyping. We had a computer and cable in the test room, and we asked users to physically plug in the cable. We noted which port they used to determine whether they'd done it correctly. In another task, we wanted users to troubleshoot a hardware problem—a

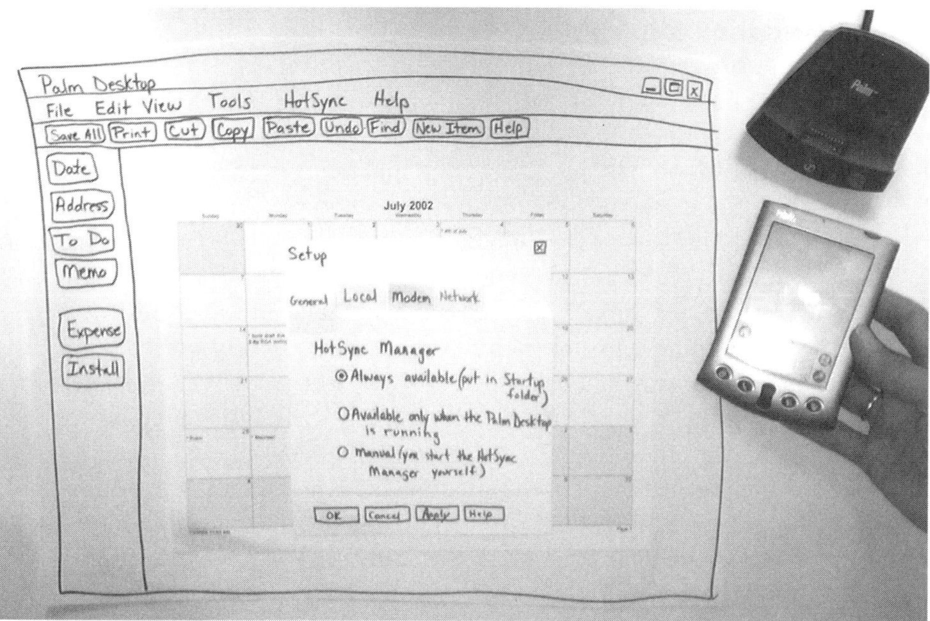

Figure 4.18 If a software interface works in conjunction with a hardware device, you can set it on the table and have users interact with it as part of the prototype.

jiggling cursor caused by a frequency conflict—that was hard to explain but easy to show. Again, we used the computer to demonstrate what the cursor problem looked like but had them solve it using the paper prototype.

One hardware prop that I don't use is a keyboard for typed input. I've never found it necessary; it's adequate to simulate most data entry by having the user write it with a pen. Sometimes it's important to know what key a user pressed—for example, Tab versus Enter to get to the next field in a form. To determine this, the test facilitator can simply ask, "What key did you press to get there?" (But once the user has given a correct answer, there's nothing further to be learned from asking this question for every field.) Unless your interface relies heavily on function keys or key combinations, trying to use a physical keyboard will only slow you down, without adding much useful information. As explained in Chapter 12, if you truly have a need to study keystroke (or mouse) level interactions, a paper prototype is probably not the best choice.

Hardware Devices

Sometimes there's no computer monitor—the user is interacting only with a piece of equipment and its set of buttons, knobs, lights, and so forth. In this case, the definition of "paper" prototyping stretches to include cardboard, Fome-Cor, or other materials used to build 3D prototypes. This technique is useful for a variety of hardware devices, including instrument panels, medical equipment, handheld devices, and consumer appliances.

In one project, researchers Säde, Nieminen, and Riihiaho (1998) were asked by a manufacturer to help design a can-recycling machine for consumers. There were two main ideas for the design—a "manual" version where the user had to insert the can horizontally a certain way so that the machine could read its bar code and an "automatic" version where the machine could read a vertically inserted can regardless of its orientation. The interface was very limited (no text, just a diagram and three indicator lights) and the design goal ambitious: All supermarket customers must be able to instantly use the machine.

After making a mock-up of each design (shown in Figure 4.19), the researchers tested both versions at a supermarket. Volunteer shoppers were given a bag full of cans and asked to recycle them. One of the researchers was obviously visible behind the machine to accept or reject the cans while another stuck colored bits of paper on the front to simulate the indicator lights. Although crude, this method of testing was sufficient for the researchers to conclude that there was a significant difference in usability: The automatic version worked well, but about half the participants would not have been able to recycle their cans with the manual concept. They also discovered some unexpected user actions, such as placing rejected cans on top of the machine. The manufacturer built a prototype of the automatic version that incorporated the findings from the mock-up, and it also performed well in usability testing. Eventually this machine went into production and is still being used today.

"Incredibly Intelligent Help"

My mentor, Jared Spool, taught me one of my favorite paper prototyping tactics, called *incredibly intelligent help.* It can be used before the online help or print documentation has been developed. This tactic is used not only to refine the help or manual but in many cases to improve the interface itself.

When users gets stuck, the facilitator prompts them to ask a question about what's confusing them. One of the product team members (designated ahead of

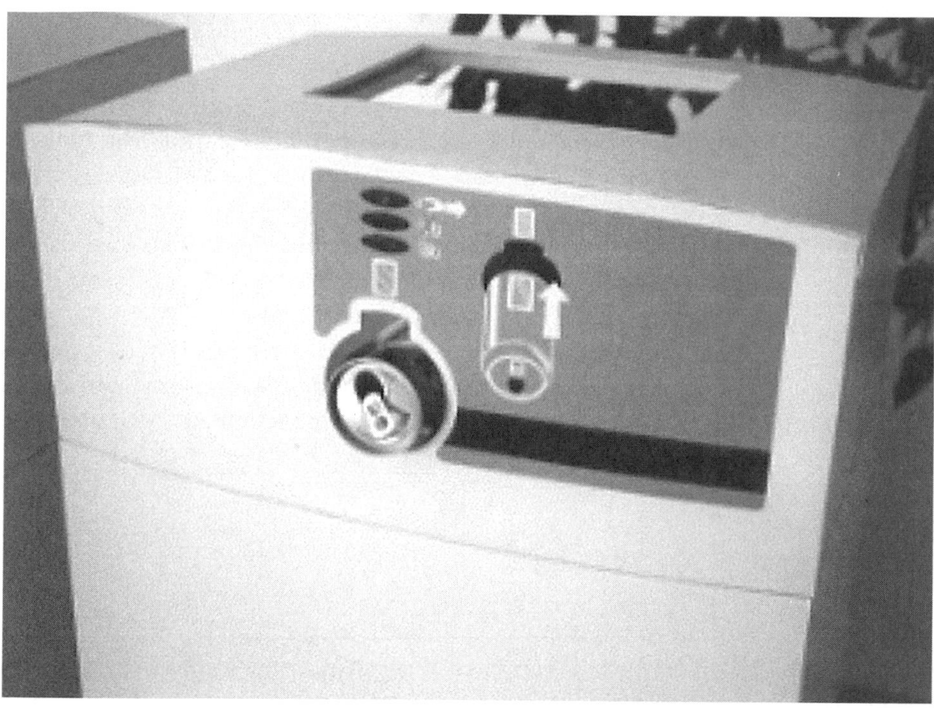

Figure 4.19 The mock-up of the manual version of the can recycling machine. In testing, a visible researcher stood behind the machine to accept or reject each can while another used colored pieces of paper to simulate the indicator lights.

time as the "Help System") gives a terse answer. The Help System should resist the temptation to answer questions that users haven't asked yet—wait and see whether the short answer solves the problem. If the users are still confused, they can ask another question and the Help System will provide a bit more detail, and so on.

The purpose of incredibly intelligent help is to find the piece of information that makes the lightbulb go on in the user's head.

The purpose of incredibly intelligent help is to find the piece of information that makes the lightbulb go on in the user's head—sometimes users only need a clue or two to get them back on track, not a long explanation. Write down the questions users ask and the explanations given. After the test, see whether the information users needed can be incorporated directly into the interface (thus avoiding the question in the first place), or if that is not practical then it should be included in the help or documentation.

Human Actors

Sometimes you may want to include humans in your paper prototype—as humans! For example, users might call an 800 number or initiate an Internet chat with an online customer service rep. To simulate this interaction, designate a member of the development team to play this role. (I don't recommend having users call the real customer support number unless you're willing to waste time on hold.) The catch is that this person shouldn't look at the interface during the conversation because in real life they wouldn't be able to see it.

One of the advantages of using human actors is that user questions emerge in a natural way, and you can determine the information required to answer them. As with incredibly intelligent help, the team should try to incorporate this information right into the interface.

Wizard of Oz Testing

Paper prototyping is similar in spirit to so-called Wizard of Oz testing. In essence, Wizard of Oz means any testing setup in which a human being acts as an intermediary between user and machine. It's often used to conduct testing with users before the underlying technology is developed. As the name implies, a human (often, although not necessarily, hidden) performs manipulations to make it appear as though something high-tech is happening. For example, several years ago I participated in a study to find out how people would give commands and dictation to a voice recognition system while editing documents. The users were not allowed to touch the computer but rather had to give all their commands orally to an experimenter sitting next to them who would then perform them literally. We got some interesting insights from these tests—for example, when scrolling up a page, the command "back up" actually means to go *down* the page!

A variation of the Wizard of Oz technique can be useful for paper prototyping. In rare cases, it's necessary to show the user something on a computer that is too difficult to simulate with paper (such as a very complicated graph) or that relies on inputs that can't be known ahead of time (such as live data). To do this, an expert sits at a computer in the same room as the users and paper prototype and enters the users' inputs from the paper prototype to show what the resulting output would be. The user still interacts exclusively with the paper prototype, but they see the results of their actions on the computer screen.

I have used this technique only rarely in paper prototyping. Because the tasks are created before the paper prototype is developed, there is usually a finite and predictable set of results that users might see (even when you account for likely mistakes), and thus it's possible to prepare them ahead of time. But this technique may be useful for sophisticated tools where a more intuitive interface is being added on top of a hard-to-use "expert-only" system, for example, one that previously relied on command line entry.

Documentation, Help, and Training

If you're working on documentation, help, or training for an interface, testing a paper prototype will yield useful inputs to your process of deciding what really needs to be covered, and to what level of detail. In addition to the incredibly intelligent help technique, here are some tips for technical writers and trainers.

Content and Method of Access

If you happen to already have print documentation and/or online help from the previous version of the interface, sometimes you can include this material in the paper prototype test. Think of help/doc as having two aspects—*method of access* and *content.* The method of access includes whatever the user does to get to the material: click a Help button, type a term into a search engine, or open a manual to the index. The content is what they see once they get there. Depending on the stage of your development, you might have the method of access, the content, or both. (For training, it's a bit simpler. The method of access is "the person attends a class," so trainers only need to be concerned with content.)

Here's an example where we tested the help content but not the access to it. A company called Brix Networks makes Web-based tools for Internet service providers. With all the technical concepts inherent in their product, the development team anticipated that even their sophisticated target market would sometimes want clarification of terms. For example, in setting up something called a verifier group, users had to select one of five configurations from a drop-down list. One of the developers wrote a description of each configuration on a sticky note—that was the "help content" for the task. If a question came up about the options, we plopped down the sticky note on the interface (Figure 4.20). Eventually, this information was incorporated into the online help. Note that this method didn't tell us whether or how users would access the help, but it did allow us to refine the help content.

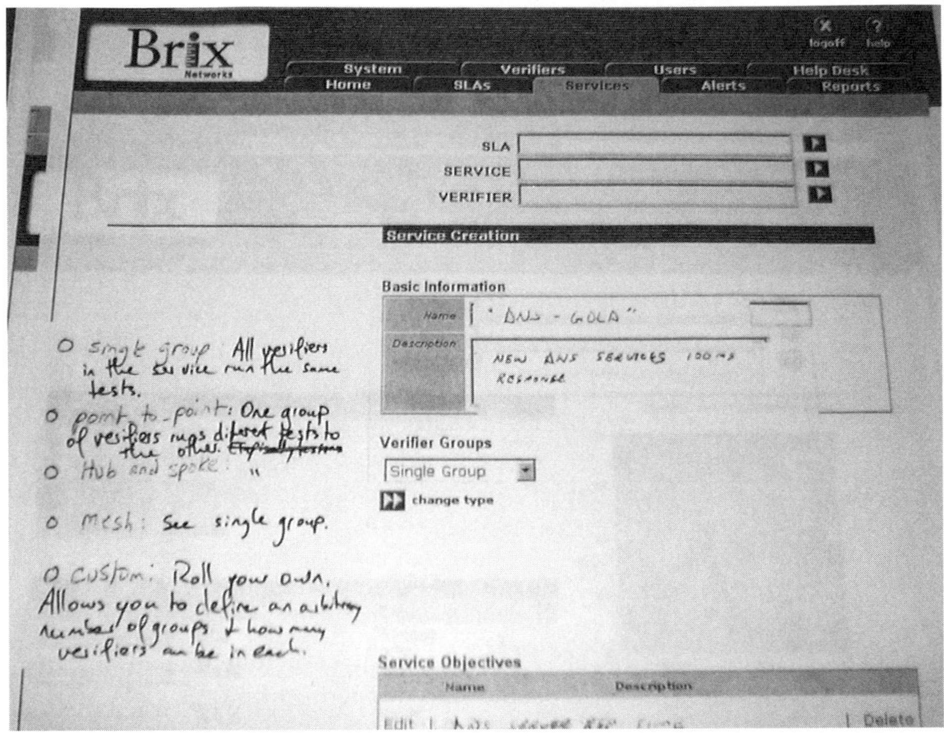

Figure 4.20 The five options for verifier groups involved technical concepts. The handwritten explanations allowed us to determine what wording would clarify the terminology. Eventually, this information was incorporated into the online help.

Preparing Material for Testing

To simulate the method of access, if you have an existing manual index that has most of the right terms in it, you (or rather, the person facilitating the usability test) could give it to the users and ask them to show you how they'd look up their question. Similarly, if users say they'd go into online help and there's no context-sensitive help topic for their current screen, the facilitator could ask them what they'd type into the search engine. In any case, you should pay attention to the users' language and the terms they naturally use—these are prime candidates for index and search terms, even if users don't use the "correct" terminology.

If you don't prepare any content ahead of time, you can use the incredibly intelligent help technique. If you do have time to draft some content, review the tasks and look for the top five or so areas where you anticipate the user running into difficulty (especially in regard to concepts as opposed to the mechanics of accomplishing a task) and start with those. There may be material from the existing interface you can scavenge, or you might want to quickly write something. You don't need to cover everything, however, and don't spend a lot of time documenting an interface you haven't tested yet. The prototype is likely to change rapidly, so wait until it has stabilized before making the documentation consistent with it.

Although I often suggest hand-drawing a paper prototype rather than creating it on a computer, I make an exception for documentation; because of the greater amount of text, it's probably faster to draft the content in a word processor and print it out. Whether handwritten or typed, avoid the temptation to do a lot of formatting—first-level headings are about the right level of detail for now.

Prioritizing the Informational Needs

If you're a writer or trainer, testing a paper prototype will show you what information users truly need, as opposed to what's nice but not necessary. You'll also get a sense of where users look for information (for example, do they notice the context-sensitive help?) Years ago I helped conduct some tests of Lotus 1-2-3 with a couple dozen spreadsheet users, and we found that no one had trouble changing font size, color, style, and so on. This was true even for people who weren't familiar with the application. Naturally, the manual had a whole section pertaining to cell styles, but not one user looked at it. On the other hand, there were some tasks that users found more difficult, and for those they did turn to the manual.

I'm of the belief that not everything needs to be documented. I like to joke that the tech writers at Lotus could have replaced all the nouns in that chapter with names of vegetables and no one would have noticed. Although that's a funny image, the serious issue is that someone had spent time documenting functionality that was self-explanatory, whereas harder-to-use functions remained undocumented. Even tech writers who believe that everything should be documented may still find it useful to know the relative priority of all the material they're responsible for. That way, they can devote more time to the things that are harder for users.

Summary

This section of the book has introduced paper prototyping—what it is and some reasons why it's useful—and provided many examples. Chapter 2 presented several case studies and their findings; this chapter has taken a widget-level view to get you thinking about how you might create a prototype of your interface. Now it's time to climb out of the details and look at the larger process of creating and testing a paper prototype.

Process: Conducting a Usability Study with a Paper Prototype

The chapters in this section describe the process of using a paper prototype to conduct usability tests for an interface. This is all the "how-to" material, and it assumes that you've made a decision to try paper prototyping on a real project. If you still haven't made up your mind whether paper prototyping is an appropriate technique for your interface and situation, read Part III and then come back here when you're ready to try it.

Chapter 5

Planning a Usability Study with a Paper Prototype

So you've decided to give paper prototyping a try. How do you go about doing it? This chapter outlines the people, activities, and time you'll need. Some companies do their first paper prototype usability study by hiring a consultant to come in and lead all the activities. This chapter and the others in this section cover much of what I do as a usability consultant—theoretically, it should put me out of business!

I'm not being facetious. I believe that the best way to make interfaces more user-friendly is to close the feedback loop between product teams and users by teaching people how use paper prototypes to communicate, ask questions, and find answers. Once everyone knows how to do this, I'll find some other way to earn a living!

If you're not a usability specialist, you may be doing some of these things for the first time. If you already have a process for conducting usability studies, this chapter will help you identify the activities that are different from what you typically do. (On the surface, the only thing that's different about using a paper prototype for usability testing is that you have to create the paper prototype. But there may be some other differences from your typical process, such as leaving time for changes between tests and less need for formal reporting.)

The process described in this chapter has worked well for me on dozens of projects, but it certainly isn't the only way to do things. There are other books that go into detail about the activities involved in usability testing; the book by Dumas and Redish (1999) is a good one to start with, and you'll find others in the References section.

Overview of a Usability Study Using a Paper Prototype

Table 5.1 shows the "view from 30,000 feet" of a usability study using a paper prototype. (As a reminder of the conventions I'm using, a usability *study* is a series of tests conducted with a given interface and set of tasks. A usability *test* is just one session with a user or user pair.) There's more detail about each activity later on. Reduced to its essentials, the process looks like this:

- Determine the goals of the testing—what do you want to learn?
- Who are the users? Define them so recruitment can begin.
- Create tasks around things that those users do.
- Create the paper prototype pieces needed to perform those tasks.
- Hold internal walkthroughs to prepare for testing.
- Conduct several usability tests, refining the prototype after each test.
- Establish priorities for the issues found.
- Plan additional changes to the interface in the short term and/or track them so that they can be resolved later.
- Communicate your findings to others who weren't directly involved.

Notice that you don't start the process by creating the paper prototype. Rather, you first agree on high-level goals and concerns, then develop usability tasks around those things, *then* develop the paper prototype and test it. How early can you start? If you're sketching screens on a whiteboard, you're far enough along to start paper prototyping. If you have questions about what users will like, understand, or accept, you can throw together a prototype and get answers.

Table 5.1 Overview of a Paper Prototyping Project

	What Happens	*Who*	*Time*
Kickoff meeting	◇ Discuss goals, risks, and concerns ◇ Agree on user profile ◇ Determine "core team" ◇ Set schedule	All stakeholders	3 hours

Table 5.1 Overview of a Paper Prototyping Project—cont'd

	What Happens	*Who*	*Time*
User recruitment	⟐ Find people who match the user profile and schedule them	1–2 people if you're doing this in-house; some companies outsource this	Depends; a 2- to 3-week lead time is typical
Task design	⟐ Create the tasks to be used in usability testing	Core team plus anyone with important input about what gets tested	3–5 hours
Prototype creation and walkthroughs	⟐ List interface elements that are needed to support the tasks ⟐ Split up the work ⟐ Hold periodic walkthroughs ⟐ Formal run-through *without real users* prior to usability testing	Core team; others can come and go as schedules allow	$\frac{1}{2}$ to 5 days total
Usability testing and iterative refinement	⟐ Perform usability tests (most last 1–2 hours) ⟐ List issues after each test ⟐ Revise the prototype before the next test	All stakeholders	2 days total
Prioritizing issues and action plan	⟐ Prioritize unresolved issues ⟐ Discuss top issues and possible solutions ⟐ Create action plan to address issues ⟐ Track issues	Everyone who attended one or more usability tests can help prioritize; the rest is up to the development manager and/or team	3 hours

Continued

Table 5.1 Overview of a Paper Prototyping Project—cont'd

	What Happens	*Who*	*Time*
Communication of results	As needed: ◇ Write summary of "top 10" issues ◇ Post results on intranet ◇ Write report ◇ Give presentation of results ◇ Create a walkthrough video ◇ Create an interface spec	1–2 team members (often, but not necessarily, the usability specialists)	1 hour to several days depending on the activities

www.paperprototyping.com has a document containing Table 5.1 that you can use as a blueprint for your own plan. Modify it as needed, and hand it out at your kickoff meeting.

People to Involve

Paper prototyping and usability testing should involve all members of the product team, not just those who have "designer" or "usability" in their title. Every day of a project, dozens if not hundreds of decisions are made that affect some aspect of the user experience. Even under-the-surface technical factors such as database design can have an impact on the user interface (and vice versa). Practically speaking, the number of decisions that affect the user is too large for one person or even one department to handle. If only one or two people in the company are responsible for the entire user experience, their limited ability to collect and disseminate usability data will quickly become a bottleneck. Instead, it's usually better to have many people participate in usability activities and get the data firsthand. This section explains who should be involved and to what extent.

Terminology: Designer and Developer

As I start tossing around words such as *designer* and *developer*, I'm going to run afoul of differences in how people define these terms. At some companies, the same person who designs the interface also codes it, tests it, and maybe even helps document and support it. Other companies distinguish between designers and developers. Furthermore, there are graphic designers and interaction designers and software designers and instructional designers—see the problem? I'm going to adopt some role-based conventions:

- A *designer* figures out what it should do or be. (The "it" depends on the context—usually I'm talking about an interface, but these terms also work for documentation, training, and so on).
- A *developer* makes it happen.
- *Technical* means "understands the constraints of the technology and tools used to implement the interface."

Using these conventions, someone from Marketing might be considered a designer, and a trainer wears the developer hat in the context of creating a course. People from a variety of departments might be considered technical depending on what they know—for example, some writers are very savvy about technology. I am deliberately using broader definitions than many people are used to because it underscores my philosophy that creating a product is a multidisciplinary process. You know who you are—if it sounds like I'm talking about you, assume that I am, even if I'm not using the title you're accustomed to.

The "Core Team"

If you have a large development team, it's a good idea to designate two to five people as the "core team" for the activities in a usability study. When it comes to scheduling, it's unlikely—and probably not even desirable—that the entire development team can be involved in every aspect of the prototype preparation and testing. Plan the activities around the availability of the core team and invite others to participate in whatever they're able to.

The core team consists of those people whose involvement is crucial to preparing and testing the prototype. Typically, the core team includes the designer/developer(s) responsible for the interface and a usability specialist if the team has one. One of these people takes the leadership role in planning and conducting the activities. The development manager or product manager may be part of the core team, although if this manager oversees several projects he or she may delegate the responsibility to one of the people mentioned earlier. It's also quite common to have a tech writer, marketer, and/or graphic designer on the core team.

Technical Expertise

For a moment, I'm going to divide the world into two types of people:* those who are technical as I've defined it and those who are not:

- If you're the technical type, realize that other people have good insights about what users want and need, and you really want to get those insights *before* development is in full swing. The ideas that come from nontechnical people aren't always useful or workable, but the paper prototype will sort the wheat from the chaff. Be open to prototyping something even if you're not sure how to make it work—maybe you'll be able to use the idea in another form if it works well for users.
- If you're not technical, remember that interface design is a skill as well as an art. You have a lot to contribute, but not all of your ideas will be practical within the constraints of your development process. Sometimes you'll have to defer to the techie types when they say, "The architecture doesn't support it" or "That goes against our style guide." But don't be afraid to pick up a pen and scribble a screen if inspiration strikes.

It's important to have at least one person on the core team who has the technical perspective—knows the system architecture, the limits of the technology, what is easy, and what is hard. This will prevent the team from developing a prototype that is impossible to implement. This person(s) should have the final word on whether and how something is included in the prototype.

The Rest of the Team

Paper prototyping is a multidisciplinary activity and should include people in addition to those who are directly responsible for the interface design/development. In particular, seek out those who have direct contact with users: sales, mar-

---

* There are two types of people in the world: those who believe you can divide the world into two types of people and those who don't.

keting, tech support, trainers. These people often have valuable insights about what users want and what confuses them. So do writers and QA/QE/test engineers because they are often among the first people to use the interface, albeit in a lab setting.

A Note about the Graphic Designer

If there's a graphic/visual designer assigned to the project, it's great to have that person involved, possibly as part of the core team. But the rest of the team shouldn't be intimidated by the presence of someone whose doodles could be framed and sold as art. When a team member has artistic ability, others may be tempted to let that person do all the prototyping work "because it will look nicer." Remind everyone that it's fine if the prototype looks like it was drawn by a 10-year-old because the point is *not* to spend time making things look pretty when you'll want to change them tomorrow anyway. The graphic designer shouldn't have to do more of the work than anyone else.

Kickoff Meeting

When starting a paper prototyping project, get everyone together to discuss the goals of the testing and the method. Here's a typical agenda for this meeting:

- Provide an overview of activities
- Discuss risks and concerns
- Create a user profile
- Determine the schedule

Provide an Overview of Activities

The first time you do paper prototyping or even usability testing, it's natural for people to have questions about these activities. You might print out a version of Table 5.1 and take it to the meeting. You might even make a paper prototype of an application everyone is familiar with, just to show them what you're talking about. Paper prototyping is one of those visceral things that can be hard to explain, but everyone knows it when they see it in action.

People who are not part of the core team may wonder which activities they need to be involved in. I recommend that they attend the following:

- **At least one walkthrough,** preferably the last one before testing begins. People get more out of observing tests if they're familiar with the prototype beforehand.
- **At least two usability tests.** Mathematically speaking, you can extrapolate in any direction from a single data point. If someone observes only one usability test, he or she may prematurely conclude that the interface has a problem and that other users will have the same difficulty (or conversely, that this user represents an outlier and that there really isn't a problem with the interface). But if that observer watches another usability test, he or she will see similarities and differences, which provides a better perspective on reality. Even if some people can observe only one test, that's still much better than nothing—just caution them that what they see may not be typical and that they should compare their observations with what happened in the other tests.
- **The debriefing meeting.** Because this is when the issues are prioritized and discussed, it's a good way to find out what happened at the other tests. If there will be a report of the findings, you might suggest reading the report as an alternative to attending the debriefing meeting, although the downside is that the person won't be involved in prioritizing the issues.

Discuss Risks and Concerns (Finding the Rattlesnakes)

As the saying goes, it's not the rattlesnake you see that will bite you. The real value of paper prototyping comes from its ability to point out problems early in the development process, while it's still easy to avoid them. Thus, you should design your usability tests around whatever aspects of the user experience you are most worried about (or know the least about). This is called *risk management.*

This kind of thinking is backward from how software is often developed. To have a solid base of code to build on, developers often start with the pieces that are well understood, just to get something running. Aspects of the design that are still up in the air are postponed until later, thus providing ample cover for the rattlesnakes. But because paper prototypes don't depend on functioning code, they allow you to do the opposite—start with whatever you have the most questions about, mock something up, and get user feedback. As soon as you have a handle on a particular issue, you can turn your attention to whatever's next on your list of things to worry about.

Paper prototyping is an excellent tool for risk management because it helps you clarify what you do and don't know about how well your interface will work, and it can help the team make important decisions. Ronnie Thomson, Director of Engineering, describes Centra's prototyping experience before the first release of their Web application Symposium: "There was an undercurrent of doubt about whether we were doing the right thing [with the 3D interface]. Paper prototyping helped the company address these issues and change technical direction. Without it, these decisions would likely have taken 6 to 12 months longer."

At the kickoff meeting, ask everyone to discuss what things they're concerned about and/or would like to know more about. The exact questions, of course, depend on the circumstances of your project, but following are some questions you might use to get people started:

- What are you least sure about?
- What are the greatest risks from a business perspective?
- What problems keep you up at night?
- What important design decisions do you still have to make?
- What have we gotten the most negative feedback about?
- What tasks are critically important to users, even if they're done infrequently?
- What parts are new?

If you have an existing version of the interface, make sure to get input from trainers and/or customer support, who will likely have a good idea where the trouble spots are. If your team is designing something new, these questions may be harder to answer. You may not even know where your biggest risks lie—in essence, this is your biggest risk.

Write down everyone's concerns on the whiteboard, and ask someone to type it up at the same time. It's fine if people don't agree on what the problems are. Don't discuss, just list. The next chapter on task design explains how you use these concerns as inputs into the process of creating tasks. (Although you could wait until the task design meeting to have this discussion about risks, I find it's useful to do it at the kickoff meeting because it helps people understand the purpose of paper prototyping and usability testing.)

Discussing your concerns first may help clarify the type of user you want to focus on, which is the next activity in the kickoff meeting. However, it's possible that these steps should be reversed for your project—the things you're most concerned about might depend on which user(s) you're talking about. If you find yourselves getting bogged down in the discussion of risks, you may want to switch gears and talk about users, then pick up your discussion of risks once you've agreed on the user profile.

Create a User Profile

It's important to get consensus from the development team about which kind of users you want to recruit for the usability tests. It's common for interfaces to have more than one type of user, but if you're doing usability testing for the first time, choose only one. For example, if your interface is used by system administrators and end users, pick one of those populations to test with. The main problem with testing multiple types of users is that you're tempted to subdivide your test population too much, and it's very hard to interpret the results if you've brought in only two users from each of four target markets. You need to test with enough of one kind of user to see the patterns, and once you've done that you'll have plenty of data to digest. So pick one type of user for now—you can always do another usability study later.

There is no one best process for creating a user profile. I describe what I usually do, but you might want to do some further reading on the topic.

Start by discussing what characteristics the target users have. Following are some questions you may find helpful:

- What education or training have they received?
- What are they responsible for in their work?
- How familiar are they with the technology and concepts our product uses?
- What products similar to ours have they bought/used?

Make a list of all the characteristics mentioned. Once you've run out of steam, look at your list and identify a subset of four to six characteristics that capture the essence of this user. (Some examples are provided shortly if you'd like to peek at them now.) Typically, you'll find that some characteristics supersede others. For example, you may not care if a network administrator has a computer science degree as long as he or she has somehow gotten a job that includes responsibility for configuring servers.

Once you have agreed on a user profile, ask yourself if the people you'd like to bring in for usability testing might be slightly different than this profile. Sometimes you may be able to broaden a criterion; other times there may be certain people you want to screen out.

Example of broadening: "We'd really like to get network administrators who do the hands-on configuration and troubleshooting of the network. But it's okay if we have a couple of their managers too, because they still understand the concepts even if they don't do the hands-on work."

Example of narrowing: "We should screen out people who design or develop Web sites—they know too much so they aren't typical of the audience." (Another obvious example is people who work for your competitors. If an outside company is doing recruitment, this won't be obvious to them, so you'll need to be explicit about what competitors you're excluding.)

Examples of User Profiles

Following are some sample user profiles that are similar to ones I've used for real projects.

For a Data Security Web Application

- Works at a large organization (>1000 people) such as a hospital or Fortune 1000 company. (The size of the company isn't important per se, but it acts as a proxy for a company that has a need to protect internal data. If someone works at a smaller company but meets the other criteria, he or she is in.)
- Manages a nontechnical group (such as Purchasing, HR, Finance, Marketing, etc.). Screen out Engineering, IT, MIS.
- Approves access to sensitive resources (such as network dial-in, high-value transactions, financial accounts, employee records, medical records, and proprietary data).
- Has budgetary responsibility; approves expenditures.

For a Music Web Application

- Buys at least two music CDs per month (more is better).
- Has downloaded music from the Internet.
- Is age 18 to 34.
- Owns (or has used) a portable MP3 player: [list]
- Listens to at least one of the following radio stations: [list]

For Small Business Banking Customers

- Works at a small business with annual revenues between $250,000 and $500,000 per year.
- Does not work in any of the following industries: banking, financial services, or insurance.
- In their company, is the decision maker or influencer for the company's banking, payroll, insurance, and/or retirement plan decisions. (Ideally, we'd like people who are involved in all these areas.)
- Is not a software or Web site developer.
- Company currently has a business account with [bank].

Notice what these profiles have in common—they consist of no more than a handful of factors, they distinguish between requirements and nice-to-haves, and they also mention characteristics to screen out.

Demographics versus Characteristics

In practice, I've found that demographic factors such as age, gender, and income don't seem to have much effect on a user's ability to turn up usability problems, so I often don't include them in the user profile. Usually, if you get people who have the appropriate skills, knowledge, and motivation, demographic factors are secondary.

However, I'm not saying that demographic factors are irrelevant—they are certainly an important part of understanding who your users are. It's just that when it comes to finding people to participate in usability tests, demographic factors often turn out to be only a proxy for what you're really interested in—usually some combination of knowledge, preferences, and behavior.

For example, say you're developing a travel Web site, and marketing research has shown that your target market falls into a certain income range. But then you think of that low-income couple you know who treat themselves to a week in Aruba every spring. Perhaps the important factor isn't income, but the number of trips taken each year, in other words, their behavior. So you'd ask, "If the person buys more than one plane ticket online per year, would we want them regardless of income?" If the answer is yes, you can drop the income demographic from your user profile because it's only acting as a proxy for amount of leisure travel.

Another way to scrutinize demographic factors is to ask, "How would someone with factor X behave differently when using our interface than someone without it?" If you can't answer that question, the factor can be omitted from your profile. For example, several years ago I worked with a company that was introducing high-speed Internet access to a market. They wanted to conduct a paper prototype test of their Web site. One of the factors on their initial user profile was "Has two phone lines." Their reasoning was that people who had a second phone line for their computer would be prime candidates for another method of Internet access. This made perfect sense for their *marketing* efforts, but when we asked ourselves, "How would people with two phone lines use this Web site differently than people who only have one?" we realized it was totally irrelevant for what they wanted to test. Which was good news because dropping that requirement made user recruitment much easier.

Although I often omit demographic factors from a user profile, I'll make an exception if a factor truly is an integral part of what we're trying to study; I have tested Web sites specifically aimed at men, women, college students, parents, and so on. In these cases, the product team believed that a demographic factor had a strong effect on the validity of the data obtained from testing. (Translation: If we had tested with someone else, there's a significant risk that the usability test results would have been dismissed as atypical.)

Reality Check

Just because your team reaches consensus on the user profile doesn't mean that it represents reality. (In the more egregious cases, you get a big clue during user recruitment when you can't find those people—because they don't exist!) Take every opportunity to validate your user profile with people who know (or even better, are) users. One of my colleagues once worked at a company where the product team assumed that users would have a background in math and statistics. But when my colleague visited some training classes, he found that only about one third of the users fit what the product team had considered to be the "typical" profile. Fortunately, he discovered this in time to fix the product, which might otherwise have alienated two thirds of its target market.

Time Needed to Create the User Profile

The first time you create a user profile, it might take you an hour or three, especially if there are differing assumptions about who your users are. Sometimes you may realize that you don't have a clear picture of who your users are—this isn't ideal, but it happens. If there are uncertainties or disagreements about users, note these as areas for research.

Once you have a user profile, you might be able to reuse it for subsequent usability tests. But be sure to first discuss whether you've learned anything about users since the last usability study that might cause you to modify the user profile.

Determine the Schedule

A typical first-time usability study using a paper prototype takes a total of 5 or 6 days of effort, but spread across perhaps a month from start to finish. To recruit users, you have to know when the tests will be. Finding users has a longer lead time than preparing the prototype, so start by scheduling the usability tests and allow 3 to 4 weeks for user recruitment. (Once you have a user profile and a recruitment method established, it may be possible to test on much shorter notice.)

Like they said on Star Trek, "Space: the final frontier." Your testing schedule might depend on when you can get a place to do it. Try to reserve the same lab/conference room all day on the days you're planning to usability test; although paper prototypes are portable, they can be a pain to move.

Work backward from the first test to schedule the activities you'll need to get ready. Although you may worry that you won't be prepared, chances are you will be—in dozens of paper prototyping projects, I've never known a team that couldn't get ready in time. One of the advantages of paper is that you can throw something together at the last minute if need be.

Length of Usability Tests

Perhaps 95% of the usability tests I've done have been either 1 or 2 hours in length. For your first couple of usability studies, I suggest that you choose between 1-hour or 2-hour tests. Go with 2 hours if you have many things to cover, if the interface contains new or complex concepts, or if it supports a work flow that contains more than a handful of steps. For example, in testing software for network administrators, I've always planned 2-hour tests. On the other hand, 1 hour is usually sufficient if the interface is smaller in scope.

That's rather vague advice, but fortunately I've found that the product team usually has a pretty good gut feeling about whether their interface needs 1 hour or 2. Ask yourselves, "Can a user cover what we're interested in within 1 hour?" and trust your collective instincts. If you're evenly divided, go with 90 minutes.

Of course, tests of other lengths are possible. In my experience, tests longer than 2 hours are rarely needed—if you plan one, be sure to include time for a break. Tests much shorter than an hour may not be not practical because you'll want time at the beginning for introductions, time at the end for Q&A, and you can probably come up with enough tasks to keep the user busy for a while. Short tests might make sense if you're redesigning only a small part of the interface or you have just one or two tasks; this is more likely to be the case if you're already conducting frequent usability tests.

Number of Users

As a rule, testing with five to eight users will provide enough data for you to see the main patterns, provided that you use roughly the same set of tasks (it's okay to vary them a little) and the users are from the same profile. There is some debate on this number-of-users topic among usability professionals, and both sides are able to back up their claims with some solid evidence. Nielsen and Landauer (1993) put forth their finding that the curve describing the total number of problems found started to flatten out after about five or six users (Figure 5.1). More recently, User Interface Engineering (Spool & Schroeder, 2001), reported that when users are asked to bring their own tasks (and credit cards) to e-commerce sites, it takes considerably more users to find the major problems—on the order of dozens. This

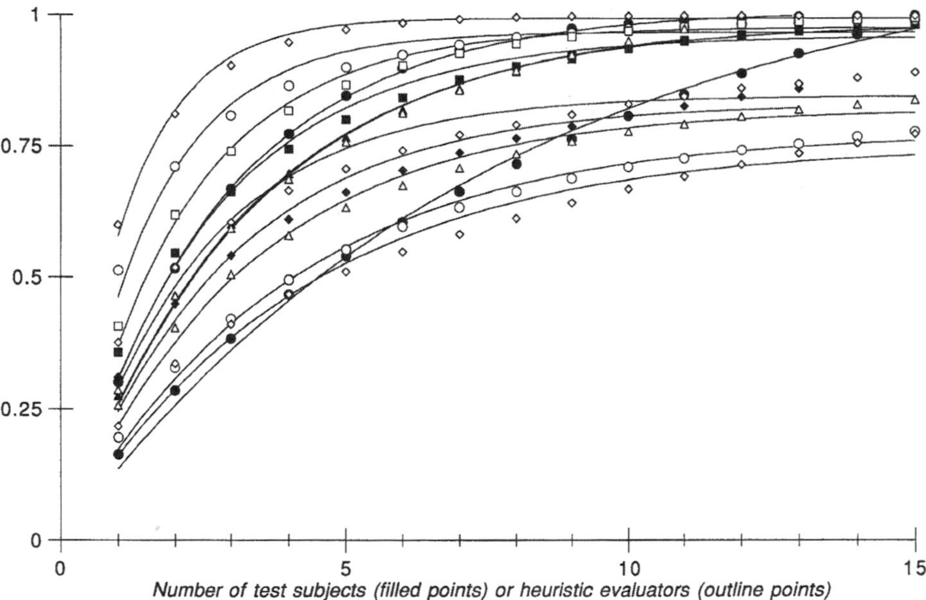

Figure 5.1 This graph from Nielsen and Landauer's work (1993) is often cited as the reason why you only need a handful of users—there's clearly a point of diminishing returns in testing with additional users.

is because when users do different things, they cover different aspects of the interface. Not only that, but when users are pursuing goals they truly care about (not to mention spending their own money), they are more sensitive to subtle issues than when they're doing a task someone else has invented.

Fortunately, with a paper prototype, the tasks are naturally somewhat constrained because you're only prototyping a portion of the interface and/or you're preparing the data the user sees. Thus, paper prototype tests tend to fall under the conditions of the Nielsen and Landauer study. Practically speaking, I find that after three or four tests I can usually see the patterns in what users are confused about and bothered by. There is no guarantee that you'll uncover all the problems, but once you have a few hours' worth of observations, it's time to step back and digest what you've learned.

So I suggest that for your first usability study, you plan no more than four to six tests. If you are using co-discovery (two users at a time, as explained in Chapter 8), you might schedule four 2-hour tests (for a total of eight users), or if you would rather test with one user a time, you could plan six 1-hour tests. With either of these schedules you can complete the testing in 2 days. Keep in mind that you can always do more tests later if you want.

Spacing of Tests

It's important to leave time between tests to review what you've learned and make changes to the prototype. If you're accustomed to conducting nonpaper usability tests, you may be in the practice of scheduling an entire day's worth of tests back-to-back, but this doesn't work as well with paper. I suggest a maximum of 4 hours of testing time per day, with a minimum of 2 hours between tests.

The schedule I've most often used is to hold usability tests from 10 AM to noon and from 2 to 4 PM on two consecutive days. That's a total of four tests, and with co-discovery that's eight users. Of course, testing can be spread over a longer period if the team expects to make substantial changes. In that case, I might leave a day in between the 2 days of testing. I rarely allow more time than that because usability testing with a paper prototype is an immersive activity. If you stop for too long, you'll lose momentum.

Estimating the Other Activities

Once you have scheduled the usability tests, you'll want to schedule the activities that precede and follow them.

Task Design

The next chapter discusses task design in detail. I've found that task design is often the most difficult activity in a paper prototype usability study because it tends to expose missing or conflicting assumptions that team members have about the product and what users will do with it. Thus, from a planning perspective I like to set aside a minimum of 3 hours (per user profile) to design tasks—and be prepared for it to take up to twice that long, especially the first couple times. It's also a good idea to have the product team review your tasks; thus, you may want to plan some time to modify them.

Creating the Paper Prototype

Creating the paper prototype takes anywhere from half a day to a week, depending on the state of the design. Start by assuming 2 days and adjust the estimate depending on various factors—less time if you're working mostly from screen shots and up to a week if it's a complete redesign or many people have input. If you think it will take longer than a week, chances are you're overpreparing. Also keep in mind that you don't need to prototype the entire interface, just enough to do the tasks.

Allocate time in half-day increments. Paper prototyping is not an activity that can easily be done in a few minutes between meetings. Because of all the pieces, it takes a while to set up the prototype and put it away. (Some teams don't like to leave their prototype spread out on the table overnight because they're afraid that the cleaning crew will throw it away!) Most paper prototypes I've worked on have been developed in three to four afternoons over a week or two. You may also want to reserve a conference room for the prototype creation sessions and walkthroughs—you want a large surface to spread out all the pieces.

Walkthroughs

Chapter 7 explains the purpose and method of conducting internal walkthroughs prior to the first usability test. Walkthroughs are an integral part of the prototype creation process, so by setting aside time for prototype creation you've also accounted for the walkthroughs. The exception is the last walkthrough before testing—you may want to schedule that because it often involves a larger group than the core team that created the prototype.

Debriefing Meeting and Action Plans

You may want to plan a short session immediately after each test to list what you saw and then make changes to the prototype. Because that session is attended by the people who observed the tests, one simple solution is to tack on a half hour to the testing time—if the tests will last 2 hours, tell people to set aside 2.5 hours for each test they attend.

At the end of the usability study, after all the tests are complete, plan a debriefing meeting with the entire product team to prioritize and discuss what you learned. People's memories fade pretty quickly (my memory has a half-life of about 24 hours), so it's best to hold the debriefing as soon as possible after the last test—I try to schedule it for the next day. It usually takes about 2 hours to prioritize the issues, sometimes less, at which point you might continue into a discussion of how to address them, or you might schedule a separate meeting for that. Once the debriefing meeting is over, there is probably some additional work needed to document and/or communicate the results. Chapter 11 covers these topics in more detail.

At this point, I return you to your regularly scheduled development process—whatever methods you normally use to prioritize and plan your work, you should input the test results into.

User Recruitment

There are many good references on user recruitment, so here I only to touch on the main factors that affect planning and scheduling. First you must decide whether to manage user recruitment internally or outsource it to a company (such as a market research firm) that specializes in doing this sort of thing. The best decision depends on the following:

1. **Time.** It's time-consuming to play phone tag with people, screen them, schedule them, send out paperwork and reminders, and so on. Some of this work can be done through email, but it still takes a nontrivial amount of time to manage the process.
2. **Money.** Depending on the user profile and your geographic area, you can pay upward of $100 per user to have an outside company do user recruitment (not

counting the money you have to pay the users). This may be outside your means, or it may be money well spent.

3. **Frequency of usability studies.** One R&D department I know of has a contractor who works 20 hours a week scheduling usability tests. This makes sense for them because the department has several projects underway at a time, and they do frequent usability studies. Consider whether others at your company might also want to conduct usability studies; perhaps you can share recruitment resources.
4. **Sources of users.** Sometimes you may have no clue where to find users, or you may want people who are unfamiliar with your product or company. (If the latter, you obviously can't put an invitation on your own Web site.) Brainstorm about how your users get their news and professional information; to reach them, you might use newspaper or radio ads or flyers posted at a local college, professional organizations, user groups, and so on. If you're still struggling for ideas on how to find users, working with a recruiting firm may be your best bet.
5. **Whether your users are customers.** If you know who your customers are, it may be easiest to just contact them yourself. (A market research firm can work from a list that you provide and save you some time, but this usually doesn't save you money because they have to do almost as much work.) Be sensitive to the politics involved in dealing with customers—if people in your Sales/Marketing department have existing relationships with customers, you should discuss your plans with them first to determine the best way to proceed.

If you work with an outside company, they will likely want you to write a screener, which in essence means turning your bullet-list user profile into a series of questions, like a flow chart, that lets the company know whether a particular person meets your needs or not. The company you're working with should be able to provide you an example of the format they'd like you to use. Creating a screener can take a couple of hours, but it can often be reused for subsequent usability tests as long as the user profile remains the same. A screener can also be useful if you are doing recruitment internally, although if a member of your core team is doing recruitment they may not need one.

If you decide to do user recruitment internally, think about who might be well suited for the task. If you have an extroverted co-worker who's good at administrative details, managing user recruitment may be a perfect career enhancement opportunity for that person, as well as something he or she would enjoy.

How Many Usability Studies?

So far, this chapter has assumed you're doing one usability study. But how many usability studies do you need to do for your product? For starters, plan just one study and let the results determine whether you're comfortable that your design works or you need to redesign and then test again. Some product teams use paper prototypes in the early stages to smoke out the show-stoppers and then plan a small usability study or two later with the real interface to find any issues that wouldn't have come up with paper.

Companies that do a lot of prototyping and usability testing tend to evolve into an iterative process that uses small, frequent usability tests throughout the development cycle rather than one or two large efforts. Following are two examples.

From the Field: Iterative Usability Testing

"Although we do a lot of usability testing, we only bring in a few users each round. On the CP Select tool [described in Chapter 2], we tested five versions of the paper prototype, but we did our first two rounds of testing with two to three users each, and they were internal users. This works for us because our tools are highly specialized and we have ready access to domain experts in-house. For the next three rounds, we tested with both internal and external users, but only a couple of each. So for the whole project we worked with maybe six external users and a dozen internal. But that was enough to see radical improvements in our design—the team was surprised at how much easier it was for users to complete tasks in the final version.

"We also need to determine when we've done enough testing. What drives each round of testing is how clear we are on what the problems are. The data we collect also tells us what can stay the same. Over time, we can chart our progress by seeing how much of the design can stay the same—we call this 'gelling.' Once a design gels, we feel comfortable going off and implementing it, because the remaining issues tend to be minor."

By Jennifer Lymneos, The MathWorks

From the Field: Iterative Usability Testing—cont'd

"On one project I did usability tests every Friday for five weeks. I started with some rough prototypes our graphic designers had created in PhotoShop and printed them out. I sat down with four to six users (one at a time) on a Friday and walked them through a series of 'functional' questions (e.g., How would you use this page to do X?). I gave them markers so they could mark up the paper screen shots as they answered my questions. I spent the following Monday and Tuesday working my notes into design changes to apply to the PhotoShop files. In week 3 I began to show them the screen shots on a monitor—I'd gotten what I could from paper and was ready to switch over to doing it on a computer. By week 5 the users were looking at HTML files rather than flat graphic files (our designers were converting the flat files to HTML during this time). At the end of five weeks the design had stabilized to the point where I was only finding small issues."

By Brent Mundy, Usability Specialist

It Gets Easier

Your first paper prototype usability test is like busting sod—it's a lot of backbreaking work for a farmer to prepare a field for its first planting. Your first experience with paper prototyping may feel like a major production. You're starting from scratch with the user profile, recruitment, tasks, and prototype creation. Your co-workers have questions about the technique, and using a new skill takes a lot of mental energy. But for subsequent "crops," it gets much easier—you'll know where to find users, some of your materials can be reused, you won't have to explain the activities, you'll learn how to do the optimal amount of preparation, and you'll be more relaxed when conducting the usability tests.

Chapter 6

Task Design

Task design is one of the most important aspects of usability testing. You don't just watch users do whatever they want with the interface; you create specific tasks that cover what you want to learn. A good task is like a spotlight that illuminates your interface, showing you the parts that work well and the issues that get in users' way. A good task provides reliable data about key issues so that you get the most from your usability study. But a poor task can mask problems or even turn up false ones. For example, if you ask users to do something that they would never do in real life and they fail, it's difficult to tell whether the interface really has a problem or if you've created an artificial one.

As important as task design is, it isn't easy to do it well. I think task design is probably the hardest part of usability testing, and even after 10 years I'm still learning. This chapter shows you what has worked for me and helps you avoid some common pitfalls.

Characteristics of a Good Task

So what makes a good task? A good task has the following characteristics. (Except as noted, this discussion applies to tasks used for any type of usability testing, not just paper prototypes.)

- Is based on a goal that matters to the user profile you've chosen.
- Covers questions important to the success of your product and business.
- Has appropriate scope—not too broad, not too specific.
- Has a finite and predictable set of possible solutions.

- Has a clear end point that the *user* can recognize.
- Elicits action, not just opinion.

I'm going to discuss the first two characteristics—users' goals and your questions—in detail when I describe the process of creating tasks. For now, suffice it to say that if a task doesn't have the first two characteristics, it is likely to give you misleading information or waste your time.

Has Appropriate Scope

The scope for a task should be large enough for the user to achieve a realistic goal and to answer one or more of your important questions. Typically, tasks of this scope take anywhere from 5 to 30 minutes to complete with a paper prototype.

If you're new to usability testing, your first inclination may be to test one screen at a time. Screens are designed one a time, but this isn't the best way to test them—you won't uncover the broader issues that arise only when the user sets out to accomplish something. For example, there may be an important function that users need. If you just show them one screen that doesn't contain that function, they may assume that you've provided it elsewhere, when in fact you aren't even aware that it exists. Sometimes your co-workers can review a screen—this is sometimes called "hallway usability"—and spot your more egregious blunders ("Dude, there's no way to delete a record"), but real users have a hard time at this because they're not used to thinking like designers. Unless they've read the functional spec, they don't know all the features that are supposed to be available.

Has a Finite and Predictable Set of Possible Solutions

If you had an entire working interface at your disposal, you might not be concerned about having a finite set of solutions, but when you're using paper you have to make all the prototype pieces to support what the user might do. Thus, you may want to introduce some constraints into your task for the purpose of limiting the amount of preparation you'll need to do.

For example, if you were testing a working version of a gardening site, you might have a task that says, "Last year, raccoons ate the crocus bulbs you planted. Are there any bulbs that don't appeal to critters?" But if there are dozens of bulbs in your online catalog, you might not want to prepare a prototype page for each one. One tactic is to alter the task to constrain the set of possible solutions: "Your neighbor told you that raccoons won't eat daffodil bulbs—is this true?" That way, you need only the product page(s) for daffodils. Another tactic is to leave the task as is, and if the user tries to look at a bulb page you didn't prepare, simply tell them what it would say about edibility. But in either case, you'd still want to keep a realistic level of complexity in the higher-level pages such as the home page and the category listings; otherwise the task would be artificially easy.

I recommend that there should always be at least one solution to a task. It's best to avoid so-called "red herring" tasks where you tell the user to attempt something you know is impossible—many usability specialists believe that such tasks are not ethical and can result in undue stress on test participants. (Chances are, they'll have a hard enough time with the things the interface does let them do.) If there is a reason you need to use this kind of task, tell the users up front that some tasks may not have solutions and they're allowed to give up.

Has a Clear End Point

It's usually best to avoid overly open-ended tasks such as "Explore this site" or "Find out something interesting about daffodils." Tasks that lack a clear end point are awkward to facilitate. The users won't be sure whether they are doing the right thing, and it's hard for you to know when to end the task, forcing you to jump in at an arbitrary point and interrupt them.

The users, not you, should decide when the task is done. Sometimes users successfully complete a task but don't realize it because the interface doesn't give them sufficient feedback. It's common for users to decide on their own to verify the results of their work, especially when using an interface for the first time. For example, say they completed all the steps needed to configure the network; chances are, they'll want to ping the devices (send a test message and look for a response) to be sure. If you stop them too soon, you might miss the fact that users need some additional functionality to verify what they've just done. (You should also watch for the opposite problem—users might think they're done, but there's a step they don't know about, or perhaps they've done something incorrectly without realizing it.)

Elicits Action, Not Just Opinion

A good task should cause the user to interact with the interface, not just look at it and tell you what they think. Often, what users say they like does not reliably indicate what they can successfully use, and vice versa. It's not that users are lying to us—often they are responding to the *concept* of a particular feature, when in reality it may not work the way they envision. For example, several years ago I tested the Function Wizard in Microsoft Excel. One user got stuck trying to create a function that would calculate a mortgage payment, and I finally had to help him. When I asked him what he thought of the Function Wizard, he said, "Now that I know how to use it, I think it's great." Then I gave him the next task, then the next, and watched him get wrapped around the axle each time. But he never wavered in his professed liking for the Function Wizard.

Most of the time during a usability test should be spent watching users work with the interface as opposed to talking about it. If you have opinion-type questions on your list of things you want to know (e.g., "What do you think of this service?"), it's best to save them until the end of the test session, if you even ask them at all. In general, usability testing is not an efficient method of soliciting opinions or other subjective data because you're working with only one or two users at a time rather than the dozens or hundreds of people you'd have with other methods, such as focus groups or surveys. Depending on the completeness of the prototype, opinion questions may be even less useful in paper prototype tests than they are in usability tests of finished products.

I usually avoid opinion questions, although I'll make an exception if someone on the product team has a burning desire to ask one and he or she understands the limitations I've just described. Often, it's pretty clear from the users' comments whether they like or dislike something.

Overview of the Task Creation Process

In a good task, the user covers the areas of the interface that you have questions about while on their way to accomplishing something that *they* care about. Tasks for usability tests come from the intersection of two lists: your questions about the product and users' goals (Figure 6.1). So let's look at how you get those two lists and then create tasks from them. The steps are as follows:

1. List the users' goals and accomplishments that can be achieved using your interface.
2. List your questions—issues, risks, and other concerns about the interface (you may have done this as part of the kickoff meeting).
3. Prioritize your questions.

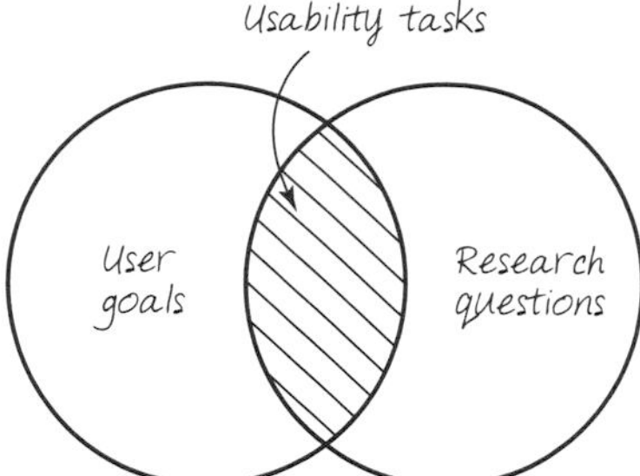

Figure 6.1 Good usability tasks are drawn from the area of overlap—users are doing something they care about, and along the way they're answering your questions.

4. Pick a user accomplishment that covers one or more important questions and turn it into a task using the template provided in this chapter. Repeat this step until you have a set of tasks that covers your questions.
5. Determine the order of the tasks and whether you've got the right amount of work to fill your testing time.
6. Write the instructions that will be given to users.
7. Reality-check your tasks.

As indicated in the previous chapter, task design should be done by the core team, plus others who have a strong interest in what is tested and/or who have knowledge about users and what they do. Although it's possible for one person to create tasks, the discussion that takes place during the task design session can be quite valuable because it will reveal all sorts of assumptions (often conflicting ones) about what users will do with the interface.

Step 1: List User Goals

If your interface works flawlessly but doesn't do anything that users care about, all your hard work will be for naught. So start by making a list of goals and accomplishments that are important to the user profile you've chosen for this usability study. What are people using your interface to do? What is important to them? How does your product make their life better? Pay attention to things that users do frequently—if you're developing an online brokerage and users can't execute a stock trade, you're sunk. Also consider goals that are infrequent but really important—if users can't use your backup software to *restore* a file, it doesn't matter how easy the backups were to do.

While attempting to list user accomplishments, some product teams realize that they really don't know what their users do. This is not the end of the world, but it indicates the need for research into users and their needs, which is beyond the scope of this book. (But not, fortunately, beyond the scope of other books in the References section.)

Even if you aren't sure what your users' goals are, you can probably make some educated guesses. Another idea is to seek out people in your company who have contact with users (for example, salespeople, trainers, customer service representatives) and get their input. Just keep in mind that it's especially important to reality-check what you come up with, as I describe later.

Functionality versus Goals

When you're used to thinking about functionality, it can be hard to switch your mind-set to think about the users' goals. You may find yourself listing functionality. When this happens, I keep asking the product team, "Why is that important?" until I hear an answer that contains a user goal.* The user's goal is often broader than the function the team started with. For example, someone may initially say that a user goal is to buy a stock—the why questions help them realize that the user's true goal is a well-funded retirement (or perhaps the excitement of gambling). Table 6.1 shows more examples for a hypothetical online job database.

Step 2: List Your Questions

Next, make a list of all the questions and concerns you have about the product. As discussed in the previous chapter, identifying risks and concerns is a helpful thing to do during the kickoff meeting, so you might use that list as your starting point. Some issues might be based on user feedback while others are just a nagging feeling in someone's mind. They are often, but not always, necessarily phrased as questions. Some issues are fairly specific, as illustrated by the following examples compiled from several projects:

* I call this the small-child tactic. Kids have an infinite capacity for asking why. Ironic that part of being a successful consultant involves behaving like a small child.

Table 6.1 Functionality versus User Goals for a Job Database

Functionality	*Why Is This Important?*	*Rephrased in Terms of User Goal*
Register and upload resume	Person wants to find a new or better job. But having a resume online is just one step toward this goal.	Decide whether this service would be useful to me in finding a new job. If it's not going to be worth my time, I won't bother uploading my resume.
Search by geographic area	Commute time is important; many job-seekers don't want to relocate.	Find all the suitable job openings within a reasonable commute from my home so that I don't waste my life driving to and from work.
Sign up for daily email notification	In a tight job market, many job postings are filled quickly.	How can I find out about new job openings before the other guy does so that I can contact the company first?
Navigate to supplemental articles (resume writing, interviewing)	Person wants to increase chances of finding a good job.	I have an interview next Monday. I haven't interviewed for a while—are there particular things I should or shouldn't do?

- Source/destination—do users understand these terms, or are they too technical?
- When the free version times out after 30 days, have we broken their expectations? Will they buy it, or just be mad at us?
- Some people print the preview, which doesn't look very good. How can we get them to print the PDF instead?
- Do users understand the Reset/Clear buttons in the Watch list?
- Tech support gets lots of calls about forgotten passwords. How can we fix this online?

Or you might find that your questions are broad or vague:

- How do people discover new music, such as music by similar but unknown artists? How do they decide what music to buy?
- Users come to the site for the free materials, but we want them to become buyers. What would help with this? Showing sample pages of new books?

- We don't know which aspects of account management our customers want to do online. Does anyone really care about account aggregation?
- We've gotten feedback that the interface is "disjointed." You can end up someplace without clearly knowing how you got there. No one can give us a specific example, though, so we're not sure what this means.

It's not necessary to separate the issues into specific and broad—I've done this to help with the next point I'm going to make. Just brainstorm a list of the things your team is most concerned about, and write them in whatever order they come up. A typical team comes up with a couple dozen issues; you might have even more.

Step 3: Prioritize Your Questions

As a rule, the specific questions are easier to answer, but the broad questions are usually more important to the success of the product. (Specific issues that are costing the company money, like the forgotten password example, may be exceptions.) So guess which questions get made into tasks first? From what I've seen, it's often the specific ones, because they're easier to investigate. But remember what's at stake—the success of the product, perhaps the entire company, may hinge on the broader issues.

Remember what's at stake—your company.

So look at your list and ask, "Which of these are most important to the success of the next release?" (Or the company—the best way to phrase this question depends on the nature of the business you're in.) One way to prioritize the issues is to have people vote for the three questions they think are most important. Often, you can't answer all of the top questions in a usability study, but at least you'll be looking at the forest, not just the trees.

Sometimes the broad questions pertain to patterns that will emerge only after you've watched a number of users do various tasks. For example, if your broad questions are "How do users navigate?" and "Why do customers complain that it's too slow?" you can't really create one specific task that will answer them. In this case, make sure that your set of tasks as a whole will let you watch users do the things that you think will yield clues, and eventually you'll start to see the patterns.

Step 4: Create a Task

This is the step that's hardest to describe in concrete terms. In essence, take your two lists (user goals and your questions) and pick a user goal that covers one or more of your most important questions. Then turn it into a task by asking, "What's a specific example of this?"

For each task, fill out the following template (which is available at *www.paperprototyping.com*).

Task #: < Task Name >	
Goals/output:	
Inputs/ assumptions:	
Steps:	
Time for expert:	
Instructions for user:	
Notes:	

- **Task name and number.** Give each task a brief descriptive name and a number. The name helps you remember what its purpose is, and the numbers are useful in usability testing because you can ask the observers things such as, "Shall we skip 3 this time and go right to 4?" without discussing the content of the tasks in front of the users.
- **Goal/outputs.** What will users have accomplished when they're done with the task? Is there a tangible output? How will they know the task is complete? What might the users do to be sure?
- **Inputs.** List all the information or resources—tangible and intangible—that a user would need to complete this task. Examples include a valid log-in, business policies, physical objects such as a textbook or a credit card, file names, and so on. Real users may have some of this information in their heads—in your usability task you might have to provide this information. For example, a network administrator probably knows the network configuration by heart, but for your task you'd need to create a network schematic with relevant details, such as server names and IP addresses.

For the inputs, outputs, and everything that happens along the way, you'll need to have consistent data that reflects a realistic scenario. For instance, if users enter information on one screen that appears in a report later, the report should match what users entered to avoid confusion (I talk more about creating data in the next chapter). During task design, start thinking about realistic data that you could use for the task.

- **Assumptions.** Assumptions are the conditions and prerequisites that are in place at the start of the task. The assumptions depend on what you want to learn from the task. For example, if a task explores how users recover from an error caused by a duplicate record, your assumptions include the condition(s) that cause the error to occur, such as, "An employee with the same name already exists in the database." Often, your assumptions will emerge when you start doing walkthroughs, so you don't have to nail them all down in the task design session—you can add more later. In practice, I sometimes combine assumptions with inputs because the distinction between them isn't crucial; they're both things that we need to consider while preparing the prototype.
- **Steps.** Write down the steps you expect the user will go through in completing the task. This helps you identify the prototype pieces that you'll need to create. Writing down the expected steps can also be helpful if there will be observers who aren't as familiar with the interface as you are.

  Keep the steps mostly at a screen level—no need to list every field on the order form, just say "order form." Don't worry about exact terminology because these steps are just for your benefit in preparing the interface. The user won't see these steps, only the task instructions that you'll write later. Some tasks have multiple paths that lead to success, so jot down any variations, such as "Search OR navigate to lawn & garden page." Put optional steps in parentheses, such as (Review privacy policy).
- **Time estimate for expert.** Estimate how long it would take an expert (someone on the core team) to complete the task. Ignore any time needed for the system to do its processing and focus on the time spent entering data and clicking buttons. Some tasks, such as composing an email, require time for thinking or creative effort, so allow time for that. In the next step of the task design process, I'll explain how to use this estimate to decide when you've created enough usability tasks.
- **Instructions for users.** Don't write the instructions for the users when you're filling in the rest of the template. Although task design works well as a group activity, writing the instructions can be done by one person after you've drafted your set of tasks. The following examples include the instructions, but keep in mind that they were written after everything else in the template.

- **Notes.** The notes section might have several types of information, including the reasons why you created the task, how you'll conduct it, specific things to watch for, and questions to ask users after the task is complete. Information to include in the notes varies depending on what's being tested. Write down whatever information you think will be useful to have on hand during the usability tests. Give copies of the completed task templates to usability test observers because this information helps them get more benefit from watching the tests. It's also quite helpful to the test facilitator.

Because task design is a group activity, you may want to draft each task on a piece of flip chart paper or a whiteboard. Ask someone at the meeting to fill out the template on a laptop as you go so that you'll also have it in electronic form.

Examples of Completed Task Templates

The following are examples of completed task templates that I've used in paper prototype usability tests. Although these tasks came from very different interfaces, you'll note the following things they have in common:

- The steps are described at a fairly high level, often tersely. These are intended for the development team, who knows what they mean.
- Each task would take an expert only a few minutes to complete.
- The length of the instructions given to users varies depending on the amount of background information the user needs to understand and complete the task. (Note: I have not yet explained how to write task instructions; that's coming in step 6.)
- For some tasks, there are detailed notes, but for others there are none.

Although three of the four examples happen to be from Web applications, tasks for other types of interfaces look much the same. In fact, when you are thinking in terms of goals and instructions for the users, the type of underlying technology shouldn't matter much, if at all. It comes into play only when you're looking at the steps, and to some extent the inputs and outputs. When the goal and task instructions are free of any references to technology or functionality, it's usually an indication that you've been successful at keeping your focus on the users rather than getting bogged down in implementation details.

Example 1: Web Application for Online College Courses

Background: This application is used by college students. When they purchase a textbook, students get access to the online version of the book and additional course content provided by the instructor. For a new book, this access comes in the form of a card containing a code. This task explores what happens in the case of a used book. Because the code can't be reused, the student must pay separately for access to the online materials.

Task 2: Used Book	
Goal/output:	Successful purchase of online access, resulting in ability to see course assignments
Inputs:	◇ Used book with expired access code card ◇ Credit card # ◇ Course ID as it might be given by instructor ◇ QuickStart Guide? ◇ Confirmation email
Assumptions:	◇ Student has previously registered but is not logged in ◇ Starting from where task 1 left off
Steps:	◇ Complete the registration process (several steps) ◇ Purchase online course access ◇ Wait for email ◇ Log in ◇ View course
Time for expert:	7 minutes
Instructions for user:	**Oral instructions: "For another class, you bought this book used at the bookstore. It came with this card, but this strip has been torn off. Find out whether you can still use this card as you did with the first course."**
Notes:	◇ Task 2 tests student registration and course enrollment as in task 1, but this time the student purchased a used book for another class and needs to use the purchase option. ◇ Let them try entering the access code and get "already been used" error. ◇ Note whether they understand what they're purchasing.

Example 2: Network Administrator Software

Background: This software application is used by network administrators to support the policies and practices within their organization, for example, controlling access to certain types of resources, prioritizing network traffic, and so on. In this scenario, the network administrator works at a college and the goal is to prevent students from using network bandwidth to download music.

Task 1: Block Napster	
Goal/output:	No one on the network is able to access Napster
Inputs/ assumptions:	◈ Network schematic with IP addresses, switches ◈ Switches consist of 1 Cajun and 1 Cisco
Steps:	◈ Log in ◈ Set up network ◈ Define (name) port ◈ Create application ◈ Set up policy ◈ Make a rule ◈ Create domain ◈ Create devices—Cisco, Cajun ◈ Assign devices to domain ◈ Deploy ◈ Verify
Time for expert:	5 minutes
Instructions for user:	**You're a network administrator at Whatsamatta U. The college president wants to prevent students from downloading music with Napster. You've just installed [the software] and you want to set it up to prevent anyone on your network from using Napster.**
Notes:	

Example 3: Web Application for Purchase/Download of Music

Background: Strangely enough, this example also deals with college students and downloading music, except in this case it's the desired activity. The users are college students who own a portable MP3 player and are in search of some good tunes to put on it. In addition to testing the mechanics of downloading music to the PC and MP3 player, in this task we also wanted to see how people went about finding and selecting music.

Task 2: Get 10 Tracks on Device	
Goal/output:	Portable MP3 player has 2 tracks on it that the users like
Inputs/ assumptions:	◇ MP3 player ◇ Has confirmation email as a result of task 1 ◇ Each user chooses 1 track according to their tastes
Steps:	◇ Go to [site].com ◇ Get to music application (from Download page) ◇ Search or browse for first track/artist ◇ Download to device ◇ Detect hardware, install ◇ Search or browse for second track/artist ◇ Download to device is grayed out ◇ Search or browse for third track/artist ◇ Download to device
Time for expert:	5 minutes
Instructions for user:	**Choose 10 songs you like and put them on your portable MP3 player.**
Notes:	◇ We'll ask the users what music they're interested in and how they'd search/browse to find it. Our prototype probably doesn't have exactly what they'd want, so at that point we'll have them pick something they recognize. ◇ If the users get "no search results," do they understand the possible causes? ◇ The first track they select will be downloadable to device, but the second track they pick will not be (to see whether they understand why). ◇ We won't actually have them download 10 tracks—after the second successful download we'll ask them if they'd use this same process if they were downloading 10. ◇ Do not explicitly ask the users about the playlist at this point; the next task is intended to encourage them to discover it ◇ Do they realize why some music isn't available (because of legal restrictions)?

Example 4: Web Application for Corporate Buyers

Background: The target audience for this application is people who work in purchasing departments at large companies. The application is intended to support the process of selecting vendors according to business rules that the company specifies; for example, vendors will be selected based on quality first, price second.

Task 1: Create RFQ	
Goal/output:	RFQ sent out to potential vendors
Inputs/ assumptions:	◇ Approved suppliers exist ◇ Product catalog exists (we may give them codes) ◇ All simple items, no compound ones ◇ Desired business rules are known ◇ Attachment exists for terms and conditions (t&c)
Steps:	◇ Create high-level RFQ (name, code, type, parameters, policy, suppliers, notes for suppliers) ◇ Create requisitions within quotation (name, code, description) ◇ Assign items to reqs (select type—simple in this case—category, product, define unique name & code, qty, max, min, price, date) ◇ Add attachments for t&c ◇ Print, get approvals ◇ Submit (define schedule info)
Time for expert:	10 minutes
Instructions for user:	**Welcome to your first day here at Consolidated Monopoly, the world's largest manufacturer of widgets. As an experienced corporate buyer, you'll be able to help us get some equipment we need.** **We need some desktop computers for our rapidly expanding development organization. We're hoping to get a better deal than the $800 apiece we've been paying at a local retailer. We need to have 500 PCs delivered in about a month.** **It doesn't matter whether all 500 PCs come from one vendor or not, and it's okay if we get the monitors from a different vendor than the CPU. The machines should include the latest versions of Windows, Microsoft Office, and Norton Antivirus.**

	There's a document on your hard disk called "terms&con.doc" that outlines our standard terms and conditions. Make sure that potential vendors receive this document before submitting a bid.
Notes:	

Step 5: Number and Order the Tasks

So how many tasks should you create? Enough to fill your allotted test time, plus one or two extra. Keep in mind that you won't have all the test time to spend on the tasks—it typically takes 5 to 10 minutes to get the user comfortable, briefed, and introduced, perhaps longer if you interview the user about his or her background or work. You may want to reserve another 10 minutes at the end of the test for questionnaires or to discuss interesting issues that arose. So the time available for tasks is typically the test length minus 10 to 20 minutes.

The Time Expansion Factor

Estimating task times is an art, not a science. Although I've gotten better at it over the years, occasionally I'm still way off. But there's a rule of thumb that I've found useful: Take that "time for expert" estimate and multiply it by a time expansion factor. This factor is a crude means of accounting for all the things that cause people in a usability test to work more slowly than an expert under ideal conditions: they're unfamiliar with the interface, they're verbalizing their thought process, they might have to wait for the Computer, and so on.

For software, I multiply the expert's time by a factor or 5 to 10 (I usually use a range, not a single number). In other words, a task that takes an expert 1 minute under ideal conditions will probably consume 5 to 10 minutes of test time. For Web sites, I've found that the time expansion factor seems to be smaller, more like 3 to 5 minutes. (I think this may be because the controls are usually simpler than for software—users are primarily clicking—but this is just a guess.) In looking at your interface, think about how much data entry is involved. Writing by hand takes time, so lots of data entry implies a bigger expansion factor. Also consider how many new or complex concepts are involved, which will affect the amount of time users need to think and/or experiment. Of course, these numbers are only rough guidelines, and your mileage will vary.

Add up the expanded task times and see whether you've filled your allotted test time. It's a good idea to create an extra task or two. Especially in a paper prototype, it's common for users in later tests to complete more tasks because your improvements to the interface make it easier to use.

Make sure that your tasks aren't too long. I've found that a task longer than 30 or 40 minutes can be fatiguing for users (not to mention observers). But there's no hard and fast definition of "too long." If you're testing a lengthy process, you might want to break it down into smaller tasks. Or the facilitator can plan to intervene after a certain amount of time, ask the users to summarize what they've done so far, and offer them a break.

Also be on the lookout for tasks that are very short—5 minutes or less. Sometimes this indicates that you're testing just one screen or function rather than a user goal. Although a short task is not necessarily bad, ask yourself if it makes sense to combine it with another task.

Dropping and Reordering Tasks

For some types of usability testing it's important to use the same tasks in the same order for each user. This is typically the case if the purpose of the testing is to collect success rates, task times, error rates, or other metrics. But metrics usually aren't the focus of paper prototype tests because the interface is continually evolving. Thus, it's usually not important to use the same tasks in the same order for each usability test—it's okay to vary them.

The purpose of paper prototyping is to provide answers to the questions you're most concerned about. As you conduct usability tests, you'll collect lots of data, and this data can cause you to be more (or less) worried about a particular issue. If you find your concerns changing during a usability study, it's appropriate to change the tasks accordingly. Here are some reasons why you might decide to drop a task and replace it with one of the extras you created:

- **You're not learning anything new.** Sometimes you learn all you need from a task by watching just the first few users complete it, especially if the interface works well (which does happen, although not as often as we might like). Once a task stops yielding new insights, it's done its job and you can send it into early retirement. Just be careful about reaching this conclusion prematurely—Users A, B, and C might sail past an issue that flummoxes User D. If there's any doubt, keep the task and gather more data.

- **You've identified a problem but aren't prepared to fix it yet.** Paper prototyping allows you to make many improvements to the interface in a short time, but sometimes you uncover problems that require more in-depth thought. If a task reveals an issue that you all agree needs to be fixed, it's not always necessary to keep banging your head against that particular wall. (However, if you are still trying to understand the nature of the problem, then you should probably keep the task.)
- **The task is too unrealistic.** If users indicate they'd never do this task, it might not be not worth keeping. But first reexamine the issues that caused you to create the task. If you had a wrong assumption about what users needed, drop the task. On the other hand, if your underlying questions are still valid, perhaps you can fix the task to make it more meaningful to users.

Step 6: Write Instructions for Users

The next step is to write the task instructions you'll give to users. Here are some guidelines.

Describe the Goal But Not the Steps

The purpose of usability testing is to learn how users approach the interface and what naturally makes sense to them. If the task instructions give them too much help, in essence you're training them, and this can mask usability problems. If you're a tech writer, you may have an especially hard time avoiding this trap because you earn your living by writing detailed instructions—it takes a conscious effort not to do this. Instead, the task instructions should explain *what* the user is trying to accomplish, but not *how.* See Table 6.2 for an example.

The exception to the rule of not providing steps is when there's an aspect of the interface that's out of your control or otherwise not interesting for you to test. In that case (which doesn't happen very often), it's okay to explain how to do something. As an alternative to doing this in the task instructions, the test facilitator can step in and help the users past this point.

Table 6.2 Task Instructions: Bad and Good Example

Bad (Explains How To Do It)	*Good (Describes Only the Goal)*
1. Start Excel 2. Go to Tools → MATLAB functions 3. Create a new function—from the list of installed MATLAB Excel builder components, load "myclass" from "my component." 4. Select "myprimes" from the list of available methods. Set up inputs/outputs for this function as follows . . . (The original task went on for 2 pages.)	You have a work colleague who created an Excel Add-In called the MATLAB Function Wizard that allows you to access certain MATLAB functionality. He's asked you to test it to find all the prime numbers between 0 and 25. (Note: The users were familiar with Excel and the product team wasn't testing Excel itself, so the explicit wording of "Excel Add-In" is appropriate.)

Avoid Wording That Reveals the Method

After all those endless meetings where you haggled over the exact wording for a menu option, you shouldn't use that wording in your task instructions because doing so could provide users with unintended clues. If you ask users to "create a graph" and you have a Create menu with a Graph option in it, you've made the task artificially easy. Use synonyms or a picture instead. (Chapter 13 has more examples of ways in which task instructions can cause a bias.)

A Picture Is Worth 1000 Words

Sometimes visual aids come in handy because they let you avoid using specific nouns and verbs—show the user a graph and say something like, "You want to make one of these for this month's sales results." Figure 6.2 shows an example of a picture we used in a usability study of an e-commerce site.

Figure 6.2 This type of coffee maker is called a French press, but we didn't want to reveal that to users because it might bias them toward using the site's search engine—coffee makers were easy to find via the search engine but hard to find using the links. So we showed them this picture and said, "Your friend has one of these and it makes great coffee, so you'd like to buy one."

Written, Not Oral

I usually give usability tasks to users in written format so that they can refer back to them as needed. This is important if the user needs to enter data from the task instructions, such as a server name. But there are exceptions to this rule. Sometimes for very simple tasks you can give the instructions orally. Oral instructions are also helpful when you don't want to reveal the spelling of a term, such as, "See if there are any new treatments for osteoporosis." But when in doubt, use written task instructions.

One Task Per Page

Print each task on a separate page and give them to the users one at a time. This gives you more flexibility to skip or reorder tasks depending on what happens in the usability test. It also avoids making users feel bad if they don't complete all the tasks (especially if you have a couple of extra tasks in reserve). I like to use 5 × 8 index cards for tasks, but regular paper works fine too. See Figure 6.3 for an example. Have an extra copy on hand in case the user jots something down on the task page.

> You've been grading essays. You're seeing the same grammatical problems over and over, don't they teach English in high school any more? You want to find some sections in The Longman Handbook pertaining to comma splicing so you can have your students read them.

Figure 6.3 An example of a task used in a study with college-level English teachers. It contains a subtle joke—can you see it?

Use Humor Carefully, If At All

Write your tasks in a professional but friendly tone. Most usability specialists agree that it's best to avoid overly clever or "cutesy" tasks. Although humor is a good thing, using it in usability testing can backfire if it accidentally strikes too close to home or the user feels insulted. I once heard of a task that read, "You've just been laid off—ha ha! See what outplacement services the HR site offers." Unfortunately, one of the users had just experienced a painful layoff and started crying. So that's definitely an example of what not to do!

On the other hand, although paper prototyping is a serious activity, it isn't necessarily a solemn one. I see nothing wrong with using subtle or lighthearted humor to help establish a relaxed atmosphere in the test setting, provided that it's appropriate for your audience. The task shown in Figure 6.3 was used in a usability study with college-level English teachers. (The joke, in case you didn't catch it, is that the second sentence contains a comma splice. To an English teacher, this is funny.) I've also seen developers draw elaborate hourglass cursors to use when the Computer needs time to find the next screen—these can make users smile. Props, such as the one shown in Figure 6.4, can also be humorous. But the bottom line for humor is to carefully consider its effect on your users and err on the conservative side.

Figure 6.4 We didn't really need this paper "credit card" for the e-commerce site we were testing, but it made people laugh.

Step 7: Reality-Check Your Tasks

Sometimes product teams lack a clear understanding of how and why users will use the interface. Although in an ideal world we'd have this information, sometimes we don't and we have to guess. Creating tasks from made-up user goals isn't inherently evil as long as you don't confuse them with reality. Perform a "reality check" by asking users at the end of the task if it's something they'd actually do and/or care about. If they say no, modify the task or omit it. Otherwise, you risk getting meaningless—or even misleading—feedback.

From the Field: When the Reality Check Bounces— A Cautionary Tale

I worked on a medical project where we tested a software prototype with radiologists. We were having a pretty high success rate with task completion. The development team was very happy with the way things were going, but I had an uneasy feeling about the results. I couldn't pin down why; it was just my subjective sense of how the users were responding.

In one of the last tests, the test participant completed the task without any problem but didn't really seem satisfied and was not terribly responsive to the follow-up questions. I finally asked him if this was how he would want to do the work described in the task. Well, the flood gates opened. "Oh no," he said, and proceeded to give a very clear explanation of what he'd actually like to do and why.

From the Field: When the Reality Check Bounces—A Cautionary Tale—cont'd

Fortunately, the development team was observing the test. It was clear to everyone at that point that the task was fundamentally flawed because real users would never do it the way we'd envisioned. This was a very important finding and we wished we'd learned it earlier.

Contributed by Cay Lodine

If you're really uncertain about the user goal that a task is based on, you might want to do the reality check before you use the task. Perhaps the people in your company who have contact with users can tell you if the task bears any resemblance to the reality they've seen. Maybe they can even put you in touch with some users so you can ask them yourself.

The process of task design can open up a whole new world of questions about your users and what they do. But don't be discouraged if you feel like you're raising questions faster than you can answer them—this is actually a good sign because it indicates that you've begun to think in a user-centered way.

Just like designing a usable interface, creating good tasks is a complex and iterative process. The internal walkthroughs described in the next chapter will help you refine your tasks as well as create your interface.

Chapter 7

Preparing the Prototype

This chapter explains how to create a paper prototype and prepare for usability testing by doing walkthroughs. The prototype creation and walkthrough activities happen iteratively—make some prototype pieces, do a walkthrough, figure out what's wrong or missing, and repeat. There are no hard and fast rules for how long to spend on each iteration, but as noted in Chapter 5 this process typically takes a total of 2 or 3 days, perhaps spread out over a couple of weeks.

List the Pieces Needed for the Tasks

Make a list on a whiteboard or flip chart of all the screens your prototype will need to support the tasks you've created—the steps from your completed task templates are a good starting point. Keep the list fairly high-level; you don't need to specify every menu or drop-down list because the person making a screen is responsible for its details. For example, the task of opening a retirement account at a financial Web site might require the following screens:

- Browser window with controls
- Home page
- Existing user log-in
- Create new account screen(s)
- Regular/Roth IRA explanation
- Account summary

- Privacy policy
- Terms and conditions
- Retirement savings calculator
- Mutual fund screener

The list doesn't have to be in any particular order because it's just for your benefit in identifying what to prepare. It's usually fastest to create this list *without* looking at the existing interface, if there is one; otherwise you risk digressing into a discussion of the current design.

Don't Forget the Data

There is likely to be some data associated with the tasks, and you'll need to prepare that too, not just blank screens. Developers are accustomed to thinking of data in terms of structure (the account description is a 20-character ASCII string) rather than content (Mike's IRA). But the content is what users care about. They enter data that is meaningful to them, and they expect the interface to reflect the information they entered. The interface is really just a means to an end, so users are likely to pay more attention to the data than they do to the widgets that make up the interface.

Often it's important for users to see how their data will appear elsewhere in the system. If a user is creating an online classified ad by filling out a form, he or she will probably want to preview that ad in the same format the system will use to display it. If you ask users to simply imagine something ("It'll let you preview your ad"), you could miss important feedback, such as, "Oh, wait—it took out those extra blank lines I wanted it to have."

The data you use should be realistic enough that users can interact with it in a meaningful way. This is especially important when users are domain experts in the subject matter of the interface. In the MathWorks cpselect case study described in Chapter 2, the team initially tried to use hand-drawn sketches to represent pictures of land masses in their prototype. They quickly learned, however, that this wasn't good enough for image processing tasks. The users got distracted trying to make sense of the sketches because image processing was what they did in their work. The team replaced the sketches in their paper prototype with aerial photographs, which were suitably realistic and worked much better. Similarly, if your users are accountants and you're testing a financial application, the numbers had better make sense.

Make sure the data "hangs together" in a consistent manner throughout the task. If you ask users to find all the three-bedroom houses for sale but you show them search results that include some four-bedroom ones, users might wonder what they did wrong. (Of course, if you're clever with the removable tape, perhaps you can cover up the four-bedroom houses, thus solving this problem on the fly.)

You should also include a realistic degree of complexity in your paper prototype. If your online hardware store sells 37 cordless drills but you pretend there are only 3, you'll design the drill page in a way that may not scale. This is not to say that you need the product pages for all 37—you might constrain the task in such a way that the users are likely to look at only 6 of them.

Where do you get realistic data? Some companies have suitably complete databases that are used in quality assurance testing, or perhaps Marketing has something they use for demos. But if your test databases contain mostly nonsense filler such as "test1" and "asdfasdf," you're better off creating your own. If you are having trouble coming up with a realistic scenario, talk to the people in your company who have contact with users. Just don't use a database that has real people's information in it—that's too realistic!

Divide and Conquer

The best way to create the prototype depends on the size and composition of the team and how far along the development is. At one extreme, if you're making a prototype of an existing interface and it has a straightforward sequence of screens, you could simply make screen captures and print them out as the basis for your prototype (this is a great task for an intern). In this case you might adjourn the meeting until the next day, when you'll have the screen printouts, and then do your first walkthrough.

If the interface doesn't exist yet or is being substantially changed, there's some design work required. So divide and conquer: Have each person on the team put their initials on the list next to the screens they'll prepare. Leave the list where everyone can see it so that they all know who's working on what—people may want to pass along ideas or collaborate.

This divide-and-conquer idea initially makes some people nervous because it feels like I'm advocating design by committee, a committee that may include some nondesigners. But in practice this is not what happens. The paper prototype is created by the core team, which by definition includes those responsible for the interface, so the prototype always remains in the appropriate hands. Most prototypes have some screens that are well defined and relatively easy to create, such as the browser background or log-in screen. What I've found is that that team members with less design expertise tend to sign up for the easier pieces, leaving the heavy lifting for the lead designer(s). The end result is that the work is split up in an appropriate way and everyone benefits by becoming familiar with the interface. (And if a suboptimal design idea does manage to creep in, usability testing will weed it out.)

It isn't wrong to have the whole prototype created by just one or two people if that's what you're most comfortable with. But it might be advantageous to divide up the work as I've described here, or even to try parallel design.

Parallel Design

Sometimes you have to come up with many mediocre ideas to get a few good ones. Because paper prototypes aren't confined to a computer screen, they lend themselves to collaborative activities in which several team members spread out their sketched designs on a wall or table. As explained later, it can be helpful to *generate* several variations of a design as a means of finding good ideas, but before you *evaluate* (usability test) the design you should probably pick just one.

In a technique known as parallel design, product team members work alone or in small groups to generate different designs and then review everyone's ideas. Interestingly, parallel design seems to facilitate the identification and development of successful ideas, even when they're contained in not-so-good designs (McGrew, 2001). Thus, parallel design with paper prototypes can provide a way for non-designers (especially those who've had a lot of contact with users) to make meaningful contributions to the interface. In the Of Interest box on p. 149, Dr. Bob Bailey describes how he used parallel design in a course on user interface design.

Avoid Competition

Although it can be a fruitful exercise to create several variations of an interface, you need to know when to stop. One of the caveats of parallel design is the temptation to turn it into a "use-off."* It's rarely productive to foster competition within a

---

* This is my term for the usability equivalent of a cooking competition, where prototypes are pitted against each other in usability tests.

Of Interest . . . Parallel Design

*Dr. Bob Bailey, Chief Scientist for Human Factors International (available at **www.humanfactors.com**)*

Several years ago I taught several "hands-on" courses on user interface design. In one exercise, students were given a specification, and used a prototyping tool to create a simple system. After the design solutions were completed, each individual in the class used everyone else's proposed systems to complete a task. Having experienced everyone else's ideas, the students then made changes to their original prototypes. The revised interfaces were always better than the original. The three most interesting observations from these classes were

(a) how many unique ideas (creative design solutions) individual students had initially,

(b) no matter how good their original interfaces, every one could be improved, and

(c) how quickly students found and perpetuated good design ideas in their own products.

---

team because this can get people focused on winning rather than collaborating to produce the best design.

There's also another reason to avoid the use-off mentality. In essence, all usability problems have one root cause: The development team didn't know something that turned out to be important. This ignorance might be about what users needed, how they would interpret a term, how they would behave, or any other sort of missing information or incorrect assumption. Until you start doing usability testing, you don't know what you don't know. If you have several versions of an interface, it's likely that all of them will share some important flaws—based on all that stuff you don't know yet.

So although parallel design can be a useful technique in coming up with ideas, I recommend that the core team settle on one design before the first usability test. When two or more ideas seem equally good, start with the one that's easiest to implement. If it works, you're done. If not, you can try something more elaborate.

Existing versus New Design?

Sometimes a debate comes up about whether it's better to test a prototype of the existing design or to scrap it in favor of a new approach. Neither answer is wrong—

a paper prototype can evolve from any starting point—so here are some factors to consider:

- **The cost of mistakes is low.** If you try something new and it flops, you haven't wasted much time. And often you'll learn information that will help you even if you keep the current design. For example, one team prototyped a wizard to help with a configuration task. They weren't sure whether their development schedule would allow time to implement the wizard, but they still got feedback about terms, concepts, and what assistance users needed to make decisions along the way. All this information was useful even though, as it turned out, they had to stick with a variation of the current design.
- **Don't redesign something you haven't tested.** If you don't have consensus on what's wrong with the current version, you might want to use it for the first couple of tests until you understand the problems you need to solve and then do your redesign. It's easy to fall into the trap of reworking and polishing a design before users ever see it, only to have the first usability test reveal some huge issue that forces you to redesign it. On the other hand, if your customers have already told you what's wrong and you have ideas about how to fix it, go for it. (As a developer once said to me, "We know this part is bad—there's no point in getting 10 people in here just to tell us it's bad.")
- **Limit time, not creativity.** You don't want to spend long stretches of time designing without getting user feedback—that would defeat the purpose of paper prototyping. One way to manage this is to establish an upper limit for the amount of time you'll spend creating your prototype. When you've reached that limit, test what you've got.

One advantage of paper prototyping is that you can prototype something without regard to whether it can actually be built. This is also one of its drawbacks. The degree to which technical constraints should be considered depends on whether you're prototyping something you plan to release in 3 months or 3 years—the longer your time frame, the more you can focus on what users need and then figure out later if and how to build it. There's a similar argument for adherence to interface style guides. If your company has a corporate style guide and it's not negotiable, it's probably best to have your paper prototype conform to the style guide. But if you're trying to make a case for changing those guidelines, you might deliberately do something different to determine whether it will work better.

Hand-Drawn versus Screen Shots?

Perhaps there's an existing version of the interface and someone suggests that you start by making screen shots. Following are four factors to consider.

- **How much do you expect to change it?** You might as well use a screen shot for something that you know you can't change, such as a screen from the operating system. However, for screens that you expect to evolve (which is probably most of them), you might want to draw them by hand so that hand-drawn changes won't stick out the way they will if you use screen shots.
- **Which method is faster?** Although it seems like it would be faster to create a prototype from screen shots, in practice this is not always the case. Consider the time to walk to the printer, wait for your screens to come out (half of them are stuck in the queue behind someone who's printing 20 copies of the functional spec), get waylaid by someone wanting to discuss yesterday's meeting, and so on. Ask yourself whether you could sketch some of the screens faster, especially the straightforward ones.
- **Where is the data coming from?** If your interface shows information from a database (for example, a product catalog) and you happen to have a suitable database on hand, printing screen shots might be the quickest way to get realistic data. On the other hand, if you have to make up the information yourself, it might be just as easy to draw the scenes by hand.
- **Will the printouts be readable?** Printouts of screen shots are sometimes difficult to read. Without getting into the technical details, the colors you see on the screen often don't come out quite the same on paper (or vice versa). Ink is a different medium than light. As shown in Figure 7.1, the gray background that works well on the screen may look muddy on a printed screen shot. Depending on the resolution of the printer, icons and images sometimes lose their clarity. So if you print screen shots and find that they're difficult to read, the easiest thing to do may be to redraw them by hand. You already have a design, so this doesn't take long.

Although I'm not aware of any empirical evidence, I believe that a mixture of hand-drawn and printed screens still adequately conveys to users that the design is in flux and thus encourages their feedback. I've also found that prototypes that start out with a nice, neat set of screen shots usually evolve into a collection of

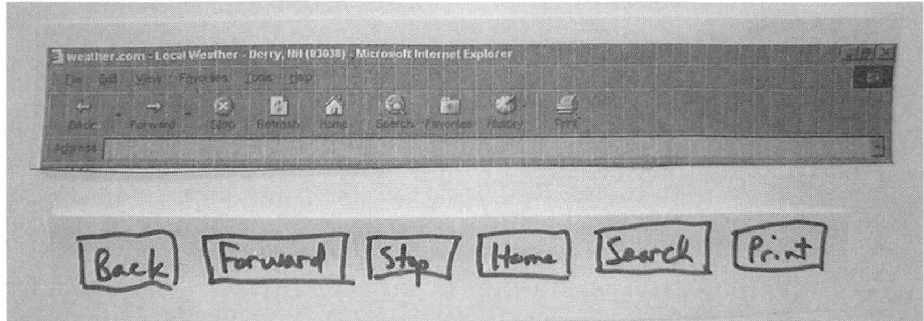

Figure 7.1 Two versions of browser buttons—one drawn by hand, and the other printed out. Notice that the hand-drawn buttons are easier to read.

screen shots, screen shots with handmade corrections, and some that have been redesigned and drawn by hand. So when screen shots are easy to make, I think it's okay to use them as a starting point and redraw screens if and when you find a need to.

If you make hand-drawn corrections to printed screen shots, occasionally users will be clever enough to realize that a hand-drawn correction is the thing they're supposed to focus on. (But there are still plenty of cases—I'd say the majority—where this doesn't seem to happen, probably because the screen still has several problems.) If you are concerned that a hand-drawn change might provide an artificial clue, either redraw several of the surrounding elements by hand also (this is where the wide removable tape is useful) or redo the screen.

Tips for Hand-Drawn Prototypes

Following are some tips to keep you from spending too much time preparing hand-drawn screens.

- **Neatness doesn't count (much).** Paper prototypes should be just neat enough to be legible, but no neater. It's fine to draw freehand instead of using a ruler. If someone else can read your writing, it's good enough. Resist the temptation to redraw something just to "neaten it up." Chances are, you'll want to change it as soon as you've tested it, so you might as well wait until you know what problems you're trying to solve. Don't refine a design you haven't tested because much of that effort will be wasted. See Figure 7.2 for an example.
- **Monochrome is okay.** As the saying goes, "You can put lipstick on a pig, but it'll still be a pig." Color can't save an inherently flawed design. In fact, it's a good

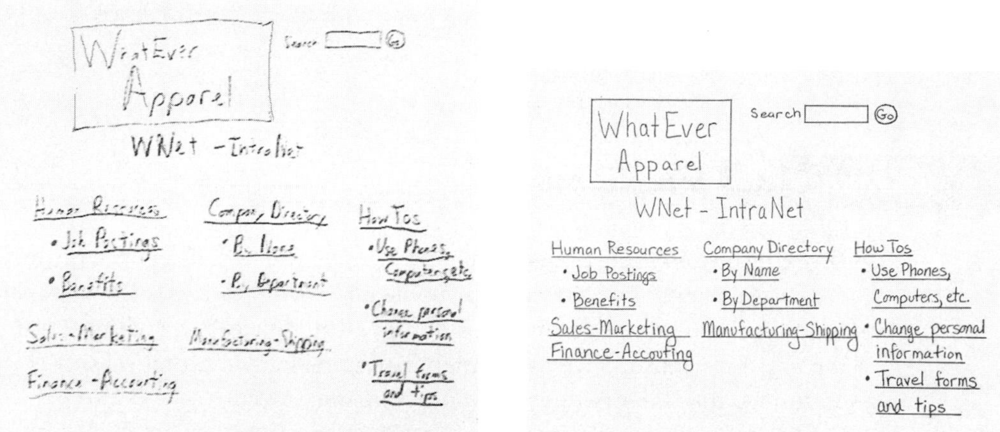

Figure 7.2 Although messy, the version on the left is legible enough to get user feedback. The extra time needed to create the neater version does not provide sufficient benefit to justify the effort.

strategy to design an interface in monochrome first. Color and other visual refinements can be added later once you're sure your design isn't a pig. But if you want to stick with black, that's fine too.

Even if you aren't adding color to the design until later, you can still have some fun with it now. If you're the type who writes with a fine-point mechanical pencil (like I did during my engineering days), getting a package of colorful art markers might help you to think more creatively. Choose a color or two that suits your personality—users don't seem to mind when one screen is drawn in blue marker and the next one is purple. But if you'd rather stick with black, that's fine too.

◇ **Size (usually) doesn't matter.** If users will be writing data on the prototype, you need to make the edit fields large enough to accommodate their writing. Drawing the prototype a bit larger than life also helps observers watch the action. Other than that, size usually doesn't matter too much. It's okay if the prototype is not drawn to scale; some screens can be relatively larger than others. As a rule, the concept of "making it all fit" should be preceded by a good understanding of what "it" consists of. If you're still determining functionality and content, you can probably postpone your concerns about screen real estate until a bit later in the process, provided that you keep your designs within reason. If you need to keep an eye on space constraints, you might want to use graph paper or simply count characters and/or lines as a proxy for space.

Greeking and Simplification

Greeking means using nonsense words to represent text. In a paper prototype, you can use squiggly lines instead of nonsense words to serve the same purpose. Greeking is not needed in many prototypes, but it's worth knowing about. Following are three reasons why you might use greeking—the first reason is the most common, and the other two are more unusual.

1. **You haven't finished designing the interface.** Because paper prototyping lets you test an interface before it's completely designed, there may be portions of the interface that haven't been created yet. For example, you might know that your software application will have View and Help menus, but you haven't yet given any thought to their contents. So you could create greeked View and Help menus where all the choices are squiggly lines (see Figure 7.3). If the user tries to go to something you've greeked, you tell them, "The squiggly lines mean that you understand everything here but it's not what you're looking for." Of course, if users keep gravitating to something you happen to have greeked, you might want to consider putting in what they're actually looking for.
2. **To simplify parts of the interface that you have no control over.** A typical example is the File Open dialog box. If a task requires the user to open a file,

Figure 7.3 You can use greeking for parts of the interface that aren't directly related to your tasks.

you can create a simplified version that contains just the file name they need for the task (Figure 7.4). There's no real benefit in watching people use a more realistic version of this dialog box if you're not going to make any changes to it. Also, greeking avoids the need to have users navigate through a file structure that is artificial to them, which is less interesting for you to watch compared with other things thcy could be doing.

3. **To prevent the user from getting drawn into the content.** For example, when realtors were usability testing a real estate application, they kept wanting to read the descriptions of the houses that we'd made up. Since we were trying to test only part of the functionality—navigation, search engine, sorting—and not the format of the descriptions, having house descriptions was a distraction. So we greeked the descriptions, making it apparent to users that the information represented a house description but preventing them from focusing on it. Figure 7.5 shows an example from a florist Web site.

You've probably seen greeking that uses the words "Lorem ipsum dolor sit amet . . ." which is actually Latin, and faked Latin at that, so I have no clue why it's called greeking. The classic lorem ipsum wording was concocted so that its ascenders, descenders, and word lengths would approximate English text. Thus, it makes better filler material for screen layouts than "text text text" or "content here." Greeking is sometimes used on Web pages with the assumption that someone else is taking care of the content—as a search on "lorem ipsum" will reveal, sometimes this assumption is mistaken!

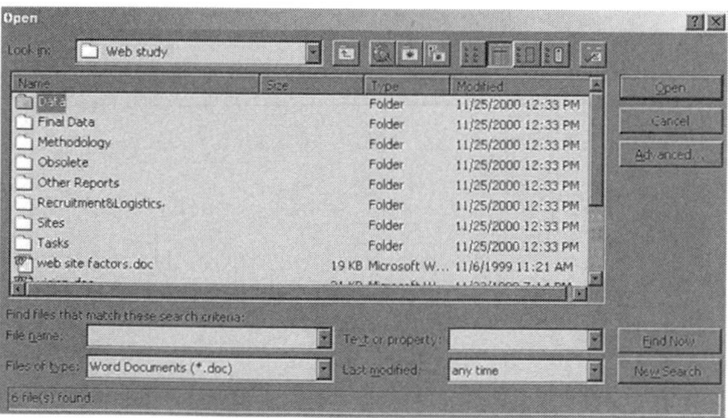

Figure 7.4 I usually use a simplified version of the File Open dialog box and greek the other files because we're not testing the operating system or the file structure.

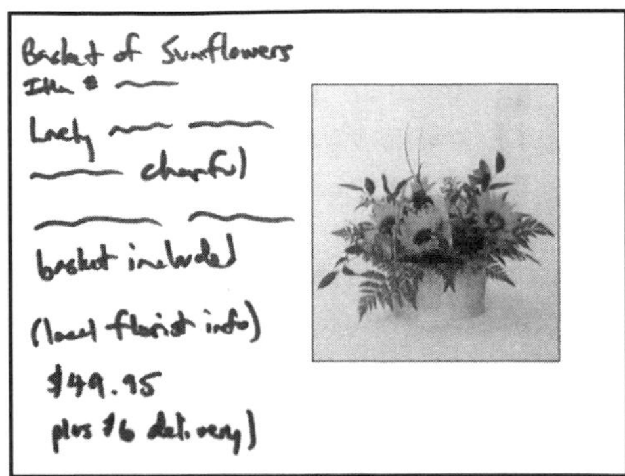

Figure 7.5 You can use greeking for content if you don't have it yet or don't want users to be distracted by detail that's irrelevant to what you're testing.

When people first learn about greeking, they're often tempted to overuse it. The previous examples should be considered as tactics to use in special cases rather than something you'd do as a matter of course. Don't greek parts of the interface that are relevant to what you're trying to test. For example, in a drop-down menu, you wouldn't want to greek all the choices except the one you want the user to select—that makes the task artificially easy, and you might fail to learn something important. It's also important in many cases to have realistic content in the prototype because it's interesting to watch users make decisions based on that content.

Using Screen Shots

Assuming you want to use some screen shots in your paper prototype, here are some things you might want to be aware of as you do your preparation:

- **Enlarge so that observers can see.** This may not be necessary if you have a really good camera setup or only a couple of observers, but if you have several people sitting around a table, most won't be able to read an actual-size paper prototype. It can also be difficult for users to write in edit fields that are sized for the screen, especially with a transparency marker. You might want to enlarge the screens by about 30% to 50% by using a copier.
- **Remove defaults** by whiting out radio buttons and checkboxes and then replacing them with versions on removable tape as shown earlier in this chapter. Radio buttons may not be too much of a problem because it's fairly clear that

the removable tape supersedes the original default state of the button. If the user unchecks a checkbox, however, it could introduce confusion later in the task if your prototype still shows an X in the box.

- Web-specific: **Clear link history** in the browser before making screen shots. If you don't, you're practically blazing a trail to show users the correct path—the visited links usually appear in a different color, even if you're printing in grayscale. One of my colleagues ruefully reported that her users quickly caught on to the visited links as being the correct path, and it undermined most of the value of the usability test.
- Web-specific: **Capture a whole page at once.** Not all screen grab utilities can do this, although this feature is increasingly common. SnagIt from TechSmith is an example of a utility that has an auto-scroll feature, or you can simply print from the browser (as explained earlier, you don't need to include the browser frame and controls if you create a browser background). Definitely avoid any tool that requires you to paste partial screens together manually.

When you take these factors into account, you may find that it's just as fast to sketch some screens by hand. Usually the best course of action is to do whatever is fastest to get your prototype together, then modify it as needed as a result of usability testing.

Separating Elements

Most interfaces, whether they're Web pages or software, have some parts that remain visible most of the time. For example, software applications typically have a row of menus and icons across the top, and perhaps some at the bottom. Some applications use a left-hand tree structure that expands and collapses. Web sites often have a persistent row of links at the top, a left navigation panel (that sometimes changes at lower levels of the site), and a content area.

Your first impulse might be to make screen shots of each whole screen, one for each permutation you expect the user to see. But if you decide to make a change to a persistent area of the screen, such as the left navigation panel, you need to make that same change on every page. Thus, it's often easier to cut up screens into their main components to facilitate revising only part of the screen, as shown in Figure 7.6. (Sometimes it can add a bit of confusion to have several pieces representing one screen, but simply telling the user, "This is all one screen" usually does the trick.)

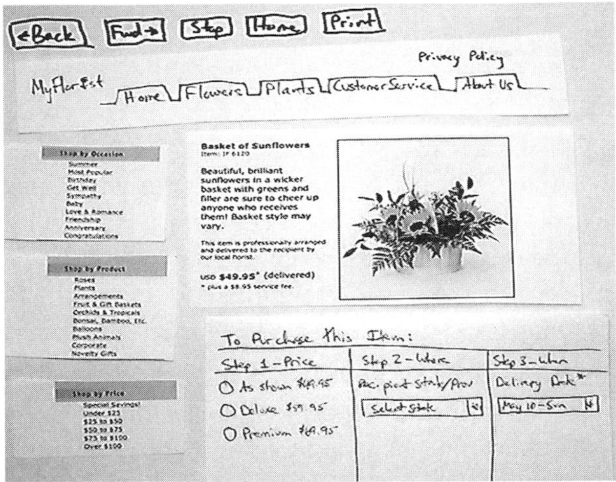

Figure 7.6 This Web page started out as a screen shot but was cut into pieces to facilitate site-wide changes. The revised tabs and ordering information (which were redrawn by hand in this example) can easily be used on every product page.

How Much to Prototype—Anticipating Paths and Errors

There are often several correct ways to complete a task, not to mention a seemingly infinite number of ways for things to go wrong. You should prepare enough of the prototype to accommodate things that users might reasonably do, but it's not necessary to anticipate everything that might happen in the usability tests.

For example, on a Web site, some users might use the search engine, whereas others navigate by clicking links. In this case it's reasonable to prepare both alternatives unless one of them simply isn't interesting for you to watch. But don't go overboard and try to prepare for every combination of terms the user might enter. Just pick the few search terms that you think are most likely and don't worry about those one-in-a-thousand edge cases. This may be inherently difficult for programmers to do because the exceptions and edge cases are often what make code complicated, and unanticipated edge cases are a common cause of bugs. But it's usually premature during paper prototyping to worry about making the code robust—you first need to make sure you have a design that works for users.

What about errors? It's pretty darn likely that some users will step off the path you envisioned for accomplishing the task. Prepare to handle the errors that seem likely, but don't make yourself crazy. It's always possible during a usability test to jot down an error message or even just tell the user what it would say. As explained in Chapter 9, there are ways for the test facilitator to respond if a user tries to do something you haven't prepared for.

Avoid putting too much effort into your initial prototype. A good rule of thumb is that you should feel about 50% ready before your first internal walkthrough and 80% to 90% ready before your first usability test. If you feel 100% ready, chances are you've put too much effort into an interface that will need to be changed anyway.

Organizing the Prototype

No doubt about it, paper prototyping is messy. One of the challenges is organizing all the pieces of paper so that the Computer can quickly find the next one. There's no right way to organize a paper prototype—each Computer will develop his or her own system for locating pieces quickly. But here are some tips.

- **Ordering . . . not!** It's usually not possible to determine the exact order in which screens will be used. Even if there's an expected sequence of steps, users may back up, jump ahead, do things that cause error messages, look up something in help, and so on. But if you can be fairly sure that users will view a series of screens in a fixed order (for example, a tutorial), it may be helpful to number them on the back.
- **Table or three-ring binder.** Most Computers I've worked with will spread out piles of paper on the table, but some people use a three-ring binder to hold all the screens and flip back and forth to the appropriate page. I've never used a binder because it seems a bit limiting—you can't look at more than one thing at a time and it may take longer to find the next screen when you can't see everything. On the other hand, a binder is more portable, so do whichever works for you.
- **Organization by task versus function.** Sometimes it can be helpful to organize the pieces by task—everything for task 1 goes in a folder (or stack), everything for task 2 in another folder, and so on. However, some pieces may be needed for multiple tasks. If you don't expect the piece to change (say, the File Open dialog box), you can simply create multiple copies of it and put one in each folder. If it is likely to change, then you have to remember to create multiple copies of the revised version as well. This can be a pain if the interface is undergoing rapid iterations, so you may be better off creating only one version of each piece and putting it in the folder where it will first be used. In later

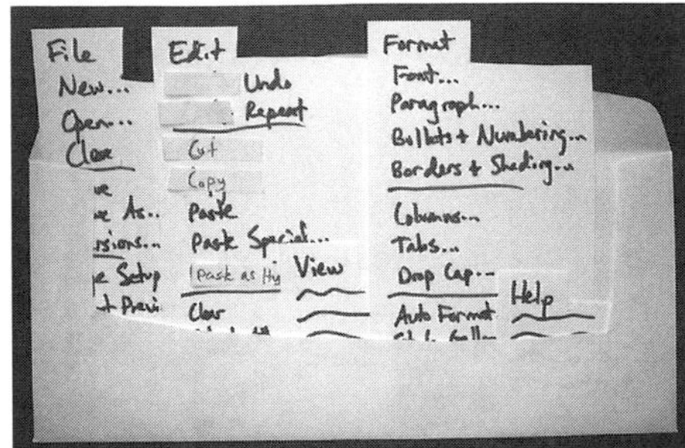

Figure 7.7 An envelope is a handy way to organize drop-down menus.

tasks, take pieces from the folders for earlier tasks as you need them. At the end of the test, take a couple minutes to put everything back where you'll want it before the start of the next test.

- **Use of envelopes.** Drop-down menus are usually written on small pieces of paper, so they can easily get lost in a folder full of larger pieces. One idea is to line them up side-by-side in an open envelope so that you can quickly find the one you need. If the pieces are small, you can even cut down the front of the envelope so that they're all visible, as shown in Figure 7.7.
- **A "Gallery of Annoying Pieces."** The smaller the pieces are, the more likely they'll get lost. This goes double for anything that's on removable tape—in the course of leaning across the table, the Computer invariably ends up with errant prototype parts stuck to his or her elbows (the record I've seen so far is three). To minimize this problem, designate a piece of paper as the "gallery of annoying pieces." All the small pieces—including those that come loose during the test—go on that piece of paper where they're easier to find later. See Figure 7.8.

Design Reviews

There can be considerable benefit to product teams in using a paper prototype to walk through the tasks themselves, without users. I'm going to distinguish between two types of walkthroughs—an *internal walkthrough,* which is used to prepare the prototype (and team) for usability testing, and a *design review,* where the

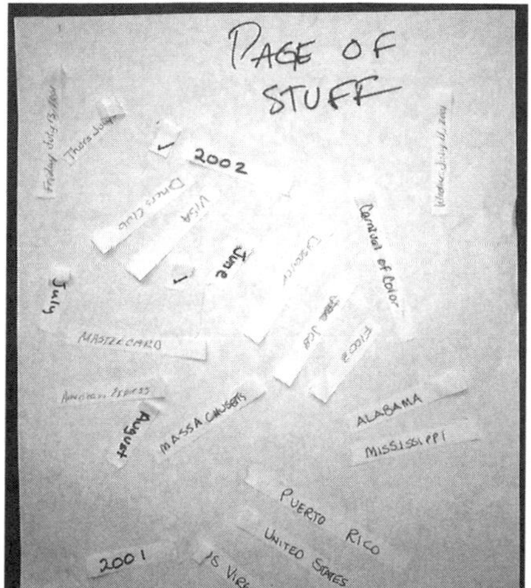

Figure 7.8 Give all those little sticky pieces a home so that they don't end up stuck to your elbows during a usability test. I call this the "gallery of annoying pieces," but this team has titled their version "Page of Stuff."

paper prototype is used as a means of discussing the interface with stakeholders. You may hear these terms used differently than I've defined them here, and to some extent they are overlapping concepts. This section briefly discusses design reviews; the rest of the chapter focuses on internal walkthroughs.

Many of my clients have told me that just the process of creating tasks and the paper prototype made them look at the interface differently—even before the first usability test, it's already been a useful exercise. Some product teams create paper prototypes and use them internally in design reviews, without ever conducting usability tests. A paper prototype can spur productive discussion, especially for those who may have difficulty visualizing the behavior of an interface from a specification. Design reviews using a paper prototype enable the product team to see the interface from a fresh perspective—they'll notice annoyances like cumbersome switching back and forth between two screens or a link that's missing. They may also identify larger issues, such as a missing requirement. Although design reviews are not a substitute for usability testing, they can help product teams identify and fix problems in the interface. So consider taking a paper prototype to your next interface review meeting.

From the Field: Paper Prototypes as a Design Aid

"One of our interfaces is used in an operating room to record data on cardiac implants. The path to get to one screen was too long given the time available to enter the data dictated by the doctor during the procedure. It's also challenging when the user has to enter data on multiple devices. Paper prototypes allow us to lay out a screen-by-screen process flow and identify where we may consolidate screens and tweak the order of screen progression."

Phillip Hash, Principal Human Factors Engineer, HiddenMind

Internal Walkthroughs

An internal walkthrough as I've defined it is an activity that helps the product team prepare to conduct usability tests with the paper prototype. A walkthrough is similar to a usability test in that you have a prototype and tasks, but in this case there are no outside users. Instead, one team member acts as an "expert user," performing the task the way the product team expects it to be done.

A walkthrough is a practical exercise that helps the team:

- Identify parts of the prototype that still need to be created.
- Prepare for different paths the user might reasonably take (correct or otherwise).
- See how the interface is intended to work, which is especially useful for those creating documentation or training or who are new to the development team.
- Give the Computer practice in manipulating all those pieces of paper.
- Identify issues pertaining to technical feasibility. Typically, these are researched after the walkthrough.

You should hold your first walkthrough as soon as you think you have most of what you need to get through at least one of the tasks. Depending on the size of the team working on the prototype, it may be easier to wait until you're ready to walk through all the tasks at once, or you may want to tackle them one or two at a time. This also depends on the complexity of the interface and the confidence you have in the design. If you're creating something new, it's often useful to put the pieces together sooner rather than later, just to make sure everything hangs together.

How to Do a Walkthrough

To hold a walkthrough, you'll need a table that's large enough to spread out the prototype. Assign people to the following roles:

- **Computer.** The person who organizes and manipulates all those bits of paper (may be more than one person).
- **Expert user.** A product team member plays this role, performing the tasks as an expert (someone who understands the interface) would be expected to do. It's not part of this role to make bizarre mistakes or other radical departures from the norm—leave that for the real users!
- **Scribe.** This person writes down all the missing pieces, issues, and questions that come up. It's not always the best use of time for the entire team to discuss each issue on the spot and come to a decision. The scribe makes a list so that these things can be addressed after the walkthrough. On small teams, the scribe role may be combined with any of the other roles.
- **Facilitator.** Strictly speaking, a walkthrough doesn't need a facilitator, although it doesn't hurt to have a designated person lead the session and make sure it doesn't digress too much. Whoever plans to facilitate the usability tests should attend some walkthroughs in preparation; walkthroughs are a great way to become familiar with the functionality and behavior of the interface. For new facilitators, it's also an opportunity to practice.

Naturally, other members of the product team can also be present to help make missing prototype pieces, identify potential issues, learn about the interface, or simply to get a better understanding of paper prototyping.

As the expert user walks through the tasks, questions and issues will arise and the scribe should write these down along with missing prototype pieces. At the end, the scribe reads the list and team members decide who will do what before the next walkthrough. Agree on the time of the next walkthrough before dispersing to do individual work. In my consulting practice, I've found that 15 to 30 minutes is usually sufficient for people to research a couple of questions and make a few screens—in other words, to make enough progress that it's worth doing another walkthrough. If you allow too much time, you risk losing your momentum.

Caution: This Isn't a Usability Test!

There's often a strong temptation to turn a walkthrough into a premature usability test by asking a co-worker to play user. Typically, someone will say, "Hey, why don't we get so-and-so to be the user? She's never seen this before, so she'd be great." Resist! There are some problems with this, both obvious and subtle:

- **You aren't ready for prime time.** The reason for walkthroughs is to *prepare* for usability testing. You're certain to find unresolved issues, some of which you'll end up discussing on the spot, which is fine for those of you who are working on the interface, but a waste of time for the person you asked to help you. He or she has better things to do than listen to you debate whether a button should be disabled or how you'll handle a particular error.
- **Co-workers aren't real users.** Co-workers are usually not representative of real users, even if they talk to users every day or used to be users themselves. Your co-workers know stuff that real users don't, such as your company's business strategy, acronyms, brand, other products, and so on. Very likely, your co-workers know more about your interface—even if they haven't seen it—than real users do. Therefore, the behavior of a co-worker usually isn't a good proxy for what real users will do. (Possible exception: You're designing an intranet or other interface specifically intended for employees of your company.) And if you bring in a co-worker who truly "knows nothing" about what you're doing, then you may run afoul of the next issue.
- **There are ethical and legal considerations.** When you usability test with internal employees you actually have *more* ethical and legal responsibilities than if they were strangers. It's one thing if you have a bad test (one where the user feels foolish or appears ignorant) with a stranger, but it's quite another if you have to see that person in the cafeteria every day. It's even worse if that person is your boss! There are even potential liability issues: If a co-worker participates in a usability test and feels (correctly or otherwise) that their performance was perceived poorly by others, you could have a lawsuit on your hands. Of course, the likelihood of this is small, but you should think twice before asking someone outside the product team to play user.

At one company that shall remain nameless, a person coming in for a job interview was asked to participate in a usability test instead when the scheduled participant didn't show up. The person believed that the usability test was part of the job interview and became distressed about being placed in a situation that made him look bad. Lawyers got involved. The case was settled out of court, but it serves as a cautionary tale about the risks of conscripting people at random to participate in usability tests.

- **You don't want more opinions.** I've yet to work at a company where there's a shortage of opinions. The whole purpose of usability testing is to gather data from real users, not yet another internal opinion. It may not be wise to redesign an interface solely on the basis of internal feedback. If a co-worker gives you feedback that you don't want to act upon (at least not yet), then you're put in the awkward position of explaining why you're apparently ignoring the valuable advice you asked him or her to give.

Keeping the aforementioned cautions in mind, sometimes it can be valuable to ask a co-worker to play user for another purpose: to introduce them to the concepts of paper prototyping and usability testing. Some of my colleagues have reported very positive results from inviting an influential manager or VP to play user after first carefully explaining the technique of paper prototyping and the purpose of the walkthrough. There's more on the topic of convincing skeptics in Chapter 13.

Who Should Be the Computer

People sometimes think that you have to be a software developer to play Computer, but that's not necessarily the case. In fact, it can be valuable for a tech writer or trainer to be the Computer because this gives them experience with the interface. It's true that the Computer needs to understand how the interface behaves in response to the user's inputs, but one can usually pick up the necessary knowledge simply by watching someone else walk through the tasks a couple of times. Just as the interface isn't expected to be perfect, neither is the person playing Computer—if the Computer makes a mistake during a usability test (which is not uncommon for more complex interfaces), there's usually another team member present who will notice and help get things back on track. (It can also take some of the pressure off users to see that the Computer makes mistakes too.)

When practical, it's good to have more than one person who is prepared to be the Computer. You don't want to cancel a usability test because your Computer is home with the flu. Also, it's fairly demanding to be the Computer. In particular, it's hard for the Computer to also take notes, which is an important thing for the lead designers to do. So try to spread out the effort a bit. Some teams have two or three people who take turns playing this role, or they may have different Computers depending on the task. I've done paper prototype tests where Person A kept all the pieces for tasks 1 and 2, Person B was responsible for tasks 3 and 4, and so on. (While the Computers are changing places, I joke with the users that we're giving them a hardware upgrade!)

Some teams have a *Co-processor* work with the Computer. The Co-processor finds pieces, puts pieces back when they're no longer needed, writes things on the removable tape, and otherwise helps keep the prototype from becoming a disorganized mess. For example, when a user clicks "Add to Cart" on an e-commerce site, the Co-processor prepares a piece of removable tape to represent how that line item will appear in the shopping cart (see Figure 7.9).

When (and When Not) to Redesign

Sometimes even an internal walkthrough is enough to expose major problems in the interface. The mere act of performing the steps as users are expected to do can reveal aspects of the interface that are cumbersome or even technically impossible. When this happens, it's appropriate to come up with an improved version of the design even before the first test. It makes sense to redesign the prototype if the

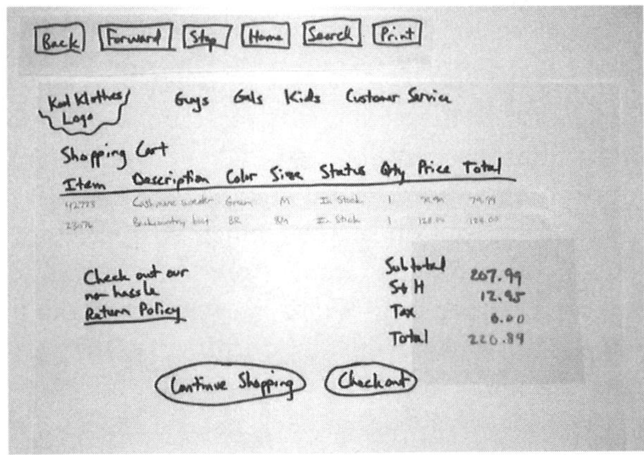

Figure 7.9 The Co-processor can help out by doing things such as writing the line items for the shopping cart based on what the user selects and recalculating the total.

team agrees that the issues found during walkthroughs are valid and serious. (As an example that may seem extreme but that occasionally happens, sometimes even one of the lead designers can't do a task.)

On the other hand, you should resist the temptation to redesign based solely on someone's opinion or the desire to try a different approach without understanding the strengths and weaknesses of the existing one. The problem with doing redesign before testing is that you don't yet know what you don't know. Once you watch users work with the prototype, you'll better understand the problems you're trying to solve. So if design ideas come up, jot them down and save them until you have some data from testing—then you'll know which of your ideas you truly need.

The Final Walkthrough–the Usability Test Rehearsal

The usability test rehearsal is basically another internal walkthrough, but with a few extra elements added. A rehearsal is not specific to paper prototyping—it's an important step in preparing for any usability test. Ideally, the rehearsal should take place the day before the first usability test. It often involves a larger group than those who worked on the prototype.

The purpose of the rehearsal is to make sure everyone (the Computer, facilitator, and observers) and the prototype are ready for usability testing. The facilitator runs the rehearsal in a similar manner to how he or she will conduct the usability test, but with several differences. Instead of focusing attention on the user (who in a rehearsal is still one of the product team members), the facilitator's goals during a rehearsal are as follows:

- **Familiarize observers with the prototype.** It's hard to get much use out of watching a usability test if you've never seen the interface before. That's especially true of paper prototypes because they change rapidly; the design you're testing tomorrow may not have existed yesterday. Because observers aren't allowed to talk during a usability test, encourage them to ask questions during the rehearsal. Once they understand the interface and the test procedure, they'll be prepared to get the most out of watching the usability tests. (Caveat: The observers aren't allowed to *redesign* the prototype at the rehearsal. If they have ideas, they should write them down and save them until the team is ready to make changes to the prototype.)
- **Collect people's questions.** Let everyone know at the start of the rehearsal that you want to gather all their questions about how well the interface will work

and what real users will do. For example, "Do users realize that they can sort by the column headings?" The test facilitator should write down these questions with the aim of getting as many answers as possible during the usability tests.

- **Estimate task timing.** Although it isn't possible to say with any confidence, "Task 1 will take 14 minutes," timing the tasks during the rehearsal will give you a sense of how long it takes to complete each task (assuming all goes well) and whether you have about the right number of tasks to fill the time allotted for the tests. During a rehearsal there is usually some discussion among the product team. To some extent, this discussion is a proxy for the amount of time that users will spend thinking aloud or getting stuck in the usability tests.
- **Decide when you'll intervene.** If there are doc/help writers on the team, they may be very interested to learn if the material they've written is useful. But many users don't go to the help or manual of their own accord. Discuss if and when the facilitator should intervene to suggest that they look something up. You might also want to agree on at what point the facilitator should step in and help users complete a task in the interest of moving on to the next one. (To an observer, it can be nerve-wracking to watch a user struggle with a task that is meticulously explained in help, to the point where that observer can no longer concentrate on what the user is doing. To forestall some of this stress, it can be helpful to discuss when and how the facilitator will assist users. You may also want to include this information in the Notes section of the task template.)

Note: Because I have 10 years of experience facilitating usability tests, I no longer need to have lengthy discussions about these things with the product team—they know that I am aware of what they're interested in, and they trust that I'll get as much of that information as I can. But if the facilitator and product team are unaccustomed to conducting usability tests, they haven't established that level of trust yet.

- **Create a "game plan."** It's not necessary to use the same tasks for each usability test—paper prototyping allows some room for improvisation in the test structure depending what you're learning. At the rehearsal, the facilitator should get a rough idea of which tasks are of greatest interest to the developers and under what conditions it may be appropriate to skip or reorder tasks. This is what I call a "game plan." An example of a game plan might be, "We'll do the first 3 tasks, and then depending on how much time we have, either go on to 4 or skip to 5." Like its sports counterpart, a usability test game plan is not a rigid structure but can be adapted depending on circumstances. For example, if a team member is very interested in task 5 but she can attend only two of the usability tests, in those sessions you might decide to do task 5 earlier to ensure she'll get to see it.

Pilot Tests

Unlike a usability test rehearsal, a pilot test is not something you'll do for every usability study, although there are situations in which one can be useful. A pilot test is a cross between an internal walkthrough and a usability test. Its main purpose is to refine the tasks and methodology used in the main tests (as opposed to a usability test, which is used to refine the interface). Unlike in a walkthrough, in a pilot test you bring in a representative user. Unlike in a usability test, you ask this user to give you feedback on the tasks and instructions, not just to do them. You can also time the pilot test to get a better idea of how long it will take users to accomplish the tasks. In a pilot test, it's appropriate to interrupt the user (politely, of course) to have a discussion with your teammates about how you want to change the tasks or methodology—this is not something you want to spend time doing in a usability test.

A pilot test is useful when you don't want to change the tasks during the usability study. For example, I tested a live Web site in the United States that was also being tested in Denmark. My Danish counterpart created the tasks, and I conducted the pilot test. I then reported back to her my results such as, "Task 2 will take more time than we thought, so we should allow up to 40 minutes. But task 3 and task 5 cover similar ground, so let's eliminate task 5." The pilot test helped us coordinate our methods so that our test findings would be comparable.

I reserve pilot tests for situations in which there is a high degree of rigor needed in the testing methodology, such as a competitive evaluation of two released products. Because a paper prototype is continually evolving, there is less need to hold the methodology constant, so I don't bother with pilot tests. However, there is no reason not to conduct a pilot test if you feel the need for one. In particular, a pilot test can be a good opportunity for a new facilitator to practice under the guidance of a more experienced one. Speaking of new facilitators, the next chapter explains the basics of usability test facilitation.

Chapter 8

Introduction to Usability Test Facilitation

It wouldn't be very useful to sit a user down at a table covered with prototype pieces and ask, "So what do you think?" People have a hard time answering abstract questions like that, especially out of context It's important to not just ask users what they think, but to see what they do. It's like the difference between looking at a car on the showroom floor and taking it for a test drive.

To conduct a usability test, you need to have users, realistic tasks, and a test facilitator to run the show in a structured yet informal manner. This chapter explains what the facilitator does during a usability test. If you're already experienced in conducting usability tests, you may want to skip to the next chapter.

In a nutshell, the purpose of the usability test facilitator is to maximize the amount of useful and reliable data from the test sessions while at the same time minimizing the stress on the users. As you might expect, these two goals can conflict with each other, so a good facilitator understands how to make the trade-offs.

Are You Dangerous?

I believe that anyone who has good social skills and a genuine interest in usability can learn the basics of facilitation well enough to be effective, although as with any skill, there are nuances that may take years to master. There's a risk that this chapter may give you just enough information and encouragement to be dangerous—fools rush in where angels fear to tread. One chapter can't do justice to all the special situations that can arise or explore the interesting debates among usability professionals about how to handle them. Before facilitating your first test, I recommend that you watch a few tests run by an experienced facilitator, do additional reading (see the References section), or take a training class. Join an organization like the Usability Professionals Association *(www.upassoc.org)* or SIGCHI *(www.acm.org/sigchi),* which may have chapters in your area. Practice your skills whenever possible and ask colleagues to give you feedback.

Facilitator Responsibilities

Here's an overview of the activities typically performed by the usability test facilitator:

- Before the users arrive, brief the in-room observers on how to behave, what to watch for, and how to take notes (Chapters 10 and 11 discuss this further).
- Greet the users, brief them, obtain their informed consent, and pay them.
- Escort users to the test room and introduce them to the Computer and any observers.
- Ask users to introduce themselves and summarize their background.
- Explain the testing protocol—how to interact with the paper prototype, work together, think aloud, and so on.
- Facilitate each task, interacting with users as needed.
- Manage the time spent on each task, covering the areas that are of greatest interest to the observers.
- (Optional) Facilitate a short Q&A session with the users (and observers, if present) to discuss interesting issues that arose during the session or ask questions not covered by the tasks.
- End the session on time.
- Thank the users and escort them out.
- Debrief the observers—list issues and make changes to the prototype in time for the next test. (This can be done by a core team member instead of the facilitator.)

Ethical and Legal Responsibilities

The goal of usability testing is to learn how to make the product better with the assistance of users—but not at their expense. As the facilitator, you have an ethical and legal responsibility to make sure that your test participants do not have an unpleasant experience.

Many years ago, the spell checker in Microsoft Word (I think it was version 2.0) did not recognize the word "usability" and suggested "suability" instead. I was highly amused at the time—I was writing a report that compared the usability of a Microsoft application to one of its competitors—but it's stuck in my head ever since as some kind of subtle cosmic warning that usability testing can land you in legal hot water.

Central to the idea of usability testing is the concept of informed consent—the user understands the nature of the session and their role *before* agreeing to participate. With the possible exception of paper cuts, there is little risk of physical harm during a paper prototype usability test. However, any kind of usability testing carries the risk of psychological or emotional harm in the form of embarrassment, frustration, or stress or feeling stupid. It's your responsibility to avoid causing this kind of harm. Just as conscientious backpackers leave their campsite cleaner than they found it, the facilitator's goal is to have users leave the session in as good or better frame of mind as when they came in. Of course, users may be more tired, but they will also have reasons to feel good, such as hearing that their perspective is valuable and how their feedback will make the product better.

As of 2002, there is no formal code of ethics for usability testing, but it is likely that one will be developed in the future. In the meantime, you may want to study the ethical guidelines used in related professions like psychology. See *www.paper-prototyping.com* for more information.

This isn't how you want a usability test to feel!
(Illustration by Rene Rittiner.)

The Informed Consent Form

The informed consent form is a contract between you and the user that states you've explained the purpose and nature to their satisfaction, including the following:

- What you'll ask them to do (i.e., work with a prototype)
- What's being tested (the interface, not the user)
- Any risks to their physical or psychological well-being (such as the presence of observers)
- The length of the session, including their right to end it at any time
- What data you will collect and how this information will be used

Ideally, the informed consent form should be sent to users ahead of time so that they have a chance to read it, contact you with any questions or concerns, and decline to participate if they are not comfortable with the test setting. If observers will be present, the informed consent form should explicitly mention that fact. If the session is being videotaped, the form should explain what the tape may and may not be used for. However, just because users receive the consent form doesn't mean they will read it, so the facilitator should go over this information when the users arrive for the session. (The next chapter contains some sample wording.)

Although the informed consent is a legal document, it shouldn't be written using legal jargon. Write in plain English so that users can form an accurate picture of what the session will be like and what's being asked of them. Figure 8.1 shows an example of an informed consent form. A document containing the most recent version (I keep evolving it as I learn more) is available on *www.paperprototyping.com.*

Nondisclosure Agreements

Depending on your circumstances, you may need to ask users to sign a nondisclosure agreement (NDA). An NDA is a legal document that prohibits participants from discussing what they saw in the usability test unless or until your company makes that information publicly available, for example, by announcing the product. NDAs are typically used when the product is new or undergoing substantial changes and the company doesn't want to leak the details. But in practice, many companies don't use an NDA for usability testing because there is little risk of anything bad happening if users discuss what they saw (make sure your recruitment

Sample Informed Consent Form

This is a study about a Web site intended for people who buy and download music from the Internet. Our goal is to make the Web site appealing, intuitive, and user-friendly. Your participation will help us accomplish this goal.

In this session, you will be working with a prototype of the Web site. We'll ask you to try several things that people might typically do on this site, such as finding music by a particular artist. Several members of the development team will sit in the same room, quietly observing the session and taking notes. We are scheduling another person to participate in the same session with you, but if this other person cannot attend for some reason, you may be the only participant in your time slot. A session facilitator will sit near you and help you if you are stuck or have questions.

All information we collect concerning your participation in the session belongs to [company] and will be used for our internal business purposes. We will not videotape or audio tape the session. We may publish our notes from this and other sessions in internal reports, but all such observations will be confidential and will not include your name. We will not ask you to purchase anything during this session, and entering any of your personal information will be optional.

This is a test of the Web site—we are not testing you! We want to find out what aspects of the Web site are confusing so that we can make it better.

To the best of our knowledge, there are no physical or psychological risks associated with participating in this study. You will receive a check for $75 at the beginning of the session, which will last approximately 1 hour. You may take breaks as needed and may stop your participation in the study at any time.

Statement of Informed Consent

I have read the description of the study and of my rights as a participant. I voluntarily agree to participate in the study.

Print Name: ______________________

Signature: ______________________

Date: ______________________

Figure 8.1 Sample Informed Consent Form.

process screens out any competitors), and sometimes the company even considers it a benefit if test participants start spreading the word. Discuss the need for an NDA with your Legal or Marketing department, or other powers that be.

If your company has a standard NDA document, it'll likely be more complicated than what you need for usability testing—most NDAs are written for contractors or companies who are potential business partners. Participants in usability tests don't receive proprietary materials such as functional specs or business plans, so some of the stipulations may not apply. On occasion I've seen a user back out of a usability test due to discomfort over an imposing legal document. If users must sign an NDA, ask if it's possible to use a simplified version that merely prohibits users from discussing what they see until the product is released.

Payment for Users

Users who have no association with your company will expect some sort of payment for their time. Expect the compensation to be in proportion to the specialization of the expertise you're looking for. In one Boston-area study in 2002, I paid network administrators $125 for a 1-hour usability test of a specialized Web application, and in another study I gave consumers $75 for a 90-minute test of a travel Web site. Talk to a market research firm to find out the going rate in your area and whether nonmonetary gifts are appropriate—a bottle of good wine might be appreciated in one culture but taboo in another. Those little marketing giveaways (a key chain or coffee mug with your corporate logo) are nice extras, but they're not a substitute for more substantive compensation.

Users are entitled to their full payment simply by virtue of showing up on time, even if you discover that a person does not meet the screener (that's the fault of the recruiter, not the participant). I like to pay users at the start of the session—it starts things off on a pleasant note, and I believe that it may reduce the perceived pressure to perform—but usability specialists are still debating the merits of paying before versus after, and as of this writing neither approach is considered wrong.

Decide on the form of payment before recruitment begins. Many participants expect cash by default. If you are paying with a check or gift certificate, make this clear up front in case the user is expecting to use the cash for cab fare home. Consider reimbursing users for transportation or parking if those expenses are nontrivial. Unless you plan to pay users more than a few hundred dollars, you probably don't need their tax ID number, but double-check this with your Accounting department. When I use cash payments, I have each user sign their name, date, and amount received on a sheet of paper, which serves as a record of what happened to all that cash.

So far I've been discussing test participants who have no association with your company. But payment may not be appropriate if users are employees or customers of your company or if they work for a government or industry that regulates the maximum gift that can be accepted—even a coffee cup may be considered too valuable (I wish I was joking about that, but I'm not). Talk with your Human Resources or Sales department to determine what is appropriate for the user profile you've selected.

Facilitator Roles: Flight Attendant, Sportscaster, Scientist

A smoothly run usability test can appear deceptively simple.* A test facilitator is like a duck—serene on the surface, but paddling like heck underneath. There are many judgment calls that the facilitator makes in every usability test. How long should you let the users struggle when they're stuck? When and how should you give them hints? What do you do when there's not enough time left to complete the task? The guidelines I provide here will help answer those questions, but it will take practice for you to build confidence in your skills.

A test facilitator is like a duck—serene on the surface, but paddling like heck underneath.

In understanding what it takes to be a good facilitator, I've found it helpful to think in terms of three roles:

1. Flight attendant—safeguard the physical, psychological, and emotional well-being of test participants.
2. Sportscaster—maximize the flow of information from the users to the observers.
3. Scientist—maintain the highest possible degree of integrity in the data.

These roles capture the essence of the facilitator's responsibilities. As you'll see later, they also provide guidance for the inevitable situations when trade-offs arise.

---

* A friend once asked me point-blank after helping me with a pilot test, "Companies *pay* you to do that?"

The Flight Attendant

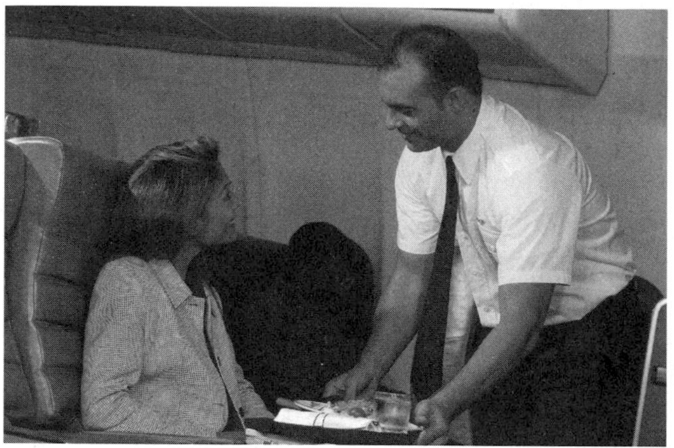

(Jack Hollingsworth/Getty Images.)

The flight attendant is the most important of the three roles. Just as a real flight attendant's primary responsibility is the physical safety of passengers (in the early days of aviation, flight attendants were trained nurses), the facilitator makes sure that the testing experience is emotionally nonthreatening for participants. In the flight attendant role, the facilitator is responsible for pretest briefing and obtaining informed consent, monitoring the users throughout the session for signs of stress, and providing reassurance and assistance as needed. Handing out those little packets of peanuts is optional.

Comfort is important too. All usability tests should take place in an atmosphere of hospitality, which helps relax the user. A flight attendant role is a service-oriented one—the test facilitator should greet users, hang up their coats, offer a beverage, and perhaps chat for a few minutes. These small courtesies establish the facilitator in the users' minds as a helpful person who cares about their well-being. I do not recommend having an assistant perform the greeter tasks and then bring the users into the test setting where the facilitator awaits; although this may be appropriate in a scientific setting, paper prototyping is an informal and "high-touch" activity, and it works best when the facilitator and users have established a rapport. If circumstances require the use of a greeter, coach him or her in the particulars of the flight attendant role.

The flight attendant also notes each user's demeanor—are they cheerful or serious? Assertive or timid? What kind of day have they had so far? Although it's impossible to make a thorough assessment of someone's personality in a few minutes, the more you can learn about a user, the better you will be able to make judgment calls when that user is stuck. I might joke with a user who was confident and upbeat, but with a person who seemed shy or tired I would avoid humor and be a little quicker to step in when he or she ran into difficulty.

The flight attendant has duties after "take off" as well. Throughout the test, the flight attendant monitors users for signs of stress. Some red flags include sighing, short answers to questions when longer answers were previously given, apologies or other self-blaming statements, and so on. The flight attendant remembers to offer a mid-test break (often appreciated by the observers as well) and a beverage refill. If a user ever appears distressed, the facilitator has the right and responsibility to pause or end the test session. (This situation should be very rare—one in a few hundred tests—so a full discussion is beyond the scope of this book. Suffice it to say that the facilitator's primary responsibility is to salvage the ego of the participant.)

*Once I have thought of the situation in terms of the **information** that is lacking, it's easier to say something to the user that sounds respectful and reassuring but not phony.*

One of the most important things that the flight attendant can do is assure the users that they are holding up their end of the bargain, even when—make that especially when—they encounter difficulty. Although we'd like it if everyone sailed through the tasks, it's more valuable for the product team to find the things that give people trouble. When users get stuck, they're really doing us a favor, albeit one that might feel painful to both them and us. It's important to acknowledge and alleviate that pain in a way that comes across as respectful. This is sometimes tricky—gratuitously positive feedback like "Gosh, you're doing great!" or "Don't worry, it's not your fault" may sound hollow or patronizing to a struggling user. There's also a risk that praise can make users think they're on the right track when they're not.

I find that it helps a lot if I refuse to think of users as dumb or ignorant. It's much more accurate, not to mention fair, to think in terms of specific knowledge that we mistakenly assumed users would have. If a user-blaming thought enters my mind (for example, "He has no clue how to do this"), I recast the issue in terms of the missing facts: "He's shown us that people need to know X, Y, and Z to do this task. We thought this user profile would know X from their jobs—maybe our assumption was wrong. And we really do need to find a better way of explaining Y and Z." Once I have thought of the situation in terms of the *information* that is lacking, it's easier to say something to the user that sounds respectful and reassuring but not phony.

It may take quite a bit of practice before it feels natural to provide feedback in an appropriate way. Over the years, I have learned to take my cues from the users.

Although some people might want reassurance that you don't blame them for the problem, others merely need to hear that you've followed the logic of what they're doing. Here are several different examples of the kinds of things I've said to users who encountered difficulty. What all of them have in common is their respectful intent based on my assessment of the user and the situation. You'll need to decide which of these examples might be appropriate for your users, and over time you'll come up with your own.

"This is exactly the kind of feedback we were hoping to get."

"It's not just you. Other people have run into this too, so it's definitely something we need to change."

"What you've done makes perfect sense, so hopefully we can change the logic of the system to support your approach."

"Thank you—you've just found something important that we wouldn't have noticed on our own."

"The developers are intimately familiar with the code, and sometimes they don't realize that they've omitted crucial information from the interface."

"You're part of our market for this product, so your perspective is valuable."

"Hmm, it never explained how to do X, did it? In real life it wouldn't be fair to expect people to use this without being told about X."

"Thanks for hanging in there . . . it appears that we made this way harder than it needed to be, and I'm sorry about that."

"This is very helpful—you're doing just what we need you to do."

Although the flight attendant is the top-priority role, it is usually not the role that occupies most of the facilitator's time. As long as all is going well, the flight attendant stays in the background so the sportscaster can have center stage.

The Sportscaster

While the flight attendant's attention is focused on the user, the sportscaster serves the observers, who are members of the development team. The main responsibility of the sportscaster is to ensure that the observers get as much useful information from the test as possible.

(Ron Case/Getty Images.)

Thinking Aloud versus Talking with Users

A common technique for conducting usability tests is the *think-aloud protocol,* where you ask the users to articulate their thoughts as they work on the task. But let's face it, thinking aloud isn't what most of us do. If someone went through their daily life explaining their every action, we'd question their sanity. So although it's fine to ask users to think aloud in a usability test, most of them aren't going to do it perfectly and it certainly can't be called natural. You know what is much more natural? Talking with users as they work. Especially in a paper prototype test, this turns out to be the way to go.

Here's the rationale. In paper prototype testing, the Computer is sitting right across from the users, so their first tendency will be to talk to the Computer. But you don't want this because then the Computer will feel a social obligation to help the user by explaining the interface. So as the facilitator, you should be the person the users talk to, and the easiest way to do that is by talking to *them.*

But do so carefully. Rather than agreeing, disagreeing, or explaining, the facilitator should be asking questions, encouraging users to elaborate, and remaining neutral toward the interface and its designers. It's easy to inadvertently give users a clue about what they're supposed to do. Confirming afterward that the users made the correct choice isn't quite as bad, but should still be avoided. So before speaking, consider what effect it might have on the users' behavior.

You may have heard the story about Clever Hans, a horse that supposedly could count by reading a number off a card and tapping his hoof that many times. Except it turned out that Hans' proud owner (and also the researchers who tested this supposedly psychic horse) was subconsciously giving him the cue to stop tapping. If horses are smart enough to play this game, it's a safe bet that humans are too.

The Play-by-Play

Although in theory the observers see and hear everything that the facilitator does, there are some reasons why this may not be true in practice. The facilitator usually has the best vantage point because he or she sits close to the users and the prototype. People who are sitting farther away or in another room may not be able to read the error message that just came up or see which menu option the users clicked on. Observers who are writing notes may have missed what the users just did. Some users speak softly, and observers can't hear them.

So one thing the sportscaster does is what I call the play-by-play—verbally reinforcing any user action that might not have been obvious or visible to observers. For example, if the user writes something in the search field, you'd say, "So you typed 'return policy' in there." And then when the Computer hastily scrawls a "No matches found" error on a scrap of paper, you'd say, "Hmm, 'no matches found.' What does that mean to you?" Obviously, you don't want to mindlessly parrot every detail—the sportscaster uses this tactic judiciously, when there's a good chance that observers missed some information that's important to understanding the users' behavior or context. It can alter the user's behavior if you call attention to something the user hadn't noticed, so it's best to do the play-by-play for those things you're pretty sure the user is already focusing on.

Here are some other sportscaster tricks I've learned over the years.

Encourage Questions, But Don't Answer Them

One of the ironies of the test facilitation is that you want to encourage the users to ask questions, but most of the time you don't want to answer them, at least not right away. This can feel awkward, so you might want to prepare some responses ahead of time. For example, if a user asks you the meaning of a term, you might say something like, "That's a really great question but forgive me if I don't answer it yet—maybe you'll discover the answer as you go." Other tactics are to direct users' attention back to the task ("Why is that important?") or to plead ignorance ("Hmm, I'm not sure.") But do acknowledge the users' questions in some manner, or they may stop asking.

Write down all the questions that users ask. Questions often indicate something important about the functionality or usability of the interface. At the end of the test, if the users didn't find the answer to something they were truly curious about, you can enlighten them. ("Remember that undo function you wanted? It was hidden over here.")

Use the Users' Vocabulary

The words you use when talking to users can influence their behavior. Avoid the temptation to use the "right" terms—when possible use the same vocabulary that the users have already used. Otherwise, you might inadvertently provide a clue about how the interface is supposed to be used. For example, if a user refers to the corporate logo on your Web site as "the beach ball," you would call it the beach ball, too, not the home page link.

Use Open-Ended Questions

It's usually better to ask open-ended questions rather than closed-ended ones because the former encourage users to give more detailed answers. The purpose of an open-ended question is to encourage users to reveal their underlying thought process.

"What will that do?"

"What are you trying to do right now?"

"What are you thinking?" (Use a neutral tone with this one!)

"Hmm, tell me more about that."

"What does ____ mean to you?"

Although open-ended questions are often preferable, sometimes you may want to use a closed-ended question if time is short or you really do want to know something specific, such as, "Did you see this link to the return policy over here?" However, I suggest reserving such questions for the end of the session because they can change the user's subsequent behavior. In addition, you should be careful not to imply that the user has missed something "obvious."

Listen for Nonspecific Utterances

Vocalizations such as *hmm, ah, oh,* or *oops* usually represent the tip of a cognitive iceberg, and they're your cue that something important is going on inside the user's skull. Ditto for nonverbal gestures. A person who is confused or thinking may wrinkle a brow, frown, or put a pen in his or her mouth. All these cues offer a great opportunity for the facilitator to probe what's happening in a nondirective manner: "John, what's going through your mind right now?"*

Make Use of "Hourglass Time"

Paper prototype tests often have short pauses when the Computer is looking for (or creating on the fly) the next piece of the prototype. Instead of sitting in silence, you can use this time by summarizing the actions the users have taken so far (or better yet, ask them to do so) or by asking what they expect will happen next. It also might be a good opportunity to offer a break.

Learn When to Shut Up

Unlike a real sportscaster, it's not necessary or even desirable for the facilitator to keep up a nonstop barrage of questions and commentary. As a new facilitator, I sometimes pummeled users with so many questions that they didn't have sufficient time to consider their answers. When people are thinking, it's perfectly appropriate to let the silence go on for a bit—15 or 20 seconds will seem a lot longer to you than to them—before you encourage them to verbalize. When a person is conversing, his or her brain cannot be fully focused on the interface. If you're always jumping in with questions or hints, the development team may complain (with some justification) that you aren't giving the users enough time to figure things out on their own. In other words, you're part of the problem.

Let Users Decide When They're Done

As a rule, you should let the users decide when the task is done. For example, I once had a user give up on a data entry task—the information was saved automatically, but he thought he had to use the Save command, which happened to be grayed out. After 10 minutes of frustration, he gave up. This was an important usability issue, but one we wouldn't have seen if we had stopped him the moment *we* knew the task was complete.

End Tasks Early if Appropriate

As an exception to the preceding rule, on occasion you may want to end a task prematurely if the part you care about happens early. For example, on an e-commerce site, you might want to watch users complete the checkout process all the way to the confirmation screen on one task, but you don't need to see this more than once. On the next task, when the users add the item in the shopping cart, I might say, "I'm going to ask you to pause here. You've covered the part we needed to see,

---

* Just don't get too carried away. I once commented that a user was scratching his head, whereupon he fixed me with an unreadable expression and replied, "Yes, it itches."

so in the interest of time we'd like to move on to something else." (This is just my preference, but the word "pause" feels less awkward to me than "stop," which implies that I didn't like what the users were doing.) Caveat: Use this tactic sparingly (ideally no more than once per test) because users may become inhibited if they expect to be stopped at any moment.

Consider Allowing Between-Task Discussion

My usual practice is to allow observers to ask a question or two at the end of each task, although some facilitators may choose not to do this if they're concerned about maintaining control of the session. But I keep these discussions brief, usually just a couple of minutes, because one of the facilitator's responsibilities it to manage how the test time is spent. If an issue has come up that merits more in-depth discussion, I might give the observers the choice, for example, "We have about 20 minutes left. Do you guys want to continue this discussion now or do one more task and then come back to it?" Although I'm still managing the time, the observers get to decide which activity is of greater interest to them.

The Scientist

The scientist is responsible for the integrity of the data, through note-taking, videotaping, written tasks, test procedures, and so on. The scientist strives to maintain objectivity and to minimize any adverse effects on the data being collected. People who are unfamiliar with usability test facilitation may mistakenly think that this is the facilitator's primary purpose, but in paper prototype usability tests, the scientist role is usually the third priority—there are many circumstances where the scientist takes a back seat to the other roles.

I don't want to imply that being scientific isn't important; professionals in any field should always understand their methods, apply them appropriately, and seek ways to improve them. But keep in mind that paper prototyping is not a technique that's used when precise usability measurements are required. It's more of a blunt instrument. Most of the time, there isn't a need to calculate statistics. You don't use an eye-tracker or spend hours analyzing videotapes. Most of the data from a paper prototype usability test is qualitative, not quantitative.

Is objectivity important? Yes and no. Clearly, the facilitator has the opportunity to introduce all kinds of bias into the testing process, through something as obvious and deliberate as a hint or as subtle and unintentional as a smile when the user makes a correct choice. It's virtually impossible to remove the human element from paper prototype testing. Thus, the scientist's focus isn't on minimizing interaction with the users but rather on monitoring how it might affect the results.

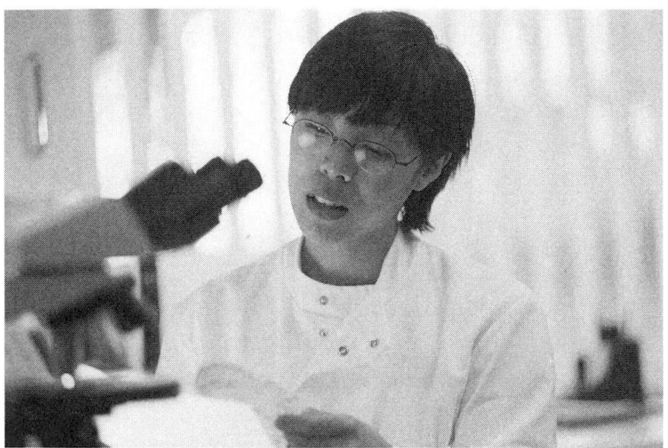

(Getty Images.)

For example, if the users are given a hint, the scientist makes note of it so that the team can discuss later how the users' behavior might have been affected. For example, "They found the answer in the help, but only after a suggestion that they look there. This is evidence that the help *content* works, but we can't conclude whether users in real life will see it." However, it is usually best for the facilitator to avoid asking leading questions or revealing his or her own opinions of the interface, so the scientist strives to maintain this objectivity. Chapter 13 revisits the topic of bias in more detail.

For beginning facilitators, it is often hard enough to fulfill the flight attendant and sportscaster responsibilities without adding note taking to the mix. I recommend that new facilitators skip the note-taking until they're comfortable managing the action. Instead, invite plenty of observers and have them take notes (which they should be doing anyway). I also know some facilitators who feel, even after several years of experience, that they do their best work when they leave the note-taking to others.

Co-Discovery (Two-User) Testing

Usability testing with two users at once is not, strictly speaking, a paper prototyping technique, but most of the tests I've conducted have been co-discovery because it seems to work quite naturally. In a co-discovery session, the two users work on the tasks together, discussing them with each other (and the facilitator) as they go.

Benefits

There are several reasons why co-discovery can be useful:

- **More comfortable for the users.** A solo user who gets stuck might blame himself or herself, but a pair of users who are stuck realize, "Okay, obviously this isn't just me." Especially when you have in-room observers, having users work in pairs can help them relax.
- **Easier for the facilitator.** Contrary to what you might think, facilitating a test with two users is often easier than working with one. In co-discovery, users talk to each other as they work through the tasks, and the facilitator may end up saying relatively little. This is fine. With only one user, the facilitator usually needs to take a more active role and be more conscious of providing positive feedback.
- **More data.** With two users, you're getting two people's thoughts and reactions at the same time. Note that you're not necessarily getting two *independent* viewpoints—User B may quickly agree with what User A said, making it hard to determine what User B really thinks. But if both users provide a plausible rationale for why they agree, that can give you more confidence about the need to change something. And when users disagree, then you usually do have two valid data points. Although this isn't very scientific, I tend to split the difference and view co-discovery as providing about 1.5 times the data of a single-user test.
- **Scheduling.** In several hundred usability tests, I estimate that I've experienced an average no-show rate of about 1 in 10 users. If you've scheduled two users and only one shows up, you can still hold the test. That's useful if you're testing on a tight schedule or have observers traveling to attend the sessions. Double no-shows are very rare—perhaps 1 in 100 tests—so with co-discovery there is little chance of having to cancel a test.

Drawbacks of Co-Discovery

Although it has its advantages, there are also some drawbacks to co-discovery:

- **Discrepancy in experience or confidence.** If one user knows substantially more than the other (or thinks so anyway), it can be awkward for the other person. Ideally, you'd avoid this during the recruitment process by not pairing people with a mismatch in experience, but this makes recruitment more complicated and it's hard to do perfectly.

- **Peer pressure.** Some participants may be more concerned about looking foolish in front of someone else in their profession than they are in a roomful of strangers that they'll never see again.
- **Slower pace.** Sometimes two users will take longer to complete tasks because there's more discussion. This drawback balances the "more data points" benefit—it's a trade-off.
- **Dominant personality.** Most people are pretty good about sharing and will work out for themselves who does the clicking and typing. Some pairs will automatically switch roles after a task or two. But a few people don't get good marks in "plays well with others" and tend to dominate the session. This doesn't happen very often, but when it does, it makes the facilitator's job harder.

Why I Choose Co-Discovery

I've found that co-discovery works well for paper prototyping—I use co-discovery about half of the time in nonpaper testing, and more like 90% of the time when testing a paper prototype. (I'm usually testing on a tight schedule, plus it's easier for two people to share a paper prototype than a computer.) In usability studies where I've done both single-user testing and co-discovery, most of the time the product team has felt that they got more benefit out of the co-discovery tests. But this is a generalization, and there are some usability specialists who believe that the drawbacks of co-discovery outweigh its benefits. Although the rest of this book assumes that you're testing with two users at a time, I suggest that you try both methods and decide which works best for you.

Friends or Strangers?

There are some advantages in pairing up people who don't know each other. Usability guru Jared Spool tells the story of how he once facilitated a test with a married couple who spent the entire session communicating in half-sentences:

> *She:* "Why don't we click on the . . ."
>
> *He:* "I was just thinking that . . ."
>
> *She:* "Oh yeah, you're right—let's . . ."

Jared dubbed this communication shorthand "married people's syndrome," but it can happen with any two people who know each other well. (There's also an ominous variation where the users know and *dislike* each other.) Strangers tend to be more thorough about discussing things, so their conversation is easier for observers to follow. It's also easier to avoid inequities in power—a manager/subordinate combination is especially risky.

Although I usually try to pair up strangers, this is not a hard and fast rule. There are some situations in which it makes sense to recruit people who know each other:

- The product is typically used by people who know each other (for example, a parent and child, or people who are playing a game together).
- The users are coming from some distance away (perhaps one of your customers) and want to share a ride.
- Users indicate that they would feel more comfortable working with someone they know.

To make the friends-or-strangers decision for your product, consider the circumstances of its use and what will be most comfortable for the user population you've chosen.

Making Trade-Offs

Let's go back to those roles of flight attendant, sportscaster, and scientist. When various situations arise in usability tests, it's often helpful to frame the situation in terms of a trade-off between two of the roles. Usually the flight attendant role has the top priority, but there are times when you might decide to let the sportscaster or scientist have their way. Thinking in terms of roles may help you understand the opposing forces at work so that you can make the best decision for each situation. Following are several examples.

Situation: *Users are stuck on a problem you haven't seen before.*

This common situation is a flight attendant/sportscaster conflict. The sportscaster wants the development team to get as much information as possible about the issue, including everything that's going on in the users' heads, but the flight attendant wants to make sure that the users don't feel stupid or embarrassed. Usually it's okay to wait and see if they can get past the difficulty on their own, but the flight attendant should provide reassurance and be prepared to intervene if necessary. (If your users are familiar with the game show *Wheel of Fortune*, you might ask, "Would you like to buy a vowel?" A bit of gentle humor can diffuse tension, and it's also a subtle reminder that the user is in charge.) Later in this chapter, I provide more tips on getting users unstuck.

Situation: *Users are stuck on a problem that also came up in the last two tests.*

Naturally, the flight attendant is concerned and should remain vigilant, but this is primarily a sportscaster/scientist trade-off. The main question to ask is, "How much data do we need about this problem?" If the team is already painfully aware of the issue, there's little point in spending valuable test time covering the same ground again. In this case, the scientist might give the users a hint to get them over the difficulty, noting the fact that he or she has done so. But if not all of the observers were present at the previous tests or there's no consensus about the severity of the problem, the sportscaster might overrule the scientist to let the observers get more information about the problem.

Situation: *Two users working together disagree on what to do next.*

The sportscaster might want the users to go down the wrong path first because it will likely be more interesting to watch them realize the error and recover from it—one hallmark of a usable interface is that it helps users get back on track. But the flight attendant must approve because it would be detrimental to foster conflict among the users and facilitator. One way to direct the users is by saying something like, "You guys have different ideas about how to proceed, which is fine because people do things differently. Why don't you try what John suggested, and if that doesn't do what you wanted, you can switch to Mary's approach." The scientist notes that the users were given this instruction (I call it a "nudge") about which way to go first. However, if time is short and there's additional ground to cover, the scientist may overrule the sportscaster by suggesting that the users take the correct path.

Situation: *The team has redesigned a screen, but the users don't take the path that will lead them to it.*

This is another situation in which the sportscaster will probably take priority over the scientist, although not immediately. The sportscaster knows that the team is eager to find out how their revised screen works, but the scientist first wants to establish whether the users would have gotten there on their own. So the scientist will avoid taking the users to the redesigned screen at first, until it's reasonably clear that they won't go there. Then the scientist can step aside in favor of the sportscaster, who directs the users to the new screen to find out how they react to it.

Other Common Testing Challenges

Writing about everything that can possibly go wrong during a usability test would be a book in itself. But here are some common situations and tips for handling them.

Getting Users Unstuck

It's usually not a question of whether users will get stuck, but rather how soon and how badly. Having users run into difficulty while attempting tasks is perhaps the most valuable part of usability testing because it indicates a problem with the interface that you can (hopefully) solve now that you're aware of it.

> *Once you explain something, you forever lose an opportunity to understand the problem.*

When users ask a question, resist the temptation to answer it. Once you explain something to a user, you *forever lose an opportunity to understand the problem.* Once the answer has been revealed, users may have one or both of the following reactions:

- ◇ They will be embarrassed at what they perceive to be their own ignorance and not want to tell you what they were thinking. "Oh, never mind, it was just me."
- ◇ They literally can't reconstruct or articulate what their thought process was in the absence of information that they now have. They'll say something like, "Okay, that makes perfect sense. It's fine the way it is."

On the other hand, you don't want the test to grind to a halt. My favorite tactic for getting a user unstuck is to ask a series of questions, starting very general and progressively getting more specific. For example, say you're testing a telephone interface and the user can't figure out how to transfer a call:

Facilitator	*User*
1. What are you trying to do right now?	I want to transfer this call to Mike in Accounting.
2. What do you think the next step is?	I want to dial 5385, but not lose this guy I'm talking to.
3. (A small hint): Do you see anything that might help you?	I'm not sure . . . if I dial the extension, won't it just beep?
4. (A big hint): What do you think the Flash button does?	I was wondering about that, but I was afraid it would hang up.

This approach is useful in ferreting out the root cause of a problem. You verify that the user:

- Is trying to do what you thought (perhaps the user assumes the caller would prefer to be given Mike's extension instead of being transferred).
- Shares your understanding of how to go about it.
- Can find and use the specific function or control needed to proceed with the task.

In this example, the root cause of the problem is insufficient information about how the Flash button works.

The User with an Agenda

Every once in a while a user will take advantage of the usability test as an opportunity to give the product team detailed—perhaps repeated—feedback on what's wrong with the interface or how it "should" be designed. Sometimes when users have behaved this way, it's been my fault for not briefing them well enough on their role. A user who has participated in focus groups may believe that they're being asked to give their impressions of what they like and dislike, which is usually not the primary goal of a usability test. An excess of opinion can also happen if the user is an influential stakeholder, such as an important customer.

Users who have interface design backgrounds are often tempted to offer their suggestions because they believe—sometimes even correctly—that their expertise is valuable to the team. Unless you're looking for a design consultant, it may be helpful to screen out potential test participants who claim to know a programming language, have created a Web page, and so on, unless of course these users are your target audience. (This is similar to the reason why people who work for market research firms aren't allowed to participate in focus groups—they know too much about the methodology, and it affects their behavior.)

Regardless of the cause, when you encounter a user with an agenda, there are a few tips for keeping him or her focused on what will provide the most value to you:

- Avoid asking the user's opinion about likes or dislikes—you'll just open the floodgates.
- Direct the user's attention back to the interface, for example, "Please show me what you'd do next."
- Let the user know you've captured his or her feedback—sometimes the person just wants to be sure the message has been heard. One way to confirm this is, "Thank you, I've made a note of that." If the user makes the same point again shortly thereafter, you might try, "Yes, you mentioned that."
- If necessary, politely curtail further discussion. My favorite way to do this is by saying, "In the interest of time, there are some other areas we want to cover." This reminds the user that there are plenty of other issues that we would like his or her feedback on.

Unusually Nervous User

Perhaps the most difficult situation a facilitator will ever face is a user who simply can't manage to relax. I have seen initial nervousness in such a variety of usability testing situations that I find it impossible to generalize about the cause—male/female, solo/co-discovery, paper/computer, lab/living room, with/without videotaping, a dozen/no observers. I believe that a few users are destined to experience initial nervousness in virtually any test setting, and we should accept this as unavoidable even as we seek ways to alleviate it.

But every now and then, a user who starts out uncomfortable stays that way. If a user doesn't relax after he or she starts interacting with the paper prototype, here are some tips:

- Provide help sooner—don't let the person struggle.
- Take a break and assess how the user is feeling. End the test if necessary.
- Give positive feedback and reassurance as explained in the flight attendant section.

- Avoid humor, especially sarcasm. In a delicate situation, trying to be funny can give users the mistaken idea that you're laughing at them. I have learned the hard way that flippant comments I aimed at the interface ("Oh yeah, like that makes sense") can strike users instead.

Mismatched Users

Another challenge in facilitating co-discovery usability tests is when one user has less confidence than the other does. (Sometimes this user has less knowledge of the subject matter, but not always.) Try to get feedback from both users. Don't allow an outgoing or confident user to speak for both—ask the other user whether he or she agrees or disagrees, or even direct questions to that user first. But if one user seems especially reticent, avoid putting him or her on the spot.

Tips for New Facilitators

Facilitating usability tests can feel awkward at first. Here are some of the things I found most helpful when I was first starting out.

- **Use a checklist.** A checklist is a bulleted list of everything you want to cover in your briefing of users, introduction of paper prototyping, and so on. A good checklist is generic enough to be used in a variety of usability studies, so you shouldn't have to keep rewriting it. (The next chapter has some examples of checklists you can use while conducting paper prototype usability tests.)
- **Wean yourself from scripts.** In a script, you write down everything you will say to the users and read it to them at the proper time. Scripts are useful in usability testing when it's important to control all the interactions you have with the users. For example, if you were testing two competing software packages, you'd want your introductions of them to use equally neutral wording. But in paper prototype testing, it's unlikely that you need this degree of scientific rigor—when an interface is rapidly changing, a detailed script can become more trouble to maintain than it's worth. I've heard of facilitators who spent so much time scripting paper prototype tests that they lost all the benefit of it being a fast technique. Although scripts are okay when you're starting, as you gain confidence in usability test facilitation, I recommend that you pare them down into checklists.

- **Practice out loud.** In any kind of public speaking (and test facilitation counts!), it's helpful to practice out loud. I recommend practicing your facilitation skills with co-workers and friends—not necessarily the whole usability test, but at least the introduction and instructions. Saying everything out loud will help you feel more comfortable, plus if something comes out wrong or you find yourself at a loss for words, that's one less mistake that you'll make with a real user.
- **Seek feedback.** Although I no longer videotape usability tests (the next chapter explains why), as a learning experience there's no substitute for seeing yourself on video. (In my first experience of reviewing test tapes that I'd facilitated, I realized that I had a bad habit of trailing off and not finishing . . .) Or invite a colleague to sit in on your tests and give you feedback; one inherent benefit of the usability profession is that we strive to be empathetic rather than critical. Whenever I conduct a usability study, I ask the team afterward what they thought went well and what they'd like to do differently in the future. If I realize I've made a mistake, such as asking a leading question, I'll discuss it as an example of what not to do.
- **Strive for progress, not perfection.** One of my experienced colleagues told me that she expects to make at least one mistake per day of testing, and she relaxes once she realizes she's made it (as in "Okay, that was my stupid thing to say today. I should be fine now.") It's always a good idea to improve your skills in accordance with whatever best practices may exist in the profession. At the same time, I don't believe that any two people will ever facilitate a usability test in exactly the same way any more than two software engineers will ever write the same code. As you become experienced in facilitating, you'll learn tricks that work well for you. And despite how carefully you've prepared, try to accept that you'll also make mistakes that you can learn from.

Chapter 9

Usability Testing with a Paper Prototype

The previous chapter covered the basics of usability testing without regard to whether the interface is being tested on a computer or as a paper prototype. This chapter discusses the variations in usability testing methodology that are specific to the medium of paper.

The Test Facility

It's not necessary to have a usability lab to test a paper prototype—I've conducted more than 90% of my usability tests in my clients' conference rooms. All you really need is a room with a door that can be closed (to minimize distractions) and a table large enough for the users and the Computer to interact with the prototype.

Tip: You might not want to reserve your best conference room for usability testing—I've learned that the fancier the conference room, the wider the table. Very wide tables make it hard for the Computer and users to work on a prototype that's between them.

On the other hand, there is nothing wrong with testing a paper prototype in a usability lab if you happen to have one. The biggest problem I've found with usability labs is that some are optimized for computer-based testing—the rooms are small, or there's restrictive furniture (such as a kneehole desk) that makes it hard for several people to gather around. If your lab lacks a large work surface, consider getting a couple of inexpensive folding tables to use when you're conducting paper prototype tests.

Seating

Obviously, you want the users to sit in front of the prototype. Put the users closest to the door so that they don't face an obstacle course on their way in and out. The Computer usually sits across from the users, which means that the Computer sees the prototype upside down—a drawback, but usually the Computer is familiar enough with the interface that it's not a problem. (And other prototype pieces waiting in the wings will be upside down to the users, and thus less likely to distract them.)

The facilitator can sit either next to the users or across the table, next to the Computer. It's easier for the facilitator to converse with users when they're across the table, but I also think there may be a subtle psychological benefit to having the facilitator literally "on the users' side." Although I usually sit next to the users, I think that both options work.

It's best to avoid having observers sit behind users because this can make some people uncomfortable. Instead, observers should sit around the table, where they can see the prototype. See Figure 9.1 for some sample seating arrangements. As explained in the next chapter, this isn't as distracting as it sounds if the observers are well behaved. A useful rule of thumb is that the less familiar an observer is with the prototype, the closer he or she gets to sit. This is exactly the opposite of what happens by default—someone unfamiliar with the interface often says, "Don't mind me; I'll just sit over here in the corner." But then that person can't follow what's going on, gets little value from observing, and doesn't bother to come again.

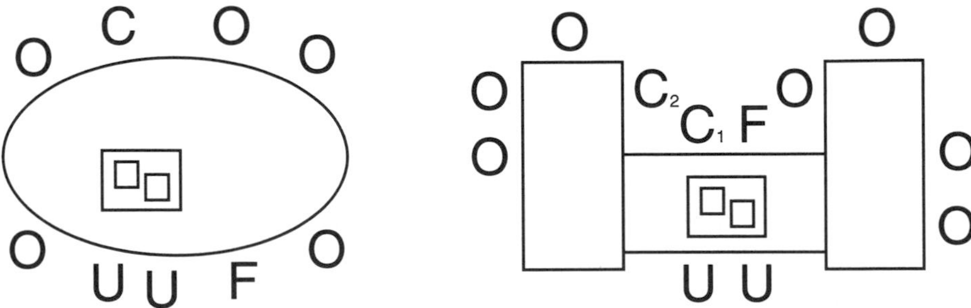

Figure 9.1 Some possible seating arrangements for a paper prototype test. The letters indicate the positions.

Videotaping

I first started conducting usability tests when I joined User Interface Engineering in 1993. Back then, we videotaped all usability tests—paper or otherwise—as a matter of course, and we gave our clients copies of the tapes. But in recent years I have almost completely stopped videotaping usability tests because most tapes of paper prototype tests simply aren't used.

Whenever I cross paths with a former client, I ask what they did with the tapes from the usability study we conducted. Usually, the person looks slightly embarrassed and admits that the test tapes were put on a shelf and have been gathering dust ever since. I estimate that at least 90% of the usability test videotapes I've made have never been watched.

Reasons to Skip the Videotaping

Videotaping a paper prototype usability test is less useful than taping a computer-based test, for several reasons:

- **The action is slowed down.** On a computer, users may perform keyboard or mouse actions faster than the eye can follow, but with a paper prototype the speed is limited by how fast the human Computer can do things. The Computer can't miss the action because he or she controls it.
- **The interface changes frequently.** Many paper prototypes are revised after each usability test, and they can evolve quite rapidly. In a fast-moving development environment, a videotape that shows problems from 2 weeks ago may no longer be relevant.
- **There is less need for analysis.** Analysis of usability test data always has a point of diminishing returns. With paper prototypes, this point comes sooner than with software, again because the prototype tends to change rapidly—some statistics might be obsolete before they're even calculated. A useful question to ask yourself is, "Will the time needed to review that tape provide more value than something else I could be doing instead?" Perhaps the answer is yes if there's an important but subtle issue you're still trying to piece together, but

often the time would be better spent revising the interface or conducting an additional test.

- **It's hard to read the prototype screens.** With inexpensive video equipment, the picture may not be good enough to read the prototype screens and sometimes screens with a lot of white space can confuse a camera's automatic focus. Although better equipment might solve the problem, I'd go that route only if it wasn't physically possible for observers to come to the test.

Reasons to Videotape

On the other hand, here are some reasons why you might decide to videotape your usability tests.

- **Not enough observers.** As long as there are at least two or three good observers taking notes, they should be able to capture many of the issues. But if your team is very small, the observers are inexperienced, or you're worried that you might miss something important, a videotape can act as your safety net.
- **Remote observers.** Although I advocate having all the observers in the same room, this may not always be desirable or practical. With observers in another room, a video camera is usually needed to relay the action because the prototype may be difficult to see through a one-way mirror. Because you're already dealing with a video camera, you might as well pop in a tape.
- **Need for a highlight tape.** Highlight tapes can be valuable to communicate the problems you found to a large number of people or important stakeholders. Seeing the users get confused and voice their concerns has a lot more impact than simply hearing someone describe what happened. But highlight tapes can be time-consuming to make unless you have good editing equipment and know how to use it—consider whether a few pithy user quotes might do the trick. (As long as the user can't be identified by what they said, this use of test information is covered by the informed consent form.)
- **Need for a demonstration tape.** A demonstration tape is similar to a highlight tape except that its purpose is to illustrate the technique of paper prototyping instead of the findings from tests. Sometimes people need to see a brief clip of a paper prototype test to "get" how the users interact with the Computer and prototype. If you don't have a suitable test tape and the users' permission to use it, one alternative is to record a "dramatization" (as is sometimes done on

television) of real events, but using your co-workers as actors. This approach requires no editing because you prepare the script ahead of time, and you probably don't need more than a minute or two of tape to show how the method works. Naturally, you would make it clear that this was a reenactment, not a real test.

- **Just in case.** For whatever reason, someone may want you to tape the session "just in case." The main downside is that if you do a lot of testing, you'll eventually have a large library of obsolete tapes. One company I know of simply records over their oldest tapes.

How to Videotape a Paper Prototype

Having discouraged you from making unnecessary videotapes, it's okay to do so if you have a use for them. Naturally, an essential prerequisite is to obtain the users' written consent, including an explanation of the purposes for which the tape can be used—you don't want a user to turn on the TV and discover that he's in a commercial giving a testimonial for your product. So think about the possible reasons you might want to use a tape: for just you, to verify something that happened? To show to the product team? To make a demo tape or a training video on test facilitation? Make your consent form as explicit as possible. If your consent form says that you'll use the tape only to verify what happened in the session and you decide later that it would be perfect for your presentation at the annual industry conference, you must contact the users and get their permission.

Here are some tips on what equipment to use and how to set it up.

- **Film from above.** I've made dozens of tapes by mounting a consumer-grade video recorder on a tripod behind the users. I place the tripod as close as practical, extend it fully, and angle the camera downward to focus on the prototype. Although this quick-and-dirty approach is good enough for many situations, it's inevitable that the camera's view of the prototype will be partially obstructed at times by the users. If you have a usability lab, a camera in the ceiling can capture the action. If you don't have a lab, look for a tripod that allows the camera to be mounted vertically above the table (Figure 9.2).
- **Determine the field of view.** You want to ensure that observers can read the screens, so the prototype should fill most of the camera's view. Be aware of what the camera can and cannot see. Tape the prototype background to the

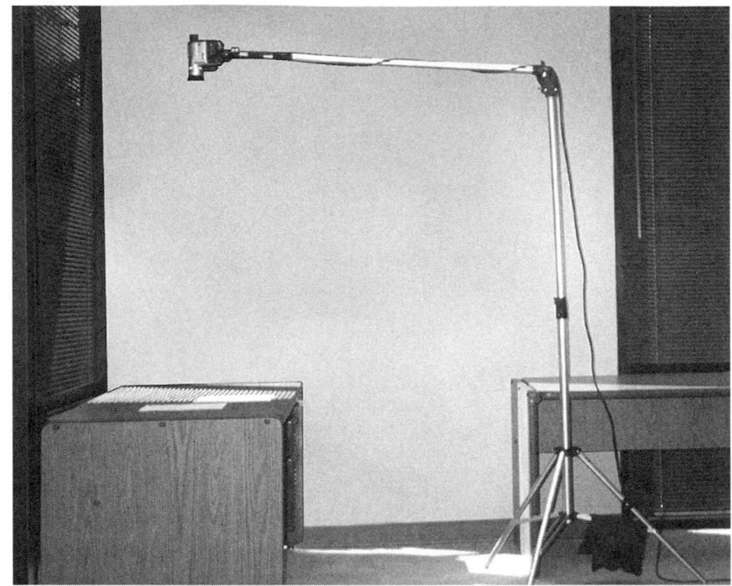

Figure 9.2 A special tripod allows you to position the camera directly above the prototype.

table to keep it in place during the test. Alternatively, you can outline the camera's field of view with masking tape and keep all the action inside this box. (A tip for those with fancy equipment: If you're using multiple cameras and a mixer to put an inset of the user's face in a corner of the recording, part of the prototype video won't be visible. Mark out that section on the prototype as a reminder not to let important action happen there.)

- **Use a trained camera operator if necessary.** If the camera is positioned and focused correctly, a human camera operator may not be necessary. However, if you have a lab technician who knows what he or she is doing, it's appropriate to make camera adjustments to help the viewers see better. But keep adjustments to a minimum. When I made my first few videotapes, my overzealousness in panning, zooming, and focusing made the resulting tapes a recipe for visually induced motion sickness.
- **Watch the wiring.** Run cables where the users won't trip over them. Ideally, everyone in the room should have a clear path to the door without having to avoid cables. (Back in the days of clip-on microphones, I once tripped over a cord and yanked the mic right off the user's collar. Neither of us was hurt, but it taught me a lesson.)

Preparing Users

So now you've got your room and equipment ready. This section describes how to prepare users for a usability test of a paper prototype. The goal is to have users feel prepared, comfortable, and in control of the session. I'm assuming that you are using co-discovery and in-room observers—if not, simply omit those instructions that do not apply to your situation.

Note: All the tables in this chapter are available as Word documents from *www.paperprototyping.com.*

During Recruitment

My advice on explaining paper prototyping during user recruitment is "Don't." Paper prototyping is an inherently visual and kinesthetic activity. Trying to explain it over the phone to a stranger (who probably knows little or nothing about usability testing) is like using mime to explain life insurance to a 10-year-old—you're using the wrong medium, and they lack the background. You'll get tongue-tied, the user will be confused, and you'll get distracted from the primary purpose of the recruitment process, which is to schedule participants who are suitable and willing.

Instead, gloss over paper prototyping by saying something like, "You'll be working with a prerelease version of the system." You want the user to understand the *goals* of the session—to find out where the interface works well and where it's confusing—but you don't need to describe your technology, or lack thereof. Here is an example of a paragraph that I gave to a market research firm that was recruiting participants to test a data security application:

> We're looking for participants for a usability study. In this study, you'd be working with a pre-release version of a web application intended for use by people who are responsible for data security and web servers. Our goal is to figure out how to make the interface more useful and user-friendly. We would ask you to perform some tasks with the application while members of the development team sit in the room, quietly observing and taking notes. We are testing the web application; we are not testing you! Depending on the session there may or may not be another participant working with you, and there will be a facilitator sitting next to you to assist you. Does this sound like something you'd be comfortable doing?

Upon Arrival

Once the users arrive, you want to prepare them for what they'll encounter when they enter the test room. Your first few minutes with the users sets the tone for the session, so strive to be professional, relaxed, and friendly. Table 9.1 shows the items you should cover in your introduction and examples of wording you might use.

In the Test Room

The observers are assembled in the room before the users come in, and the prototype is on the table, displaying the screen that we've decided to use as the starting point, even if it's just a blank background. Once the users are seated in front of the prototype, I ask the team members to introduce themselves first—this allows the users to look around the room and get familiar with the test setting before they are asked to speak. Observers should avoid giving much detail about themselves or what they're working on, especially things like "lead designer," which might sound intimidating. If in doubt, just names will suffice.

Then I introduce each user by first name (do whatever is appropriate in your culture) and have each one describe a bit about his or her background. Not only does this get the users comfortable speaking to the group, but the team can verify that the users meet the profile of the target audience for the interface. Whoever did the user recruitment should provide you with the users' answers to the screening questions, which can help you identify interesting aspects of the users' background. I usually ask two or three specific questions—in the absence of structure, some users will either say very little (bad) or will give their entire life history (worse). I also give the observers a chance to ask the users more about their background before we begin the test.

Before giving the users the first task, I explain what they're looking at and how we'd like them to interact with the paper prototype and Computer. I always end my introduction with the all-important, "We're testing the interface; we're not testing you." I say this to every user at least once before the test (even if they've participated in a test before), and repeat it if necessary. See Table 9.2 for details and examples of wording.

How Users React

No doubt about it—paper prototyping feels weird for the first few minutes. Actually, so does any kind of usability testing. From the users' perspective, it's like

Table 9.1 Pretest Briefing

Topic	*Checklist*	*Example Wording (i.e., Script)*
Greeting and introduction	◈ Welcome the users (hang up coats, offer a beverage, ask if the directions were okay). ◈ Introduce yourself and the company. ◈ Describe the interface being tested. ◈ Give users the informed consent form (ideally, they brought the copy you sent ahead of time). ◈ Explain the goals of the session. ◈ Introduce the notion of paper prototyping.	"Thank you for coming. I'm Carolyn Snyder. I'm an independent consultant, and I specialize in conducting sessions like this one. Here at [company] we're working on a product for [target market] that will help them to [basic functionality]. I'll go over the main points in this form we sent you. The purpose of today's session is for you to help us figure out how to make this interface more user-friendly before we finish developing it. But believe it or not, we aren't going to use a computer. As you'll see, we've actually created paper versions of the screens, and this guy named Carl will be playing the computer."
Their role	◈ If using co-discovery, introduce the two users. ◈ Explain what's expected of them. ◈ Remind them of their qualifications.	"Frank, this is Ernest. The two of you will be working together. We'll give you some tasks that we think are representative of what people might do in real life. [Give example.] Your job is to tell us what makes sense, what's confusing, whether it works the way you'd expect it to, etc. You are here because you know [area of expertise], so your perspective will help us make this product more useful."
Social concerns	◈ Explicitly mention in-room observers and/or videotaping. ◈ Explain that you're testing the interface, not them. ◈ Reassure users about what will happen if they encounter any difficulties.	"About half a dozen members of the development team will be sitting in the same room, observing quietly and taking notes. We're not going to be videotaping. Keep in mind that we're testing the interface—we're not testing you—so if you run into any problems it's not your fault and it means that there's something

Continued

Table 9.1 Pretest Briefing—cont'd

Topic	*Checklist*	*Example Wording (i.e., Script)*
	◇ Reiterate how valuable this is and how much you appreciate their help.	we need to change. I'll be sitting next to you, and I can help you if you want. We held our first session this morning, and we learned a lot; in fact, we've already made some changes. We really appreciate having you come and help us out."
Set expectations	◇ Acknowledge the unfinished nature of the prototype (avoid the temptation to apologize—present this as a benefit). ◇ Explain that the design will evolve. ◇ Explain that you will record their suggestions but don't promise to implement them (especially important if the user is a customer).	"The prototype still has some rough edges—we're still thinking through how it should work and some parts of it are incomplete. Before we cast it in concrete, we want to get some feedback about how well this design works. We're doing several sessions like this one, so it's likely that the final version of the interface will be different than what you see today. If you have suggestions we'll make note of them, although at this point it is premature to promise what we'll be able to include in the interface. When we get done with this series of sessions, we'll review everyone's feedback to help determine our priorities for the next release."
Paperwork and administrivia	◇ Get signature on informed consent form. ◇ Pay users (unless you have decided to pay them at the end). ◇ Escort them into test room.	"Do you have any questions about what we'll be doing today? If not, could I please get your signature on this form? And so I don't forget, I'm going to give you your payment now since you've already earned it by virtue of showing up on time. If you need to leave early for any reason, you're still entitled to keep it."

Table 9.2 Introducing the Test

Topic	*Checklist*	*Example Wording*
Introductions	◇ Direct users to the chairs in front of the prototype. ◇ Ask observers to introduce themselves. ◇ Introduce users. ◇ Have users answer 2–3 questions about their background.	"Frank, Ernest, please have a seat here. I'll let these folks introduce themselves." "Frank, you're a senior network administrator at MegaBank, right? Please tell us a little bit about your responsibilities, how many end users you support, and what kinds of data security products you've used." (Same for Ernest.) "Does anyone here have any other questions for Frank or Ernest before we get started?"
Paper prototype orientation	◇ Explain what they're looking at (usually the first screen of the site or application). ◇ (Optional) For users with limited computer experience, you might point out familiar elements such as the browser buttons, explaining that these things on their computer might look a little different, but they do the same thing.	"As I mentioned, here's the paper prototype of the Web application you'll be working with. We've assumed you typed [URL].com into the browser and this page came up. This is your starting point." (Optional) "You use AOL at home, right? These forward and back buttons here do the same thing as the buttons in AOL—they just look a little different. If you're not sure whether something is the same as what you're used to, just ask me."
Interactions with the prototype and Computer	◇ Introduce the Computer. ◇ Explain how to interact with the prototype (and each other if co-discovery). ◇ Discuss thinking aloud and asking questions. ◇ (Optional) Note that all interface functionality is available (e.g., drag & drop).	"Carl here will be playing the computer. Now Carl may seem like a pretty smart computer, but he has no speech recognition and no artificial intelligence. Since machines can't talk, he's not allowed to explain anything. If you want to do something, you'll need to interact with the prototype just as you would on a computer. Use your finger to click on

Continued

Table 9.2 Introducing the Test—cont'd

Topic	*Checklist*	*Example Wording*
	◇ (Optional) Point out any print manuals that may exist or mention that there's a help system.	links or buttons. These pieces of tape indicate places where you can type something in, and here's your keyboard (give pen). It's okay to write on this. The two of you are working together, so talk to each other as you go. It's fine if you disagree about something because there are different ways to use this. Please tell us what makes sense to you, what's confusing, and any questions that come to mind. Your questions are especially valuable, but I may not answer them right away because our goal is to change the interface so it answers them." (Optional) "Even though this is a paper prototype, assume you can do all the things you can do with a real computer, like drag & drop and right mouse menus. There's even a help system."
They are in charge	◇ Remind the users that you're testing the interface. ◇ Confirm ending time and that they can stop or take a break at any time.	"Remember that we're testing the interface—we're not testing you. We'll end promptly at 4:00, but if you need to stop or take a break before then, just let me know. Are you ready to start?"
Begin first task	◇ Hand users the first task. ◇ Clarify the task if it's confusing. ◇ If necessary, prompt the users to begin interacting with the prototype.	"Okay, here's the first thing we'd like you to do. Take a minute to read this and let me know if it makes sense. If so, then whenever you're ready please show us what you would do first."

standing on the edge of the swimming pool, worrying that the water's going to be cold. The key to getting users to relax is having them jump in the pool and realize that the water's fine. Once they start interacting with the prototype, their brains become engaged in the task and they focus less on the social nature of the setting. It's also easier for the facilitator to reassure the users that they're providing value once they're doing something besides staring at the interface. So the key to starting a test off on the right foot is to get the users "clicking" and "typing" as soon as possible. (Exception: Sometimes it's interesting to start a task by asking users to describe how they currently do it or how they'd expect to go about it to determine whether your interface supports their approach. Just keep this discussion brief.)

It's amazing how quickly users get into the task and act in a realistic manner. In one test of a video conferencing system, the task involved negotiating a business deal. We used photographs of a person in various facial expressions to simulate the other end of the video connection, and users talked to the pictures as if they were live people. Even with a human obviously manipulating the prototype, users often say things like, "Hmm, the red light came on" or "Good, it worked," which indicate that they're focusing on the *interface* as the entity they're interacting with, not the humans simulating its behavior.

I also make it a point to talk to users afterward and ask what they thought of the experience. I've found that most people seem to understand and appreciate the reason why we're testing with paper. Occasionally someone will comment that some aspect of the interface might have been clearer on a screen. I'll simply acknowledge their statement (for example, "Yes, that table will be easier to read when the columns line up") and thank the user again for his or her help. But I've never heard a user say that the experience was silly or a waste of time, and I've heard plenty of positive feedback.

How the "Computer" Behaves

For the most part, the Computer should think of himself or herself as a machine that can do only what it's been programmed to do.

Accurately Reflect the Users' Inputs

The essence of any human-computer interface is that the machine takes input from the human, does some processing, and produces some kind of output. For an interface to be usable, users need to understand the cause-and-effect relationship between their inputs and the outputs, even if the processing is a complete mystery. (I don't need to understand how my car's antilock brakes work. All I need to know is that if I keep pressure on brake pedal—even when it makes that weird rattling noise—the car will stop as quickly as it can.)

Although developers often focus on the processing—which is, after all, the part that has to be coded—users deal mostly with the inputs and outputs, so it's important to have your prototype represent them accurately. For example, if the user writes "hiking boots" into a search engine field, use that piece of removable tape at the top of the search results page to make it say "Search results for: hiking boots." If you try to rely on memory, they (or you) may forget exactly what they entered. Similarly, if you show users a screen with different data than what they entered, they can get confused unless the differences are minor and easily explained.

Wait for the Users

Avoid anticipating what the users will do. To speed things along, sometimes an overly helpful Computer will set down the next screen (or more subtle, pick it up) before the users actually do anything to make it appear. Resist this temptation unless you're absolutely certain what screen they want and how they would have gotten there.

Avoid Conversation

Since, as the Computer, you're sitting across from the users and they know that *you* know how to use the interface, sometimes users will direct questions to you. Don't answer them—it's the facilitator's job to handle this. (If this feels awkward, you might say, "I'm sorry, but computers can't talk.") However, there are some situations when it's appropriate for the Computer to say something:

- **To distinguish action from discussion.** Sometimes users will point at the prototype while figuring out what to do next. In this case, the Computer (or the facilitator) can ask, "Are you just discussing or are you doing something?"
- **To clarify what the user would see.** If the prototype is messy enough that users can't read it, or there's something that's hard to represent with paper, it's okay to state what the user is looking at, *but not why.* For example, the Computer can say things such as, "That button is gray," or, "These are tabs." But beware the word *because,* which is a red flag that you've slipped into explanation. For example, "That button is gray because you haven't selected a record yet." If you catch yourself saying "because," stop talking.

- **To provide an oral error messages.** Sooner or later, a user will take a wrong turn that you aren't prepared for. It's fine if you need to make up an error message on the fly and simply tell the user what it would say. Try to use the same content that the real system would—resist the temptation to give them additional information that would not appear in the context of the error. (Also see the discussion of "incredibly intelligent help" in Chapter 4.)

Facilitating a Paper Prototype Test

In a paper prototype test, the facilitator's responsibilities are essentially the same as in any other kind of usability test, but there are a few differences due to the medium of paper.

- **Have them show, not tell.** In the process of thinking aloud, users sometimes slip into verbal explanations, such as, "At this point I'd start over." (People do this when testing on a computer too, but it happens even more often in paper prototyping because the Computer is human.) Ask the users to demonstrate *how* they'd do that. Avoid letting the users simply talk through the task—remind them to show you. Sometimes it's okay to relax this a bit after you've established a common vocabulary. For example, if the users demonstrate that "start over" means "click Back until we get to the home page," you don't necessarily have to make them traverse all the interim pages each time if this method would work. But when in doubt, have them explicitly show you.
- **Clarify that it's okay to write on the prototype.** Sometimes users are reluctant to write on the prototype, and you may need to reiterate that you really do want them to write on the removable tape, transparency, or prototype itself. (An occasional user will go too far and put Xs on buttons to indicate clicking; gently remind them that writing only replaces typing, not clicking.) Whenever users ask if they can write something on the prototype besides data, I say yes because chances are it's something interesting, like crossing out information they don't want to see.
- **Watch for Computer mistakes.** Sometimes the Computer will make a mistake, either a simple one, such as not moving a highlight, or a major one, such as showing the wrong screen. The facilitator should try to keep tabs on the Computer's logic and note any problems. Sometimes a simple, "Is that right?" or "Didn't we change that?" is sufficient to clue the Computer in to the problem.
- **Handle valid (but unprepared-for) user actions.** Users may do something entirely reasonable that you simply haven't prepared for, such as typing a term

you didn't expect into the search engine. One tactic is to confirm that their way would have worked and then ask them to please find another. Or perhaps you can quickly sketch a screen or modify one of the screens you did prepare. For example, if you have a page of search results that contains more items than what the user's search would yield, maybe you can cross off items to approximate the list that the user would see.

◇ **Take a break if the paper prototype crashes.** Every once in a while, the users manage to end up in a state that didn't occur to the development team even in their wildest dreams (or nightmares). I can tell when this happens because the Computer will look at the other designers and ask, "What *do* we do when that happens?" This is valuable because it reveals a pitfall that the code will need to avoid. If this happens, take a short break so that the team can step out into the hall and confer. You may need to join them to hear how they'd like to proceed. Be sure to reassure the users that they've just done a very good thing in finding this problem—if the users are relaxed enough for humor to be appropriate, I'll tell them that the paper prototype has "crashed" and we need to go reboot it.

Paper prototypes can crash too!
(Illustration by Rene Rittiner.)

◇ **Answer questions when appropriate.** Given that paper prototypes are often used before the design is complete, sometimes the users raise really good questions that are outside the scope of what you're testing. If the issue is an important one and isn't going to be covered by our tasks, I'll simply answer it (or call upon the appropriate team member if I don't know the answer). For example, in a security application used by network administrators, one of them wondered whether the system would let them set the security level of the passwords created by end users ("Red Sox" is easily guessable, at least in Boston; "Ab84gh" is not). This was something we hadn't planned to cover, but it was an excellent question pertaining to functional requirements, so I let the product manager discuss it briefly with the users.

Ending the Test

Sometimes there isn't time to complete the last task of the session, especially if it's long or the users are having difficulty. In that case, I'll ask the Computer to demonstrate the remaining steps so that the users can get closure on what they were doing. As a bonus, we may still identify another problem or two if the users are surprised by something and comment on it.

I usually reserve the last 10 minutes of the test session for discussion (especially if observers are in the room) of any interesting issues that came up during the test. Although I might do this in any type of usability test, in paper prototype tests there is a greater likelihood that the observers will have questions for the users. For example, this is an appropriate time to ask users if the tasks were typical of their work or to follow up on their comments. Sometimes one of the designers has revised a troublesome screen and wants to ask if it's better. With the tasks behind us, it doesn't matter as much if someone asks a leading question, and it's okay to answer the users' questions directly. As a facilitator, I'll keep quiet if the observers and users are having a fruitful discussion.

I do keep my eye on the clock, however. It's important to let the users go when we said we would, even if the discussion is interesting. Usually I'll give a "2-minute warning" when we're running out of time, which allows for another question or two. If the users and observers are engaged in discussion, when we're out of time I will stand up as a cue that the session is over, and people get the hint. It's usually a good idea to escort users back to the lobby so that you can be reasonably sure that they've left, especially if you plan to hold a debriefing meeting immediately after the test. (It's an equally good idea to only say things about users that you wouldn't mind them overhearing, just in case a user returns to the test room to retrieve a forgotten umbrella.)

Combining Roles

In addition to users, there are three roles in a paper prototype usability test: the facilitator, the Computer, and the note-taking observers. If you have a very small team, you might need to combine roles. The best approach depends on the skill sets of the people involved—here are some thoughts.

- **Facilitator/observer.** This is probably the combination I'd try first. I believe that with practice, a facilitator can take good notes and still manage the rest of the facilitator duties, but other usability specialists feel that one or both activities may suffer. It's probably fair to say that it depends on the experience and comfort level of the facilitator.
- **Computer/facilitator.** It's difficult to test your own design. The Computer has in-depth knowledge of how the interface behaves, and often this knowledge came from designing it. Although it's possible to facilitate a test of something that you've designed, it's really hard to remain objective. Unless you're certain that you can resist the temptation to lapse into explanation/justification of the interface, it's best to let someone else facilitate. On the other hand, if you know how to facilitate but are unfamiliar with the interface, you can probably do a passable job as Computer after a couple of run-throughs, especially if a designer will be observing and can help if you get stuck. The advantage of this approach is that the designer can focus on note-taking.
- **Computer/observer.** This one isn't very practical—the Computer has his or her hands full (literally) with the prototype, so it's hard to take more than a few hastily scrawled notes.
- **Computer/facilitator/observer.** Not recommended—I did this once, and my brain almost exploded.

No matter which way you handle it, the session may go a little slower than usual if you're juggling more duties than you're used to, but it still beats not testing at all. Reserve some time after the test to jot down additional notes. You may also want to consider videotaping.

Iterative Refinement: Modifying the Prototype

With paper prototyping, it's okay to make changes as soon as you have evidence that there's a problem. It's not necessary to keep the prototype and tasks the same for each test because you're not trying to gather statistics—you're trying to identify and fix problems.

So what happens when you find a problem with your paper prototype? If it's a little problem, fix it right then and there. If it's a bigger problem (or you're not sure whether it really is a problem), wait until after the test.

Making Changes during a Test

Making changes during a usability test always reminds me of *Harold and the Purple Crayon,* one of my favorite books when I was a child (Figure 9.3). Harold is a plucky little guy who goes through his cartoon world by drawing all the adventures that he wants to have happen, such as going sailing. When his adventures get a bit too much, he grabs his trusty purple crayon and draws his way out of danger. So when a user says, "I want to look at the return policy, but I don't see a way to do that," you can grab your equivalent of a purple crayon and write "Return policy" on the screen so that the user can click it. Similarly, it's fairly simple to change wording, rearrange items (with your purple scissors), add or remove a control, and so on. You'll get immediate feedback on whether the change helps, and if so it's already in place for the next test.

After he had sailed long enough, Harold made land without much trouble.

Figure 9.3 Like Harold with his purple crayon, sometimes you can change your interface on the fly to support what users are trying to do. (This page is my favorite because of the pun on "made land.")

Caveat: Users Aren't Designers

As a rule, it's best not to give users the virtual purple crayon and let them redesign screens in a usability test. Although users are good at describing problems, most are not good designers. My favorite illustration of this comes from an episode of *The Simpsons* in which Homer, egged on by a rabid marketer, is given free rein to design his dream car (Figure 9.4). Naturally, when he finished adding features the car was a rolling fiasco.

> *Homer:* I want a horn here, here, and here. You can never find a horn when you're mad. And they should all play 'La Cucaracha.'
>
> *Advisor:* What about a separate soundproof bubble-dome for the kids with optional restraints and muzzles?
>
> *Homer:* Bullseye!

With that caveat, sometimes it is useful to ask users to mark features or content they're most interested in or to cross off things they don't want. One Web site I tested used six tabs at the top for each of its major content areas. At the end of the usability test, I gave users a pen and told them they had 10 votes to distribute across those six tabs to indicate the value they perceived in each. Although this experiment was crude, there were some useful patterns, like the fact that one of the tabs contained stuff that none of the users cared about. If you are interested

Figure 9.4 Homer Simpson knew exactly what functionality he wanted in a car, but he was still a lousy designer. (© Fox Twentieth Television.)

in more information about ways to involve users in the design process, you'll want to read other books and papers about participatory design (see the Reference section).

Making Changes between Tests

Hopefully, you'll be conducting a handful of tests with your paper prototype. You should allow yourself some time between tests—say 2 or 3 hours—to make more substantial changes than what you were able to do on the fly. (If the design is still in its infancy or many changes are expected, you might even designate a day in the middle of your usability study for rethinking the design.) Rearranging screens, simplifying a screen, adding an example—these kinds of changes often help considerably and aren't difficult to do. Even when more substantial redesign is called for, it often doesn't take as long as the initial design did because your brain has a better grasp of the problem.

- **Problems first, then answers.** One method that works well for making changes efficiently is to first list the issues on a whiteboard—everything that the observers saw during the test that indicated a problem. (If you do this in the same room that you're testing in, remember to erase this list before the next users arrive!) Then divide and conquer, just as you did to create the prototype—people put their initials by the things they want to solve. With this approach it's possible for a team to make fairly substantial changes to the paper prototype in an hour or so. If you're doing this over lunch, order a couple of pizzas for the team and then you'll have plenty of help.
- **Include information in the interface.** The interface is the first and often the best place to explain things to the user. Always ask yourself whether a particular usability problem can be solved by directly changing the interface rather than writing instructions somewhere else. Try to make the easiest change first, which often means wording. For example, in testing a Web application for teachers, we found that users were confused by what to do next. We solved this problem by adding a sentence to the bottom of the page suggesting the next step. This worked so well that we called these "magic sentences." (See Figure 9.5.)

Note: These users were English teachers, and their willingness to read instructions online was perhaps a bit greater than usual. But I have seen equally good results from changes of similar scope—adding an example next to a field or reformatting a page to put the most-needed information at the top.

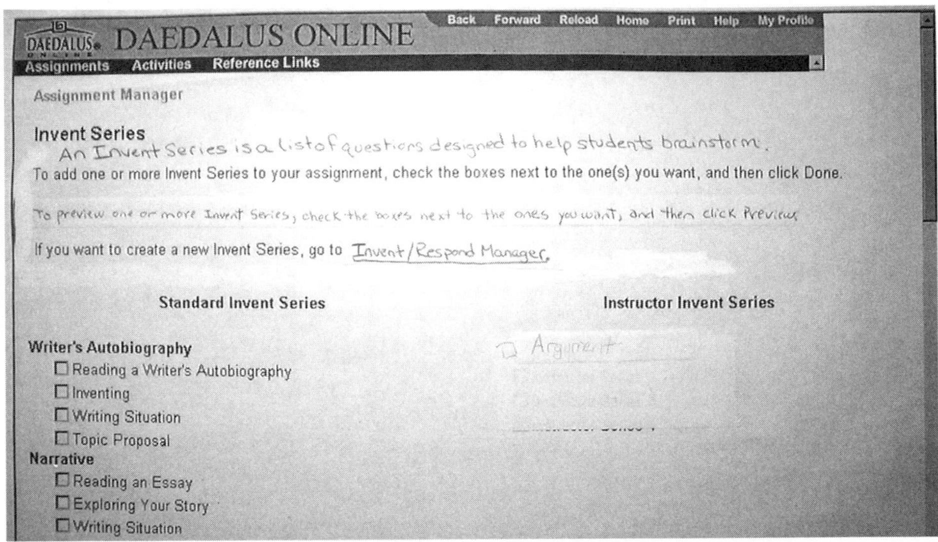

Figure 9.5 The hand-written part is what we called a "magic sentence." These brief explanations helped users understand the concepts and/or next step.

Figure 9.6 Make sure you're not just tweaking your interface to create the illusion that you've solved a particular problem.

◇ **Don't suboptimize the tasks.** Although your paper prototype is built around a particular set of tasks you've created, don't forget about all the other tasks that users might be doing in real life. Sometimes it's tempting to suboptimize the interface, in other words, tweak it so that users will get through a specific task better. For example, users aren't seeing a menu option that falls below the fold of the site, so you move it up. But to make a change like this, you also have to decide what gets pushed *below* the fold. Take a step back and be sure this makes sense for the interface as a whole. Otherwise you're only creating an illusion that you've solved the problem (as the cartoon in Figure 9.6 illustrates), and the illusion will shatter as soon as the user does a different task.

This chapter has discussed what the facilitator and Computer should do in a paper prototype usability test. The ways that you set up the room, greet users, introduce the concept of paper prototyping, and facilitate the session are all important. But don't forget that the main purpose of usability testing is to provide data to other members of the team so that they can make the product better. The next chapter focuses on the observers.

Chapter 10

Observers

If a tree falls in the forest and no one is there to hear it, does it still make a sound? If a usability test is conducted and no one observes it, does it still provide value? I'm still pondering the tree conundrum, but I'm pretty sure the answer to the second question is no. The main goals of usability testing are to get information from the users about how to make the product better *and to deliver that information to the people who can act upon it.* A fast and efficient means of achieving that goal is to have product team members observe the usability test.

Benefits of In-Room Observers

Given 21st century technology, perhaps there will come a day when people who appear to be sitting across the table may in fact be across the world. But until that day comes, we are stuck with the fact that long distance just isn't the same as being there and an observer who is in another room might as well be halfway across the world. The more that observers are separated from users, the more data they will miss—facial expressions, tone of voice, gestures, and so on.

Although a usability lab with good equipment theoretically allows observers to hear clearly and to see both the interface and the users, it's still possible to miss many nuances. My colleague Donna Cooper has facilitated many tests where she sat in the room with the user, and observers watched the test via a video camera from a separate room with another facilitator. Donna reports that in the debriefing meeting she sometimes feels like she's seen a different test than everyone else—she may be keenly aware of the user's frustration when the observers (and sometimes even the other facilitator) didn't notice it.

Although any observation is better than no observation, I believe there are some distinct benefits of having observers in the same room as users so that everyone can see and hear each other. These benefits are described in the following sections.

Users Feel Respected and Listened To

It can be gratifying to have a roomful of people hanging on your every word and appreciating your insights. Usability specialist Betsy Comstock said it beautifully: "Observers can model through their serious and interested attention the fact that the participant is making a very important contribution to the development of the product" (personal communication).

Especially if the users are already customers, in-room observers can send a powerful and positive message about the team's commitment to improving the product. Even a simple chorus of thank-yous at the end of the session reminds the users that they've made a contribution.

Observers Pay Closer Attention

When I've conducted usability tests in labs with separate observation rooms, I've noticed that as soon as the user does something interesting, the developers immediately start discussing the issue and how to solve it. As a result, they may miss the next several (and possibly more important) issues. With one client, every time I went next door to the observation room to see whether they had any questions, I found them talking on the phone, reading email, passing around the bag of pretzels—pretty much everything but watching the usability test. When observers are in the same room, there are fewer distractions and they tend to pay much closer attention to what the users are doing. (Another solution to this problem is to have a second facilitator sit in the room with the observers.)

Observers Ask More Questions

Although a prepared facilitator will know in advance many of the areas that the product team would like to probe, interesting and unanticipated things happen during usability tests. The nature of paper prototyping makes it a natural technique to use in the earlier stages of design, when the product team is still working out the best approach or perhaps still getting a full grasp of the problem that their interface is a solution for. Sometimes it's valuable for the product team and users to discuss things directly, especially when the facilitator is not a subject matter expert but the users are. Although it's possible for the facilitator to run next door to an observation room (or use a phone or other equipment) to gather questions from observers, I've found that observers in these situations ask fewer questions than when they're in the same room. (Note that it is not appropriate for observers to *interrupt* a task with questions. As mentioned in Chapter 8 the facilitator decides when questions are allowed and how long discussions should continue.)

The Facilitator Can Observe the Observers

Effective usability test facilitation contains a feedback loop: Users provide data to developers; developers respond by taking notes, through body language, and by asking questions; and the *facilitator makes adjustments* to help the observers get the most out of the session. For example, I might see that all the observers are busily writing notes. This lets me know that they've noticed an important issue, so I might slow down the pace until they've captured it. (Plus, I don't have to harp on that issue later—I know they've gotten the message.) On the other hand, if observers are sitting there passively, either they already have ample data on the issue or the current line of investigation isn't of interest. Knowing that, I can respond by assisting the user, moving to a different task, or changing the topic of discussion.

The facilitator should be aware of how observers are reacting and make adjustments accordingly. (Illustration by Rene Rittiner.)

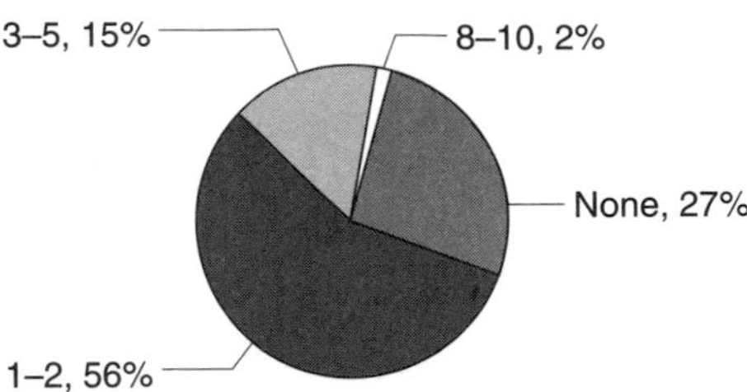

Figure 10.1 Answers to the survey question, "What is the maximum number of observers that you feel are appropriate to have in the same room with the user(s) during paper prototype tests?"

My effectiveness as a facilitator is hampered if I can't see how the observers are reacting—I'm dealing with an open feedback loop. My worst example was when I went next door to the observation room at the end of a test to see if the observers had any questions, and instead of the half-dozen people I was expecting, there was *no one* there. I had no idea when or why they had left, what they'd seen, or if anyone had bothered to take notes. I felt like that lonely tree that fell in the forest.

There Are No Hidden Watchers

Although you might assume that it's more intimidating to have observers present, some users have told me the opposite—the thought of hidden watchers can be unnerving. At the time of this writing, many companies are clarifying their policies regarding the use of personal information collected from customers. In the future, as people become more savvy about their rights to safeguard their information and privacy, it is possible that unseen observers and videotaping may become less acceptable to people than they are today. On the other hand, if video surveillance of public places becomes more common, people may come to think of their lives as one big reality TV show. Either way, the social and legal issues around this question bear watching (no pun intended).

Concerns about In-Room Observers

Figure 10.1 shows how 169 usability professionals answered a question about in-room observers. As you can see, most respondents feel that it's acceptable to have a few in-room observers, but not a lot. As Table 10.1 shows, the concerns I've heard about in-room observers fall into three categories.

Table 10.1 Concerns about In-Room Observers

Concern	*Explanation*	*Discussion*
Disruptive observer behavior	Observers may not behave appropriately, interrupting to help the user, defending the design, expressing dismay that the person doesn't "get it," etc.	This can indeed be a problem, but it's a solvable one. Observers can be trusted to behave appropriately, especially when they are taught about the effects of their behavior on users. After all, we're talking about fully functioning adult members of society here, not a troupe of baboons.
Changing user behavior	In a paper prototype test, the Computer and facilitator are necessarily present. But having nonparticipating observers may cause users to behave differently than they normally would—inhibiting their willingness to explore, causing them to be less forthcoming with criticism, etc.	It's always good to question how your methods may affect your results. Effects due to observers can't be eliminated because users must be told if the session is videotaped and/or that people are watching from elsewhere. In practice I find that properly briefed users are quite willing to offer feedback, so I'm not worried about that issue. Other effects attributable to in-room observers are certainly possible, but practically speaking I don't think they would reverse many of the findings I've seen from paper prototype usability tests. Chapter 13 talks more about various sources of bias, including some that I think are more problematic than in-room observers.

Continued

Table 10.1 Concerns about In-Room Observers—cont'd

Concern	*Explanation*	*Discussion*
User stress (a.k.a. ethics)	Users may feel uncomfortable being under close scrutiny, especially when (not if, since it almost always happens) they are confused about something or get stuck.	True, and this is the bottom line. Causing the users more stress than they have consented to would be at odds with the ethics of usability testing. You have to make your decision about in-room observers based on your best understanding of the benefits/risks, the personalities of the individuals involved, and your own comfort level (it's difficult to make someone feel at ease in a situation where you're uncomfortable yourself). Ethical questions are complicated, so talking them over with colleagues is a good idea.

Learning from Disaster

On weekends I teach beginners how to ride motorcycles according to a curriculum developed by the Motorcycle Safety Foundation (MSF). The MSF course draws heavily from the findings of a 1981 research study of motorcycle accidents in California.* For every significant accident cause, the course has corresponding material aimed at reducing that risk. For example, the study found that in two thirds of multiple-vehicle accidents, the driver of the other vehicle violated the motorcyclist's right of way. Thus, the course discusses several ways for a motorcyclist to be more visible to other drivers.

Although I haven't done a scientific study of in-room observers, I try to copy the MSF approach—whenever I hear about a "crash" (unpleasant incident) that was caused by an observer, I ask myself whether my methods (the observer rules discussed later) are theoretically able to prevent it. In doing research for this book, I deliberately set out to collect the worst examples I could find about in-room observers, and the three on pp. 227–228 are typical.

---

* The study's informal name, "The Hurt Report," refers not to its ominous subject matter but to its lead researcher, Dr. Harry Hurt of the University of Southern California.

From the Field: In-Room Observer War Stories

Anecdote	**My Comments**
"I remember one unfortunate incident. One of the observers was a technical documentation person who had written the installation manual for a product whose installation we were testing. He got very frustrated that the users were having trouble, but were not using the manual. At one point he said loudly and angrily, 'But they're not even using the manual!' The users felt bad and started using the manual (obviously a departure from their natural behavior)." *Betsy Comstock, Polycom*	*This observer hadn't been told that it's possible to gather data about what should go in the manual without having the users actually use it. I also would have discussed the "game plan" with him to get his agreement on when/if users would specifically be asked to use the manual.* *And Betsy concurs: "I learned to more carefully instruct the observers about the purposes of the testing, how to behave during a session, and what their expectations should be about the use of the data."*
"A couple of years ago, one of the stakeholders insisted on being in the room while the user testing took place. The test team didn't think it was a good idea, and we did caution the person not to interrupt what was going on and not to react to anything that happened. During one of the tests, a user hesitated and then chose an option that we hadn't anticipated. The facilitator was waiting to see what happened next. The stakeholder got up, strode across the room and informed the user, 'That's not how it's done—*here's* how it's done' and proceeded to demonstrate the interaction as we had designed it." *Professor Rosalee Wolfe, DePaul University*	*Here's my favorite line for preventing observers from helping: "Once you start explaining the interface, you no longer have a usability test but a very expensive training session."* *And this observer learned this. As Rosalee reports, "To the stakeholder's credit, this person has since embraced our efforts after we explained the value of letting a user struggle. Now the person is able to be in the room and observe without interrupting the test. As a bonus, this person now takes excellent notes."*

Continued

From the Field: In-Room Observer War Stories—cont'd

"I often conduct usability studies with observers in the room. One day we were testing a feature that 'Joe' had put together. The participant was running into all the same problems as the previous participants. At some point, Joe just couldn't take the fact that people didn't know how to use his feature at all. He stood up, pointed at the participant, and started yelling, saying that he was too stupid to use our software or to have the job he was in. I was finally able to get Joe to sit down and be quiet and work on calming down the participant and building his ego back up. In the end, everything was fine but it was an eye opener for me on what can happen during a study like that. (Yes, Joe had been briefed that he wasn't allowed to talk.) The participant is still a customer, luckily."

Anonymous

This story underlines how stressful usability testing can be for the observers. Part of the facilitator's responsibility includes not making the observers feel picked on. After seeing the same issues a few times, I might have asked Joe if we had enough data from that task and then substituted a different one. Although Joe's frustration is understandable, his means of expressing it is extreme—I've worked with hundreds of observers and never seen behavior like this. Joe may have had an anger management problem or otherwise lacked the social skills to relate well to people. If I knew there was a "Joe" on the team, I would ask some of the observers sit in another room and tactfully suggest to Joe that he might find it less frustrating to observe from afar.*

* Oddly enough, Joe later decided to change careers and become a minister. We wish him well in his new vocation.

Keep in mind that the potential for observers to wreak havoc doesn't magically vanish when you confine them to an observation room. Colleagues have told me about observers who disrupted usability tests by laughing loudly (most observation rooms aren't soundproof), barging into the test room to explain something to the user, or even throwing M&M candies at the one-way mirror. So no matter where the observers are located, it's important to brief them on appropriate behavior.

Who *Shouldn't* Be in the Room

It may not be appropriate to have a particular observer present if that person's presence might be intimidating to users. In one usability study I conducted, the users were subscribers to a professional magazine and one of the observers was a highly regarded editor of that magazine. The users knew the editor by reputation, although none had actually met him. We decided to have the editor observe the tests from the room next door so that his demigod presence wouldn't cow the users.

Similarly, you should tread carefully in any situation in which a user and observer know each other, especially if there is a difference in power (manager-subordinate) or an ongoing relationship (account manager-customer). In these situations, unless both parties agree that they're fine with the idea, it's best to ask the potentially intimidating observer not to attend that test.

Weighing Risks and Rewards

Many activities, whether professional or personal, have both risks and rewards—investing in the stock market, having a baby, and starting a business all come readily to mind. Intelligent people study the inherent risks, seek ways to minimize them, and then weigh them against the rewards before making a decision.

I'm a firm believer that it's okay to have observers sit in the same room with the users. This is how I learned to conduct usability tests, and I've done it successfully hundreds of times. In my experience, the benefits are considerable and the risks avoidable. Although I don't expect that everyone will agree with me, I do hope that a better understanding of in-room observers will encourage others to try this approach.

Thus far, the discussion of in-room observers applies equally to both paper prototyping and computer-based usability tests. But with a paper prototype test, there are always going to be at least a couple people in the room with the users, namely the Computer(s) and facilitator. Even if the observers will sit elsewhere, I recommend that the Computer and facilitator understand the risks and benefits discussed in this chapter. And given that paper prototyping is inherently a social activity, I don't believe that the *incremental* risks associated with a few well-behaved observers are compelling enough to outweigh the benefits that can be realized by face-to-face contact between those who develop interfaces and those who use them.

The Rules

Allowing observers to interact willy-nilly with the users is a recipe for disaster. Assuming you'd like to have observers in the same room, let's take a look at how to

manage them effectively. I require that everyone, even the CEO, attend a pretest briefing where I hand out and explain the following list of rules (also available at *www.paperprototyping.com*). Observers who haven't been briefed can't sit in the room—they are loose cannons and I have no idea what they might do.

Rules for Usability Test Observers

Everyone who observes a usability test is asked to abide by a set of rules. The purpose of these rules is to minimize stress for the test participants and to maximize the amount of information we get from the usability tests.

Stay for the Entire Test

The goal is to have the users forget that anyone else is in the room. Having people constantly coming in and out is distracting, and users may get the mistaken impression that you're leaving because they've done something wrong (like walking out in the middle of a movie). While you are observing a test, you are not available for any interruption short of an emergency. If you can attend only part of a test, discuss this with the facilitator beforehand to determine whether there is a way to accommodate this.

Please turn off cell phones and pagers!

Remain Silent While the Users Are Working

Usability testing gives you a whole new perspective on the interface. You may notice a problem so surprising that you are tempted to laugh or exclaim out loud. This is not unusual.

Unfortunately, the users might think you are laughing at them. Please do your best to keep as quiet as possible. The facilitator will give you opportunities to ask questions after each task and at the end of the test. If you have something to tell/ask that truly can't wait, pass a note to the facilitator. (Exception: If a user intentionally says something funny, it's okay to laugh!)

Be Conscious of Your Body Language

Although most usability tests are interesting, not every moment will be fascinating. If something is happening that isn't of interest to you but may be to others, sit quietly without fidgeting. (If inactivity makes you sleepy, one trick is to write down every word that users say.) But if you already thoroughly understand the issue that the users are stuck on and would like to see them move on to the next task, pass a note to the facilitator.

Don't Reveal How Many Tasks We Have

We may well run out of time before users finish all the tasks. If users get stuck on a task, that means that there is a wealth of information we should be fervently taking notes on. It is often more useful to explore an area of difficulty in detail rather than try to "get through" all the tasks. The facilitator will keep an eye on the clock so that we can cover as many of the important areas as possible.

No Helping

During the test, it's likely that users will have problems using the interface, and it is normal to feel a temptation to help. Please don't. Instead, try to understand why it was that the user got stuck or went down the wrong path. It's the facilitator's role to get users back on track if they get really stuck. And if the facilitator poses a question during the test, he or she is asking the users, not you—please don't answer unless the facilitator specifically directs a question to you.

Avoid "Design Questions"

You will have an opportunity to ask questions after each task. Questions that ask the user their opinions about how to design aspects of the application (such as, "Where would *you* like to see these navigation buttons?") can take a lot of time to answer and produce only limited results. Instead, focus on trying to understand the *problem*—we'll come up with solutions later, outside the test.

Respect Participants and the Confidentiality of Their Data

We have promised the participants that their participation is confidential. This means that we should not include their names in any reports or other communication such as email, and we should refrain from discussing them by name outside the test setting. Do not make negative comments about people—there is always a risk that a derogatory comment could be overheard or otherwise make its way back to the user.

How to Explain the Rules to Observers

I suppose I could just hand observers the Rules and say, "Do this or else!" But people are more likely to adhere to the spirit of the rules when they understand their purpose and importance. So I start out very seriously. A good way to drive home the purpose of the rules is to describe a worst-case scenario, like the one that happened to Jared Spool (see the From the Field box on p. 232). Empathizing with the user's shame and embarrassment creates a "teachable moment" where people are much more inclined to think about the consequences of their behavior.

From the Field: The User Who Cried

"I once had a user cry during a usability test. This was years ago, before I had much experience with usability testing. Basically, it happened because we'd done just about everything wrong. When our scheduled user didn't show up, someone grabbed an employee to fill in, without explaining what the session was about—that was the first mistake. Turns out it was this woman's first day on the job, and we figured she'd be a good candidate because she knew absolutely nothing about the product. Not only did she know nothing about the product, but it wasn't even in her area of expertise—she didn't fit the user profile at all. That was the second mistake. There were a bunch of observers sitting in the room who hadn't been briefed on how to behave (third mistake), including the woman's manager (fourth mistake). And last but not least, we hadn't done a rehearsal beforehand, so we didn't realize that the first task we wanted the user to do was, in fact, impossible.

"Once the user started running into difficulty, everyone except for her quickly realized that the task was ridiculous, and they all started laughing at their own stupidity. Unfortunately, the user thought they were laughing at her and she started crying. We all felt horrible, and after that I took the time to hand out a written set of rules and go over them with every observer before they're allowed to sit in the room. Thankfully, nothing like this has ever happened to me again."

Jared M. Spool, User Interface Engineering (www.uie.com)

I don't usually find it necessary to discuss each rule in detail, but there is no harm in doing so, especially when usability testing is new to a company. (I usually do remind people that when I ask a question, I'm asking the users. Otherwise, it's common for a helpful team member to pipe up with the answer.)

As an outside consultant I have the advantage (deserved or not) of coming into a company as the de facto expert in usability, and as a result I find that observers are willing to follow my instructions. But if you are self-taught in usability and everyone on your team knows it, that kind of credibility—and the authority that accompanies it—may be a bit harder to come by. One excellent suggestion from veteran usability specialist Chauncey Wilson is to have observers sign a copy of the rules once they've read and understood them. Chauncey notes, "The commitment of a signature seems to work, even with senior managers." To put it another way, it turns the situation from "You must do as I tell you," into "I agree that these are the ideals we're trying to uphold." Another tactic for raising awareness is to ask the observers to brainstorm what might happen if someone violated each of the rules.

Observers Are People Too

Right before a usability test, a developer once joked with me that he wished he had a cast iron lining in his stomach because he was so nervous about what the test would reveal. This from a guy who wholeheartedly supported the idea of usability testing, and after the first couple of tests had found only minor problems! With all the focus on users, it's easy to lose sight of the fact that observers have feelings too.

Usability tests can be nerve-wracking, especially to those who had a direct hand in designing the interface. So I end my observer briefing by acknowledging that a usability test can be stressful and frustrating for observers as well as for users. As a facilitator, my job isn't to beat up the interface (and, by proxy, the people who designed it) but to shed light on what's happening inside the users' heads. I emphasize that part of our purpose is to find the parts of the prototype that are working well, not just the flaws. This is something that's easy for beginning facilitators to forget in their enthusiasm for uncovering problems.

In June 2001 Bruce Tognazzini wrote a brilliant, biting, and all-too-true column on this subject called "How to Write a Report without Getting Lynched." It's on his Web site at ***www.asktog.com****. His opening sentence is, "The finest set of recommendations will be rejected if the form in which they are received is seen as hostile or belligerent." This article should be required reading for anyone who conducts usability tests or reports their results.*

When to Brief Observers

For several years, I made it a point to brief all observers right before every test, just to be on the safe side. Although I no longer think this is necessary, I might still do this if there were individuals I was concerned about but didn't want to single out. What I usually do now is designate one or two 10-minute briefings on the first test day—maybe one first thing in the morning and one after lunch—and tell observers that they must attend one of them before coming to a test. If someone can't attend a briefing, I'll either arrange a special briefing for that person or I'll "deputize" a trusted observer to do so.

Relaxing the Rules

When I'm not busy conducting usability tests, one of my hobbies is motorcycling. I've found that the best passengers are those who are just a little bit scared because they will do *exactly what I tell them.* But if they get too relaxed back there, they're more likely to do something dangerous. The worst passenger I ever had was a proficient rider who was so comfortable that he kept forgetting his actions affected my control of the bike—like the time he leaned over to scratch his ankle and almost dumped us both onto the pavement.

I've seen a similar problem with usability test observers. Most observers are initially conscientious about their behavior, especially after hearing the story of The User Who Cried, and they follow the rules to the letter. But sooner or later the observers become comfortable with the test format, and they start to bend the rules. It starts in fairly innocuous ways, such as interrupting a task with, "Can I ask just one question?" (It's difficult to say no because the observer genuinely wants to know, and I've never been able to bring myself to use the flippant response, "Yes, and you just did.")

But this is a slippery slope, and it can affect the facilitator's control of the test session. One or two interruptions may not spell disaster, but they open the door to similar behavior that eventually might. The worst case I experienced was when observers managed to start separate conversations with the two users, and the test fragmented into a rudderless meeting. After that incident, I carefully rebriefed the team again, telling them, "Even though we're quite comfortable with how a usability test works, we have to remember that it's all new to the users." This line is a good reminder to experienced observers that their behavior can have consequences they didn't intend.

Having said all this, sometimes no harm comes from relaxing the rules a bit, especially if there are only a couple of observers, it's a Friday afternoon, and the users are in a jovial mood. In a case like this I sometimes allow a bit more conversation and even an occasional interruption. But the facilitator retains the right to allow or prohibit this to the extent that he or she feels is appropriate. With new observers (or facilitators), it's best to manage the user-observer interactions strictly at first—it's easier to relax discipline than it is to make it more stringent.

Working up to In-Room Observers

Is there a limit to how many observers you can have? It depends on several factors: the size of the room, whether you're doing co-discovery, the user population, and the experience of the facilitator. Cram six observers into a small room with one timid technophobe and the psychological discomfort will be so palpable that you could cut it into blocks and build a retaining wall. But put those same six observers in a larger conference room with a pair of confident domain experts and the session is likely to be relaxed and fun. My rule of thumb is about half a dozen team members (including the Computer and facilitator) per user, although sometimes I have allowed more. In practice it's rarely feasible to have more than 10 observers because it's too difficult for them to see the prototype.

As Figure 10.1 shows, my position on in-room observers is at the upper end of the spectrum compared with that of many of my peers. However, I have a decade of experience in training observers and in helping users feel at ease. One way to get started is to have a small number of observers—one or two—in the room, and the rest elsewhere. Start by inviting the people you think will be easiest to have in there with you, and afterward have them compare their experiences with those of the people who sat in the other room. People can take turns being in-room observers, and you can gradually increase the limit if and when you are comfortable doing so.

Preparing the Users

It would be inappropriate—not to mention unethical—to lead the user into a roomful of observers that they weren't expecting. (It is equally unethical to not tell the users that they're being watched and/or videotaped.) If you review Chapter 9, you'll notice that the presence of the observers is mentioned to users three times:

1. During recruitment (whether done by you or an outside agency)
2. In the informed consent form
3. During the pretest briefing given by the facilitator

In essence, users should have several opportunities to opt themselves out of the experience (or at least find out more about it) if they're concerned that it might be uncomfortable. If for any reason you are concerned about a particular user group or test setting, be proactive about dealing with it ahead of time. For example, when testing a health information Web site, I was worried how users would feel about discussing their personal health issues in front of a roomful of strangers. A market research firm had recruited the users, but I also called them to explain the test setting and find out what topics they'd feel comfortable discussing. In the tests, I was amazed at how relaxed the users seemed, and I believe this was partly due to the extra time I spent explaining the social nature of the setting and double-checking that they were okay with the topics we planned to cover.

Observer-User Interactions: Questions to Avoid

I think it's great for observers to directly ask questions of the users, for the kinds of reasons described earlier in the "benefits" section—for example, the facilitator can't know all the questions in advance. But observers need some guidance to understand the difference between a good question and a bad one. A bad question is one that

- Reveals the answer.
- Belongs in a focus group.
- Asks users to imagine.
- Asks users to explain their cognitive process.

Each of these is discussed further.

Questions That Reveal the Answer

For some reason, the way that a question naturally pops into one's mind is usually not the best way to ask it. For example, "Was it clear to you that Purge would delete all the records?" reveals to the user what the desired answer is. To avoid doing this, one trick I've learned is to formulate the question mentally, pay attention to the second half of it (where the true question usually lies), and then turn it around so that it's nonleading, for example,

Original question: "Was it clear to you that Purge would delete all the records?"

(Hmm, second half says: "Purge deletes all the records." Oops, I don't want to tell them what Purge does, I want to ask them.)

Reformulated question: "What did you think Purge would do?" Possible follow-up if needed: "And what did it do?"

Learning to ask questions in this manner takes practice, so it's unfair to expect perfection from anyone, including the facilitator. If someone accidentally asks a leading question and the user spits back the encapsulated answer, it just means that you can't draw any conclusions from it. But sometimes the user will bail you out by saying, "You know, that never occurred to me—what I really thought was . . ." And then you *can* trust the answer, despite the leading question.

Questions That Belong in a Focus Group

Usability tests of paper prototypes are not an especially good way to gather data about whether users like a product concept enough to buy it, how much they'd pay for it, and so on. In a usability test, the primary purpose is to determine how well the interface does what users need it to do, and often you also end up learning valuable things you didn't know about the users and their requirements. To gather this kind of information, you need to remain open to all feedback, both positive and negative. Once you start asking questions like how much they'd pay for the product, the nature of the discussion changes from "How can we make this better for you?" to "How can we sell this to you?" Users will recognize that you've put on your sales and marketing hat, and it may affect the nature of the feedback that you get from that point on. Even if you reserve these questions until the very end, usability testing is an inefficient way to get this kind of data because you've got one or two users and several product team members—in a focus group, the ratio is reversed.

Questions That Ask Users to Imagine

Beware of questions that take the form, "What if we did X and Y. Would that be better?" Unless it's something you're showing to the user, you're asking the user to use his or her imagination to envision the improvements. But it's hard to know whether the user is envisioning the same thing as you are or shares your understanding of the terms you're using—every profession has its jargon and high tech

What the Developer Asks

The questions we ask sometimes aren't the same as the ones users hear. (Illustration by Rene Rittiner.)

has more than its fair share. To the user, these questions tend to sound like, "If we made it better, would you like it more?" They'll answer yes, but this tells you nothing. The risk is that you might go to a lot of work to implement something that doesn't help users.

Questions That Ask Users to Explain Their Cognitive Process

My favorite bad example: "Did you click that Sign up button because it's yellow?" Human beings are notoriously bad at explaining their own cognitive processes. Very often we can't articulate why we did something, or in our desire to please we may invent post-facto explanations for our behavior that have nothing to do with reality. It's usually best to watch what people do and listen to what they say as they're trying to do it (which helps you understand their intent) but not to ask them to dissect their behavior and come up with a reason for each action.

Ever been on a camping trip and tried to hang up a flashlight? Those clever little ones have a hole in their base designed for exactly that purpose, but in the dark it's almost impossible to put a string through it—no matter how you manipulate the flashlight, the light insists on shining out the opposite end from where you want it. That's kinda what it's like to examine your own cognitive process—by the very act of trying to shed light on it, the part you're interested in slips into darkness.

What Observers Should Do

So far, this chapter has been primarily about the things that observers shouldn't do. But there is one very important thing that they *should* be doing: taking notes. The next chapter explains how to take good notes and what to do with them afterward.

Chapter 11

Data: Capturing, Prioritizing, and Communicating

So far this book has been about the paper prototype and the people involved in creating and testing it. But the heart of a usability study is its data—all the stuff that you learn. This chapter looks at some ways of capturing the data from paper prototype usability tests and what to do with it afterward. The ultimate purpose of collecting usability data is to make the interface better, so a good method is one that accomplishes this goal quickly and effectively. Naturally, every company is different, so a technique that is ideal for one product team may be unsuitable for another.

Capturing the Data (Note-Taking)

I ask all usability test observers to take notes. Not only does this ensure that we capture as much information as possible for the debriefing meeting (which I discuss in this chapter), but it also helps the observers focus on what the users are doing.

What Observers Should Look For

For starters, give each observer a copy of the tasks, especially if you've filled in the Notes section of the template as described in Chapter 6. This information will help observers understand the purpose of each task and some of the specific things you want to look for. If all the observers had a direct hand in creating the paper prototype, they'll already have plenty of their own questions, so you might not have to brief them on what to look for. However, if there are observers who were less involved, you might want to fill them in on the issues that arose during your walkthroughs.

But in general, what should observers look for? Cases where users are confused, don't understand a term, or misconstrue a concept are quite common and worth writing down. User quotes are often useful. Anything that surprises you is likely to be important because it indicates that users are behaving differently than you expected—if you expected the users to zig and they zagged instead, there's something going on at that decision point that you should understand better. And last, but not least, it's important to note the things that worked well in the interface so that you don't waste time redesigning something that doesn't really need it.

I occasionally find it helpful to give some observers specific assignments: "Gina, you watch whether they use context-sensitive help. Ali, you write down every error message the Computer gives them out loud." I tend to do this when the observers are unfamiliar with the interface (it gives them a productive way to become involved) or when the team has a lot of specific questions.

Observation, Inference, and Opinion

It sounds like a tautology to say that observers should write down observations, but in my experience some people don't understand what that means. It's important for observers to record data in a form that won't be subject to contentious debate later. It's natural for us to filter information through our own set of ideas and prejudices, but this subjectivity means you're now dealing with opinion rather than data—and you probably had all the opinions before you got started. So let's look at the differences between an observation, an inference, and an opinion.

Observations are objective, factual statements of something the user said or did. Observations are the "what," "when," and "how" of the action, for example, "User chose Landscape orientation," or "User said, 'I can't tell what it did.'" Observations by their nature are not subject to debate—any two people who watch the same test should theoretically walk away with the same set of observations. (In practice, they won't, because it's not possible to write down everything, so each observer chooses a subset of observations based on perceived importance.) Most of your usability test notes should consist of observations—what did the users type, click, and say? But observations do not describe the why, in other words, the causes, of problems or anything that goes on inside users' heads. Those are inferences.

Inferences are conclusions based on some observations and possibly some assumptions as well. Examples of inferences are "User is lost" or "This dialog box is confusing." Unlike observations, inferences are not fact; two observers can and do draw opposite inferences from exactly the same observations. As a way of checking whether something is an observation or an inference, ask yourself, "How do I know that?" If it could be verified from a videotape exactly as you've described it, it's probably an observation. But if it contains an assumption about what was going on inside the user's head, it is probably an inference. For example, the statement "He likes this version better" is an inference unless the user actually *said,* "I like this version better," in which case then it is indeed an observation.

An **opinion** is something you think should be done about your inferences or observations, such as, "Search results should by sorted by increasing price" or "We need to show an example." (The words *should* and *need* are often clues that you've written an opinion in your notes.) Ideas that occur to you during usability tests are not necessarily bad, but you don't want to confuse them with things that users have asked for.

Note: Sometimes I do deliberately include inferences or opinions in my notes, but I flag them (for example, with "???" or "idea") so that I know these are just my thoughts, not necessarily reality.

If you're not aware of these distinctions, especially between observations and inferences, it's easy to confuse them when looking back over your notes. The problem with inferences and opinions is that two observers can see the same thing but put a different spin on it. Here's an example of several possible inferences that could be drawn from one observation:

Observation: User paused for several seconds before entering "My IRA" in the Description field for the account.

Inference 1: He didn't know whether the description was required.

Inference 2: He wasn't sure whether spaces were okay.

Inference 3: He wondered whether this description would appear in his portfolio instead of the account name.

Inference 4: He wasn't confused; he was just deciding what to call it.

And so on. As you can see, the people making these inferences have drawn very different conclusions about what the problem is (or whether there is one) and will go on to formulate different opinions about how to solve it. Thus, I think of inferences and opinions as "argument seeds" planted in one's notes, because they're likely to sprout into disagreement later.

A good test facilitator encourages users to articulate what they're thinking and doing, thus turning what would otherwise be inferences into observations. (This is the essence of the sportscaster role.) For example, if the user paused for more than a few seconds, the facilitator might ask, "What's going through your mind right now?" The user's answer should reveal which of these situations is happening.

Inferences and opinions in your notes are "argument seeds," likely to sprout into disagreement later.

At some point you probably do want to start determining the possible causes of problems, but it's best to wait until the debriefing meeting to do this. Let's assume that everyone wrote down the observation that the user paused. Some possible reasons for this might be supported by additional observations; for example, if the user later said, "Good, it took it" then that observation might support inference 2 about whether the description could include spaces. Sometimes there will still be disagreements, but if everyone offers their inferences as fact, it becomes much harder to figure out what really happened.

I'm not advocating that we should overanalyze everything to ridiculous lengths. I deliberately chose a rather trivial example of a momentary pause to illustrate the point that some problems are more important than others. As I explain later in this chapter, by first prioritizing the issues that were found in the usability tests, the team will avoid dissecting the minor ones.

Overanalyzing details to ridiculous lengths reminds me of the joke about a scientist who takes a train trip with a friend. Gazing at the passing scenery, the friend remarks, "Look, that flock of sheep has just been sheared." The scientist scrutinizes the flock and cautiously assents, "So they appear to have been . . . on this side."

Taking Notes

There is no one right way to take notes—each observer will have his or her own conventions and shorthand. This is fine unless you plan to read each other's notes in their original format, in which case it can be confusing unless you know what each other's conventions are. Table 11.1 shows some notes I took from a usability test of a travel Web site. Other than spell checking and some minor editing for clarity, these are typical of the notes I take. As shown in the Discussion column, subtle wording can mask some of the differences between observations and inferences, and further underscores the risks of interpreting someone else's notes.

Table 11.1 Example Test Observations from a Travel Web Site

Observation (from my notes)	*Discussion*
Next trip he's taking? Going to Chicago in September for a wedding in Barrington. A friend had told him a particular place—Amerisuites. What other factors would he consider? Says he prefers a pool. Wants a restaurant since he's not going to have a car. Shuttle service to the airport would also be good. I ask about price: "I like to be under $100, unless I'm on vacation."	This is the sort of speech I tend to paraphrase—the factors the user is listing give us some background on how he'll approach this task, but in this case his exact words aren't crucial.
Clicks NW suburbs. "It gave me a list of 43 properties, hotels in the northwest region of Illinois. Since I know I'm going to the Amerisuites, I'll probably do a search off the first page." He backs up to try that approach.	Saying that the user backs up is an observation; the reason why is an inference. In this case the user's subsequent actions happened to confirm it, but before the fact it can only be an inference.
Types barrington in city, Hotel name—amerisuites. "That would be a problem if I don't know how to spell it." He knows the exact dates of his trip, enters them in the search.	The phrase "he knows the exact dates" appears to be an inference. However, earlier in the test the user had said when his trip was, so in the larger context of the test this is actually an observation. If I were rewriting this for a report, I would clarify by phrasing it as two observations: "User had mentioned exact dates earlier; he entered those dates in the search."
No matches found. Says he thinks he spelled amerisuites wrong . . . or maybe it's not in Barrington. Gets rid of the hotel name and it returns one property in Barrington.	If the user didn't say what he was thinking, I might write "(Not sure of spelling???)" to indicate that I'm making an inference. If I had asked him, my notes would say, "I ask about spelling."

Laptop versus Hand-Writing

I tell observers to take notes in whatever form is most comfortable for them, and most people bring a notebook and pen. Some teams write their observations directly onto sticky notes, which as I'll explain can give you a leg up on analyzing the results. I prefer to use a laptop for note taking because I type quickly and can capture far more information. The notes I take by hand don't have as much detail, and thus it's easier to blur the difference between observations and inferences.

One potential concern about a laptop is that it can be intimidating or distracting to users, but I haven't found this to be the case. It helps if you:

- **Type quietly.** Some keyboards are noisier than others, and fingernails can make additional noise. The quieter the typing is, the less distracting it is.
- **Type continuously.** If the room is quiet and suddenly I start banging on the keyboard, that could alert the users that they've just done something interesting (which they will probably assume is a mistake). But if I keep up a fairly constant stream of typing, it becomes part of the background noise and thus is less salient.

I've found it useful to learn to type without looking at my screen—not too hard once you accept that you'll make a liberal number of typos; that way you can keep your eyes on the action. (As a note-taking facilitator, I have learned to type one thing while saying another, which is much more difficult and takes practice.) Whether your notes are handwritten or typed, if you follow my suggestion to leave at least 2 hours between usability tests, you should have time to go through your notes. Fill in details and repair any especially unintelligible passages while the events are still fresh in your mind.

Although it is uncommon (it's never happened to me), if a user ever asks to see your notes you should allow this because users have a right to know what data you've collected about them. The implication is that you should never put anything in your notes that you'd be uncomfortable letting users read.

Capturing User Quotes

I tell myself that the user's voice speaks 100 times louder than my own. One or two user quotes are usually worth whole paragraphs of my own opinions about something—it's hard to argue with a good user quote. But even though I type fairly fast, I can't keep up with speech, so sometimes my quotes turn into paraphrases. (For those who don't type fast or want to be certain they've gotten a quote right, a tape recorder might be a useful backup.)

As with observations and inferences, you want to be able to distinguish after the fact which is which, so my convention is to use quotation marks to set off wording that I'm certain I've captured verbatim. When I fall behind and have to start paraphrasing, I'll end the quote but continue with the gist of what the user

The user's voice speaks 100 times louder than my own.

said. Or, sometimes I use ellipsis (. . .) to leave out the words I didn't capture exactly, then pick up the quote farther on. One of the risks of paraphrasing is that it can be hard to tell afterward how accurate you were. One trick I've learned is to use "says" in my notes when the user is talking and I'm fairly certain I'm capturing the meaning but not the exact words—in other words, I believe a videotape would confirm what I'm writing but I wouldn't bet a year's salary on it. If I'm less certain (or am certain that I missed something), I use "Something about . . ." which is a reminder for me later to ask the other observers if they can fill in what I missed.

Including Context

This has happened to me more times than I care to admit: I'll have some awesome quote in my notes such as, "Oh, wow, it's like they read my mind" and 2 days later, *I have no idea what the user was talking about.* In the heat of the moment, between asking questions and listening to answers and all that, I forgot to include enough contextual cues in my notes to reconstruct what happened. In particular, context means keeping track of what screen the users are looking it and what data they enter. You may also want to write down what the facilitator says, to help you distinguish between a spontaneous comment and one that was prompted by a question—the former usually carry more weight.

Debriefing Meeting: Prioritizing the Issues

Usability testing is like getting a drink from a fire hydrant—there's a whole bunch of data, coming at you at high speed. So what do you do with it all? It's important to get the product team together at the end of a usability study and sort out what you learned. Even if you've been listing issues and making changes after each test, it's still useful to step back and look at the larger picture. This happens at the debriefing meeting.

There are two main outputs from the debriefing process: prioritization of the issues and an action plan for addressing them. Some teams do both things at one meeting; if some observers aren't involved in implementing changes, they can participate in the prioritization but leave when you're ready to create the action plan.

Because it's usually not practical for everyone to observe every test, people may arrive at the debriefing meeting with different ideas about what happened.

So the first order of business is to share everyone's observations and agree on priorities. Then and only then should you start discussing what to do about the issues.

Affinity Diagram

A technique called an *affinity diagram* is useful for identifying the patterns in qualitative data. Figure 11.1 shows what one looks like, and Figure 11.2 describes the process (a handout is available at *www.paperprototyping.com*). Here's a brief overview: Everyone picks their top observations from their notes and writes them on individual sticky notes or blank index cards. (At this point I remind people that their inferences and opinions are best saved for later, although inevitably a few of them will creep in.) Tape all the cards to a wall. Everyone reads all the observations, and then you sort them into groups, name each group, and then vote on which group(s) have the greatest impact on the success of the next release.

Figure 11.1 In an affinity diagram, the team sorts individual observations into related groups. Putting flip chart paper on the walls first as shown here makes the whole thing easily portable to another wall.

1. Observers go through their notes and identify the unsolved issues that they believe are most important to the success of the next release. They write those issues, *one per card,* onto index cards (or sticky notes). You may want to have a rule that the number of tests affects the number of cards from each person—perhaps about 5 per test.
2. Tape all the cards to one wall in random order.
3. Everyone reads all the cards. Don't worry about duplicates or issues that were solved by subsequent prototype changes—keep those issues in the process. (Variation: A person who discovers a card that covers the same issue as one of their own is allowed to remove *his or her own* card, but not someone else's.) If people think of additional issues they're allowed to add cards.
4. Sort the cards into groups, *without discussion.* (Discussion doesn't necessarily improve the quality of the end result but it's almost guaranteed to make the process take longer.) Keep the groups far enough apart that it's clear what is grouped with what. If someone disagrees with the way a group has been set up, he or she should simply move the cards. In particular, look for large groups that could be subdivided and small groups that have the same theme. This step ends when all the cards have been placed in a group (a solo card or two is okay) and no one is making further changes to the groups.
5. Using sticky notes (I'll assume yellow ones), name each group. The name should reflect the theme of the group. Each participant has the opportunity to name each group, and each group can have any number of yellow stickies. But if you get to a group and it already has a name that you agree with, there is no need to create a duplicate.
6. Everyone reads all the group names. On a piece of scratch paper, everyone writes down the three groups that they believe have *the greatest impact on the success of the next release.* Ask yourself, "If we had time to address only three of the groups, which three would I pick?" Choose your top three regardless of whether the work must be done by you or others—these priorities are for the project, not individual to-do lists.
7. Voting: Look at your three choices and rank them in order, with 1 being most important. On the yellow stickies, put an X to indicate your third choice, XX for second, and XXX for most important.
8. Find all the yellow stickies containing X's. The number of X's indicates the group's consensus about the priority of that category of issues. If you find duplicate categories, combine them. (If there is disagreement that two categories should be combined—as when one group is a subset of another—it may be more useful to keep them separate.)
9. Reality-check the results by asking, "Does everyone agree that these priorities make sense?" Discuss any dissenting views.
10. Start at the top of the priority list. Discuss each category in turn: the observations it contains, the insights you learned, and (if appropriate given those present) how to solve remaining issues.

Figure 11.2 Affinity Diagram Process

Note: There is no one "right" way to use this method. The steps in Figure 11.2 describe the way I conduct this process with my clients, but I think it's fine to experiment with any variation that also accomplishes the goal of reaching a group consensus. For example, you can use different color stickies to represent different kinds of information, give those on the core team more votes than outsiders, and so on.

An affinity diagram isn't specific to paper prototyping—it's a technique that works well whenever there's a group of people with a lot of information to sort and prioritize. (A client once told me that she uses the affinity diagram technique described in this chapter to make family decisions with her four children!) There are also methods of prioritizing issues other than the affinity diagram; see the following From the Field box.

From the Field: Prioritizing Issues with Sticky Notes

"I ask everyone to write issues on sticky notes as they observe the tests. Afterward, we go around the room. Each person reads through their stack of sticky notes and we agree whether each one is an issue, a bug, or an anomaly. Duplicates are discarded. At the end of this process we have one stack of stickies that's much smaller than the piles we started with. When an issue comes up and it's clear who should solve it, that person gets the sticky note. Sometimes everyone walks away with their set of things to solve, and there's nothing to write up afterward. Other times, we take the single stack of issues and prioritize those by an affinity diagram. The prioritized issues go into a spreadsheet—in a later meeting we'll read through the issues and assign them. This variation is helpful when a lot of data is obtained because it postpones the discussion of how to solve the issues until priorities are agreed upon."

Mary Beth Rettger, The MathWorks

Why a Group Method?

You may wonder why you'd want to do the prioritizing process as a group, especially if there are only a couple of people who'll be implementing the changes. Here are some reasons to consider.

- **Pooling observations.** No one person can take complete and perfect notes. Because each observer captures a different subset of observations, there's less chance that an issue will slip through the cracks.
- **Recognizing patterns.** Most usability test observations are qualitative in nature—they're not something you can measure with a yardstick or a voltmeter. The key to analyzing qualitative data is to identify the patterns over several users' worth of tests. Although I don't know much about pattern recognition as a science, I do know that it's a skill and some people are better at it than others. Similar to how a group stands a better chance of wilderness survival than any of its individual members, having several people look at the big picture usually means a greater chance of correctly identifying the most important issues.
- **Choosing optimal solutions.** It's easy to get focused on your particular area of responsibility and lose sight of the larger picture. When this happens, problems may not get solved in the most effective way. For example, a tech writer's first reaction to an inscrutable error message might be, "Gee, I'd better document that." (Or perhaps, "Let me improve the wording of that error message.") But a developer sitting in the same room might suddenly realize, "You know, I could put a check in the code to prevent that problem from happening at all." Conversely, the team might decide that documenting an issue really is the only feasible way to address it. By having the team discuss the options, there's a better chance of finding an efficient solution. An additional benefit is that the left hand will know what the right hand is doing—if the developer says that the error message will be eliminated, the tech writer won't waste time documenting it.
- **Disseminating results.** The more members of the product team who attend the debriefing, the less need there may be for formal documentation of the results via reports, highlight tapes, or other time-consuming activities.

A Note about Granularity

Some people record their issues directly onto the index cards or sticky notes while they observe the usability tests. I think this is okay, but be aware that it can have an effect on the granularity of the observations you collect. Not all usability issues occur at the level of a confusing field label—some unfold as a series of events over several minutes or longer. For example, perhaps you initially thought that the users made a mistake but later realize that they had a different and valid way of going about the task. I find that I sometimes have to look over a few pages of my notes to piece together an issue that is subtle and/or happened in the context of several screens. If you use stickies to record your notes, it might be a good idea to spread out all your stickies in order, see if any larger issues jump out at you, and if so then summarize them on stickies of their own.

Success Rates and Statistics

You may have noticed that so far I've said little about calculating success rates, error rates, and the like. Although I'm not opposed to metrics and statistics, I have not found them to be especially useful in analyzing the results of paper prototype tests. For example, it's hard to understand the meaning of the statement "Five out of seven users completed task 3 successfully" if the interface was different each time.

But sometimes simple statistics can be helpful in determining the importance of an issue or how to solve it. For example, I might be curious to know how many users looked for a link to the return policy on the shopping cart page, so I might go through my notes and count how many times it happened. Although it's often difficult to know ahead of time what issues you'll want to count (the most interesting ones tend to be the ones you didn't anticipate), if your notes are sufficiently detailed you may be able to extract some useful information. However, I have done this less often in paper prototype studies than when I'm testing a working version of the interface.

Action Plan

I don't believe it's an overstatement to say that you'll never fix all the problems you find from a usability study. It's just not practical to make an interface work perfectly for everyone, all the time; eventually you reach a point of diminishing returns. Your project also has constraints on the time and people resources that can be devoted to making changes.

I'm assuming that you already have some kind of process for managing your product development. I don't want to turn this into a book on project management, but here are a few thoughts to keep in mind as you discuss your action plan with your fellow team members.

- **Consider practicality.** One drawback of paper prototyping is that you can sometimes fix an issue in the prototype in a way that's not practical to implement. It's worth discussing the successful changes to the interface to ensure they are doable. If not, since usability testing gave you a better understanding of the problem, you'll at least be in a position to come up with an alternative idea.

- **Funnel usability issues into your regular process.** As a rule, I don't believe there's much benefit in setting up a separate system for managing usability issues if the people who fix them also do other development activities. Usability issues should be managed the same way as the rest of the work for the project. For example, if you've got the equivalent of a bug database (one company I worked for preferred the more delicate term *incident*), you'll probably want to funnel the unsolved usability issues into it.
- **Don't start tracking too early.** Because paper prototyping is a fast-moving, iterative activity, it can be premature to record every issue in a database—some problems will be fixed before you've even entered them. One company I know of doesn't bother trying to capture the issues until the design has shown signs of stabilizing, at which point they begin entering usability issues in their bug-tracking database.
- **Divide issues into "now" and "later" piles.** If your next release is quickly approaching, you may have to draw firm lines. One useful question is, "Which of these issues are important to the success of the next release?" Anything that doesn't pass that test goes into the bug database at a lower priority.
- **Consider allocating time for usability issues.** One valid concern about usability testing is that it's hard to know ahead of time how long it will take to fix the issues you find. One way to manage this is to set aside a predetermined amount of time to focus on the issues from usability testing—give each person a prioritized list and have them fix as many as they can in a certain amount of time. The interface may still go out the door with known usability problems, but at least you've given it your best shot. (Caveat: This approach only works for non-critical issues, not showstoppers such as "No one can successfully install the product.")

Communicating and Documenting the Results

It usually isn't practical to write a detailed report of paper prototype test results—in 10 years as a usability consultant, I've never done a detailed report for a paper prototype, although I have occasionally written such reports for more formal usability studies. However, it's important to communicate your findings to people who couldn't be there and/or will need the information later. Once you're ready to move into the implementation phase, the paper prototype contains a lot of information that you may need to document in some way. There's additional information in the Computer's head about how the interface behaves, and you don't want to lose that either.

This section contains several ideas for communicating the results of a usability study. They differ in their formality, the situations in which they're useful, and the effort needed to do them. You'll need to consider the particulars of your company culture in deciding which one(s) are right for you.

Top-10 List

The first thing I do after the debriefing meeting is to take the prioritized list of issues and create a short summary of the top issues. Typically I'll write one to two paragraphs about each issue that summarize our discussion from the meeting. The resulting report is usually no more than two to three pages; when I do it in email it's even shorter. For some product teams this is all the reporting that's needed.

Methodology Report

You might find it helpful gather all your methodology-related documents (user profile, screener, tasks, and so on) into one document to make things easier for next time. Because "methodology report" sounds overly stodgy, I sometimes I call this the "paper trail" report. Its primary purpose is to keep you from reinventing wheels because user profiles and tasks can often be reused in subsequent usability studies. Alternatively, you might simply collect all these documents into one (real or virtual) folder for safekeeping.

Highlight Tape

A highlight tape uses clips from the paper prototype tests. I rarely make highlight tapes because they're time-consuming, and they're usually unnecessary if you can get people to observe the tests. So consider this a technique to use only on rare occasions (for example, to accompany a presentation you're giving to 30 co-workers in another city) and make sure you've obtained the users' consent for that purpose.

Walkthrough Video

A walkthrough video can be an efficient means of summarizing what you learned from a paper prototype usability study. A walkthrough video is especially useful when the development team is in multiple locations. I've worked on several projects where the design part of the team was in Boston but the developers were in California, Russia, or Israel. Unlike a highlight tape, a walkthrough video is scripted and it shows a member of the development team instead of real users.

To make a walkthrough video, first jot down what you want to cover—how users reacted to various aspects of the interface, what you changed, how successful those changes were, and so on. Then turn on the video camera, focus it on the prototype, and start doing a show-and-tell explanation of what you learned. (If the development team is located in another country, consider making the tape in their native language.) There's no need to do everything in one take, so stop the camera whenever you need to gather your thoughts. A typical walkthrough video is 10 to 15 minutes long and can be created in an hour or so.

Interface Specification

To some extent, a paper prototype itself is a kind of an interface specification because it is a collection of screens. But you might need to tie the images together in a way that shows the sequence, with explanations of behaviors and underlying processing. A quick-and-dirty way to do this is to scan the prototype pieces and use them in the spec. The image quality will leave something to be desired, but this method is fast. Alternatively, some companies render the prototype pieces in a way that shows the final appearance—this takes more time, but sometimes high-fidelity visuals are needed, especially if an outside group is doing the implementation. Companies differ in the degree of detail they require in specifications, but ask yourself whether the paper prototype might be a useful starting point.

Documentation of the Interface Behavior

Paper prototypes show the elements of an interface. But information about how those elements interact—as well as the behavior of hard-to-prototype elements such as cursors—is often found only in the head of the Computer. A team at The MathWorks created a method for capturing and managing this information. During prototyping and design sessions, team decisions about how the prototype would behave were recorded on index cards ("When the user clicks, the selection rectangle recenters."). During usability testing, the team looked for places where hard-to-prototype behavior was confusing or hadn't been clarified, such as how to make a control point visible on top of a complex image. They created additional index cards for these.

The original intent of the index cards was as a way to track problems to be solved, as well as to help translate the users' actions into specific functions in the technical design document. (As it turned out, they made a good "cheat sheet" for the Computer as well.) But the quality engineer and the documentation writer for the project—both of whom were involved in the prototyping exercise—found additional ways to use the index cards. By the time the developers created a working version of the software, the quality engineer had used the cards to create a test plan and the documentation writer had a first draft of the tool's documentation.

Summary

The seven chapters in this part have walked you through the process of planning a usability study, creating tasks and the prototype, conducting usability tests, and using the results. In a nutshell, this is what I do as a usability consultant. The nuances can take years to master, but my hope is that I've given you enough information and confidence to get started. Don't forget that more resources can be found in the References section and on the Web site. Good luck!

Part III

Deciding Whether to Use Paper

Now that you know the basics of conducting a paper prototype usability study, it's time to revisit the larger questions about when and if this makes sense for your project. Paper prototyping, like any technique, works well in some situations but may not provide sufficient value in others. The next three chapters give you a more in-depth look at the strengths and weaknesses of paper prototyping, the political issues you may face when introducing paper prototyping into your organization, and factors that can argue for or against the use of paper prototypes in real-world project situations.

Chapter 12

What Paper Is (and Isn't) Good For

Saying that paper prototyping is a good technique is like saying that hiking boots are a good type of footwear—you have to specify *for what purpose.* Hiking boots are great for a walk in the woods, but they'd suck for ballet. In this chapter I discuss the kinds of problems paper prototyping is likely and unlikely to find in an interface. I also describe some issues for which usability testing in general (whether paper or computer) is not the best means of discovery.

Dimensions of a Prototype

So exactly what is a prototype, anyway? I know that's a funny question to be posing this far through a book on paper prototyping, but understanding the nature of a prototype helps you decide what method is suitable for what you need to learn. In essence, a prototype is a representation of a design concept, but that definition is too high-level to provide much insight, so let's break it down.

Prototype Fidelity: A Misleading Concept

First, I want to describe a way of classifying prototypes that I have found to be more problematic than useful, although I still hear it used fairly often. Years ago I was taught to think in terms of "high-fidelity" (hi-fi) and "low-fidelity" (low-fi) prototypes. In his paper, Tullis (1990) defines fidelity* by how it appears to the

---

* Strangely enough, a few years after he started using the term *fidelity,* Tom Tullis went to work at Fidelity Investments. Coincidence? Clairvoyance? Or even . . . conspiracy?

user, which may or may not reflect the extent of the working technology supporting it. Hi-fi prototypes were coded to look and act a lot like the real thing, perhaps using some kind of prototyping software. They were often good enough to be mistaken for the actual interface. Low-fi prototypes, on the other hand, were obviously faked—no one who sees a Computer shuffling pieces of paper thinks they're looking at software.

Although fidelity is a useful concept, it's misleading to apply it to an entire prototype because fidelity takes what is actually several dimensions and rolls them up into one. This can lead to confusion—person A's definition of a low-fi prototype may be significantly different than person B's without either of them being aware of it. To avoid this confusion, I've stopped using the term *fidelity* when I'm referring to an entire prototype. I use it only when I'm referring to a specific aspect of the prototype; for example, a screen created using graphics software has a high-fidelity *look*. And whenever I hear "low-fidelity prototype," I'm careful to find out what the speaker or author means by that term.

Four Dimensions of a Prototype

So let's expand this one-dimensional view of prototyping. There are different ways to look at prototypes, but the one I've found most useful consists of four dimensions—breadth, depth, look, and interaction (I got this idea from the 1996 paper by Virzi, Sokolov, and Karis). As you'll see, some of these prototype dimensions are more important than others in terms of helping you answer the questions you have about *your* interface.

Breadth

*Breadth** refers to the percentage of the product's functionality that is represented in the prototype. Some prototypes contain all the functionality that will be present in the real design, whereas others have only a subset. In terms of usability testing, a prototype needs sufficient breadth to cover the tasks that have been created, but usually not much more.

Breadth is a relatively easy concept to understand, but it's not especially interesting to our discussion because any kind of prototype can be broad or narrow.

---

* If you read my descriptions of breadth and depth and wonder, "Isn't she talking about horizontal and vertical prototypes?" the answer is essentially yes. The terms *horizontal* and *vertical* are common in prototyping literature—I chose to use *breadth* and *depth* simply because it's more expedient to use nouns for the dimensions instead of adjectives.

Regardless of the method you're using, there is a fairly linear relationship between breadth and the effort required to create the prototype—if you want a broader prototype, you'll have to do more work. Although this factor is certainly important to an understanding of prototypes, for the most part I'm going to ignore breadth because it doesn't help us differentiate and choose among prototyping methods.

Depth

As Joel Spolsky said in Chapter 3, the user interface is only the tip of the software iceberg—beneath the surface are databases, networks, security, error handling, hardware, and more. The degree to which these things are in place is depth. Whereas breadth relates to the percentage of functionality that is represented, depth is the extent to which that functionality is fleshed out and, well, functional.

By *depth,* I mean not only the level of detail that's implemented but also its robustness. Say there are 10 options that users could choose from a drop-down list. One low-depth prototype might be hard-coded to ignore what users pick; it assumes that a particular choice has been made. Another low-depth prototype might allow users to pick any of the 10 options, but half of them cause the prototype to crash because they are incompatible with other choices users have made. From the perspective of users who choose one of those unsupported options, the net effect is the same: The interface doesn't do what they told it. On the other hand, a high-depth prototype would have logic and error handling to gracefully prevent, detect, or explain any combination of choices that didn't make sense. Thus, the high-depth prototype would proceed in accordance with what users chose.

Depth turns out to be a key factor in usability testing because it affects the amount of exploration the user can do. Experimentation is a part of learning, and depth (along with breadth) is the factor that makes it possible. Without sufficient depth, the user must be constrained to walk a narrow path and/or make numerous assumptions about whether the interface would behave as expected (not to mention the time spent waiting for a crashed prototype to be restarted). In any case, there's a good chance that important usability issues might be missed if the user isn't getting the full experience.

Look

The look factor is the easiest to determine by inspection and is probably what gave rise to the original concept of prototype fidelity. *Look* refers to whether the visual aspects of the prototype accurately represent the intended appearance, including fonts, colors, and graphics. Something hand-drawn would obviously get a low score in the look department, and even printed-out color screen shots may earn only a medium score if they look substantially different from how those same screens will appear on a computer monitor—it's possible for a printout to look better than the same thing on a monitor, or vice versa. Also note that software prototypes don't automatically earn a high score for look—they may use different colors, graphics, spacing, and so on than the real thing. They just happen to have recognizable fonts and straight lines.

When it comes to look, don't automatically assume that a higher score is better. As discussed in Chapter 3, a rough-looking prototype can encourage users and other stakeholders to respond in a more creative manner. Especially in the early stages of a project, you might deliberately choose a prototyping method with a rough look to get this benefit.

Interaction

Interaction refers to the way that the prototype handles the inputs and outputs with the user—are the I/O methods simulated in a realistic manner? On a desktop computer, the input devices are typically the keyboard and mouse, and the monitor is the output. For a piece of medical equipment, the user might turn dials. For a handheld device, its weight and the spacing of the buttons might be important.

Time is an integral part of interaction, so consider things such as response time, cursor changes, flashing lights, and animation. There also may be senses other than sight involved—some interfaces use sound, and physical devices have tactile components.*

Note: Some people confuse interaction with depth—the former refers to the *methods* used to interact, whereas the latter is the *degree* to which the prototype responds as the real interface would.

Comparing Prototyping Methods

Now let's consider four different methods of prototyping and how well they do at representing the dimensions of look, similarity of interaction, and depth. Of course, these are not the only kinds of prototypes—I chose them because they illustrate interesting differences. For this example, I'll assume that the interface being prototyped is an e-commerce Web site, since that example is easy for people

---

* I hope to be safely retired from the usability business before I'm asked to test an interface incorporating smell and taste!

Table 12.1 Comparison of Prototyping Methods for an e-Commerce Web Site

Kind of Prototype	*Look*	*Interaction*	*Depth*
Working version (e.g., Dreamweaver)	Medium-high	High	Low-high
Slide show (e.g., Microsoft PowerPoint)	Medium-high	Medium	Low-medium
Paper prototype	Low-medium	Low	Medium-high
DENIM	Low	Medium	Low-medium

to relate to. Table 12.1 shows a summary of how the four methods compare; you may want to refer back to it as you read the following sections.

Working Version

Any less-than-complete version of the site can be considered a working prototype if it supports the tasks needed for usability testing. In the case of a Web site, the interface might be created in a WYSIWYG editor such as Dreamweaver or FrontPage.

The *look* depends on the extent to which graphic design was included—the prototype might be text-only or it might be designed down to the last pixel, but it's usually at least medium because it has straight lines and legible text. The *interaction* of a working prototype is nearly the same as a functioning site (although the response time might be different compared with the real Web server), so it gets a high score. The *depth* can range from low to high because it depends on the amount of time spent coding the site's behavior, such as getting product information from databases or processing an order form. Some so-called working prototypes are just a linked set of screens with nothing beneath them (low depth), whereas others have all of the underlying functionality in place to the point where they're indistinguishable from the real site.

Slide Show

Some prototypes are created as fairly static "slide slows," for example, by pasting screen shots into Microsoft PowerPoint. In the simplest variation, clicking the mouse anywhere advances to the next page, although it is possible to provide more complex branching. (For interfaces other than Web sites, something similar

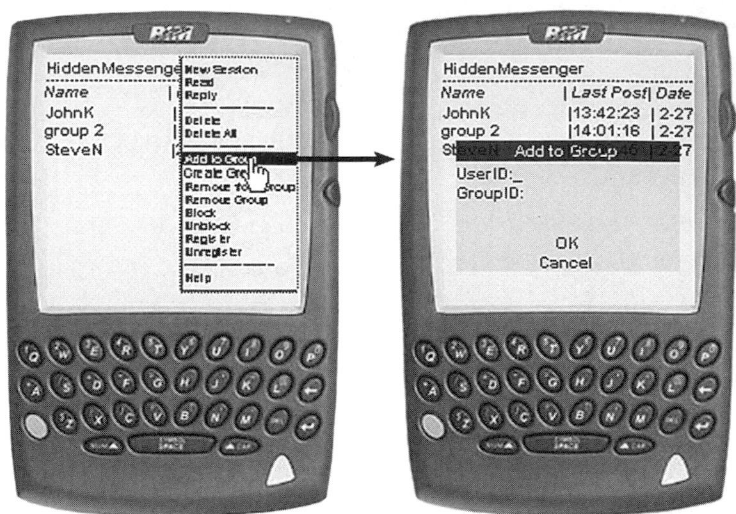

Figure 12.1 Two pages from a fixed sequence HTML prototype of a PDA application shown side-by-side. This runs in a browser, but because there are only one or two hot spots per page, in essence this prototype behaves like a slide show.

can be done using screen shots in linked HTML files as shown in Figure 12.1—naturally, if you did this for a Web site it would *be* a Web site as opposed to a slide show of a different type of interface.)

The *look* is usually in the medium-high range: high if screen shots are used, medium if wireframes are used. I've even heard of people using scanned sketches, which would of course be low. The *interaction* is only medium because you can't type, only click. The slide show usually has low to medium *depth*—the user is constrained to a subset of all the possible paths through the interface, and the controls don't work.

The main drawback to the slide-show approach is that users can't explore the interface, although you might be able to have some useful discussion based on the concepts they can see. But the lack of interactivity will limit the amount and nature of the feedback you can get—people stop exploring after the first few dead ends. You can only ask, "What do you *think* that would do?" a few times before the enthusiasm tapers off. This kind of prototype may be sufficient to expose relatively obvious errors or omissions in the design, but if you get vague positive feedback of the "Looks good!" variety, take it with a large grain of salt. The From the Field box illustrates why I believe that low-depth prototypes are more suited for demos or groups reviews than for usability testing.

From the Field: Usability Testing a Slide Show

"When I was new to the usability profession, I had a bad experience when I tried to conduct usability tests using a series of linked HTML files. The intent was to ask users what they'd click on and what they'd expect to see, and then proceed to the next page once they'd found the 'right' link. But once the users caught on that there were only one or two live links per page, the usability test quickly deteriorated into a game of 'find the hot spot.' The sessions were a complete waste of time. It really damaged the credibility of usability testing at my company, and for subsequent efforts I faced an uphill battle."

Anonymous

Paper Prototype

The *look* dimension can vary a lot for a paper prototype—hand-drawn Web pages would get a low score, grayscale printouts of professionally designed screens would be medium, and color printouts might even be high. The *interaction* factor has obvious differences—touching isn't exactly like clicking, writing isn't typing, and the human element is artificial. Although working with a paper prototype can be highly interactive, it's quite different from working with a computer, so the paper prototype gets a low score here. But what's interesting about paper prototypes is their *depth* because people take up the slack—the Computer decides what to do based on the user's inputs. Even if those inputs weren't what was expected, the Computer can (to borrow my own words from the earlier discussion of depth) gracefully prevent, detect, or explain any combination of choices that didn't make sense. So paper prototypes often have good depth.

It is worth mentioning that paper prototypes support breadth only up to a point. Although in theory you could create a 5000-page Web site out of paper, it wouldn't be practical. So if an interface (or more precisely, a particular task for that interface) requires a large number of screens, it may become overwhelming for the Computer. Although I've never counted, I estimate that most paper prototypes I've worked on have had anywhere from a few dozen to a couple hundred screens, which provided sufficient breadth and depth for the tasks the product team needed to test.

Note: Although you might hear both the PowerPoint slide show and the paper prototype referred to as "low-fidelity" prototypes, Table 12.1 reveals that they tend to have opposite characteristics. This further illustrates why the term *low-fidelity* can be misleading.

DENIM

Interestingly, there are some computer-based sketching tools that let you draw screens by hand (using a pen-and-tablet input device) and link them into functioning computer-based prototypes. One such tool is DENIM, which can be downloaded from *guir.berkeley.edu/projects/denim.* The DENIM project is headed by Dr. James Landay of the University of California at Berkeley. The idea behind DENIM is to provide Web site designers with a unified approach to various tools, such as site maps, storyboards, and individual page design. DENIM supports sketching input and a visual language—draw an X on top of a widget, and it disappears. As of 2002, DENIM does not provide support for all the widgets and interaction found in HTML forms and traditional graphic user interfaces, although enhancements are planned. See Figure 12.2 for an example of a prototype created using DENIM.

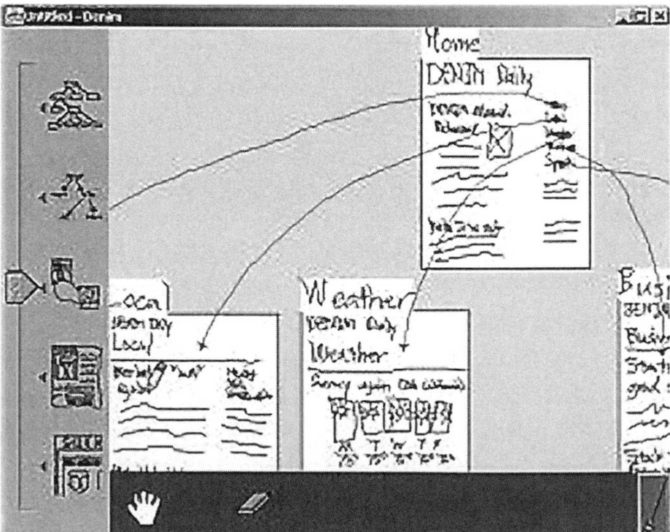

Figure 12.2 Computer-based sketching tools like DENIM allows you to draw using a pen input device and then link pages together to make a "hand drawn" prototype, which can then be tested on a computer.

Thus, a DENIM prototype has a deliberately rough *look* because its goal is to support sketching. I would rate its *interaction* capability as medium and its *depth* as low to medium because it doesn't fully support all types of interface widgets, but these scores might change as more functionality is added to DENIM.

When it comes to usability testing, a tool like DENIM may not offer any compelling benefits over a paper prototype other than removing the human Computer from the equation. And that may not even be its intent—much of DENIM's functionality is aimed toward providing a productive environment for designing, not necessarily for usability testing. To me, one of the intriguing aspects of a tool like DENIM is that it may enable researchers to tease apart the effects due to the *medium* of the prototype (paper or computer) and the *completeness* of the design.

Methods Don't Stand Alone—What Are *You* Prototyping?

Table 12.1 was created in the context of an e-commerce site, so it may or may not be relevant to what you're doing. The prototyping methods alone don't completely determine the score for each dimension—it depends on what you're prototyping. For example, you could make an HTML prototype of a handheld device as shown in Figure 12.1 and its interaction would be only medium because clicking a button with a mouse isn't the same as poking it with your finger. So if you're prototyping a handheld device, you might conclude that HTML prototypes get a medium score for interaction. On the other hand, if you're building a Web site, an HTML prototype would get a high score for interaction.

Here's an ironic example: You'd think that a paper prototype would get high marks in interaction if you were prototyping a touch screen device, but this isn't the case. Touch screens are complicated by factors such as calibration and parallax, which affect how the computer and human interpret each other's behavior. In practice, there are some important subtleties about touch screens that you can't adequately simulate with a paper prototype. Funny, huh?

So what are you prototyping? If you're feeling ambitious, you might make your own version of Table 12.1 for your interface and the prototyping methods you're considering.

Which Dimensions Matter?

As discussed in Chapter 5, when planning a usability test, you should always begin by asking what things you're most interested in learning. Table 12.2 shows some categories of questions (applicable to most software and Web sites) and which of the four prototyping dimensions are most important in answering them. Of course, you will have plenty of questions that don't appear in this table, especially if you are testing a different kind of interface—the strategy here is to think about which dimensions you need get the answers to *your* questions.

Table 12.2 Categories of Interface Questions and Paper Prototype Dimensions

	Dimensions Needed				
Category of Questions	*Breadth*	*Depth*	*Look*	*Interaction*	*Examples*
Concepts and terminology	✓	✓			◇ Do users understand the terms used in the interface? ◇ Are there concepts they gloss over or misconstrue? ◇ For new concepts, is the user able to figure them out?
Navigation, work flow, task flow	✓	✓			◇ Are users able to find their way around? ◇ Will they search, use links, or both? ◇ If there's a work flow or sequence of steps, does it match what users expect? ◇ Do you have the fields in the order that users expect? ◇ Do they have to keep flipping back and forth between screens? ◇ Does the interface ask for inputs that the users don't have, or don't want to enter?
Content	✓	✓	✓*		◇ Does the site/interface provide the right information for users to make decisions? What things do they look for? ◇ Is it useful and/or interesting to them?

Table 12.2 Categories of Interface Questions and Paper Prototype Dimensions—cont'd

Category of Questions	*Dimensions Needed* *Breadth*	*Depth*	*Look*	*Interaction*	*Examples*
					◇ Is there extra content that they don't need, or that annoys them?
Documentation, help	✓	✓	✓*		◇ What assistance does the user need to successfully complete tasks? ◇ What's the best way to provide that information? ◇ Can users quickly find the information they need, and make sense of it?
Requirements, functionality	✓	✓	✓*	✓*	◇ Does the interface do the right set of things for its target audience? ◇ Do users have additional needs that aren't being satisfied? ◇ Is there anything you could do to make the user's life easier? ◇ Are you planning to implement something that users don't really need?
Screen layout	✓		✓		◇ Is the amount of information per screen overwhelming, not enough, or about right? ◇ Do users miss seeing something that's important? ◇ Are there elements that need to be brought out more in the visual design? Any that distract the user? ◇ Has white space been used effectively? Images? ◇ Do we have the right stuff "above the fold?"
Brand	✓	✓	✓		◇ Does the interface reflect the qualities that the company wants to convey? ◇ Does the user experience match what the designer intended?

Continued

Table 12.2 Categories of Interface Questions and Paper Prototype Dimensions—cont'd

	Dimensions Needed				
Category of Questions	*Breadth*	*Depth*	*Look*	*Interaction*	*Examples*
					◇ Are there frustrations or obstacles that can be removed? ◇ Do users like it?
Colors, fonts, and other graphic elements			✓		◇ Can users see/read everything well enough? ◇ Do the most important elements stand out? ◇ Are there any considerations pertaining to lighting, vision difficulties, or color blindness? ◇ Is the interface aesthetically appealing? ◇ Do users understand what the icons mean?
Widgets and controls				✓	◇ Do the rollover menus work for users or do they have trouble? ◇ Do users notice the status line message? ◇ Can they figure out what the cursor changes mean? ◇ Will multiple windows be a problem? ◇ Do the slider controls have the right granularity? ◇ Did we pick the best keyboard shortcuts?
Response time, performance metrics				✓	◇ Does the system respond quickly enough to satisfy users? ◇ Do the pages load fast enough? ◇ Does the display change quickly enough when the user manipulates a control? ◇ Are there any download or processing delays that users might find annoying or unacceptable? ◇ How quickly can users complete this task?

Table 12.2 Categories of Interface Questions and Paper Prototype Dimensions—cont'd

Category of Questions	*Dimensions Needed*				*Examples*
	Breadth	*Depth*	*Look*	*Interaction*	
Real-world use	All these factors, plus the real context of use				◇ How does this tool fit with others that users have? ◇ What things will annoy power users after 6 months? ◇ Which of these functions are people really going to use? ◇ What happens when the user is interrupted mid-task?

* Sometimes.

Notice that breadth appears in about half of the columns in this table, so obviously it's an important factor in a prototype—there has to be enough of the interface for users to get a realistic idea of how it works. When it comes to usability testing, breadth is essentially a function of the tasks that you have created. As mentioned earlier, breadth can be incorporated in any kind of prototype and thus it's not useful as a means of choosing among methods, except in the unusual case where you need more breadth than a paper prototype (or rather, its human Computer) can handle.

What if your team has questions in most of the categories from Table 12.2? This happens often. Does it mean that you need to wait until the real product can be tested? Usually not. It might be helpful to divide your questions into "now" and "later" piles—those that can be answered with a paper prototype now and those that require a prototyping method (or the real interface) that would take more time. If the "now" pile is big enough to make paper prototyping worthwhile, go for it. (The next chapter discusses a somewhat more quantitative way of making this decision.)

Table 12.1 illustrates that paper prototyping's main strength is depth—the human Computer can simulate much of *what* the interface will do. So if depth is an important factor in researching a question, a paper prototype is likely to provide some answers. On the other hand, paper prototypes don't do so well in terms of interaction because it's hard for the Computer to accurately mimic exactly *how* a machine will respond. The look factor is somewhere in the middle because a paper prototype can be either hand-drawn or use highly designed screen shots.

Let's look at each of these categories—depth, look, and interaction—more closely. For purposes of this detailed discussion, I'm sticking with the example of an e-commerce site. Naturally, if you are designing a different type of interface, you should scrutinize whether the logic I'm presenting in each section applies to your situation or not.

What Paper Prototypes Will Likely Find (Depth Issues)

Looking at Table 12.2, there are several rows that have Depth as one of the factors. As a generalization, these are the types of questions that paper prototypes are well suited to answer.

Concepts and Terminology

Unclear concepts and confusing terminology are common—I don't think it's an exaggeration to say that I've seen these types of problems in every interface I've ever tested. Sometimes even one ambiguous word can prevent users from completing a task. For example, one user who was testing an e-commerce site refused to buy a cordless drill because it was described as a "kit" and he couldn't figure out what the kit included besides the drill. To probe problems pertaining to concepts and terminology, you need actual wording and often the supporting help or documentation as well, and these are depth factors. On the other hand, look and interaction usually aren't as important; if users don't understand the meaning of a field label or they need to see an example, this will be apparent regardless of whether the label is handwritten or typed.

Navigation, Work Flow, Task Flow

Breadth is an important dimension in determining whether users can navigate the interface or perform their work tasks because there is often more than one correct path, as well as a large number of incorrect ones. One way to think of it is that you should provide enough of the interface to confuse users. (More properly, the goal is to ensure that users aren't confused, but if you make a simplified version of the interface you can't tell when you've accomplished that goal.) To evaluate navigation, it is essential for users to have the ability to go where *they* want next, which may or may not match the path you envisioned when you created the interface. Depth is important because users sometimes step off the correct path and it's useful to know whether the interface succeeds in guiding them back onto it. Or sometimes the users' path is different but also correct—with a low-depth prototype, you may not be able to watch them do it their way.

Content

Content issues pertain to interfaces where users seek information and make decisions based on it (as opposed to an interface used primarily for data input). Similar to concepts, content questions are primarily a function of breadth and depth. In usability testing, if you want to watch users make decisions, it's often important to show them the real content, not greeked or approximated by wording such as "guarantee goes here." As discussed in Chapter 7, it may be easy to draw the content by hand or print it out, so a paper prototype doesn't have any inherent advantage or disadvantage over other methods when it comes to content—it depends mostly on where your content is coming from.

Sometimes you need breadth to understand content issues. If an interface or its content is very complex or large in scope, a paper prototype may fall short of the degree of realism you need. For example, a music Web site might offer thousands of albums—a paper prototype of the site has no realistic way to represent how all this content would appear to users or how they would interact with it. Although you might learn many useful things from paper prototype testing, there may be some questions you can't answer, such as whether users in real life would prefer to search or browse to find music.

To what extent is look part of content? If you're selling flowers online, color is indeed part of the content because users care whether the roses are red or yellow. But if you're selling life insurance, color has little to do with the content of the site, although it will undoubtedly be present in the graphic design. Similar logic could be applied for every aspect of your interface's visual design—the more of these factors that pertain to the content, the more concerned you're likely to be about the look factors that are discussed later in this chapter.

Documentation/Help

The issues for documentation and help are similar to those for concepts and terminology, which is typically what the doc/help are helping *with.* When a paper prototype of an interface is being tested, it's possible to gather useful information about what questions users have, what information is needed to answer them, and equally important, what doesn't need to be explained. By listening to the terminology they use, you can glean terms for your index.

If along with the interface prototype you are also testing a prototype of the documentation, its look may matter because formatting can aid the user's ability to find and use information. But it's usually not important to duplicate the final appearance of the help system or manual—drafting the content using your favorite word processor and adding a few headings is sufficient for a paper prototype test.

Requirements/Functionality

Most functionality is expressed in terms of what the interface does, rather than how it looks while it's doing it or the specific interaction methods used (although there could be exceptions to this rule). But it's pretty much a no-brainer that if you've built the wrong thing, it's going to fail with its intended audience. Ideally, you should have a decent understanding of user requirements and functionality before you begin the design of the interface. But if you've missed a requirement or gotten one wrong, a paper prototype can help you find it.

Screen Layout

You might think I've mistakenly put this section under paper prototype's strengths because questions pertaining to screen layout seem like they'd require a prototype with a realistic look. But many questions don't—a designer first needs to understand what elements should appear on the screen and also something about their relative priority. For example, if users who sign up for a service wonder whether there's a cost, you'd want to make sure that the word "free" jumped out at them in the final design. But until you did some usability tests, you wouldn't realize users had this question.

In essence, the findings from paper prototype tests can provide useful *inputs* to the process of designing screens because they will help you determine whether you have the right set of information in the right order, whether you've forgotten anything, and what elements need to be emphasized. On the other hand, once you're to the point of trying to determine whether you've used enough white space or if the Next button stands out enough, then you do need a more realistic visual representation.

Brand

Brand applies to the user's whole experience with the site or product, not just its appearance. A car may look great in the showroom, but you won't notice a problem with its suspension unless you drive it. Breadth and depth are often important to the brand, sometimes even more important than the look. If an interface is tastefully designed but doesn't let users do what they want, ultimately it won't create or reinforce a good impression in the user's mind.*

Although one can no longer argue, as some usability specialists did back in the mid-1990s, that graphic design is unimportant, neither can you take a flawed user experience and fix it by adding rainbows and puppy dogs. (I realize that no self-respecting graphic designer thinks this way, but occasionally I run across other people who do.)

A rough-looking paper prototype with sufficient breadth and depth can go a surprisingly long way toward revealing the ways in which the interface will support or interfere with the brand image that the company would like to convey (see the Of Interest box on p. 276). Once you have a solid foundation in terms of making the interface do what users need, then the look can build upon it in a way that supports and enhances the user experience.

What Paper Prototypes May Find (Look Issues)

When it comes to look, you first need to examine the questions you have that are specific to the visual aspects of the interface. As described in the previous section, for many types of questions, the look plays only a secondary role. But naturally many aspects of the visual design can be important depending on the circumstances. Here are three examples.

---

* Remember that famous line from the movie *2001: A Space Odyssey* where the computer HAL seizes control of the ship? It didn't matter one iota that HAL politely said, "I'm sorry Dave . . ." before dropping the bombshell " . . . but I can'let you do that."

Of Interest . . . Look and Brand—Not Inseparable

Look isn't always the most important factor in conveying a brand. I once tested two versions of a prerelease financial Web site. The first version tested had all the navigation and most of the text but lacked the graphic design—all pages had black text on a white background with no images. In other words, it was functional but ugly. The second version, which was ready a couple of months later, added the professionally designed colors, fonts, and images of smiling people.

We tested each version with half a dozen users in each of two populations (consumers and small business owners). At the end of the session, users were given a list of adjectives and asked to agree or disagree with whether they described the site. The adjectives represented the brand that the company wanted their site to have: reliable, accurate, honest, and so on. Interestingly, the brand perception didn't seem to change very much after the graphic design was added—users perceived the same flaws in the site's content and organization despite the fact that the second version looked much nicer than the first.

(Caveat: This study had a small number of users and there were other differences between the two versions besides the graphic design. In other words, this is an anecdote, not scientific proof. But it's intriguing that we saw no evidence of what we expected—that the brand perception would be improved by the addition of professional graphic design. I would love to see more formal research to help us understand when and how graphic design has the sort of positive effect that we instinctively believe it has.)

- **Alignment.** One paper prototype used a tree structure with multiple levels of indenting. Because the items in the hand-drawn paper prototype didn't line up very well, users had to work harder to understand the hierarchy that was being represented. After the test, one of the users commented that it probably would have been clearer on a computer screen, and I agreed with him.
- **Font size.** A colleague told me a funny story about font size in a Web site intended for use by teenagers. After their initial launch, the designers discovered that the large font they'd chosen could be read by a parent halfway across the room, which was unacceptable to the teenage target audience!
- **Photographs.** Some interfaces have photographs as part of the content, such as a picture of a sweater on a clothing Web site. If photographs are important, you can paste them onto an otherwise hand-drawn interface. (This is what The MathWorks did with their prototype described in Chapter 2.) On the other hand, if the interface uses photographs for a primarily decorative purpose, it's probably safe to omit them from a paper prototype.

Other things that are hard to simulate to a high degree of accuracy with a hand-drawn prototype include colors, shading, contrast, readability, white space, icons, dense layouts, and complex graphics. Because I find that this is pretty self-evident to most people, I won't belabor the obvious by providing lots of examples. If you have important questions that *depend on* specific visual elements like these, then a hand-drawn paper prototype probably isn't going to answer them to your satisfaction. (And if there are enough differences between how your design appears on paper as compared with on the screen, maybe printed screen shots aren't good enough either; in that case, it would be important to test the design on a computer.)

What Paper Prototypes Won't Find (Interaction Issues)

Paper prototypes are a rather blunt instrument when it comes to detecting many interaction problems. Following are several types of problems I've seen in testing real interfaces that I doubt I would have found with paper. This list is by no means complete—I'm willing to bet that there are many others.

Small Changes

On some interfaces, small areas of the screen change in response to the user's actions. For example, some applications use the status line area at the bottom of the window to display messages, or an e-commerce site might update a persistent shopping cart to show the number of items in it. These changes are often subtle on a computer screen; with a paper prototype, it's much more obvious because the Computer leans over the table and sticks something on the prototype. Thus, with any sort of small or subtle change, a paper prototype can only tell you if users *understand* the change, not whether they would *notice* it—you can't draw any conclusions about the latter.

Scrolling on Web Pages

On some Web pages, users don't scroll down, and thus they miss a link or content "below the fold" that's relevant to what they're trying to do. You might try simulating the fold literally, by folding the Web page where it would fall at a given resolution. If the user says he or she would scroll down, unfold the paper so that the rest of the page can be seen. Another method is to use a cutout as shown in Chapter 4. These methods may help you determine whether you've succeeded in placing the most important information above the fold, but they're rough measures at best.

Because a folded piece of paper is more salient than the scroll bar on a Web page, if users "scroll" on the paper prototype it's risky to assume that they also will on the real site. On the other hand, if users *don't* scroll with the prototype and miss something important that's below the fold, then this perhaps does indicate a problem with the page layout that you'll want to do something about.

Long Documents and Lists

Interactions with a long document or list are difficult to simulate adequately with a paper prototype. In one usability study, I watched users navigate through a series of online documents containing industrial regulations. As long as users clicked the down arrow they were fine, but the minute they moved the scroll bar directly they'd end up in another chapter—given that there were hundreds or even thousands of pages, even a small movement of the scroll bar landed the users several dozen pages away. This problem was painfully clear from watching users use the real interface (and confirmed the team's decision to limit scrolling to just the current document rather than the whole series), but we wouldn't have seen it with a paper prototype.

Similarly, I've seen users have difficulty selecting the item they wanted from a long list. When a user scrolls through a long list by clicking repeatedly, their attention is on the items in the list, not the down (or up) arrow they're clicking. If the mouse cursor drifts off the scroll bar control, the user's next click will land either within the list (selecting an item the user didn't want) or outside of it (causing the list to disappear). Alternatively, the user might try to use the keyboard—it's common for users to type the word they're looking for, such as "fr" to find France in a list of countries. Some interface elements (such as the URL field in Internet Explorer) support this behavior, but drop-down lists don't. Many users aren't aware of the difference and are surprised when typing the R whisks them off to Romania.

The "False Top" Problem

A false top is a Web page problem that's a combination of visual design and interaction. On some Web sites, once the users scroll down, they are inhibited from scrolling back up all the way to the top because at some point the page appears as though it's already there. (The scroll bar elevator does not seem to be a sufficient clue that more of the page is out of sight above.) I call this a *false top* (see Figure

Figure 12.3 Example of a page with a false top—the left image shows the true top of the page, and the right image shows how the page also appears to be at the top when the user has scrolled down, part way up, and then stopped. You probably won't find a false top problem with a paper prototype.

12.3). A false top can cause usability problems (although usually minor ones) if the user has trouble finding top-of-page navigation that's needed for the task.

Keystroke or Mouse Errors

Although the term *user error* is no longer considered politically correct, people do hit the wrong thing sometimes even when they know perfectly well how to use the interface. Premature form submission is one example of a keystroke error—the user accidentally submits a form by hitting Enter instead of Tab. Speaking of tabs, sometimes the tab order may not match the order in which users expect to fill out fields, or auto-tab may cause data to be entered into the wrong field. Because in a paper prototype the user isn't using a keyboard, chances of finding these problems are slim.

For an example of a mouse error, look at the options in Figure 12.4 that McAfee Personal Firewall gives me when it detects an unauthorized attempt to access my computer. The "Trust this address" option, which I never use, is sandwiched right between the two options I do use, and sometimes I click it by mistake. (This type of error is sometimes called a 1-off problem.)

Size of Controls

In a paper prototype, users simply touch what they want to click and we make the assumption that they did it correctly. But in real life this assumption can be wrong, and a paper prototype won't tell you how large a button or other clickable area

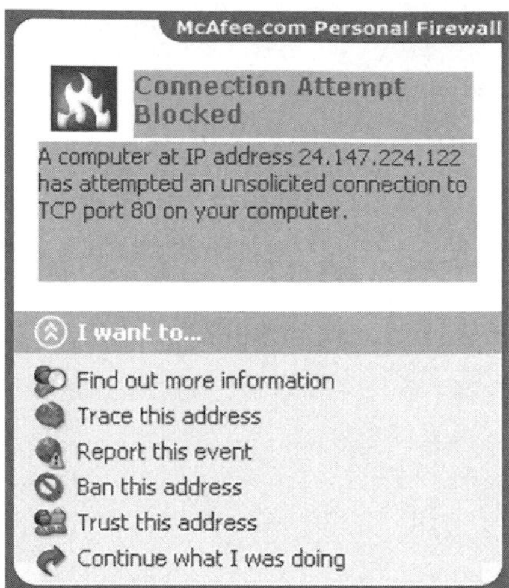

Figure 12.4 As I have learned to my chagrin, it's not hard to click "Trust this address" by mistake when I'm going for "Ban this address" instead. This is another problem I wouldn't have found with a paper prototype.

needs to be. In one usability test of a Web site, I watched a user who had great difficulty clicking on anything small (for example, the state of New Hampshire in a map of the United States). I noticed that she seemed to be clicking too high, and I finally figured out that she was centering the arrow cursor over the target she wanted to click rather than putting the *tip* of the cursor in the middle of the target. When the target was small, the hot spot ended up above the thing she was aiming at.

A computer screen faces the size issue in only two dimensions—with a handheld device or manually operated equipment, the problems become more complex. Even a three-dimensional prototype may not provide enough realism to adequately investigate issues pertaining to control size, placement, operation, tactile feedback, and repetitive stress.

Mouse versus Keyboard Preference

With a paper prototype it's hard to answer the question "Do users prefer the mouse or the keyboard?" or to spot places where they're slowed down by having to switch back and forth. In watching users complete order forms on real e-commerce sites, I noticed that very few users navigated a list by using the arrow keys—almost everyone used the mouse. Thus, when a drop-down list was placed in a form containing edit fields, the keyboard-mouse-keyboard transition slowed users down. Would I have seen this with paper? Nope, because the users' hands take the place of both mouse and keyboard.

Rollover and Cascading Menus

A *rollover menu* is one that appears when the user positions the cursor over a top-level menu option. Rollover menus can give users trouble by popping up unexpectedly (sometimes obscuring the page underneath), and some users don't understand how to use them. A *cascading menu* refers to multiple menus linked together in hierarchical fashion, like the Windows Start menu. They're difficult to use because users must move the mouse at 90-degree angles rather than taking the hypotenuse to the desired submenu choice. Because the behavior of rollover and cascading menus depends on the positioning of the mouse cursor and the timing of its movements, they're too subtle to test with a paper prototype.

Download Time or Other Response Time

Because a person simulates the behavior of the computer, the "response time" is artificial. And it can be off in either direction; on one hand, a person shuffling paper might be slower than a computer, but on the other hand a paper prototype eliminates delays due to processing, servers, and so on. Because the Computer's speed does not accurately represent the machine's, measurements of task times, error rates, and the like can be skewed by testing with a paper prototype.

Response time usually depends on technical factors, so with a paper prototype you probably can't get data about whether the interface will respond quickly enough to satisfy users. (And sometimes it's hard to answer these questions even with the real interface unless you watch users work in their own environment, doing something they care about.)

Finding Problems through Inspection

Some types of usability problems can be found simply by looking for them—the false top, cascading menu, and keyboard-mouse issues are ones I can often predict just by looking at a screen. However, there's something of a Catch-22 here: To find a problem by inspection in a paper prototype, you have to know to look for it and that knowledge only comes from having seen examples of it in real interfaces and/or interface guidelines. To the extent that you're able to educate yourself about common usability issues, you may be able to use that expertise to partially compensate for some of paper prototyping's deficiencies. But don't expect "armchair usability" to replace the real thing because there are many, many important problems that you'll never find if you look only for the problems you know about. (If you want examples, reread Chapter 2.) Usability testing is useful way to check your blind spots.

What Usability Testing Won't Find (Real-Life Situations)

Usability testing, whether of paper prototypes or real products, has blind spots of its own. So far, this chapter has mostly been about the method of paper prototyping and what problems it will and won't find. A similar analysis could be done for other methods of prototyping, but we're still talking about how well the methods do at eliciting information *in the context of a usability test.* Although a full discussion of this topic is beyond the scope of this book, I'd like to touch on some of the things that are difficult to discover in a usability test.

- **Long-term use.** Once people learn to use it, how well can they remember how to do things? How efficiently can they get things done? How easily can they focus on the task and forget about the interaction with the system? What can be streamlined? What "little" things become huge annoyances when users encounter them every day?
- **Integration and compatibility.** How does this interface fit with others that the target market is using? Does it "play nice" with the operating system and other hardware and applications? Does it have inconsistencies with those things that bother users?
- **Real-life context and needs.** Do users' goals and tasks really correspond to those things we asked them to do in usability testing? How often do users get interrupted in the middle of using the interface or have to leave it to go look something up? How much work do they lose as a result? Do they use all the functionality? Is the product really making users' lives better in the way we envisioned? Especially if the users' goals are complex or take a long time to accomplish (for example, using chemical modeling software to create a new drug), you aren't going to get the whole picture in a 2-hour usability test.

Showstoppers can lurk beneath the surface of any of these questions, but you aren't going to find them in a lab. When I claim that paper prototyping can find many important issues, sometimes people respond "But not all of them." And that's true. But it's true of any method. Although paper prototyping and usability testing are marvelously useful techniques, they are a complement, never a substitute, for other methods of understanding users and their needs. (See the References section for more information.)

Summary

This chapter has outlined the reasons why paper prototypes are better at finding some types of problems than others. Every prototyping technique has strengths and weaknesses, and every interface has a unique set of questions that the product team would like to investigate. To summarize the strategy presented in this chapter:

1. List the kinds of questions you have about your interface in terms of the four dimensions (breadth, depth, look, and interaction).
2. Determine which dimensions are needed to address your most important questions. (Refer to Table 12.2.)
3. Choose a prototyping method that has strengths in those dimensions. (Refer to Table 12.1.)
4. Accept that one method won't find everything.
5. Reality-check your findings whenever you come into contact with users.

Think of a paper prototype as a coarse screen that you use to sift out problems. Now that you've read this chapter, you should have an idea of which problems your paper prototype will catch and which might "fall through" to be found later or with other methods.

Chapter 13

The Politics of Paper Prototyping

Paper prototyping is not a difficult technique. The real challenge often lies in convincing others to try it. It isn't too hard for most people to grasp the benefits of testing a design without having to code it first. But even people who recognize that paper prototyping is useful often have concerns about it. When I teach classes about paper prototyping, I ask participants to write on index cards all the questions that they or their colleagues have about the technique. Then we create an affinity diagram using the method described in Chapter 11. The results come out looking something like this, in order of importance:

1. **Validity.** Does paper prototyping find real problems? Does it find the same problems as testing the real interface?
2. **Bias.** Does paper prototyping introduce false problems? Does it change users' behavior or feedback in such a way that we can't trust the results?
3. **Professionalism.** What will others think of this technique (and us for using it)? Will the prototype be perceived as sloppy or amateurish?
4. **Resources.** Do we have time for this? Is there a payoff here, or is this just extra work? Why not just wait until the real thing is ready?

Some of these fears, especially in regard to validity and professionalism, tend to diminish once people have additional information. Other issues have more depth to them and merit a closer look. The material in this chapter provides a framework for discussing these questions with your team. I end this chapter with some tips for dealing with those who remain skeptical.

Validity

Validity is probably the biggest concern people have—they're afraid that because a paper prototype doesn't look realistic, the results from usability testing it aren't realistic either. I'm often asked whether paper prototyping finds important problems. Although this is an area where more research would be helpful, the evidence I've seen supports the generalization that paper prototypes will find the same number and types of problems as a more high-tech method. (I discussed some exceptions in the previous chapter.)

Research

Some people may be convinced of paper prototyping's legitimacy simply by virtue of the fact that there's a book on the subject. (I wish!) Other people may be swayed by the case studies and examples that I have liberally sprinkled throughout this book, especially because they comprise the experience of people at many different companies. But the more scientifically minded among your colleagues may hunger for something more substantial than anecdotal evidence. They'll identify themselves by two words: "Prove it."

I'm not a scientist, and you probably aren't either. There is a vast body of HCI (human-computer interaction) literature, some of which is relevant to paper prototyping. Following I provide information from several published papers pertaining to paper prototyping, and there are more in the References section. I'm not attempting to be exhaustive; I'm assuming that you are a practitioner who doesn't

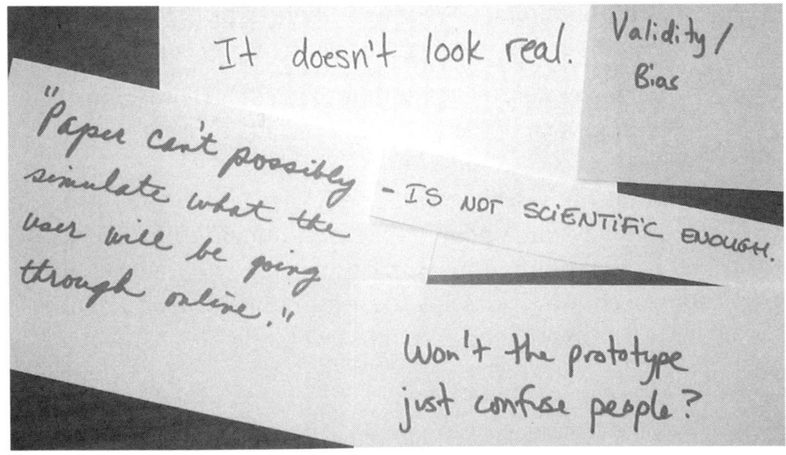

need a lot of depth on the research, just the reassurance that there is some legitimate basis to paper prototyping.

Although I'm not a scientist, I do respect science. It's quite difficult to design a solid experiment, especially for something that's vague and hard to quantify, like "usability problems." I have just enough knowledge of experimental design to know that I'm not qualified to analyze the strengths and weaknesses of the following studies from a methodological standpoint. I can, however, attest that their findings ring true from the perspective of someone who's done a lot of paper prototyping. Without further ado, here are abstracts from some research studies that pertain to paper prototyping's validity.

Virzi, Sokolov, and Karis (1996)

Abstract: "In two experiments, each using a different product (either a CD-ROM based electronic book or an interactive voice response system), we compared the usability problems uncovered using low- and high-fidelity prototypes. One group of subjects performed a series of tasks using a paper-based low-fidelity prototype, while another performed the same tasks using either a high-fidelity prototype or the actual product. In both experiments, **substantially the same sets of usability problems were found in the low- and high-fidelity conditions** [emphasis added]. Moreover, there was a significant correlation between the proportion of subjects detecting particular problems in the low- and high-fidelity groups. In other words, individual problems were detected by a similar proportion of subjects in both the low- and high-fidelity conditions. We conclude that the use of low-fidelity prototypes can be effective throughout the product development cycle, not just during the initial stages of design."

The researchers also write: "Both techniques uncovered the same usability problems for the most part, and at about the same level of sensitivity, as witnessed by the high positive correlations in the two studies between the proportion of low- and high-fidelity subjects finding particular problems. That is, when a problem was found by a high proportion of subjects in the high-fidelity group, it also tended to be found by a high proportion in the low-fidelity group. However, some problems that were found in the high-fidelity condition were not found in the low-fidelity condition, and vice versa. This is true for both studies."

In addition to their published findings, Bob Virzi told me about some further exploratory analysis of their data. They compared the high-fi prototype to the low-fi one in several ways: the number of successfully completed tasks, the average time on a task, and the number of steps taken. These three measures seemed to suggest few differences between the two kinds of prototypes, although this conclusion requires additional scrutiny before being granted the same scientific weight as the published paper. In other words, users were able to do the same tasks, in about the same number of steps, regardless of the kind of prototype. There was a greater variability in task times, but the relative relationships were preserved—if task 6 took longer than task 1 in the hi-fi prototype, those two tasks showed the same relationship in the low-fi prototype. From a practical perspective, these results imply that if something is hard to do with the paper prototype, it's probably hard to do with the real interface as well.

Catani and Biers (1998)

> *Abstract:* "This study investigated the effect of prototype fidelity on the information obtained from a usability test with potential users of a software product. Users engaged in a series of structured tasks using one of three prototypes which emulated a Microsoft® Windows 95™ based library search computer system and which differed only in their fidelity (low = paper, medium = screen shots, high = interactive Visual Basic prototype). **Results indicated there were no significant differences as a function of prototype in the number and severity of problems encountered nor in the subjective evaluation of the product** [emphasis added]. More importantly, there was a high degree of commonality in the specific problems uncovered by users using the three prototypes."

The authors also make an interesting conjecture: "However, in the real world, as the product moves through the development cycle, prototypes change not only in fidelity but also in content and structure. Perhaps it is this difference in content and structure which leads to the common belief that different usability problems should emerge as a function of prototype fidelity." In other words, because later-stage designs tend to be better than early-stage ones, some people might misattribute the interface problems to the prototyping method rather than the completeness of the design.

Novick (2000)

> *Abstract:* "This paper introduces low-tech simulation as a technique for testing procedures and their documentation. The key idea is to test the interface-procedure-documentation set in the early stages of development, where changes can be still be made easily, using extremely low-cost simulation materials. Using this low-tech method, developers can test and improve the usability of documentation for user interfaces that are still being designed. An extended example, involving a new aircraft cockpit interface for text-based air-traffic control communication, presents a look at the low-tech approach in use. An evaluation of low-tech simulation shows that the approach was practical. Qualitative analysis indicates that low-tech evaluation produces results that are dif-

ferent from those obtained using the cognitive walkthrough for operating procedures and similar to those obtained using traditional high-tech simulation."

Although this study focused on documentation, in practice the interface and its documentation are not easily separable—Novick created a paper prototype of the interface as a means of testing its documentation. Even though only one user tested the paper prototype, Novick found that the simulation was good enough to "elicit unexpected [user] behaviors that shed light on ways to improve the procedures and their documentation." The problems found with the paper prototype were later confirmed by testing with six users on a high-tech simulator. Perhaps most interesting of all, both the paper prototype and the high-tech tests found some problems that had not been predicted by the six analysts who conducted the cognitive walkthrough. Novick did note some of the deficiencies of the paper prototype approach—its timing wasn't realistic, it didn't show color accurately, and it probably wouldn't scale up to an entire airplane cockpit—but concluded that the overall approach was practical.

Strictly speaking, these studies don't "prove" that a paper prototype will find the same set of problems as a more realistic one. Rather, they indicate that the sets of problems overlap to a considerable degree and there don't appear to be important differences in the problems that are found with one method versus another. However, these studies don't really scrutinize whether paper prototyping is less useful in finding certain kinds of problems, as I described in the previous chapter (although Novick seems to have theories similar to mine). I believe that such effects do exist, but research studies to date have not been designed to reveal them. As with any field of study, subsequent research should be able to fine-tune the questions under investigation and yield more detailed insights into exactly what paper prototyping is and isn't good for. As it stands, the evidence suggests that paper prototyping is as valid a technique for uncovering problems in an interface as usability testing the real thing.

Case Studies

The problem with finding real-life examples of paper prototyping's validity is that there's usually no point of comparison—because companies are busy trying to get products out the door, they don't have the luxury of conducting usability studies with a paper prototype and comparing the results to those obtained from testing the real interface. The From the Field box by M. David Orr (on p. 291) provides an interesting anecdotal example of someone who found himself in a position to do such a comparison.

Here's a slightly more scientific example: Chapter 4 described a study where researchers Säde, Nieminen, and Riihiaho (1998) tested a 3D mock-up of a can-recycling machine. Later in the study they tested a functional prototype with a larger number of users (50 instead of 10) and found no statistically significant differences in the severity of problems encountered in using the interface—the mock-up had accurately predicted that most users would have little or no difficulty with the "automatic" version of interface. (Note that the functional prototype had some improvements over the 3D mock-up, so this is not entirely an apples-to-apples comparison, but at least they didn't find any worms in their apple.)

This is just one example—as shown in the References section, there are many papers and articles about real-world experiences with paper prototypes. In most cases there is no point of comparison because paper prototyping was the only method used, but I have yet to find an article that concludes, "We tried paper prototyping, and it was a waste of time."

Summary: Does Paper Prototyping Find Real Problems?

As you can see, the evidence of paper prototyping's validity ranges from scientific to anecdotal, and I'll add my own experience to the latter. Over a 10-year period, I have conducted several hundred usability tests of software and Web sites, at least 100 using paper prototypes. At the end of each project, I meet with the development team to categorize and prioritize the problems, then I write a report. When I go back and reread those reports, I don't see any systematic differences in the type of findings. (A better test would be to see if someone else could find a difference.) To a large extent, I believe that I have found the same kinds of problems with paper prototyping as I've found when testing the real thing.

The real question, however, is what does it take to convince *you* (or your co-workers)? Some people don't care what research says; they need to try a method and see for themselves. Other people may need far more detail about the research than I've presented in this chapter, including a scrutiny of the methods used to conduct it. Still others may make up their minds about paper prototyping based on the opinions of people they trust. Whenever questions of paper prototyping's validity arise, the best way to answer them depends on what type of person you're dealing with; I've provided you several different approaches but you may only need to use one of them.

From the Field: Comparing Paper Prototypes and Reality— An Informal Case Study

"I'm a tech writer, instructional designer, and usability specialist who works for a consulting firm. My company had been contracted to design and develop a software system for customizing documentation. Our client manufactured 2-way radios. Each customer purchased only a subset of the radio's features, so the manufacturer needed a way to generate documentation based on the selected features.

"Because the end users were internal, a number of them were involved in the design process but the manufacturer hadn't budgeted any time to conduct usability tests. Fortunately, I teach usability courses at a local university, so I had my class conduct a usability test on a software prototype. Only one user participated, but he uncovered a handful of potentially serious problems—it was hard to know where to start, there was a lack of feedback, and an important radio button had confusing options. I estimate that the prototype had taken about 100 hours to develop, and perhaps another 20 hours were needed to fix the problems before the first version of the interface was deployed. Eventually, a rev 2 version was developed, which fixed additional problems and added features.

"About a year later, I was teaching another usability workshop and I asked my class create and test a paper prototype of the original rev 1 interface. The class conducted the testing in small groups (with a student playing the role of user) and then the groups compared their findings. Even though these 'users' had a different background than the real user population, they still were able to identify most of the same problems found by the real user, including all of the serious ones. In addition, the students had several suggestions for improving the interface that (unbeknownst to them) had actually been incorporated into the rev 2 release.

"Had the paper test been done prior to programming, the first version of the product would have been much stronger, and the second version might have been unnecessary or could have focused on enhancing the feature set."

M. David Orr
(dorr20@earthlink.net)

Bias

Another common concern is whether paper prototyping might introduce usability problems where none exist. In essence, they're talking about bias. Does paper prototyping bias the results from usability testing? You betcha . . . and so does everything else.

Usability testing is an inherently unnatural (although useful) activity *that always contains multiple forms of bias.* The trick is to recognize various forms of bias that may be present and consider their effects on the data collected from usability testing. Let's first consider several forms of bias that are often present in usability tests: users, tasks, test setting, facilitator, methodology, data analysis, observers, and bugs. Last but not least, I'll zero in on paper prototyping.

Bias: Users Who Don't Fit the Profile

If a test participant doesn't fit the profile of the target market, you can get misleading results from any kind of usability testing. Let's look at two examples: subject matter expertise and familiarity with the technology.

Subject Matter Expertise

If you test with users who don't know or care enough about the subject matter, they might not reveal important problems. For example, when I tested a Web site that sells toys, one of the tasks asked users to buy a beanbag toy for a 2-year-old. Some of the users did not have children (I was testing a variety of sites in this study), and the users without children found some issues with the site's navigation and checkout process. But it was a parent who found the showstopper: "It doesn't say whether beanbags are suitable for children under 3—no way would I buy it without knowing that." People who have in-depth knowledge of a topic are more likely to realize when functionality or content are missing, problems that are often difficult for non–subject matter experts to find.

There's a flip side to this problem: Users who lack the necessary background in the subject matter may uncover "problems" that aren't really problems for the intended audience. Many professions have jargon and concepts that are incomprehensible to an outsider. For example, when I first became involved in usability, I went on a crusade to remove the word *node* from some of the applications at my company, on the theory that it was an overly geeky term. Well, I was wrong; the users, who were engineers, had no problem at all with the term *node* and would have been confused if I'd succeeded in getting it changed to something else.

Familiarity with Technology

If you are developing an interface for people who work outside of high-tech, it's very risky to usability test with tech-savvy co-workers or friends because they know too much about the ins and outs of the type of platform you're developing for. I've seen on many occasions that users who know something about Web site design can readily use things like rollover menus and multiple browser windows that often stump a less technical audience. If your test population has more technical knowledge than your typical user, you're likely to mask out a technology-related subset of problems. On the other hand, if you're developing a product for network administrators, you don't have to worry about whether they can use a mouse.

*I once received a contemptuous email from someone who completely disbelieved an article I had written called "Seven Tricks That Web Users Don't Know" (available at **www.ibm.com/developerworks/usability/library-us-tricks**). He was a system administrator in Silicon Valley. He contended that everyone he knew, including his 10-year-old daughter, was smarter than the people I'd tested with and concluded that I should "get out more" into the real world. In my reply, I explained to him that all the usability tests I conduct are with strangers who are recruited by an outside agency in accordance with the user profile determined by the client. I refrained from touching the point about which of us should get out more.*

As discussed in Chapter 5, deciding on the profile of test participants is a necessary prerequisite for usability testing. Conducting a test with a user who doesn't fit this profile carries a significant risk of causing dissent among the product team because it's unclear to what extent the test results are credible. Worst case, the team may simply dismiss the findings (perhaps correctly so) as irrelevant.

Bias: Bad Tasks

Because I believe that task design is one of the most important and difficult aspects of usability testing, I already devoted all of Chapter 6 to this topic. Tasks can be a subtle and insidious source of bias. As I've learned from my own mistakes, it's

Figure 13.1 The search form used in testing a hotel reservation Web site.

easy to give unintended hints that can conceal usability problems in the interface. On the other hand, unrealistic tasks can cause users difficulty, but that difficulty may not be indicative of what they would experience in real-life use.

Sometimes the clues contained in task instructions are blatant (at least in retrospect), and other times they can be subtle. Figure 13.1 shows a search form on a travel Web site. In testing this site, we used the following task: "You and your significant other are planning a visit to Madrid, Spain. You're arriving September 9th and staying for 7 nights, departing the morning of the 16th. A friend recommended the hotel Husa Princesa. Please use the Web site to book a room." (The purpose of this task was to find out how a user would react to the error message telling them that one or more of the requested nights was unavailable.) As Table 13.1 shows, there are several subtle biases lurking in even this simple task.

This example is a fairly simple one; you can imagine how the potential for bias might increase for more complicated tasks. Unlike when you test with a non-profile user (which your team members will readily notice and complain about), bias due to tasks can lurk undetected beneath the surface of your findings. Because it's virtually impossible to eliminate bias, you should at least look at your tasks and question whether there is a bias that might interfere with the most important things that you're trying to test.

Table 13.1 Possible Sources of Bias in Task Instructions

Possible Bias	*Discussion*
The instructions reveal that Madrid is in Spain.	We did this deliberately—the team assumed users would already have done some research about their destination and we didn't want to waste test time if they didn't happen to know where Madrid was. But otherwise, this bit of information might have masked a problem with the country being required, or possibly users' need to see a map.
The instructions give the spelling of the hotel name.	Also deliberate—the team already understood the problems caused by spelling variations, and we wanted to ensure that they'd use this particular hotel because it lacked available rooms on the dates in question.
The task assumes that the user has a certain set of information when they use the site, such as exact travel dates.	An important issue—if the search requires users to enter information they don't have, they'll be stuck. But if we give them all the inputs, we won't see this problem. (In this study, we had an earlier task where we asked users to find a hotel for a vacation they were planning in real life, so we'd already gotten data about this, including the fact that people didn't always have exact dates.)
The order of the information in the task was different than the order of the fields in the search form—the dates and hotel name were reversed.	We didn't realize this. One user made an error because she followed the order in the task instructions and submitted the form after entering the dates. (Only a minor issue in this case, but it could have been important if we were testing the search form.)

Bias: Unrealistic Test Setting

Real people don't do their work in a usability lab. In the user's natural environment, there a myriad of factors that may influence how they use the interface: lighting, interruptions, other software, performance measures in their jobs that they're rewarded for, and so on. As mentioned at the end of the previous chapter,

Usability testing is an inherently unnatural activity. (Illustration by Rene Rittiner.)

there is a whole set of problems that you're unlikely to find by bringing in users; you need to go to their environment and watch them.

Here's one of my favorite examples. A few years ago, one of my colleagues consulted with a company that was working on speech recognition software. The designers were trying to improve the accuracy of the recognition and were puzzled because the beta test version would do well for users for a while but then the recognition rate would suddenly deteriorate. They couldn't reproduce the problem in their lab. When my colleague went to watch the beta users, she noticed that they closed their office doors while they were doing dictation. When interrupted by a knock or someone opening the door, users would put the system in "sleep" mode and then talk to their co-worker. In a flash of insight, my colleague realized that the speech recognition software was trying to interpret the door-knock sounds as words, and that's what made the recognition accuracy go haywire. In essence, something that was supposed to be outside the bounds of the system was interfering radically with it.

You can make your test setting more realistic (or at least understand the ways in which it's different) if you go to the effort to do so. There's a method called *contextual inquiry* where you set up site visits for the purpose of understanding what kinds of problems your users face, how they solve them, and the environment in which they do it. The insights you gain from contextual inquiry might cause you to set up your test environment differently the next time you conduct a usability study.

Note: In creating tasks and setting up the test environment, there is a balance to be struck between realism and control—to find specific things, sometimes you have to set up your test in a certain way. A paper prototype is an obviously artificial construct, but any experiment has its artificial aspects. In a good experiment, the artificial aspects are there deliberately; in a bad experiment, they're accidental.

Bias: Test Machine

Test machine bias is a subset of test environment bias. When testing on a computer, it's likely that the computer that the user is accustomed to will be different than your test machine. For example, an America Online user may navigate to Web sites using their Favorites folder, which obviously you won't have. Their method (or lack thereof) for filing bookmarks and documents will be different than yours, and so might their screen resolution, double-click speed, font size, and so on.

I've found that bias introduced by the test machine is usually less problematic than other causes, but every now and then it can bite you. In one study of a prelaunch version of a Web site, we set the default home page in the browser to the site we were testing (it was running on a development server, so we couldn't use the real URL). So this meant that the browser's Home button went to the home page of the site. We did this as a convenience for ourselves, but some users picked up on this and used the browser's Home button to get back to the home page of the site instead of the logo link intended for this purpose. In retrospect, we realized that we'd introduced a bias that made their navigation artificially easy, and we wished we'd used a bookmark instead (or typed in the URL for them, since it was too complicated to memorize easily).

You can have "test machine" kinds of problems with a paper prototype too. I've also seen users click the hand-drawn Home browser button, mistaking it for a link to the home page of the Web site. Whether paper or machine, problems of this nature are often false ones. When I facilitate usability tests, I'll step in and help users if I believe the problem they've encountered is an artifact of the test machine or paper prototype rather than the interface itself. But I'll also discuss it with the team afterward to make sure everyone agrees it was probably a false problem.

With a paper prototype, you have the option of eliminating some kinds of test machine problems, assuming they aren't relevant to what you want to test. For example, to get around the fact that the users' directory structures will all be different, you can artificially simplify your prototype so that when they go to open a file, the one you've told them to use magically appears without the need to browse for it. (You may be able to do similar things in software, but sometimes it's more trouble than it's worth.)

Bias: Facilitator

A careless facilitator can contaminate the very data he or she is collecting. Even after 10 years of experience, I sometimes catch myself asking leading questions. A facilitator's mannerisms and body language can provide clues to the user, such as nodding before the user makes a choice. (Nodding afterward, although it also constitutes a bias, is not quite as bad.) As described in Chapter 8, sometimes there are situations when a facilitator will deliberately alter users' behavior, for example, by suggesting that they look in help. To some extent these human variables are inevitable in usability testing, so it's good to be aware of how they're affecting your data. (Caveat: Self-awareness can be difficult, both cognitively and emotionally, so think of it as a process rather than an event.)

A usability test is a social setting, and that can influence users' behavior, as illustrated by the following From the Field box.

From the Field: Usability Testing in a Social Setting

"I was running people through a study on finding information on a Palm PDA. The tasks involved reading a question and looking through the text until you found the answer. One of the answers was located in the first sentence of the file. (Q: What was earnings per share? Text: Earnings per share from continuing operations were $3.05 compared to . . .) Most of the people found that number right away and made comments like 'Maybe . . . but I better scroll down just to make sure.' The times for this question were way out of line with the other tasks. In a real-world setting, the person probably would have grabbed the answer and gone with it right away. But they wanted to make sure they answered the question right. Their goal was not 'find earnings per share' but rather 'answer this question correctly for the nice experimenter,' a distinction that makes a big difference in how to interpret results."

Loel Kim and Michael Albers, the University of Memphis

(From "Web Design Issues When Searching for Information in a Small Screen Display." SIGDOC'2001. © 2001 Association for Computing Machinery, Inc. Reprinted with permission.)

In Michael's case there was some concrete evidence (the task times) that pointed to a false problem. In a paper prototype test the evidence may not be as clear, but you can still use the qualitative analysis method that I describe later in this chapter to help you decide whether you've found a valid issue or not.

Bias: Test Methodology

There are many possible ways to conduct a usability test. In the classic "think aloud" method, you ask the users to articulate what they're doing and thinking. In co-discovery, the users are working together and talking to each other. You might interact with the users a lot or very little—at one extreme, you could simply let users work uninterrupted, postponing all discussion until the end of the session. You might script every word you say or not use a script at all. You might give the users questionnaires to gather additional information. You might ask the users to review the videotape of themselves working and explain the things that confused them.

These are all different—and valid—methods of conducting usability tests. And each method carries its own risk of bias. For example, if you ask users to think aloud, it may change their behavior if it causes them to weigh their decisions more carefully. On the other hand, if you let users work uninterrupted and have them review the video later (a technique known as retrospective analysis), users may not remember perfectly what was going through their minds at the time or may even invent reasons for their behavior.

Bias: Data Analysis and Reporting

Human beings filter and prioritize information, and to some extent this is unavoidable. When we have a set of usability test observations in front of us, we continue the filtering and prioritizing process and may or may not be aware of the methods we are using to do so. For example, in the previous chapter I described several interaction problems that are hard to find with a paper prototype. Let's say that you found the "false top" problem particularly interesting because the possibility hadn't occurred to you before. Next week a friend asks you to review his Web site and you notice it has a false top. It's very likely that you will mention that problem, and perhaps even assign more importance to it than it deserves, simply because you recently heard about it and found it interesting. That's a reporting bias.

I suspect that all humans are guilty of this type of bias, and I'm dead certain that usability professionals are! The abstract of the Catani and Biers paper quoted earlier concluded by saying, "Other noteworthy results were that: (1) usability professionals (through informal heuristics analysis) and users differed in the incidence and commonality of problems identified, and (2) usability professionals did not agree in their ratings of problem severity." My colleague Rolf Molich, who coordinated some experiments known as the Comparative Usability Evaluation (CUE) studies, found much the same thing (Molich et al., 1998, 1999). It turns out that it's difficult for any two people to report the same set of usability problems or assign them the same severity. As a profession we are still working on this challenge, but in the meantime the implication is that the person conducting and/or reporting on a paper prototype study may have more effect on its findings than does the technique itself. (This is one reason why I encourage product team members to observe as many usability tests as they can—they keep me honest.)

On the other hand, a bias in analysis and reporting isn't always a bad thing. As a consultant, I sometimes deliberately investigate and report problems that I know my clients are interested in while downplaying others. For example, on one Web site I tested, the client knew that users were leaving the site after seeing the search results page. This problem was costing them money. In the usability study, I made every effort to determine the causes of this problem. Along the way I found many other problems, some of which I didn't even bother to report because fixing them would have amounted to rearranging deck chairs on the Titanic. If I had known nothing about the company's business priorities, my findings would have been less biased, but they also would have been less useful.

Bias: Observers

Awareness of being observed can change a person's behavior. I'm not a social psychologist, but I can describe some of the effects I've witnessed. Some users may be more nervous, less likely to explore, or more likely to provide favorable feedback compared with how they'd respond in real life. I've also seen users who clearly liked being "on stage" and responded in exactly the opposite manner. These are just a few of the possible effects.

As covered in Chapters 9 and 10, the things you do to prepare users for the test setting go a long way toward making them feel at ease, and proper preparation of the observers reduces the possibility that they will cause negative effects. I'm not really very concerned about the possibility of users being less willing to offer negative feedback in the presence of observers—in my experience properly briefed users understand that they provide value by speaking up when something's not working for them, and they do so.

One of the questions people sometimes have about observer bias is how aware the users are of the observers' body language—nodding, scribbling notes, frowning, and so on. Naturally, if you're sitting in a roomful of people who are blatantly reacting to everything you say or do, it's going to change your behavior. In practice, I've found that the secret is to keep the users' attention focused on the prototype. The more engaged that users are in working with the prototype (and to some extent, the Computer and facilitator), the more overt action it will take to distract their attention.

I remember one example vividly. The two users were discussing what to do next. One user said, "Maybe we should click Apply." Out of the corner of my eye, I saw all the observers (who were seated within the users' peripheral vision) nodding their heads vigorously. I had asked them not to talk, and they were following my instructions to the letter, but they were understandably rooting for their interface to do well. However, the users were completely oblivious to this clue because they were looking at the paper prototype and talking to each other. They went on to try something other than what the observers had wanted.

Bias: Bugs

Bugs are yet another form of bias. I was testing a Web application for data security where users had to create combinations of security methods, called a policy, that were then used to protect internal data resources. When users named the policy, we were curious to see whether they named it after the security methods it used (Password and Retinal Scan) or after the thing they were trying to protect (Recipe for Special Sauce). After one test, a bug somehow crept in that left us unable to delete the policy the users had created. So the users in the next test saw the policy left over from the previous test, and they gave theirs a name that was similar. This constituted a bias—we couldn't be sure whether they would have chosen the same name in the absence of seeing what the previous users did. We had to ignore the data from these users on this issue.

"Bugs" can happen in a paper prototype too, when the Computer makes an error. As with software bugs, the effect can range from benign to completely undermining a conclusion.

And Yes, the Paper Prototype Introduces Bias Too

Last but not least, let's look at how a paper prototype may change what happens in a usability test. It's possible that paper prototypes may:

1. Cause false problems.
2. Slow down the action, possibly inhibiting users from exploring the interface.
3. Affect users' impressions of the interface.

False Problems

Sometimes the paper prototype can introduce some confusion into a usability test if the users have to decipher the nature of what they're looking at. I once conducted a test of a prototype that had an expandable list where items representing different types of devices were indented in a three-level hierarchy. We had used removable tape for each line item, but due to sloppy placement it wasn't always clear what lined up with what. And each line item had a hand-drawn icon to represent the device type, but the icons looked different depending on who had done them. In testing, we saw users puzzle over the structure that the paper prototype was trying to show them. In this case, because both the alignment and icons were part of the data, it's likely that the paper prototype did introduce some degree of confusion.

Another example comes from the Pingtel case study described in Chapter 2. Hal Shubin explains: "On the paper prototype, test participants tried pressing button labels instead of the buttons. That happened in the 'soft phone' [emulator software] too. In the 3D version of the phone, there are cues not present in the paper or software versions; the screen is recessed and the buttons stand out." In both these cases, the development teams decided to downplay or dismiss these particular "problems" found in the paper prototype.

Sometimes it's unclear whether it's the medium of paper or the human Computer that's responsible for false problems. In an experiment, Uceta, Dixon, and Resnick (1998) created a hand-drawn paper prototype of an interface for ordering fast food. They scanned their sketches and made a linked PowerPoint presentation—in other words, a prototype that still looked hand-drawn but could be tested on a computer. In testing they found a few more problems with the paper version, but eventually decided the extra problems were false ones. (As you read the following explanation from their paper, note that the person they refer to as the facilitator was also the Computer.)

"The results of the analysis indicated that the paper prototype found 55% of the usability problems with the interface while the computer based prototype found 35% of the usability problems. Given that both interfaces were exactly the same, (besides the medium of presentation), the results were surprising. However, upon further analysis, the discrepancy was attributed to the presentation environment. We suspect that the users were more frustrated at the level of fidelity and the lack of feedback with the paper-based prototype. This became evident after careful review of the videotapes, which showed that between the five participants for the paper prototype test, **there were 45 separate instances where the user was distracted in some way by the facilitator** [emphasis added]. It is ironic that this method can introduce non-existing usability problems. It seems the facilitator's presence can also create a highly artificial environment in which the user behavior can be manipulated (albeit unintentionally to the benefit or deficit of the design). Taking this condition into consideration, statistical analysis indicated that no differences were found between the sensitivity of both methods for finding usability problems."

Slower Action, Inhibiting Exploratory Behavior

Bob Virzi explained to me that he noticed some evidence of a behavioral effect in the data from the study he conducted with Sokolov and Karis. On one task that was particularly difficult, some users of the high-fidelity prototype started "thrashing"—rapidly and repeatedly taking various incorrect actions. This behavior was not in evidence with the paper prototype, where users were more deliberate. I have witnessed this effect myself on occasion, where users have said that they normally try lots of things when learning a new interface but then don't when they're testing a paper prototype. There may be a social effect here, in other words, not wanting to make the Computer do extra work. Or perhaps the Computer's slower reactions simply make rapid explorations impractical.

Whatever the cause, a paper prototype may sometimes inhibit the user from "banging on" or exploring an interface the way they normally would. However, it's difficult to predict what effect this has on usability testing results. On the one hand, if the user is working more deliberately, he or she may think through a problem more carefully and end up solving it. On the other hand, if the user is deprived of the additional information gained by experimentation, he or she may fail a task in a usability test setting but succeed in real life.

I do believe that paper prototyping can reduce the opportunities for serendipitous discovery. In tests of Web sites, I have watched users stumble upon the drop-down arrow next to the Back button in Internet Explorer (that gives access to the

10 most recent pages), comment that they've never noticed that feature before, and then go on to use it successfully. That's serendipity (and also, possibly, a bias due to the test machine if the browser they're accustomed to lacks that feature) and I don't see it when testing paper prototypes. However, I don't believe that reducing serendipity constitutes much of a problem in usability tests. In fact, if the difference between success and failure is determined by a fortunate accident, that's usually a good indication that you have plenty of bigger problems to worry about.

Liking (or Disliking) the Paper Prototype

A paper prototype can indeed affect users' perceptions of the interface, but as with timing it's hard to be certain which way the effect goes or even whether it is important. Naturally, if we ask people which prototype looks more attractive or professional, we would expect them to choose the variation that appears to be finished. In their paper, Hong, Li, Lin, and Landay (2001) confirmed that "formal representations of design were perceived to be very professional, close to finished, and less likely to change. Informal representations were perceived to be unprofessional, incomplete, and very likely to be changed."

Although it's tempting to assume that people will like the entire product better because its prototype looks more polished, that's not necessarily the case—Hong and colleagues went on to say, "Both formal and informal representations were rated similarly functional." And the Catani and Biers paper succinctly notes, "There was no significant difference on any of the 15 subjective questions as a function of prototype fidelity." Apparently, the users in these studies were able to perceive the same capabilities in an interface even when a prototype had a low-fidelity appearance.

It's also possible for people to like a paper prototype more than they will like the real product. Wiklund, Thurrott, and Dumas (1992) examined the relationship between the aesthetic refinement of a prototype and its perceived usability. They created four versions of an electronic dictionary that varied in how realistically they represented the appearance of the product. Participants rated the prototypes on a variety of scales, including ease of use and ease of learning, both before and after using them. The degree of realism didn't affect these ratings. They also had participants use the real device and provide the same ratings. But because the prototypes hadn't accurately represented the slow response times for some aspects of the real product, the usability ratings for the prototypes were more positive than those for the real thing.

There's also the question of whether you even want the users' subjective opinions. Unlike other techniques, such as focus groups or surveys, in usability testing there is more emphasis placed on what users are able to accomplish and less on their opinions. We don't just show them the interface and ask if they like it; we give them a task and watch them *do* it. Although we care what users like, we need to beware of confusing users' opinions with whether the interface actually gets the job done for them. This sort of disparity between perception and reality is quite common in usability testing. Chapter 6 described an example of a user who kept saying that he liked the Excel Function Wizard even though he wasn't able to use it without my help. This user may have been responding to the *idea* of the Function Wizard as something that would help him create formulas, but the reality was that the existing design didn't work for him.

The bottom line: Asking people if they like a paper prototype is probably not a useful exercise. It's very hard to discern exactly *what* they are liking or disliking: the appearance, the perceived capability, or the experience of using the interface. Because it is so difficult to separate these effects, I rarely ask subjective questions in usability tests, whether of paper prototypes or real products.

Examining Bias: Qualitative Analysis

The purpose of any type of usability testing is to *predict* the *possible* problems that real users will have. The question to ask yourself is, "Do we think users would have this problem in real life?" closely followed by "Why or why not?" In other words, the issue is whether one or more forms of bias may be strong enough to justify reversing the tentative conclusion that the interface has a problem.

You can't eliminate bias, so be vigilant in questioning its effects on the data you're collecting from usability testing. Although this qualitative analysis method may be overkill for most problems, it can be helpful if team members disagree about whether a legitimate problem has been found. The steps are as follows:

1. List all the **sources** of bias that might have played a role in getting a particular result from testing. Consider all the sources listed earlier, although you may decide that there are only one or two that are relevant to your situation. For example, if you found a particular problem in the only test that had a non-representative user *and* someone thinks that the paper prototype contributed to the confusion, you would have two sources to consider.

2. Determine the **direction** of each effect—does the bias act to strengthen your premise that there's a problem or weaken it? Both effects are possible. For example, if your product is intended for use by research chemists and one user who was only a chemistry student had trouble understanding some terminology, that bias acts to weaken the conclusion—more subject matter expertise might have helped the user succeed. But sometimes the presence of a bias can strengthen a conclusion rather than weaken it. For example, hand-drawn corrections to a screen shot stand out. Thus, if you make a hand-drawn correction to something you want users to notice and they still don't respond to it, you have stronger evidence that there's a problem with the interface than you'd have gotten by testing it on a computer.
3. Estimate the **magnitude** of each effect. Although this is hard to do in absolute terms (and that's why I'm calling this method a qualitative technique rather than a quantitative one), you might decide that one source of bias is relatively weak while another is strong. Try to weigh all the factors before drawing your conclusion about whether the interface has a problem.

From the Field: Bias—A Case Study

My client, Pearson Education, has a Web application called CourseCompass where college instructors create online courses to supplement their classroom activities. In a usability study, we watched users complete the registration process using a paper prototype that used screen shots printed in grayscale. In our scenario, the users were teaching an introductory psychology course and we showed them the physical textbook they'd be using. (There was also an online version of the book that accompanied the course; we had to choose the book ahead of time because its contents appeared in the paper prototype). Although the registration and course creation process were the same regardless of the subject matter, none of the users were psychology teachers—most taught English.

Once users had finished registering and defining some general information for their course, they saw a page like the one in Figure 13.2. At this point, they were supposed to access their newly defined course by clicking the Intro to Psych link to create a syllabus, assignments, and so on. Instead, users clicked the Modify button (which let them modify the information they had already entered) or the Create a Course button (which was for creating *another* course). Most users

From the Field: Bias—A Case Study—cont'd

needed a clue from the facilitator to realize that the course name, Intro to Psych, was the link to the place where they could create their course materials.

Our observation was, "Users aren't clicking the link." Our premise based on that observation was "The interface has a usability problem." In discussions with the development team, the question arose whether this problem really would have happened on a computer screen. Several interesting points arose about potential biases, some of which acted to strengthen our premise while others weakened it.

Possible Bias: Lack of color

Explanation	*Direction of Effect*	*Magnitude*
The paper prototype used screen shots printed in grayscale, so although the link was underlined, it didn't appear in blue as it would on a computer screen. This constituted a potential bias if users were less likely to notice a link that wasn't in the standard browser blue.	Weakens the premise that the interface has a problem.	Opinions differed, but the team was in agreement that the lack of color may have had some effect.

Possible Bias: Artificial data

Explanation	*Direction of Effect*	*Magnitude*
One of the developers wondered if users weren't drawn to the Intro to Psych link because they weren't psychology teachers and this wasn't the name of their real course. This was an excellent point. Artificial data may affect the way users interact with the interface. Thus, there was a potential bias due to the artificial nature of the task.	Weakens the premise that the interface has a problem.	Hard to say, but probably less than other factors. (However, the team recognized the value of using subject matter that matched what the users taught in real life and decided to do this in future tests.)

Continued

From the Field: Bias—A Case Study—cont'd

Possible Bias: Artificial motivation

Explanation	*Direction of Effect*	*Magnitude*
The users' motivation to figure out the solution might have been stronger in real life compared with that during a usability test. Or the opposite argument—users might try harder in a usability test than in real life because they're paid to be there.	Because Pearson was concerned about adoption rates, the conservative approach was to treat any barrier to successful use as a potential problem.	Probably not as strong as other factors.

Possible Bias: Visual design

Explanation	*Direction of Effect*	*Magnitude*
We observed that users tried clicking the "Manage" and "Create a Course" buttons before clicking any of the links. The buttons seemed to draw the users' attention more strongly than the link. Some users even said that they noticed the buttons first and figured that one of them had to be the right way to proceed. (If we'd tested a hand-drawn prototype with a sloppy link and neat buttons, then that might have been yet another bias.)	Supports the premise that the interface had a problem.	Relatively strong, especially in light of what users said and did.

The team's conclusion? Yes, the lack of color in the paper prototype might have contributed to the problem, but probably not enough to reverse our conclusion that we'd found a problem with the link versus buttons. It's interesting to note that of the four sources of potential bias we discussed, only one—the lack of color—was specific to the paper prototype. The other three sources of bias—including the visual design, which the team ultimately agreed was most important—would all have been present if we'd been testing on a computer.

From the Field: Bias—A Case Study—cont'd

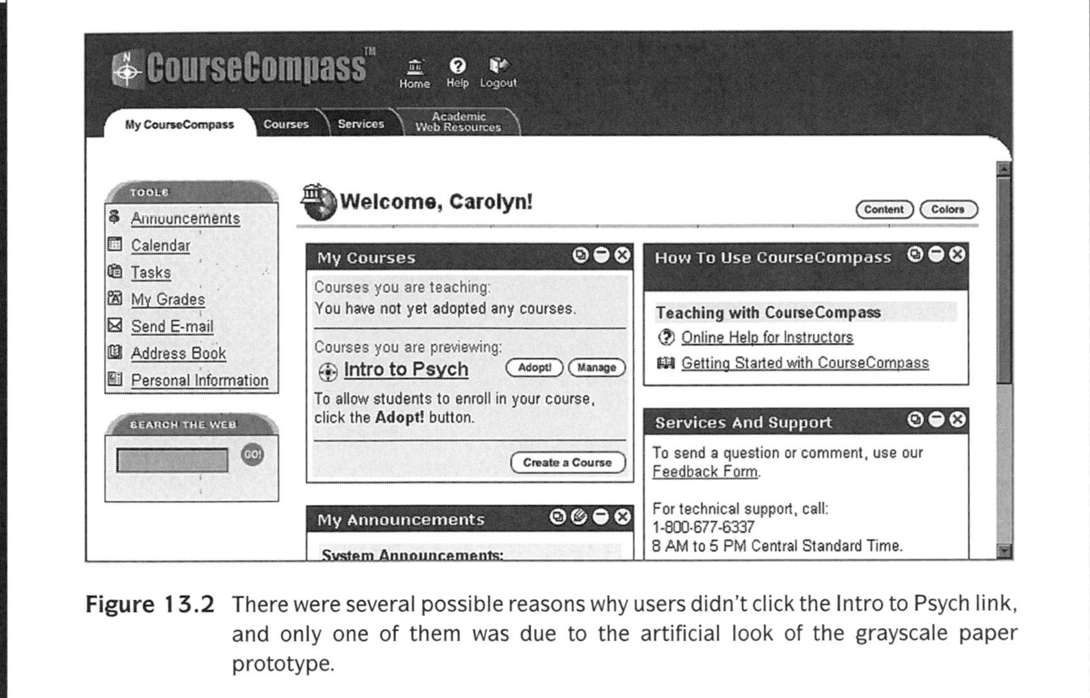

Figure 13.2 There were several possible reasons why users didn't click the Intro to Psych link, and only one of them was due to the artificial look of the grayscale paper prototype.

Do you need to do this kind of detailed analysis for every problem that arises in usability testing? Of course not. In my experience, most problems found in testing paper prototypes are quite believable (sometimes blatant) and there's consensus among the product team that they're real.

But when someone asks, "But wouldn't it have been different on a computer?" my response is to ask them to explain *why* they think it might have been different. When there's a specific reason, such as "It took the Computer too long to find that screen, so the user forgot what he'd clicked," I'm inclined to agree that we might have found a false problem. But when the rationale can't be articulated beyond a vague, "I just think it might have been different," then I'm less willing to simply dismiss the problem. Similarly, an elaborate explanation of how the users were supposed to behave may indicate wishful thinking.

Whenever someone doubts the results from usability testing, it's prudent to double-check whether the user fit the profile and if there were any problems with the task or the way it was facilitated. Sometimes a seemingly free-floating anxiety about the results from a paper prototype test is valid but is caused by something other than the prototype. In other words, people can tell that something smells fishy before they've learned to identify which type of fish it is.

Note: By this point I may have given you so many things to worry about that you'll avoid usability testing altogether out of fear of doing it wrong! But take heart—imperfect usability studies are all we've got, and they're far better than nothing. And because good usability professionals are by nature both analytical and empathetic, help is available for the asking via professional organizations and discussion lists.

Professionalism

The thought of showing an unfinished—or even flawed—design to outsiders makes many people uncomfortable. I believe that there are some valid reasons for the fears people have, based on cultural values that many of us hold. It's important to recognize the causes of such feelings so that you can respond to them appropriately.

The Fear of Negligence

In many cultures, we face pressure for our work to be complete and error-free. As children, we were taught to cross our T's and dot our I's. In many cases there are

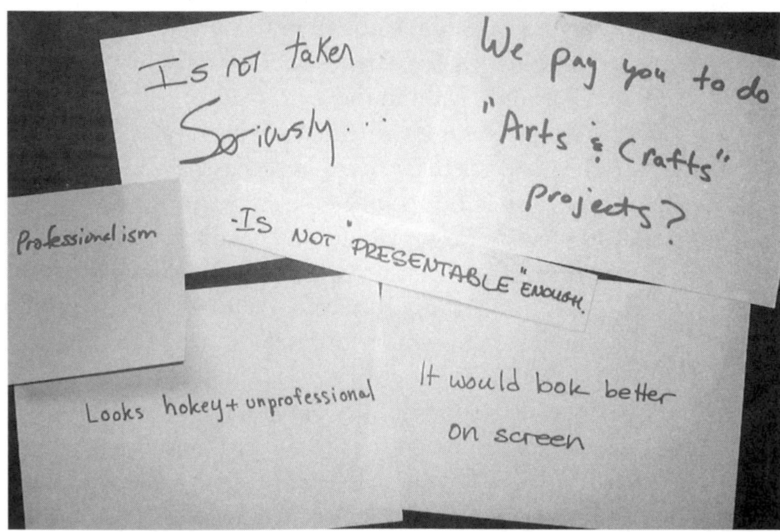

legal obligations to complete work, even for a task as seemingly trivial as shoveling the sidewalk in front of one's house. In a U.S. Supreme Court decision involving negligence, Justice Benjamin Cardozo wrote, "The hand, once set to the task, may not be removed with impunity."

On top of what our society already expects, many developers are perfectionists by nature and training, and their jobs reward this trait. Quality assurance concepts like "six sigma" emphasize that the tolerance for errors in a professional environment is (or at least, should be) very low.

Addressing Concerns about Professionalism

Given these pressures, it's natural for developers to be concerned that others will perceive their work as unprofessional if all they see is a sloppy and incomplete paper prototype. There are several tactics for alleviating these concerns, and all of them support the same strategy: setting expectations appropriately.

1. Position paper prototyping to the product team as a technique for gathering answers to their questions, as opposed to a way to find flaws in their work. (If usability testing is conducted in an overzealous manner, it can feel like a fault-finding crusade. Paper prototyping and usability testing should never be used to make someone look bad.) Emphasize that an essential part of usability testing is to identify what's working well, not just issues that need fixing.
2. Reassure the development team that it's absolutely appropriate for them to have a number of unanswered questions about the interface at this stage and that no one is expecting them to have a completely thought-through design. Trying things that don't work is a necessary part of innovation—before creating the first successful lightbulb, Thomas Edison claims to have discovered 10,000 ways to design a lightbulb that *didn't* work.
3. The team may be understandably concerned about seeming to promise something before knowing whether it can be delivered. Explain to both the development team and users that prototyping something does not constitute a commitment to build it—decisions and action plans come later, after the team has had a chance to digest the findings from the usability tests.
4. Set users' expectations that the design is still on the drawing board and that the final version may be considerably different than what they see. When participants arrive for a usability test, I explain that we know the design has some rough edges (sometimes literally!) but that we want to get their feedback before we've the invested the effort required to build it.

5. Last but not least, make sure the development team knows how the users will be briefed. I might tell the team, "The users will be told that the design isn't done, so they aren't expecting it to be perfect. If we find a spot where you haven't finished thinking things through, I won't let them beat you up for it. We'll just note it and move on." Remind them to resist the temptation to apologize because the unfinished nature of the design is actually a benefit and users will perceive it as such.

This may sound like a lot of bother, but it's not something you have to keep doing—once people have experienced paper prototyping for themselves, concerns about its professionalism should diminish.

Note: I'm not claiming that paper prototyping is appropriate in all professional contexts. Although there are many times when you can wear jeans, sometimes you need to don your best suit. If you're going before the board of directors to give them a progress report, I think there's some sort of unwritten law that you have to show them a PowerPoint presentation. (Although if you recall the story from Chapter 3 about Jack Zaientz and the government review committee, maybe you'll have the courage to show a few prototype screens on an overhead projector.) Likewise, if you're trying to sell something (either literally or in the sense of persuading someone), you'll want it to look slick. But for most people involved in product development, these situations are less common than the ones in which we want to collaborate with our customers and peers. For those cases, paper prototyping is sufficiently professional.

Resource Constraints

I've never worked on a project that didn't have resource constraints; every development effort has limits on the time, money, or people that can be devoted to it (usually all three). So it's natural that some people are uncomfortable about anything that sounds like additional work, even if they recognize the benefits. Chapter 5 covered the activities in a usability study and how to estimate the time you'll need. But some of your co-workers' concerns may not be addressed simply by having a schedule for all the activities. The main way to counter these kinds of concerns is to look for a point of comparison. In other words, to ask, "How will paper prototyping affect us *compared with what we're already doing?*" Let's look at three common concerns.

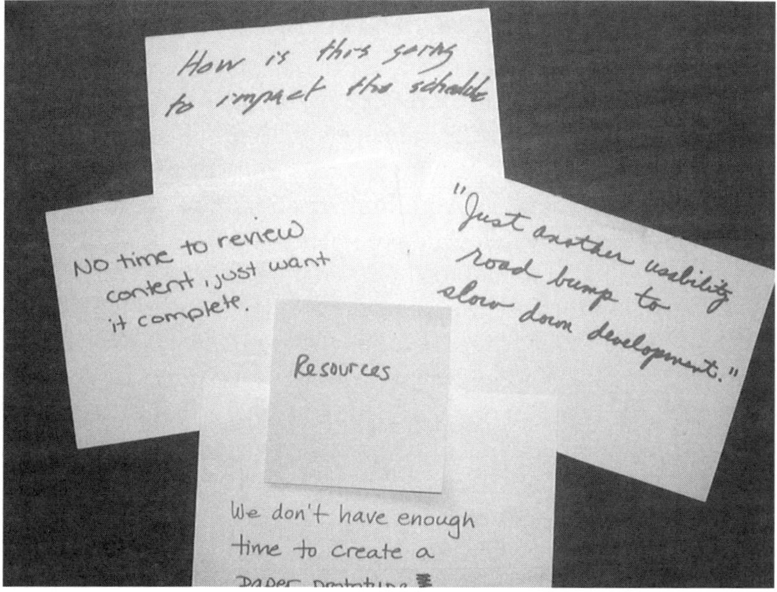

Won't It Result in More Work?

If you're testing to find problems, you're going to find problems, and obviously someone will have to fix them (or make a deliberate decision not to). It's hard to argue with the logic that the amount of time you'll need to spend responding to user feedback is directly proportional to the amount of feedback you ask for, which implies that paper prototyping (or any other form of usability testing) can result in additional work, at least in the short term.

The key to this question is to agree on what your time frame is. If you don't do any usability testing and problems with usability and functionality are found after release, you still have all the work associated with fixing them, but this work happens in the next release instead of the current one. (Unfortunately, this idea can be attractive to those who don't plan to remain at the company.) But you might be able to think of examples where postrelease usability problems came to light and caused havoc for technical support or were difficult to fix. In particular, look for problems of the types that paper prototypes are likely to find and make the case that it would have been possible to fix them before release. But tread carefully here—avoid sounding smug or berating others for mistakes that were "obvious" in retrospect. If possible, consider choosing an example from your own work.

How Will This Affect *Our* Development Process?

You already have a development process in place. Even if your process is an undocumented, ad hoc mess, it's still a process. *Process* simply refers to what you do, not necessarily what you'd like to do or are supposed to do! Here are some questions that'll get you thinking about how paper prototyping might alter the way in which you develop products.

- **"How long will we spend designing the interface if we don't do a paper prototype?"** One way or another, the interface has to be designed—and often redesigned. Paper prototyping may not be so much an additional activity as a different way of doing something you're already doing. (You might refer back to Chapter 3, which discussed the designing, rendering, and coding aspects of prototyping.) Don't forget to consider the time needed to document the design—at some companies, the paper prototypes themselves form the basis for interface specifications, whereas at others there's a need for more formal documentation.
- **"How long do spec reviews take?"** It can take several days to send an interface spec out for review and get people's comments back—with a paper prototype, the walkthroughs (and the usability tests) function as review activities in that they let you solicit and incorporate feedback from key stakeholders. Consider the effect that paper prototyping might have on your process for approving a design. Will it take less time for a person to approve a design if they have first attended a couple of the usability tests? (Or on the flip side, will attending tests take longer than the cursory reviews that person usually does?) Will a paper prototype help you get feedback from someone who normally doesn't read specs?
- **"At what point do we start asking for user feedback, and how long do we allocate for responding to it?"** To some extent paper prototyping may simply shift some activities that normally happen late in the project (after coding is complete) into the earlier stages (before or during the coding stage). For example, if your company plans long beta tests because that's the first time you find out what your customers *really* need, perhaps you could use a paper prototype early in the project to get customer feedback and then have a shorter beta test.

As you can see, it's hard to get an accurate answer to the question of whether paper prototyping takes extra time because there are several factors to consider. For some teams it might, whereas for others paper prototyping may partially replace activities they're already doing.

It is certainly possible to put too much time into a paper prototype—I've heard of people who spent weeks preparing their prototype and an elaborate script for usability testing. If people are concerned that paper prototyping requires an effort of this magnitude, the information in Chapter 5 about planning a usability study may be of use.

We Can Prototype Just as Well with ___________

Some people may contend that a computer-based prototyping tool is just as fast and provides the same benefits. This argument is really about efficiency, although it's rarely stated that way. To consider efficiency, you have to weigh what you put into the technique with what you get out of it. Start by estimating three things:

1. **Percentage of problems you'll find with a paper prototype.** Make a list of your most important questions about the interface, then look at the previous chapter to see which questions are answerable using a paper prototype. Estimate the percentage—is it 50%? 90%?
2. **Time needed for a paper prototype.** How long would it take to create a paper prototype, to the nearest day? (Answers of 2 to 4 match my experience; answers greater than 5 are unusual and suggest that too much effort is being spent on the prototype.)
3. **Time needed for a computer-based prototype.** How long would it take to create a working mockup of the same functionality, including time to set up the test environment?

Now calculate what I call the *efficiency ratio* by dividing the percentage of problems found by the days of effort. (For simplicity, testing a working version of the interface is assumed to find 100% of the problems, although no method provides 100% accuracy. If your software prototype is incomplete in some way, you might want to estimate a lower percentage of problems found for it as well.) Compare the ratios you get—larger numbers are better because they indicate more problems found relative to the amount of effort. Finally, consider how sensitive the result is to errors in your estimates. In most cases the best course of action should be pretty clear-cut, but not always. Here are some examples.

Example 1: The cpselect tool from The MathWorks discussed in Chapter 2. Because most of their questions were about how users would work with the tool and only a minority pertained to the visuals and interaction, let's estimate that they could answer 70% of their questions with a paper prototype that would take 3 days to develop, as opposed to taking a month (20 days) to make a working version. So the calculation is as follows:

Paper 70% ÷ 3 days = 23

Working version: 100% ÷ 20 days = 5

It's easy to see why The MathWorks uses a lot of paper prototyping—it's almost a no-brainer for them given that their software is highly conceptual and complex to build. Even though I made up these estimates, you can see that the numbers would have to change a lot (for instance, building the working version in 4 days instead of 20) to yield the opposite conclusion that they'd be better off building a working version first.

Example 2: A complex information visualization interface. Say you're developing a Web site that displays real-time display of U.S. stock market data. Blocks representing companies appear in varying shades of red and green to reflect their current stock price. In this case, the paper prototype might not do a good job of portraying the subtleties of the display and interaction—assume it would answer only 60% of the team's questions. At the same time, this paper prototype might be time-consuming to develop because a display that changes would need to show many variations. Assume there's a working prototype that would need a week's worth of work to prepare for testing.

Paper 60% ÷ 4 days = 15

Working version: 100% ÷ 5 days = 20

In this case there may be a stronger argument for testing the working version, although the decision could easily go the other way if the estimates are off—if the working version ends up taking 8 days instead of 5, the team might have been better off testing with paper. The team might want to make the decision by considering the factors I discuss in the next chapter (for example, the stability of the software).

Example 3: An e-commerce site. Screens are being developed in Dreamweaver. Layout is important, so the team wants to test using screen shots. It'll take a couple of days to mock up all the necessary pages and print them out, but at that point it would only take 2 days more to link them and get the order form to work. The team's pretty comfortable that either method would answer most of their main questions; there are just a few aspects like rollover menus and some animation that won't work well in paper.

Paper 90% ÷ 2 days = 45

Working version 100% ÷ 4 days = 25

In this example the paper prototype wins at first glance, but given the small incremental amount of work to make the mocked-up site work, there might not be much risk in going that route. This is a case where probably neither decision is wrong—if no other factors argue for or against using paper, you could even flip a coin!

I find that sometimes the efficiency ratio is an illuminating tool and other times it's useless. It also ignores the benefits and drawbacks of each method (for example, paper prototypes allow for more creativity, but they don't generate code). Your answer may be quite clear in regard to one technique over the other and thus lend you confidence about the best way to proceed. But if the results aren't so clear or you have a lot of uncertainty in your estimates, the efficiency ratio may not be a helpful tool for you—feel free to ignore it. Just keep in mind that one definition of a good prototyping method is one that provides sufficient value in return for the effort you put into it.

Tips for Dealing with Skeptics

When you propose using paper prototyping in your organization, it's unlikely that everyone will embrace the technique without question. Here are some suggestions for dealing with those who remain skeptical despite your most convincing reasons.

- **Respect skepticism.** This one is first for a reason: Paper prototyping isn't a perfect technique, so it can actually hurt your case if you argue too vigorously in favor of it. Listen to people's concerns—try to separate the valid ones from the fears that arise from unfamiliarity with the technique. The material in this chapter will help with some of the questions and misconceptions people typically have, but it won't be enough to satisfy everyone. Skeptics have a right to hang onto their concerns until they can replace them with firsthand knowledge.
- **Make a sample paper prototype.** Some people resist paper prototyping simply because they can't quite picture what you're talking about. Take an existing application that is small in scope, print some screen shots, and even hand-draw a few. (This preparation should take less then an hour—if you think it'll take longer, pick something simpler.) Bring the prototype to a meeting, have a willing co-worker play user, and show people how it works.
- **Have influential people try it out as mock users.** Several people have told me that this tactic was successful in getting paper prototyping accepted into their

From the Field: Introducing Paper Prototyping

> "Back in the mid-90s, paper prototyping wasn't widely known and there was a lot of skepticism initially. Paper prototyping wasn't very credible in the eyes of managers. So I asked some managers to participate in early test sessions and pretend to be end users. After they experienced paper prototyping as a user, they realized that it worked, and there was a lot less resistance to using it."
>
> *Timo Jokela, formerly of Nokia*

organization; see, for example, the From the Field box above. (Caveat: Chapter 7 mentioned the risks in having a co-worker act as a user, so don't treat this situation the same way you would a usability test. Causing influential people to feel foolish can be a career-limiting move. One suggestion is to take more of a walkthrough approach—tell the person each step to take but have them do all the interaction with the prototype. The person will still get to see what users experience, but isn't put on the spot.)

- **Seek support from sympathetic departments.** If you're a developer or usability specialist, note that technical writers, trainers, and customer support reps are likely to be staunch supporters of usability testing—without it, usability problems become *their* problems. Invite them, and other sympathetic souls, to everything you do regarding paper prototyping and/or usability testing. Don't worry about whether you have the authority to request their presence, just make them aware of your plans and trust that they'll do their best to be involved.
- **Just do it.** Because paper prototyping can be done with as few as two people, you may not need to get a whole lot of buy-in before you start trying it. Think about whose permission you truly need, see if you can set up a couple of usability tests, and invite people to come and watch. In companies where paper prototyping is new, I've noticed that it's common for the third or fourth usability test to be much better attended than the first—once a person sees firsthand the value of the data that they get, they insist that their manager/co-workers/staff attend subsequent tests.
- **Ask for feedback.** If someone is skeptical but still agrees that paper prototyping is worth trying, promise them that afterward there will be an opportunity for everyone to give their feedback on how well the method worked, whether they want to use it again, and anything they might want to do differently. In fact, I make it a point to do this at the conclusion of every usability study.

Chapter 14

When to Use Paper

Chapter 12 looked at the kinds of questions that paper prototypes can (and can't) answer about your interface. In this chapter we look at circumstances of your project that can nudge you toward or away from using paper. In this chapter I assume that you've decided paper is a viable technique for what you want to learn but you're still debating whether testing a paper prototype would make sense for your project as opposed to testing some other version of your interface. If you've already made your decision about using a paper prototype, you can skip this chapter.

War Stories

In 10 years of usability testing, I've collected a number of "war stories" of usability tests (and sometimes whole usability studies) gone horribly awry, with consequences ranging from funny to frustrating. Here's a sample that will give you a sense of what can happen. All of these stories are true, although details have been omitted to protect the embarrassed.

War Story 1: Honey, I Shrunk the Functionality

This case involved a revision to an existing software product, so there was a large body of underlying code already in place. The team had been working very hard on some new functionality, and it was a focus of the usability test tasks we'd created. But 2 days before the first usability test, the latest build was so unstable that we had to drop back to a previous build that lacked the new functionality. That version was buggy as well, causing delays in the usability tests when the system behaved strangely or crashed. Because customers were coming from out of town to participate in the tests, we didn't want to inconvenience them by rescheduling. The tests still provided useful information, but the team was conscious of how much more they would have learned if they had had all their new functionality ready in time.

War Story 2: Ready, Fire, Aim

We'd successfully conducted three usability tests of an e-commerce site running off the company's development server. The planned launch was a month away, and development was proceeding at a feverish pace. Right before the fourth test, someone accidentally uploaded the wrong thing and wiped out the most recent 3 days' worth of work from the entire team. That was the end of that usability study—with so little time available and a snafu on top of it, no further usability tests could be scheduled. We were just glad we'd managed to conduct three tests before it happened.

War Story 3: It's Coming (and so Is Christmas)

Another prelaunch Web site. Development was being done by an outside company who didn't like to announce every little schedule slip, especially because they'd been working long hours to meet an aggressive launch date. At 6 pm the evening before the first day of testing, the team finally admitted that they weren't going to be ready. Testing was postponed from a Thursday to the following Tuesday. Six participants had to be rescheduled. Not all of them could attend the new date, so replacements had to be recruited on a tight schedule. (And even when things can be pulled together in time, it can be harrowing—my record for the closest I've gotten to usability testing before seeing the interface for the first time is 2 hours. Hearing a developer ask, "What time does the first test start?" is never a good sign!)

War Story 4: Network = Not Work

In this case, the problem wasn't with the Web site we were testing but with the network connection in the room we were using as a temporary usability lab. Right before the first test, the network became a "not-work." I spent the first half hour of our test session chatting with the user while several people wrestled with intransi-

This is never a good sign! (Illustration by Rene Rittiner.)

gent cables and hardware. When they were ultimately unsuccessful, we moved the test to the development manager's office. Only three observers could fit in the office—half the number that had wanted to attend the test. The really frustrating thing about this case was that, being somewhat paranoid about hardware, I had insisted on a thorough test run the day before and everything had worked flawlessly.

War Story 5: Accidental Pornography

I was testing the e-commerce site of a reputable company. The user was completing an order form and through a rather bizarre sequence of actions managed to access a porn site by accident. I was very thankful that she and I were the only ones present and that she recovered her composure (mine was pretty shaken as well) after I figured out what had happened and explained it to her.* In addition to being embarrassing, there was some legal exposure (pardon the pun) here as well—earlier in that same study, a user had arrived at the test facility without having signed the consent form. She first wanted to ask me about what kinds of sites we would be

* The sequence of events: After entering her last name, the user hit the Tab key. Instead of going to the address field, the cursor went to the URL field in the browser. The user typed the first 2 digits of the street address—19—before noticing that the cursor wasn't in the address field. She clicked in the field and resumed typing. A couple fields later, she mistakenly hit the Enter key instead of Tab, which activated the URL field, and we visited 19.com, a porn site.

visiting because she was uncomfortable with some of the material available on the Internet. In an alarmingly prophetic choice of words, I reassured her that if these sites were movies they'd all be rated G. If the porn accident had happened to this user, she could have sued me.

Paper Prototype War Stories

You may have noticed that none of these war stories feature a paper prototype. In case you're wondering where those war stories are, so am I! Honestly, I don't have any—in 10 years I have yet to experience a situation where a paper prototype prevented a usability test from taking place. (I've had to cancel paper prototype tests when users didn't show up, but that can happen in any usability test.) I've also worked with development teams who were concerned that they weren't going to be ready in time, but in the end they always were. Hmm.

My experience suggests that paper prototype tests are less vulnerable to some kinds of problems than usability tests that rely on machines and other capricious entities. But equally important, I can think of many cases where product teams tested prerelease interfaces and *didn't* have a disaster or where the benefits of paper just weren't that compelling. So let's look at various aspects of your project—the people involved, the stability of the technology, the kinds of tasks you want to test—so that you can be proactive in identifying factors that might bollix up the usability study that you're planning. If a factor doesn't seem to apply to your situation, feel free to ignore it. At the end of the chapter, I summarize these discussions in a checklist.

People and Logistics

First let's consider the people—who's on your development team, where they're located in relation to users, and how difficult your target user population is to (re)schedule.

Composition of Development Team

Paper prototyping seems to work well when the product team is large and/or interdisciplinary. Many people who have useful ideas lack the technical ability to implement them, such as customer support reps, Marketing, QA, and writers. With a paper prototype there is no technical barrier to prevent ideas from coming from a variety of sources. Although it's possible for the designer to go to these people to get their input, it may be more efficient to gather the people together and let them contribute their expertise directly to the prototype. (Naturally, you'll want to take a look at the individuals who make up your team to decide whether this is a good thing or not!)

The converse is somewhat true—if the development team is small and very proficient with their tools, the benefits from using paper may not be as great. I've seen teams with two or three developers who could make substantial changes fairly rapidly. At one company, after each usability test the room would immediately empty as the developers rushed back to their desks to make changes before the next test. (Unfortunately, this was the same company featured in the "Ready, Fire, Aim" war story, who also proved their capability to make substantial *mistakes* on short notice!)

Location of Development Team and Users

Usability tests involve a whole cast of characters—users, the facilitator, the Computer, and observers. In a paper prototype test, you have to get the whole cast together in the same room. Unless everyone is already at one location, it can be inconvenient to reschedule a usability test. I've known cases where customers traveled considerable distances to participate in usability tests, like a guy who flew across the United States for a 2-hour usability test and went back home the same day. It's also not unusual for development team members from another city to come in for a couple days in to observe usability tests. The more people who assemble for the test, the farther away they're coming from, and the more influential they are, the more painful it is when something forces you to reschedule. But if you're developing an intranet and your users are right down the hall, postponing a usability test is no big deal.

Remote Usability Testing

It's difficult to usability test a paper prototype unless the Computer and users are in the same room. However, some of my colleagues have experimented with ways to test prototypes remotely, by preparing materials in either paper or electronic form and then walking through them with the user on the phone. See the From the Field box on p. 324 for examples.

From the Field: Remote Usability Testing

"I once did paper prototype testing over the telephone with excellent results by sending the participants a paper prototype booklet that I asked them to open only after our phone conversation began. The booklet supported the use scenario, so the participant could say 'Now I'd press the OK button,' and I could say, 'All right, now you see the screen shown on page D.' I was surprised at how well it actually worked, and it enabled us to include many more participants at next to no cost. (Note that the application we were testing was quite simple; this technique might become unwieldy with an interface containing more screens.)"

Betsy Comstock, PolyCom

"Rather than sending the papers, I created a set of prototype images and stored them on a Web server. Each image URL is encrypted so the user won't be able to guess what the next image would be by tweaking the URL on his/her browser. The users were connected via ICQ for text communication and we even managed to connect to a participant in Russia! Every time I asked the user to work on a page, I sent him the image URL by ICQ and gave verbal instructions over the phone. In that way I could guarantee that we were in sync."

Shawn Zhang, usability specialist

Remote usability testing is an intriguing idea, but it may not yield the richness of data that you get by being in the same room with users. There may be interaction drawbacks if the user has to flip pages or take other special action to get to the next screen. On the other hand, if travel isn't feasible, remote testing is much better than nothing, and it may allow the product team to get feedback from a larger number of users than they'd be able to see in person.

Rescheduling Costs

Rescheduling users can cost money. If you pay an outside agency to do user recruitment, they may charge you a fee for rescheduling the same users to a different day. They almost certainly will charge for each qualified person they recruit, including those that couldn't be rescheduled. Some companies don't blink at wasting far larger sums than the few hundred dollars needed to reschedule a usability study, but other companies have tight budgets and throwing away money is painful.

Development Context

As you can tell from the war stories, a lot of things can prevent you from conducting usability tests. The factors discussed in this section will help you estimate the likelihood of a technical snafu interfering with your testing plans.

Dependence on Technology

Prerelease stuff is buggy. As Murphy's Law says, anything that can go wrong, will go wrong. This state of affairs is normal during product development, but it can wreak havoc with your usability testing plans. The more modules or applications that have to play nicely together, the more vulnerable you are to technical problems—and the effect is multiplicative. Say you have a task that utilizes four software modules. Each performs reliably 90% of the time and crashes the other 10%. Put these four modules together, and your chance of getting through the task without crashing is $0.9 \times 0.9 \times 0.9 \times 0.9$, or only about 66%. It's kind of like Murphy's Law with multiple Murphys. In contrast, paper prototypes don't rely on databases, networks, servers, or any other form of technology, which eliminates most of the things that can go wrong. I've even done paper prototyping during a power failure!

You programmers out there, I know what you're thinking: "But this is my application. I'm the one writing the code." Yes, but until you're well into the debugging stage, your code (or code written by others that yours depends on) may not be stable enough to allow users to do meaningful work without crashing. Bugs happen, and software development is sometimes a process of taking two steps forward and one back.

It is possible to conduct usability tests with buggy software, and I have done this many times. If the development team knows where the land mines are located, the facilitator can usually steer users safely around them. If the users find a land mine we didn't know about, perhaps it's not difficult to restart the system and get back to where they left off. But these situations can be nerve-wracking, not only for the users but also for the product team. As a facilitator, I sometimes find

We often aren't quite as in control of software development as we would like. (Illustration by Rene Rittiner.)

myself mentally chanting, "Stop him before he clicks Submit, stop him before . . ." Which is not so bad—it's part of the facilitator's job—but the real issue is that the observers have the same chant going through *their* heads. I've seen developers who were so focused on the survival of their interface that they didn't get much value from watching the usability tests. If you're concerned that a buggy interface will be too distracting to the product team (or upsetting to users, who may disregard assurances that it isn't their fault), consider using a paper prototype instead.

Usability Testing versus Development

I deliberately put the "versus" in the heading because sometimes that's how it seems to me—it's possible for usability testing to interfere with the development process and vice versa, especially in its later stages. The degree to which a project is vulnerable to this depends on whether there's a separate environment that can be used for testing. If the usability tests rely on the latest build on the development server, development must come to a carefully orchestrated pause so that someone submitting a "minor" change doesn't accidentally break the very thing you're trying to test. This can have a detrimental effect on schedules, unless the entire development team plans to attend the usability tests or wouldn't be submitting any changes during that time anyway.

But if you use a paper prototype, usability testing and development are completely separate and can proceed in parallel without risk of hurting each other. I've known a few development teams who chose to conduct paper prototype tests late in the project—when a reliable version of the interface was available—simply to alleviate any risk that the development schedule would be impacted.

You might respond that a good project manager is capable of handling all these circumstances, especially with decent version control software. That's true, but not all project managers are that good—when I was a project manager my sanity was fragile enough as it was, and the need to maintain a stable environment for usability testing would have pushed me right over the edge. If your development process runs like a Swiss watch, paper prototyping may not offer you any advantages. But for those who are already logistically challenged, paper prototyping can make life easier.

Test Environment—Hardware and Facility

One way to avoid conflicts with ongoing development is to set up a separate test environment with all hardware, software, network connections, and so on needed to do the tasks. Maybe you're lucky enough to have a fully outfitted usability lab. Or your QA department or training facility may have something like this, although if they use it every day you may not be able to borrow it.

You may be thinking, "What's all the fuss about a test environment? I'll just run it on my laptop." If your interface runs in a simple and self-contained environment like that, then you're right, you don't really have this problem. But some test environments require lots of technology—think servers, multiple computers, hardware devices, and the like. The harder it is to create a good, realistic test environment, the stronger the argument in favor of using a paper prototype to avoid going to all that trouble (and possibly expense because hardware isn't free).

Test Environment—Accounts and Databases

For some testing situations, it's easy to set up dummy accounts and databases for users to use when performing tasks. Other times this isn't as feasible. For example, one financial services Web site didn't have a test database for usability testing (the developers had one but it wasn't possible to share it), so for testing purposes we had to use the real Web site, which naturally accessed the real customer database. For tasks that assumed the user already had an account, we needed a real account. There was a VP at the company who allowed his account to be used for this purpose (provided we didn't buy or sell anything!), but this guy was in no way a typical user—he owned dozens of stocks. Thus, users had to wade through a large amount of unfamiliar data, which made some of the tasks artificially complex. And since we couldn't transact, we were limited in what we could test.

Tasks, Data, and Test Scenarios

The usability tasks that you want users to do can have a bearing on whether paper will offer advantages over testing the real thing. Paper prototypes can sometimes give you greater flexibility with your tasks than you'd get with the real interface. In other cases they're a poor substitute for reality.

Control of Content

You don't just need control of the technology—for usability testing purposes, you often need some degree of control over what the user sees, such as information that comes from a database. For live Web sites, don't forget content such as ads that may change without warning (not to mention the risk of accidental pornography). If some of the content isn't under your control, think about whether this could have a detrimental effect on your usability tests.

Between-Test Reset Procedures

In setting up a series of usability tests, consider what you need to do between tests to *reset* the test environment. For a Web site, this may be as simple as clearing the link history in the browser and deleting cookies. For software applications, it may be easy enough to delete all the files the user modified during the test session and replace them with fresh copies. But not always. One Web application had an underlying work flow involving several users and databases—when Person A was done handling a request, it resulted in database changes and work being sent to Person B via email. To simulate the work flows needed for our tasks, one of the developers created some elaborate procedures that we had to run between tests, and in one case even between tasks. (And because he couldn't attend all the tests, he also had to train others on those procedures.) I asked him afterward to estimate how long he'd spent on all that setting up and resetting; he said about 15 hours. Because this interface was fairly simple, we could have created a paper prototype in perhaps half that time.

Installation and Configuration Tasks

Tasks involving installation or configuration are a special case of reset procedures—they can be a pain. Say you have a test scenario where the user installs a software application. Perhaps in task 1 you'd test the ideal case where everything goes smoothly, and in task 2 you want to throw the user a curve in the form of a compatibility problem they have to resolve. To do task 2, you'd have to uninstall the software and set up the conditions that would cause the incompatibility. Or you could save an image of the pristine test machine on a server and restore it, although in my experience this can result in several minutes of downtime (which may not be a drawback if you can hold a discussion with the users in the meantime). With a paper prototype, you could simply start task 2 by telling the user, "Assume you're doing the same thing on a different machine."

Real-World Consequences

I once visited a prospective client that was developing a Web application for booking corporate travel. They knew that their interface lacked feedback, and rather shamefacedly admitted that on a couple of occasions while testing the interface they had accidentally bought plane tickets . . . nonrefundable ones, naturally. That's an example of a real-world consequence. Similarly, some software applications control physical equipment. If you're testing an interface for medical equipment or some other potentially dangerous device, you may have a situation in which users can blithely get themselves into real-world trouble. I once taught paper prototyping to some engineers who worked on process control for heavy machinery used in processing steel. One of them remarked that you got a whole new appreciation for the effects of a bug when it could result in sheets of steel spewing across the factory floor at 200 mph. Obviously, paper prototypes avoid such problems.

Lengthy Processing Delays

It's not a big deal in a usability test if the user occasionally has to wait a few seconds for a page to download or a large file to be opened. But if there is processing that takes any longer than the time needed to offer the users a refill of their coffee cups, you might be wasting too much time by testing the real interface. For example, in a usability test of software for network administrators, users were asked to set up some tests of the network that would take several hours to execute in real life. With the paper prototype, we just told them, "It's now the next morning, and here's the report." (Sometimes with software you can do something similar, but other times it's just too much of a pain.)

User-Defined Tasks

In a paper prototype test, it's a given that you know what the tasks are because you came up with them before creating the prototype. But sometimes it's important to watch users doing their own tasks—something that they care highly about—rather than tasks you invented. When users work on their own tasks, they may uncover subtleties that you weren't aware of (or even entire *tasks* you weren't aware of). Unless the data and/or functionality of the interface is quite limited, user-defined tasks usually aren't feasible with paper because you need breadth—you can't predict where users will go. For example, you may need the entire pet products catalog rather than just the section devoted to ferret toys.

Timing and Scope

There are good times in the project cycle to use paper prototyping, and there are better times. There are even a few bad times.

Stage of Development

In the early stages of development, before implementation begins, paper prototyping may be your only viable option for doing usability tests. In the middle of development, you might have the option of testing either a paper prototype or a working version of the interface. But right before a release? Yuck. In my opinion, the most difficult time to do any kind of usability testing is in the month before launch—the development team is focused on fixing bugs and getting the product out the door, so it's difficult to get any bandwidth from them to observe usability tests. Even if a few tests can be squeezed in, there may be little opportunity to fix problems before the release, which can be demoralizing. In essence, testing done in the month before launch might really be testing done for the *next* version of the interface, so if you find yourself in this situation, you might think about waiting until then. If you're still primarily concerned about this version, make every effort to do your testing as early as possible.

Although paper prototyping may be most common during earlier stages of development, it isn't wrong to use it in any situation in which the logistical advantages described in this chapter are sufficiently attractive.

Scope of Planned Changes

If you're designing something brand new, paper allows you to do several iterations of a design before you start implementation. The flexibility of paper as a design medium isn't a compelling advantage if you're not in a position to make substantial changes—perhaps you've already committed to a particular approach and you're just refining some of the details or maybe you've already done some usability testing and have a good handle on the issues. But if you know the current design will present you with some challenging problems to solve, paper will give you freedom to experiment.

Making Your Decision

The checklist in Table 14.1 summarizes the factors that this chapter has covered. (For a printable version, see *www.paperprototyping.com.*) This checklist isn't a definitive decision-making tool that will tell you whether you should use a paper prototype. Its goal is more modest—to ensure that you've thought about the risks particular to conducting usability tests with your interface. Hopefully this checklist will prevent your project from becoming a war story like the ones at the beginning of this chapter.

The number of check marks in each column isn't especially important, and not all the factors will apply to every situation. The main thing you should do is look for showstoppers in testing the working interface. If your software application depends on the stability of several modules being developed by an outside firm, you're moving to a new building 2 days before the first usability test, and the users are flying in from Singapore, the chances of a trouble-free usability study are vanishingly small. Go with paper and save yourself the aggravation. On the other hand, if the interface you want to test is under the control of two whiz-bang developers and the users are down the hall, there are relatively few inherent risks in testing the real thing.

Table 14.1 Checklist: Working Interface versus Paper Prototype

	Working Interface	*Paper Prototype*
People and logistics	❑ There are only a few people working on the design, perhaps 3 or 4 at most.	❑ The product team is larger.
	❑ The people directly responsible for the design are already proficient with a computer-based tool like VB, Dreamweaver, etc.	❑ Using a computer-based prototyping tool would require a learning curve before we were proficient enough to prototype what we envision.
	❑ Everyone working on the design has a technical (i.e., programming) background.	❑ There are nonprogrammers on the team whose input is important, such as tech writers, customer support reps, or Marketing.
	❑ The development team and users are all located within a reasonable commuting distance, or remote testing is a viable option.	❑ We aren't all in the same geographic area and remote testing isn't a good option—if we're going to do usability testing, someone has to travel.
	❑ The users are readily available. They won't be upset if we have to reschedule a test, and a few rescheduling fees won't break our budget.	❑ The recruiting firm charges us a fee to reschedule users, or the users are people we don't want to inconvenience.
Development context	❑ The interface is a standalone piece of software or other technology.	❑ There are many software modules required for successful completion of the tasks.
	❑ All the software modules needed for usability testing are stable, or we're confident we can test around the problems without too much difficulty.	❑ Some software modules are under development, are of uncertain reliability, or otherwise not under our direct control.
	❑ It's not a problem to pause development for a couple of days to do usability testing.	❑ People are constantly submitting changes—we either have to ask them to hold off for a few days or we'd need to set up a separate test environment.

Table 14.1 Checklist: Working Interface versus Paper Prototype—cont'd

	Working Interface	*Paper Prototype*
	❑ It's not difficult to set up a test environment, including hardware, databases, accounts, etc.	❑ It would take time and/or money to set up a test environment, or it would be hard to create one that's sufficiently realistic.
	❑ We can control everything the user sees, including product databases and ads.	❑ Some of the content comes from sponsors, manufacturers, or other outside sources, and we can't always predict or control it.
Tasks, data, and test scenarios	❑ Reset procedures are minimal—transactions can be easily faked or reversed.	❑ Resetting the test environment between tests is complicated—transactions are real, high consequence, or difficult to undo.
	❑ Installation and configuration are not being tested.	❑ Tasks include installation or configuration.
	❑ There are no long delays for the user to sit through—a minute at most, and usually less.	❑ The user may have to wait more than a minute or two for the system to do its processing.
	❑ We want users to bring their own real tasks to the test session.	❑ The set of tasks is known in advance; we've created them.
Timing and scope	❑ Usability testing can wait until the middle or end of the development process.	❑ Usability testing before or during development is desirable.
	❑ There is a previous working version of the interface.	❑ The interface doesn't exist yet or needs to be substantially redesigned.
	❑ We can't make huge changes at this point, just a few tweaks.	❑ We know there are significant problems, or we'd like to experiment with solutions.

Hybrid (Paper + Software) Testing

If you're having trouble deciding, why not take the best of both worlds? When a design is new or is being overhauled, it probably makes sense to do all your prototyping with the same method. But sometimes, especially if you've already done some usability testing, there may just be isolated parts of the design that you're working on. You may want to consider a hybrid prototype, where you use the real interface for most of the tasks but switch to paper for a screen or two as needed. (If you're up for a bit of Wizard of Oz, have the users write inputs on the paper. Then you can ask them to close their eyes while you "magically" replicate their actions in the software and then have them open their eyes and continue testing with the software.) Figure 14.1 shows an example where a single paper

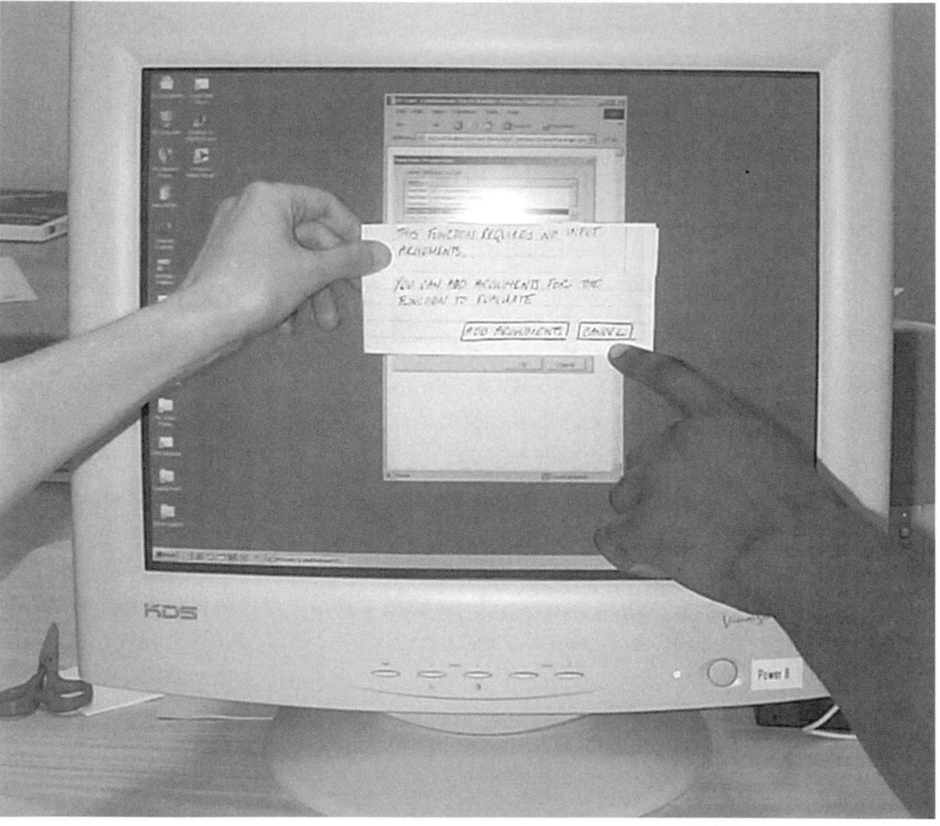

Figure 14.1 When you have only isolated screens to test, you can use a hybrid approach of software and paper.

prototype screen is held in front of a computer screen; it's also possible to put a few paper prototype screens on the table next to the user.

Hybrid prototyping may not be the best choice for companies that are just getting started with usability testing. The hybrid approach is somewhat awkward when the paper prototype consists of more than a couple screens or you do a lot of switching back and forth. I once conducted a usability study of a Web application where we alternated each task between a paper prototype and a laptop. This worked reasonably well, but the logistics were complicated—when users were working on the laptop, we also had it projected on the wall so that the rest of the team could see. When we switched to the paper prototype, however, we had to turn off the projector, move the laptop aside, and rearrange our seating. We lost some test time due to the constant shuffling of people and equipment, although the users didn't seem to mind.

I would use the hybrid approach again, but I would first make sure that it was truly needed, in other words, that there was a set of questions that called for each method. Otherwise I'd probably vote for doing the whole prototype one way or the other—in this case, the problems we found from testing on the laptop would also have shown up in a paper prototype.

Part IV

Broadening the Focus

Most of this book has focused on the details of what paper prototyping is, what it's good for, and how to do it. Now let's zoom out a bit. Paper prototyping fits within the larger context of user-centered design, which also includes techniques like contextual inquiry, personas, and participatory design, to name just a few. Although the techniques themselves can be sophisticated, they share an innate simplicity: They help product teams understand users.

Chapter 15

Examples of User-Centered Design

Let's look at some examples of how people use prototyping as just one part of the larger picture of user-centered design. I asked three usability specialists to describe how they have used paper prototyping and other user-centered techniques at their company or clients. You'll notice that the examples have some things in common:

- **Early feedback.** These companies recognize the value of figuring out what's needed *before* building it, so they seek feedback from users and internal stakeholders.
- **Several techniques.** Paper prototyping is an important technique, but not the only one. In particular, there are other user-centered activities that precede the first prototype.
- **Fast and iterative.** Designs go through multiple revisions. There's no expectation that the early designs will be perfect, only that they'll improve each time around.
- **Small and informal.** No big budgets, no huge research studies, no fancy reports. Just do it, learn from it, do it again if needed (and schedules allow), and then move on.

Example 1: The MathWorks

By Mary Beth Rettger

I'm Director of the Usability Group at The MathWorks, a developer of technical computing software. At The MathWorks, we use several user-centered design techniques to help us understand what our users need and to ensure that what we build actually meets those needs. Here's how we applied contextual interviewing, paper prototyping, and usability testing to the development of MATLAB 6.

Contextual Interviewing

It's important to watch and/or interview customers in their own work environment, where they can easily show us examples of what they are trying to accomplish. This process is called contextual interviewing. Rather than just getting a laundry list of new features users want, they show us how they hope to use a new feature or explain what problems they are trying to solve with the current product. Armed with a thorough understanding of the problem, our software designers can come up with targeted solutions that address the users' needs.

During MATLAB 6 development we undertook a research project with the assistance of undergraduate students enrolled in an Engineering Psychology class at Tufts University. The project was a win-win situation—we obtained a lot of data with relatively little effort from within the company, and the students received course credit for their work. After some training in contextual interviewing techniques by our usability team, the students interviewed about 20 MATLAB users. The students wrote formal reports summarizing the "top 10" issues observed during the interviews. They also provided us with detailed interview results, including artifacts such as samples of users' work, outputs, and photos of the users' work environments. Finally, the students created several "Meet Our Users" posters that graphically illustrated several typical users and their work. (This is similar to the technique of creating *personas,* although personas are usually made-up examples of typical users instead of actual people.)

All this information was valuable to the development team. Developers who were eager to get a fresh perspective on the problems our users faced appreciated the top 10 lists and the user posters. The individual interview transcripts were even more important—developers pored through this information to get specific data with which to prioritize their efforts. Several key themes came out during these interviews, including requests that we improve MATLAB's Printing, Plot Editing, and help system. That's where the work artifacts came in handy: Seeing examples of real work that users were trying to do (or had difficulty doing) helped the developers gain a better understanding of where to focus their efforts.

Because the students were not MATLAB experts, we were still left with the task of determining which changes to make to MATLAB. Several development team members (including tech writers and quality engineers) went out on a handful of follow-up interviews with users, getting answers to questions that had arisen from the student interviews. This combination of efforts helped us come up with an excellent list of priorities for MATLAB 6.

Usability Testing of Paper Prototypes

Once they understood what users wanted, developers were eager to begin coding new solutions, so we moved on to paper prototypes. Most often, the basic design was hand-sketched, and other user interface elements such as drop-down menus, dialog boxes, and error messages were created using sticky notes, tape, and glue.

Thanks to the contextual interviews, we had a good idea of what "realistic tasks" were for our users. Team members worked with one task at a time and walked through the process of completing it with the prototype. Because the developers were focused on the users' tasks, they had to think hard about the purpose and value of each feature. This ensured that only the essential parts of the interface were created—no need to add extra features if they weren't relevant to the users' work.

The MATLAB 6 release contained several tools, so it was practical to test each tool with only a small number of users. We selected customers who would typically use the feature we were testing. One or more developers acted as the Computer, responding nonverbally to the user's interactions with the interface. Each user was instructed to "think out loud" to help us understand what they were expecting from the product. Although users often gave us puzzled looks to start with, they quickly got involved and had fun with the game-like aspects of working with the prototype. More important, most users had no problem making the connection between the paper version and the end goal of a more usable product designed for them.

Members of the development team sat in the room and observed each usability test. Sometimes only one team member observed; other times there were half a dozen. After—or sometimes even during—each usability test, we made changes to the prototype. We did as many rounds as we needed to feel confident that we were on the right track (or in some less ideal cases, as many as we had time for), and the developers went on to code the functionality that had been hammered out on paper.

Usability Testing of Working Software

It was important for us to retest designs after they were implemented in code. In some cases, there were features that truly didn't test as well on paper as online.

Also, once implementation started, there were inevitable changes and compromises necessary to express the design in code. So we needed to validate the more finished designs.

Much of this testing was done in our usability lab: a two-room lab, with rooms separated by one-way glass. We generally had one developer and a usability specialist sit with the user in the testing room, and additional team members observed from the other side of the one-way glass. As with the paper prototypes, we gave users realistic tasks to complete, asked them to "think out loud" while they worked and to let us know if they experienced frustration or satisfaction with the feature being tested. The usability specialist or developer sometimes prompted the user for more information along the way.

All the team members were involved in observing the test sessions, although not every person observed every test. Team members took notes during test sessions on sticky pads, writing down one issue per sticky. At the end of all the test sessions, we held a debriefing meeting involving the whole team where we conducted an affinity diagramming exercise, grouping issues from these sticky notes into like categories. Once the categories were established, it was easier for the team to review the issues and decide what actions to take. Because the entire team was involved in learning what was working (or not) in the interface, everyone could contribute to the solution. Thus, the process not only improved the interface but also served as a useful team-building exercise.

Usability Nights

We've also had a lot of success with what we call "Usability Nights," which are a fast way to get informal usability feedback from a group of users. Basically, we take over a training room for an evening and bring in a teamful of developers and a bunch of local customers. Instead of having everyone work on a problem at the same time, we set up stations for each tool or interface, staffed by the development team member(s) who's working on it.

We usually ask the users to bring in examples from their jobs to work on. Typically we're only getting feedback on one or two interfaces, but on one occasion we tested several development efforts at once. Users rotated through each station, spending about 30 minutes at each. Depending on the stage of the project and what the developer wants to learn, they might have used a paper prototype, working software, or even a hybrid approach combining a paper prototype with the real software.

Usability Nights are a fast way to get a lot of information, and our customers enjoy them as well. They appreciate the opportunity to be involved in the development of the products they'll eventually use in their own work.

Example 2: IBM

By Thyra Rauch

At IBM, our human factors specialists use a variety of user-centered design techniques throughout the design and development process. Our push has been to move more and more to the front of the process, working early with users and iterating on early design solutions. Paper prototyping is one of those techniques used successfully by many groups in IBM at various points in the process. Here are some examples from some of my recent projects.

When I began work with Tivoli Systems (a company later bought by IBM) several years ago, we had to work very quickly on a novel project—a piece of software that our customers had no experience with. The problems we were trying to address could be solved in a number of ways, so first we wanted to get those thoughts down and run them by our customers.

Storyboards

Before we began prototyping, we often used storyboards to capture more of the scope and flow of the design proposal. Storyboards are much like paper prototypes, but typically broader in scope and not generally intended for input from the customers. We tend to do them on big sheets of paper that capture the narrative of the customer stories, questions that need to be asked, issues that need to be addressed, assumptions, user information, decision points, and the like. These documents become a record for the team, and the ideas that we have captured on them remain to be explored later as resources free up. We've gone back to storyboards as much as several years later because they are such a rich source of information.

Paper Prototypes

Following our storyboarding exercises where we explored the domain, we created some very rough paper sketches of several alternatives and went prepared, with a team comprised of human factors and visual design specialists, to do some "design on the fly" if necessary. The beauty of this approach is that we could do this kind of activity virtually anywhere: at our development lab, at the customer's site, or at one of their trade shows or conferences. In many cases, none of the alternatives we had sketched fully met the needs of the customers, so we did a lot of quick sketching, with the customers telling us what to draw. In some cases, the customers got

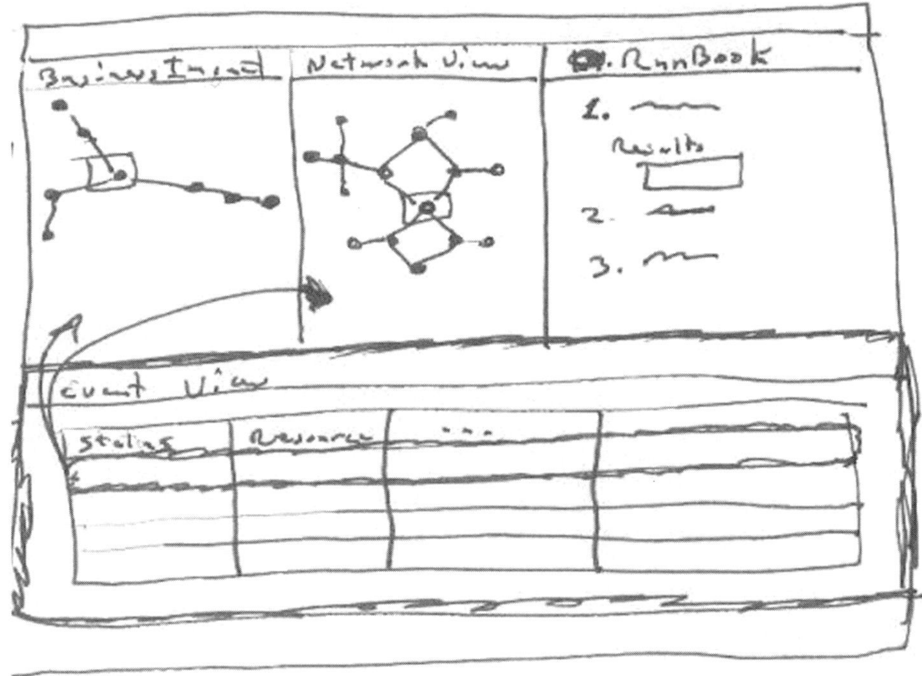

Figure 15.1 A very rough paper prototype screen that was used in usability testing.

so excited they grabbed the pens and started sketching themselves, which is part of the magic of this medium—anyone can participate.

Using rough forms such as the one shown in Figure 15.1, it's very easy to get people engaged in the process. On one hand, it's good to go in with a straw man because:

1. It shows you have done your homework in the domain.
2. It gives them something to react to, which seems to be easier them coming up with something from scratch.
3. It scopes the level you want them to work at by providing an example.

On the other hand, using paper prototypes encourages them to work with you to *evolve* the design, not just nod their heads in acceptance. The rougher the prototype, the better (to a point) because it readily conveys the idea that the design is open to input versus it's already been designed and is now cast in concrete with you merely getting their approval to proceed.

PowerPoint Presentations

Another technique we used a lot was to use paper screens printed off from PowerPoint slides. The slides included screen captures of existing product panels, screen captures where we did some cut-and-paste to make suggested changes, pencil sketches that were scanned in, and simple blocks with arrows for navigation and blobs where stuff goes. Again, the three main notions were being "open for input," "fast to produce and change," and "portable."

We've used a lot of PowerPoint prototypes in the past several years to communicate quickly and easily among team members and customers in remote locations because it's easy to distribute the prototypes online and then have everyone on a teleconference discussing them. At that point, the prototype really isn't "paper" anymore, but more in a class that we started terming "mid-fi" a number of years ago.

Mid-Fi Prototypes

At that point, I was part of a small multidisciplinary team that was working on one of the first Web applications. The product, BookManager BookServer, was an online document system. At that time, the notion of Web applications was pretty new, and we wanted to get the concepts of the system across to folks in as interactive a way as we could, as quickly as we could. We got bogged down trying to use low-fidelity or paper prototypes because they were not really interactive enough to show the power of our search engine, but we didn't want to spend the time to code high-fidelity prototypes, so the notion of medium-fidelity, or "mid-fi," prototypes using HTML was born. Our team, which included a programmer and an online help writer, could very rapidly mock things up for our customers, and even make changes on the fly. This project is described further in a paper I co-authored called "Web-Based Prototyping for User Sessions: Medium-Fidelity Prototyping" (Leone, Gillihan, & Rauch, 2000).

Summary

What all these methods have in common was that they allowed us to refine our understanding of users and what they needed. Storyboards captured our own preliminary ideas (and lots of questions) about how the interface needed to work, paper prototypes encouraged dialog with users, and mid-fi prototypes were useful for those questions that paper couldn't answer.

Example 3: Dictaphone

By Hal Shubin

I'm a usability consultant at Interaction Design *(www.user.com)*. One of my clients is Dictaphone Corporation, a provider of innovative voice technologies. Dictaphone is developing a handheld microphone used in conjunction with software called PowerScribe Workstation. Doctors use the microphone to dictate notes after each contact with a patient. The software converts the speech to text, which the physician can then edit via a combination of keyboard, voice commands, and buttons on the microphone. For example, the spoken phrase "Dictaphone: ankle sprain" alerts the speech recognition engine to put appropriate standard text in the dictation display. The physician can then navigate among fields to replace placeholders—indicate which foot was injured, what medication was prescribed, and so on. The microphone has functions like Dictate, Rewind, and Insert text, plus navigation controls used in conjunction with the software.

Developing hardware can be riskier than software because it's expensive to fix mistakes once the device has reached the manufacturing stage. The Dictaphone team used several rounds of prototyping, using progressively more realistic techniques. The methods allowed many internal stakeholders to participate in the design process, including members from several disciplines, such as software engineering, mechanical engineering, manufacturing, and a physician who acted as a proxy for the target user population. Here's a summary of what we did.

Usage Scenarios

In the earliest stages of design, I created some rough layouts and then Bob Hanson, the industrial designer, prepared scale drawings. Then we began working with a set of three usage scenarios we had created for a previous project—Dictaphone is proactive about understanding customers and their needs. Each scenario contained a fictional but realistic description of a doctor and a description of how he or she would use the PowerScribe Workstation. (An example is shown in Figure 15.2.) The scenarios helped us walk through several common tasks that we expected our target user population to do. Although this is not a substitute for usability testing, this scenario-and-walkthrough technique provided a context for our design discussions. We had one scenario that represented physicians who were not very comfortable using computers. This scenario came directly from the people we had met during usability tests of the PowerScribe Workstation software and was a good way to remind us to limit features and keep the design simple.

Goal	He's concerned about accuracy, both for the patient's sake and because of his dexterity problems.
Computer use	Average
Dictation	He dictates notes after each patient encounter, although he often reviews his dictation at the end of each day.
Affiliation	Family Health Care, Boulder, CO
Notes	Dr. Manos has difficulty using his hands due to a recent neurological problem. He gets a little support from the nursing staff during patient visits but can use a computer reasonably well. He represents some classes of handicapped users, but also people who simply have lessened dexterity.

Dr. Ramesh Manos
Pediatrics

Dr. Manos found the telephone-based dictation system easy to use. Because of his disability, he wore a headset instead of holding the handset and has a telephone with large buttons that are easier to press. The new PowerScribe Workstation set him back a little, until he worked out some accommodations. For example, when his hands tire, he holds the microphone with one hand and presses the buttons with the other. That's easier than trying to manipulate buttons with the hand he's holding it with. When possible, he uses voice commands for navigation . . .

Figure 15.2 Excerpt from a usage scenario for the PowerScribe Workstation. The scenario continues to discuss usage for a few more paragraphs, then has a table showing how Dr. Manos would use each proposed feature of the microphone.

Collaborative Design: Wood Blocks and Stickers

Bob and I wanted to show the development team our drawings, but first I wanted to have a group design session. Successful design is a collaborative effort—they bring us consultants in for our design knowledge, but the team members have the domain knowledge. An activity where people make something concrete is a great way to transfer that knowledge. A design exercise forces people to be explicit about their ideas, so you get better and richer information than when they just talk. We decided to do this exercise before showing them our drawings so that our ideas wouldn't influence them.

So we had them build microphone models. Bob prepared blocks of wood that were about the size of the microphone. We gave the team members pens and blank stickers in various sizes. We began the session with a discussion of the features they wanted on the device, just to get ideas going. As always, there was some skepticism—people are always a little leery when they have to do something that reminds them of art class! But once we got started, everyone really got involved. Some samples are shown in Figure 15.3.

At the end of the meeting, Bob and I showed them our schematics. Turns out that some of our drawings weren't valid any longer because our brainstorming discussion had simplified the design by moving some features from the microphone to the base it would sit in. So this exercise was very successful. It was hard work for them to turn their ideas into something tangible, but they realized that we had discussed the design in far more detail than before.

I think it's important to accept design advice from my clients because they've thought about the problem longer than I have. Team members had great ideas about arranging controls that helped Bob and me in our next round of design. Bob

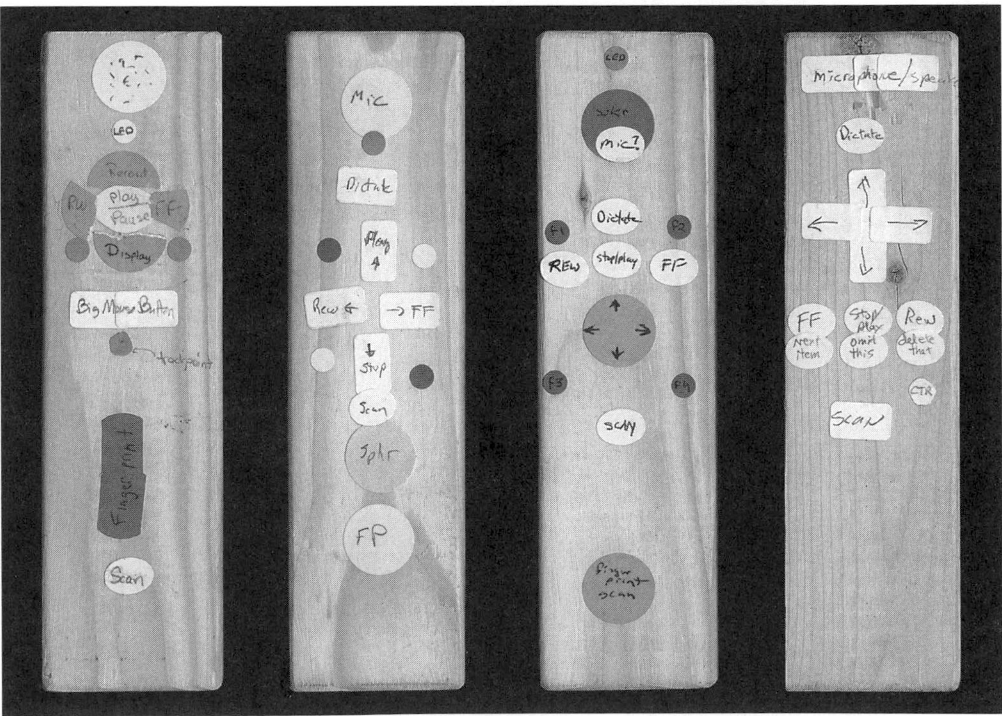

Figure 15.3 Using wood blocks and stickers, the team members experimented with button layouts and discussed their ideas. This exercise led to several changes in the assumptions about the design.

and I walked away with four complete prototype designs to use in our subsequent design work. It doesn't matter that we didn't develop all of the ideas—our job is to come up with a good design that makes the product successful.

Fome-Cor Mockups

We were concerned about the possibility of hand fatigue if users used the microphone for long stretches of time. The design schedule called for making full 3D foam models at this point, but they're expensive and take a week or two to make. We wanted some quicker feedback first. We had a pretty good idea of the relative importance of the buttons, and realized that it'd be okay for users to reach a little for the less-used ones. Our goal at this stage was to identify problems due to button location. Where would the user's hand rest? How hard would it be to reach the various buttons? Would it be okay to adjust one's grip to reach some buttons?

Bob made models of some button layouts using Fome-Cor (polystyrene foam sandwiched between two pieces of paper, available in various thicknesses). He drew the button layouts on Fome-Cor and cut them out to fit over the lower half of an existing microphone shell. Bob created about eight of these, representing five different configurations with three minor variations (such as a four-way rocker versus four separate buttons). Some examples are shown in Figure 15.4.

Here's where the usage scenarios came in handy again—by holding a model and pressing its buttons in accordance with anticipated usage, we literally got a feel for which designs were more comfortable to use even though the buttons themselves were only two-dimensional. We also got some insights about which buttons needed to be near other buttons. For example, our simulations showed us that we could increase efficiency by putting the button to initiate dictation near the one used to display the dictated text. At this stage, we also considered how complex the design looked, as well as some conventions such as having the Rewind button on the left and Fast Forward on the right. In a review meeting, we were able to rule out five of the eight models, leaving us with three.

Foam Models

Next we enlisted a model maker to build true 3D models so that we could further explore the look and feel of the microphone. We were able to settle on a single overall form, but the layout of the button arrays was still in flux. One change was to move the buttons so that they'd be easier to press when one picked up the micro-

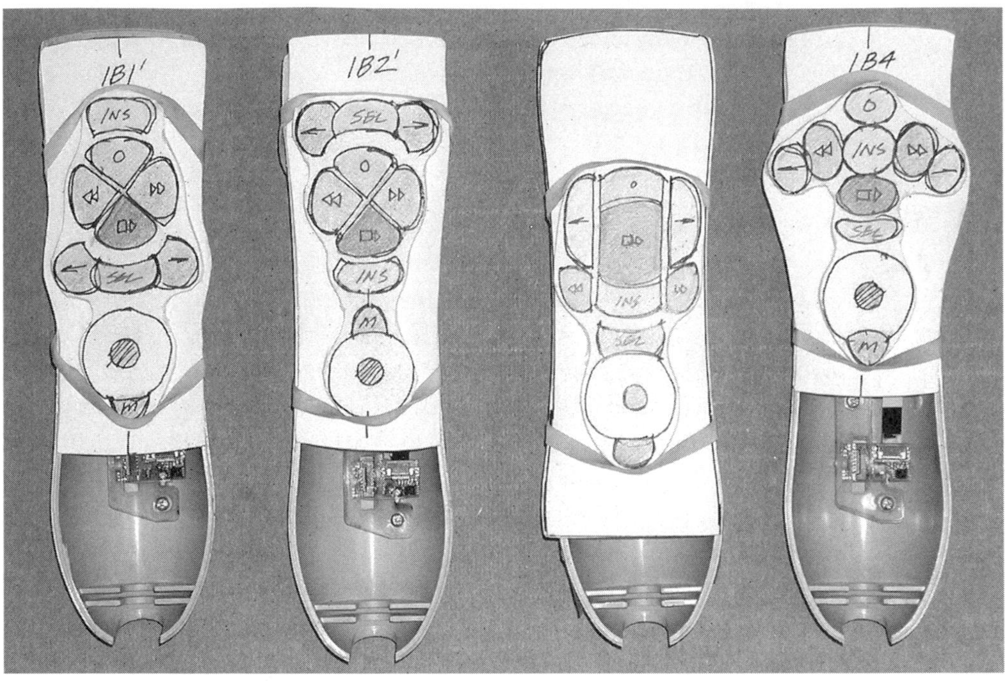

Figure 15.4 These prototypes (made of Fome-Cor, paper, and a microphone shell) enabled the development team to explore what it would be like to hold the microphone and use its buttons to perform various tasks.

phone. We also wanted to limit "regripping," although eventually we decided it was okay for secondary features.

The industrial designer and model maker then produced a final set of models, like the one shown in Figure 15.5. Bob came up with a very pleasing circular layout for the button array. He had the model maker create one microphone body with four replaceable alternatives for the button arrays. Some of the differences were concave versus convex button shapes and relative sizes of related buttons. I knew we were on the right track when the product manager picked up the model and a great smile came over his face! We also sent models to team members in other states, who gave us useful feedback about spacing and button sizes.

Looking Forward, Looking Back

As of this writing, the microphone is still under development. The mechanical and electrical engineers are working on the PC board and suggesting modifications that will make manufacturing easier. Bob is working with the mechanical engi-

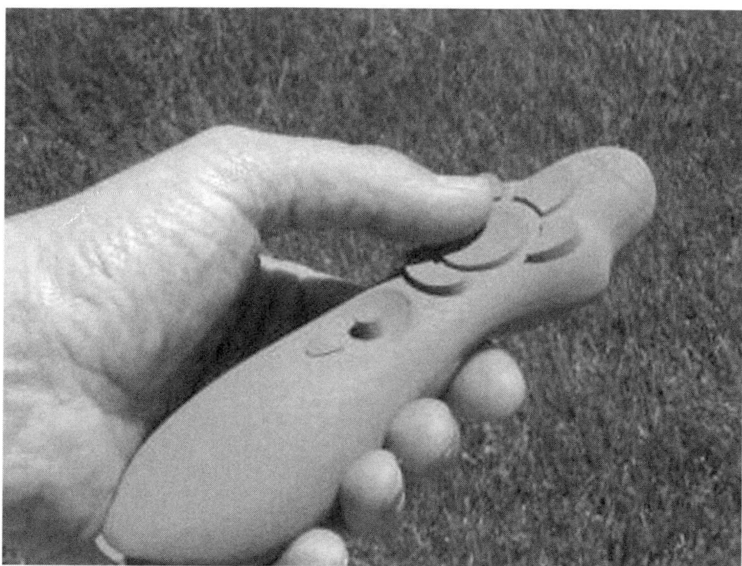

Figure 15.5 Foam models allowed the team to experiment with different button layouts.

neer to create a CAD database so that they can do the tooling for manufacturing. The model maker is creating a new button-array insert with greater tactile feedback between the buttons. I also plan to conduct usability tests, using the most realistic model that's available at the time.

Although all this prototyping may sound like a significant effort, any design mistake that made it into production would be very expensive due to manufacturing costs. David Pearah, Dictaphone's Senior Product Line Manager, Speech Products, sums it up:

> "The benefits of going through the prototyping steps are almost too obvious to mention. The design exercise with wood blocks gave us a good forum for discussing our ideas. The drawings, Fome-Cor models, and foam models each improved our understanding of the designs that Bob and Hal were creating.
>
> We are building something that physicians will hold all day long. Without a 3D model, there's no way to know how comfortable it will be. Designing the microphone was more complex than we thought it would be because curvature, button spacing, and tactile feedback all make a difference in the user experience. We needed multiple models to discover the subtle things. It's important to know when to stop making prototypes though; at some point you have to actually make the thing. It can never be 100% perfect. There are long cycles in hardware development and foam models are the cost of reducing risk. Although it increases time up front, it can save time later on. The process Hal describes worked well for us."

Chapter 16

Final Thoughts

This is the end of this book, but certainly not everything you need to know about user-centered design, and perhaps not even everything you'd like to know about paper prototyping. It's certainly not the end of what *I'd* like to know—in writing this book I realized that I still have many questions about paper prototyping, including:

- How does paper prototyping change the process of design? Does it allow designers to work in a fundamentally different way?
- Do the benefits of using paper prototypes in usability tests depend more on the medium of paper or the unfinished nature of the design?
- Exactly how does a paper prototype affect a user's behavior compared to testing the real thing? Is there a better way to spot false problems due to the paper prototype or Computer?
- Do teams that use paper prototypes truly spend less time on coding? How much money does the technique save them?
- What's the best way to funnel the results from paper prototype testing into the development process? When everything is changing rapidly, what's the best way to capture the insights that the team is learning?

And so on. Now I understand what Einstein meant when he said, "As our circle of knowledge expands, so does the circumference of the darkness surrounding it." Despite any unanswered questions, I hope that this book has given you a good understanding of how paper prototyping works and how you can use it to benefit your product development process. I'll leave you with these thoughts:

- Paper prototyping is a useful technique, but it's just one of many under the larger umbrella of user-centered design.
- This book has provided an introduction to usability testing—you should read other books, join discussion lists, and learn from others with experience. The usability profession is graced with many generous people who will take the time to help a newcomer.
- Don't be afraid to try paper prototyping and usability testing—you won't do it perfectly (no one does), and you'll learn from your mistakes. Just as your interface will benefit from several iterations of feedback, so will your usability skills.

And finally, as Oscar Wilde said, "Life is too important to be taken seriously." Have fun!

References

If this were a paper prototype, you'd be able to touch the URLs in these references and the Computer would magically take you there, but since this is only a book, we can't do that. But if you visit *www.paperprototyping.com,* you'll find links to the articles and papers that are available online.

Papers and Articles

Cited in Text

Catani, M. B., and D. W. Biers. 1998. Usability evaluation and prototype fidelity: Users and usability professionals. In *Proceedings of the Human Factors and Ergonomics Society 42nd Annual Meeting,* pp. 1331–1335. Santa Monica, CA: HFES.

Hertzum, M., N. E. Jacobsen, and R. Molich. 2002. Usability inspections by groups of specialists: Perceived agreement in spite of disparate observations. In *Extended Abstracts: Proceedings of Conference on Human Factors in Computing Systems: CHI '02* (Minneapolis), pp. 662–663. New York: ACM Press.

Hong, J. I., F. C. Li, J. Lin, and J. A. Landay. 2001. End-user perceptions of formal and informal representations of Web sites. In *Extended Abstracts: Proceedings of Conference on Human Factors in Computing Systems: CHI '01* (Seattle), pp. 385–386. New York: ACM Press.

Leone, P., D. Gillihan, and T. Rauch. 2000. Web-based prototyping for user sessions: Medium-fidelity prototyping. In *Proceedings of the Society for Technical Communications 44th Annual Conference,* pp. 231–234. Toronto, Canada: STC.

McGrew, J. 2001. Shortening the human computer interface design cycle: A parallel design process based on the genetic algorithm. In *Proceedings of the Human Factors and Ergonomics Society 45th Annual Meeting* (Minneapolis/St. Paul), pp. 603–606. Santa Monica, CA: HFES.

Molich, R., N. Bevan, S. Butler, I. Curson, E. Kindlund, J. Kirakowski, and D. Miller. 1998. Comparative evaluation of usability tests. In *Proceedings of UPA98* (Usability Professionals Association 1998 Conference), pp. 189–200. Washington, DC: UPA.

Molich, R., K. Kaasgaard, B. Karyukina, L. Schmidt, M. Ede, W. van Oel, and M. Arcuri. 1999. Comparative evaluation of usability tests. In *Extended Abstracts: Proceedings of Conference on Human Factors in Computing Systems: CHI '99* (Pittsburgh), pp. 83–84. New York: ACM Press.

Nielsen, J., and T. K. Landauer. 1993. A mathematical model of the finding of usability problems. In *Proceedings of Conference on Human Factors in Computing Systems: INTERCHI '93* (Amsterdam), pp. 206–213. New York: ACM Press.

Novick, D. G. 2000. Testing documentation with "low-tech" simulation. In *Proceedings of IEEE Professional Communication Society International Professional Communication Conference and Proceedings of the 18th Annual ACM International Conference on Computer Documentation: Technology & Teamwork* (Cambridge, MA), pp. 55–68. New York: IEEE.

Rudd, J., K. Stern, and S. Isensee. 1996. Low vs. high-fidelity prototyping debate. *Interactions* January:76–85.

Säde, S., M. Nieminen, and S. Riihiaho. 1998. Testing usability with 3D paper prototypes—Case Halton system. *Applied Ergonomics* 29(1):67–73.

Schumann, J., T. Strothotte, S. Laser, and A. Raab. 1996. Assessing the effect of non-photorealistic rendered images in CAN. In *Proceedings of Conference on Human Factors in Computing Systems: CHI '96* (Vancouver, British Columbia, Canada), pp. 35–41. New York: ACM Press.

Spool, J., and W. Schroeder. 2001. Testing websites: Five users is nowhere near enough. In *Extended Abstracts: Proceedings of Conference on Human Factors in Computing Systems: CHI '01* (Seattle, March 31–April 5), pp. 285–286. New York: ACM Press.

Tullis, T. S. 1990. High-fidelity prototyping throughout the design process. In *Proceedings of the Human Factors and Ergonomics Society 34th Annual Meeting,* p. 266. Santa Monica, CA: HFES.

Uceta, F. A, M. A. Dixon, and M. L. Resnick. 1998. Adding interactivity to paper prototypes. In *Proceedings of the Human Factors and Ergonomics Society 42nd Annual Meeting* (Chicago), pp. 506–511. Santa Monica, CA: HFES.

Virzi, R. A., J. L. Sokolov, and D. Karis. 1996. Usability problem identification using both low- and hi-fidelity prototypes. In *Proceedings of Conference on Human Factors in Computing Systems: CHI '96* (Vancouver, Canada), pp. 236–243. New York: ACM Press.

Weiss, S. 2002. *Handheld usability.* New York: John Wiley & Sons.

Wiklund, M. E, C. W. Thurrott, and J. S. Dumas. 1992. Does the fidelity of software prototypes affect the perception of usability? In *Proceedings of the Human Factors and Ergonomics Society 36th Annual Meeting,* pp. 399–403. Santa Monica, CA: HFES.

Other Papers and Articles

Buchenau, M., and J. F. Suri. 2000. Experience prototyping. Symposium on designing interactive systems. In *Conference Proceedings on Designing Interactive Systems: Processes, Practices, and Techniques,* pp. 424–433. New York.

Chandler, C. D., G. Lo, and A. K. Sinha. 2002. Multimodal theater: Extending low fidelity paper prototyping to multimodal applications. In *Extended Abstracts: Proceedings of Conference on Human Factors in Computing Systems: CHI '02, Student Poster* (Minneapolis), pp. 874–875.

Coble, J. M., J. Karat, and M. G. Kahn. 1997. Maintaining a focus on user requirements throughout the development of clinical workstation software. In *Proceedings of Conference on Human Factors in Computing Systems: CHI '97* (Atlanta), pp. 170–177. New York: ACM Press.

Grady, H. M. 2000. Web site design: A case study in usability testing using paper prototypes. In *Proceedings of IEEE Professional Communication Society International Professional Communication Conference and Proceedings of the 18th Annual ACM International Conference on Computer Documentation: Technology & Teamwork* (Cambridge, MA), pp. 39–45. New York: IEEE.

Hakim, J., and T. Spitzer. 2000. Effective prototyping for usability approaches to prototyping. In *Proceedings of IEEE Professional Communication Society International Professional Communication Conference and Proceedings of the 18th Annual ACM International Conference on Computer Documentation: Technology & Teamwork* (Cambridge, MA), pp. 47–54. New York: IEEE.

Kavanaugh, R., and J. Soety. 2000. Prototyping using Visio. *Usability Interface* 7(1).

Kyng, M. 1994. Scandinavian design: Users in product development. In *Proceedings of Conference on Human Factors in Computing Systems: CHI '94* (Boston), pp. 3–9. New York: ACM Press.

Lafreniere, D. 1996. CUTA: A simple, practical, low-cost approach to task analysis. *Interactions* Sept/Oct:35–39.

Muller, J. J., and R. Carr. 1996. Using the CARD and PICTIVE participatory design methods for collaborative analysis. In *Field methods casebook for software design,* eds D. Wixon and J. Ramey. New York: Wiley.

Muller, M. J., and S. Kuhn. 1993. Communications of the ACM Volume 36, Issue 6 (June 1993): *Special issue on graphical user interfaces: The next generation participatory design,* pp. 24–28. New York: ACM Press.

Muller, M. J. 2001. Layered participatory analysis: New developments in the CARD technique. In *Proceedings of Conference on Human Factors in Computing Systems: CHI '01* (Seattle), pp. 90–97. New York: ACM Press.

Muller, M. J., J. Hallewell Haslwanter, and T. Dayton. 1997. Participatory practices in the software lifecycle. In *Handbook of human-computer interaction.* Amsterdam, North-Holland: Elsevier Science.

Ovaska, S., and K. J. Raiha. 1995. Parallel design in the classroom. In *Extended Abstracts: Proceedings of Conference on Human Factors in Computing Systems: CHI '95* (Denver, May 7–11, 1995), pp. 264–265. New York: ACM Press.

Rettig, M. 1994. Prototyping for tiny fingers. *Communications of the ACM* (April). 37(4):21–27.

Säde, S., and K. Battarbee. 2001. The third dimension in paper prototypes. In *Design by people for people: Essays on usability,* ed R. Branaghan, pp. 203–212. Chicago: UPA.

Virzi, R. A. 1992. Refining the test phase of usability evaluation: How many subjects is enough? In *Proceedings of the Human Factors and Ergonomics Society 36th Annual Meeting,* pp. 457–468. Santa Monica, CA: HFES.

Virzi, R. A. 1989. What can you learn from a low-fidelity prototype? In *Proceedings of the Human Factors and Ergonomics Society 33rd Annual Meeting* (Atlanta), pp. 224–228. Santa Monica, CA: HFES.

Wilson, S., and P. Johnson. 1995. *Empowering users in a task-based approach to design.* New York: ACM Press.

Books

Barnum, C. M. 2002. *Usability testing and research.* New York: Pearson Education.

Beyer, H., and K. Holtzblatt. 1998. *Contextual design.* San Francisco: Morgan Kaufmann.

Donoghue, K. 2002. *Built for use.* New York: McGraw-Hill.

Dumas, J., and J. C. Redish. 1999. *A practical guide to usability testing,* rev ed. Portland, OR: Intellect.

Hackos, J. T., and J. C. Redish. 1998. *User and task analysis for interface design.* New York: Wiley.

Landauer, T. K. 1995. *The trouble with computers: Usefulness, usability, and productivity.* Cambridge, MA: The MIT Press.

Mayhew, D. 1999. *The usability engineering lifecycle: A practitioner's handbook for user interface design.* San Francisco: Morgan Kaufmann.

Nielsen, J. 1994. *Usability engineering.* San Francisco: Morgan Kaufmann.

Nielsen, J., R. Molich, C. Snyder, and S. Farrell. 2001. *E-commerce user experience.* Freemont, CA: Nielsen Norman Group.

Norman, D. A. 2002. *The design of everyday things.* New York: Basic Books.

Preece, J., H. Rogers, and H. Sharp. 2002. *Interaction design: Beyond human-computer interaction.* New York: Wiley.

Rosson, M. B., and J. M. Carroll. 2002. *Usability engineering: Scenario-based development of human-computer interaction.* San Francisco: Morgan Kaufmann.

Rubin, J. 1994. *Handbook of usability testing: How to plan, design, and conduct effective tests.* New York: Wiley.

Schrage, M. 1999. Serious play: *How the world's best companies simulate to innovate.* Cambridge, MA: Harvard Business School Press.

Schuler, D., and A. Namioka (eds). 1993. *Participatory design: Principles and practices.* Hillsdale, NJ: Lawrence Edbaum Associates.

Spool, J. M., T. Scanlon, W. Schroeder, C. Snyder, and T. DeAngelo. 1999. *Web site usability: A designer's guide.* San Francisco: Morgan Kaufmann.

Web Sites

Snyder Consulting ◇ *www.snyderconsulting.net*

Author Carolyn Snyder's Web site.

Bruce Tognazzini ◇ *www.asktog.com*

Papers and articles by Bruce Tognazzini.

Human Factors International ◇ *www.humanfactors.com/downloads*

Articles on usability and past issues of the UI Design Update newsletter.

DENIM ◇ *guir.cs.berkeley.edu/projects/denim/*

The DENIM Project, led by Prof. James Landay, is focused on researching tools for designing user interfaces through informal interaction such as sketching. DENIM can be downloaded from this site.

DialogDesign ◇ *www.dialogdesign.dk/reportsandpapers.html.*

Usability reports and articles by Rolf Molich, including the Comparative Usability Evaluation (CUE) reports.

IBM developerWorks ◇ *www-106.ibm.com/developerworks/usability/*

IBM's resource for developers. Includes technical content in addition to usability articles.

Jakob Nielsen ◇ *www.useit.com*

Features Alertbox, Jakob's biweekly column on Web usability, plus links to reports, seminars, and other resources for Web professionals.

National Cancer Institute ◇ *www.usability.gov*

A resource for designing useful, usable, and accessible Web sites and user interfaces. Checklists and guidelines, links for Web statistics and trends, accessibility resources.

Society for Technical Communication ◇ *www.stcsig.org/usability*

This Web site is a forum to share information and experiences on issues related to the usability and user-centered design.

Usability Professionals Association ◇ *www.upassoc.org*

Links to usability resources, plus archived issues of UPA Voice, the organization's Web newsletter.

Usable Web (Keith Instone) ◇ *www.usableweb.com*

A collection of links about information architecture, human factors, user interface issues, and usable design specific to the Web.

User Interface Engineering ◇ *www.uie.com*

Articles and white papers.

Index

E

F

G

H

J

K

L

P

Q

R

S

U

V

W

X

Figure Credits

Figure 1.1 courtesy of Mary Beth Rettger, The MathWorks.
Figures 1.2–1.8 courtesy of Timo Jokela.
Figures 1.9 and 13.1 courtesy of WorldRes.com.
Figure 1.10 courtesy of Neil Wehrle, Razorfish.
Figures 1.11 and 15.1 courtesy of Thyra Rauch, IBM.
Figure 2.1 courtesy of The MathWorks.
Figure 2.2 courtesy of Mary Beth Rettger, The MathWorks.
Figures 2.3 and 2.4 courtesy of Centra.
Figures 2.6 and 2.7 courtesy of Pingtel.
Figures 2.8 and 2.9 courtesy of Samantha Lizak and Kristin Grasso.
Figure 4.19 courtesy of Simo Säde.
Figure 4.20 courtesy of Brix Networks.
Figure 5.1 from Nielsen, J., and T. K. Landauer. 1993. A mathematical model of the finding of usability problems. In *Proceedings of Conference on Human Factors in Computing Systems: INTERCHI '93* (Amsterdam). New York: ACM Press. © 1993 Association for Computing Machinery, Inc. Reprinted by permission.
Figure 7.2a courtesy of Joe Grant, Grant Consulting, *http://www.grantconsulting.com.*
Figure 9.2 courtesy of Mitchell Gass, uLab/PDA, *http://www.participatorydesign.com.*
Figure 9.3 from Crockett Johnson. 1998. *Harold and the Purple Crayon.* New York: HarperTrophy. Reprinted by permission.
Figure 9.4 from *The Simpsons*™, episode 7F16, "Oh Brother, Where Art Thou?" © Fox Twentieth Television. Reprinted by permission.
Figures 9.5 and 13.2 courtesy of Pearson Education.
Figure 9.6 © 2000 Randy Glasbergen. Reprinted by permission.
Figure 11.1 courtesy of The Hiser Group.
Figure 12.1 courtesy of Phillip Hash, HiddenMind.
Figure 12.2 from *http://guir.berkeley.edu/projects/denim/.* © 1998–2002 by the Regents of the University of California. Used by permission.
Figure 14.1 courtesy of The MathWorks.
Figure 15.2 courtesy of Dictaphone Corporation. Photo: Getty Images.
Figures 15.3–15.5 courtesy of Hal Shubin, Interaction Design, *www. user.com*.

About the Author

Carolyn Snyder earned her experience in unusable interfaces the hard way—the first 10 years of her career were devoted to creating them, first as a software engineer and then as a project manager. After a decade spent face-down in the code, she discovered that there were real people out there who actually used those interfaces. And thus was a usability specialist born.

In 1993, Carolyn joined User Interface Engineering, a prominent U.S. usability consulting firm founded by Jared Spool, where she specialized in usability testing and paper prototyping. In 1999, she started Snyder Consulting (*www.snyderconsulting.net*) to focus on the work she loves most—the hands-on involvement with development teams that empowers them to make usable and successful products. Carolyn has worked with dozens of clients, ranging from Fortune 500 companies to start-ups. She also teaches seminars and writes articles about usability topics.

Carolyn has a BS in Computer Science from the University of Illinois and an MBA from the University of Chicago. She is co-author of two usability books: *Web Site Usability: A Designer's Guide* and *E-commerce User Experience*. In her spare time, she rides her pink and black tiger-striped Harley, reads sci-fi/fantasy novels, and volunteers at an animal shelter.